The
Quotable
Spirit

The Quotable Spirit

A Treasury

of Religious and

Spiritual Quotations

from Ancient Times

to the Twentieth

Century

Compiled and Edited by
Peter Lorie and
Manuela Dunn Mascetti

Macmillan • USA

MACMILLAN
A Simon & Schuster Macmillan Company
1633 Broadway
New York, NY 10019

MACMILLAN is a registered trademark of Macmillan, Inc.
Design by Rachael McBrearty

Library of Congress Cataloging-in-Publication Data
The quotable spirit : a treasury of religious and spiritual quotations from ancient times to
the twentieth century / [compiled] Peter Lorie and Manuela Dunn Mascetti.
    p. cm.
ISBN 0–02–861206–X
1. Religion—Quotations, maxims, etc. 2. Religions—Quotations, maxims, etc.
3. Spiritual life—Quotations, maxims, etc.
I. Lorie, Peter. II. Dunn Mascetti, Manuela.
BL48.Q48 1996
291.4—dc20   96–13514
                                                                                    CIP

10 9 8 7 6 5 4 3 2 1
Printed in the United States of America

Contents

To Osho

Preface

I might repeat to myself, slowly and soothingly,
a list of quotations beautiful from minds profound;
if I can remember any of the damn things.
　　　　　　—Dorothy Parker *(1893–1967)*, The Little Hours

This is the Spiritual Domain. This is the Spirit World. This is the world
of God. God is not merely invisible and inside us. This is the
manifestation of God.
　　　　　　—Da Free John (Adida) *(Contemporary)*,
　　　　　　The Fire Gospel

*W*estern civilization, during the last years of the twentieth century, has become more and more conscious of the beauty of spiritual mysticism, derived from both the ancient and modern cultures of the East and West. What is more, the flavor of this particular kind of mystical beauty and the texts that it has engendered are totally different from other forms of literature, because they are largely born out of expressions of the divine heart—rather than from purely intellectual, poetic, or emotional sources. Mystical literature is essentially inspirational, and is sought by those who enjoy the very real thrill of listening to God.

There are many now who seek inspiration from the words of both Western and Eastern religious leaders, masters, gurus, sadhus, and wise men and women of civilized cultures that often predate our own by many thousands of years. Unfortunately, these words are not readily available in the standard collections of quotations. We are still, in much of Western society, dominated by the Judeo-Christian ethic in one form or another, and as such, miss a wealth of literature that casts a far wider net than any belief structure created in the last two millennia.

The Quotable Spirit contains selections of words of the great spiritual masters and writers of virtually every time and culture and every religious creed, great and small. The selection is made not only to exemplify the great names of our past and present, but also to reflect the sense of the divine heart and soul that humankind possesses; something that in this age of science may often seem lacking. There is much in these pages that will be entirely unfamiliar to many readers: material that was written thousands of years ago by authors and teachers who lived in remote kingdoms, and who certainly never reached the kind of audience available today. For example, the obscure work known to some as *The Book of Nothing*, more properly entitled *hsin hsin ming— Discourses on the Faith Mind*, written by the Third Zen Patriarch Sosan, was first published only as a thin, wire-stapled pamphlet from a private press in England. I found a copy of it in a mystical library at the heart of the Osho commune in Poona, India, tucked between two equally obscure and ancient Hindu scriptures. And yet its content is as profound, fascinating, and illuminating as anything ever recorded in the standard works of religious scripture. There are many words of wisdom from such remote sources in these pages. And they stand alongside the "kings" of scripture—the Upanishads, the Rig Veda, the Bible, the Bhagavad Gita, the Egyptian Book of the Dead, T. S. Eliot, Alan Watts, and Ramana Maharshi. These works and extraordinary individuals have given us their words of wisdom to help us on our own paths through the difficulties of everyday life, and in all my own travels through some of the toughest terrain in existence, I have derived more satisfaction, peace, and stillness, more genuine meditation, from such works than from any other source.

The idea of *The Quotable Spirit* has been in my mind for almost two decades. While many people will read a good novel for inspiration or satisfaction, I will sit reading religious and inspirational writings from the old masters. I once spent an entire "skiing" vacation, while my young wife was speeding up and down the Swiss Alps, sitting on a bench three thousand feet up, surrounded by snowy peaks, overlooking the most glorious valleys in the world—reading *Krishnamurti's Notebook*!

For all of us, I believe, there is inspiration in the words that derive from an enlightened being. Otherwise we would not have fostered the growth of the great organized religions—Christianity, Islam, Buddhism, Taoism, and so on. All these faiths grew from the need of the individual to discover God or some form of divinity that helps each of us to rise above the humdrum activities of daily routine. Much of this seeking finds satisfaction in the words that gave rise to the faiths.

In a sense, however, these "words of God" can hardly be called literature at all. There seems to be a kind of inspirational theocracy of the written word—a hierarchy of inspiration. At the bottom of this scale one might put pornography, while farther up we could find formula fiction and then, higher still, the great fiction of such writers as Dickens or Mailer, and still higher are levels attained by poets. On the next, still more elevated level of this "spiritual Richter Scale" we find philosophical and theosophical writing by such authors as Alan Watts, Ram Dass, and Aldous Huxley, where the work has grown out of a strong connection with a divine spirit, even if, in some cases, the words may have been aided by chemical substances.

And at the top level of our scale we find the greatest among us from a literary as well as human standpoint—enlightened beings who have surpassed us all on the journey to awakening and consciousness—Jesus, Mahavira, Buddha, Krishnamurti, Osho, Gandhi, Lao-tzu, Chuang Tzu, and a surprisingly large number of others through the ages. Here, on the scale, is the difference between the intellectual and the spiritual, and in a sense the difference between literature and wordlessness—the mind and the heart.

These words are the ones that can raise our own spirits even higher than that of poetry and song, that can actually aid us to move farther down our own faltering paths toward understanding and self-realization. For these are the words, in effect, of God. The great enlightened mystics of our past and present do not, I believe, speak to their disciples as teachers. In some senses the purpose of these "holy" words of wisdom are not to stimulate the brain at all, but to go into the body via another route that leads directly to the soul. The spiritual master Osho once said that we must listen to the silences between the words, like looking at the spaces between the fingers, for it is these silences that actually affect us, that touch our souls. So in the reading of the divine texts that are quoted in this book, we might wish to "read between the lines," and listen to the silences that lie therein.

The whole "spiritual movement," or what was originally known as the New Age movement, has gathered speed in the last years of the twentieth century. It has gone from being a small fringe interest in subjects once considered flaky—such as astrology, aromatherapy, prophecy, and crystal gazing—to what is now a mainstream market in which religion has become a best-selling area of interest, with far larger sectors of the public paying attention to books such as *The Celestine Prophecy*, something that in the early 1990s might have hardly gotten any attention at all.

This elevation of the spirit is also enhanced, no doubt, by the upcoming millennial end, and the human tendency to pay attention when God appears to be getting disturbingly close. Humanity creates calendars, imagines future catastrophic events, assigns a time to them, and then proceeds to fear their arrival. God probably forgot what date it was long ago.

But in a more serious vein, the incredible growth of science and the passion that mankind has developed for rational precision have both contributed to a dearth of awareness of the more irrational spirit. Witchcraft and God's glory were subjugated by scientific inquiry and the Age of Reason, so somewhere the human spirit forgot to drink of the well—and indeed, the well became covered over.

My own meanderings into the New Age, and therefore, I guess, the beginnings of the research for this book, began in the late 1970s when I first visited India and smelled the unique air of Eastern mysticism in that land where life and death live as close friends. After almost two years there, traveling and living in an ashram just south of Bombay, there was no turning back, and my task became obvious through a name given to me by the master of the ashram. This name—Purvodaya—means "the rising of the East," and by Indian legend the giving of the new name signifies a new pathway to bring Eastern understanding to the Western world—a task I happen, seemingly by chance, to have undertaken ever since.

In the early 1980s, working as a publisher and writer, I began meeting with American publishing houses in New York and San Francisco with the intention of getting books on "odd" esoteric subjects published. I found, at that stage, most editors were unwilling to take the risk in an area that was still regarded with some suspicion, but eventually the first book that I authored (*Nostradamus—the End of the Millennium*) on a New Age subject was published. This book formed part of a series that sold more than two million copies in the following years, thus proving that the New Age was indeed being born.

As we worked through the task of selecting the quotations for this volume, it became evident just what a plethora of material exists that has not seen the popular light of day for centuries. Ask the average person in the street for names of spiritual writers and the list would probably stop after Jesus, Buddha, and Mohammed, yet ask that same man or woman about the joy experienced in moments of divine understanding—in a church, in Muir Woods surrounded by redwoods, in the silence of reading beautiful writing—and there is no lack of enthusiasm. We all seek God in our own way. We all wake in the night wondering what life is about. We may all be preoccupied with career, finances, and success, but we all also know that secret yearning that has no name.

I am keenly aware that the following pages are peppered with inaccuracies and exclusions and that we have not been able to sufficiently provide everything. I hope to add to and update a future edition. We will continue to collect material in that hope.

I would like to thank my co-compiler, Manuela Dunn Mascetti, for her research, inimitable Swiss order, and love in this project; as well as Julie Foakes, for her research help and constant suggestions after digging around looking for books that probably haven't seen the light above the "dungeons" of the London Library and British Museum for centuries! Finally, and of course, I thank my editors Mary Ann Lynch and Olga Herrera Moya, because for sure chaos was turned to order by them.

And as I continue to strive along this bizarre pathless path, which gets narrower and narrower, preventing me from going off track, I begin to realize why I am so much in front of the computer, looking for words of wisdom, both from myself and others. I am trying to tell a story—a story of an ancient time when wisdom was actually far greater and more beautiful than it has been allowed to be in the past two millennia. There is a history behind these words that was in some strange way interrupted by man when the need for organization overcame truth. We forgot, so to speak, the true face of Jesus, and in our desperation to formulate the future, we painted a fake masterpiece. Now, at a time when disillusionment has become so important to us, we begin to look back beyond that past and see that perhaps there were profound civilizations that contained the wisdom and true face we seek. Here, in these pages, I hope there is a taste of that true face of God.

> *There is a being, wonderful, perfect;*
> *It existed before heaven and earth.*
> *How quiet it is!*
> *How spiritual it is!*
> *It stands alone and it does not change.*
> *It moves around and around, but does not on this account suffer.*
> *All life comes from it.*
> *It wraps everything with its love as in a garment,*
> *and yet it claims no honour, for it does not demand to be Lord.*
> *I do not know its name, and so I call it Tao, the Way,*
> *and rejoice in its power.*
>
> *Lao-tzu*

Peter Lorie
August 1996, London

Introduction

*T*he primary "rule" by which we have selected the quotations in this book is governed by the need to inspire. Unlike a political, literary, poetic, or humorous quotation, the spiritual quotation has only truly one motive in existing beyond the mouth that spoke it or the hand that recorded it: to make a connection with the divine or inspire the reader into some fundamental, internal change of view, however small.

This rule can be applied, of course, across many different—if not all—religious and spiritual persuasions. There are no rules to this rule—we are all quite different in what we find appealing and inspiring in religion, so the choice of words can be broad.

It is not that we can only choose quotations from religious leaders such as Jesus or Buddha; many hundreds of writers and speakers have found ways of expressing the divine spirit without ever having enjoyed any formal or informal religious qualification. So the choice is wide.

The choices can also be made from virtually all ages of humanity. We can go back to ancient Egypt or the Upanishads, the Sanskrit teachings that were composed nearly three thousand years ago in India, and find a plethora of material to inspire us. Or we can look into the origins of Sumeria, which grew out of the city of Ur during the third millennium BCE.

Equally we can visit recent centuries and find as much power from the mouths of Georg Gurdjieff, Carlos Castaneda, Hermann Hesse, or D. H. Lawrence, the sole criterion being the presence of the soul criterion.

The book is arranged in themes, with each theme including the authors in chronological order by birth date, or, in the case of quotations from works such as the Koran, where there is no known author or several authors, by approximate first publication date. The thematic device is intended to help the reader indulge whatever particular aspect of the divine appeals, and the chronological order is designed to give a timeline of spiritual history and some idea of who lived during the same eras in different cultures and nations.

Each quotation (as far as is possible) is given its bibliographical source within the text.

Some of the quotations, of course, are derived from sources that are "as old as the hills," so that it is not always possible to date them accurately, or indeed necessarily provide an author or source of any kind. But the vast majority of the quotations are sourced.

The Key-Phrase Index is intended to source interesting and relevant material in the book for readers who have no particular quote or author in mind, but have some sense of the kind of "feeling" desired from the quotes. It can be instructive, and even fun, to simply scan this index and follow the lead that the words provide to the pages indicated.

Angels

❂ PHILO OF ALEXANDRIA
(1ST CENTURY BCE)

Not only is it [the air] not alone deserted by all things besides, it is rather like a populous city, full of imperishable and immortal citizens, souls equal in number to the stars. Now regarding these souls, some descend upon the earth so as to be bound up in mortal bodies . . . Others soar upwards . . . While others, condemning the body to be a great folly and trifling, have pronounced it a prison and a grave. Flying from it as from a house of correction or a tomb, they have raised themselves aloft on light wings toward the aether, devoting their whole lives to sublime speculations. Again there are others—the purest and most excellent of all—who possess greater and more divine intellects and never by any chance desire any earthly thing whatever, being, as it were, lieutenants of the Ruler of the universe, as though they were the eyes and ears of the great kings, behold and listen to everything. Philosophers in general are apt to call these demons, but the sacred scriptures call them angels, using a name more in accord with nature.

On Dreams

❂ NEW TESTAMENT

Be not forgetful to entertain strangers: for thereby some have entertained angels unawares.

Hebrews 13:2

❂ THE KORAN
(7TH CENTURY)

Each has guardian angels before him and behind him, who watch him by God's command.

❂ JALAL AL-DIN RUMI
(1207–1273)

One day in the mid-morning a noble-man ran into Solomon's judgment-hall, his face pale with anguish, his two lips blue, Solomon said to him, "Sir, what has happened?"

"Azrael, the angel of death," said the man, "has looked upon me so angry and baleful." "Well, what is your wish?" asked Solomon, "Declare it."

Said the man, "Command the wind, O lord-protector, to transport me hence into Hindustan; it may be that coming there, your slave will save his soul alive." Solomon ordered the wind to bear him swiftly over the waters to the depths of Indis.

The following day, when his court was in session, Solomon spoke to Azrael thus: "Did you look on that true believer so balefully to drive him a wanderer far from home?"

Said Azrael, "When did I look on him balefully? I beheld him with astonishment as I passed by, for God had commanded me, saying, 'This very day seize you his spirit in Hindustan!' I said to myself in wonder, 'Even though he had a hundred wings, for him to be in India this day is a far journey.'"

From whom shall we flee? From ourselves? Impossible!

From whom shall we snatch ourselves? From God? How impious!

Tales of the Masnavi, Solomon
and the Angel of Death

✿ BRIDGET OF SWEDEN
(1303–1373)
I beheld a Virgin of extreme beauty wrapped in a white mantle and a delicate tunic . . . with her beautiful golden hair falling loosely down her shoulders. . . . She stood with uplifted hands, her eyes fixed on heaven, rapt, as it were, in an ecstasy of contemplation, in a rapture of divine sweetness. And while she stood in prayer, I beheld her Child move in her womb and . . . she brought forth her Son, from Whom such ineffable light and splendour radiated that the sun could not be compared to it. . . . And then I heard the wonderful singing of many angels.

Book of Questions

✿ FRANCIS BACON
(1561–1626)
The desire of power in excess caused the angels to fall; the desire of knowledge in excess caused man to fall; but in charity there is no excess, neither can angel or man come in danger by it.

Essays

✿ WILLIAM SHAKESPEARE
(1564–1616)
I tell thee, churlish priest,
A ministering angel shall my sister be
When thou liest howling.

Hamlet, V, i, 242

✿ ROBERT BURTON
(1577–1640)
Every man hath a good and a bad angel attending on him in particular, all his life long.

Anatomy of Melancholy

✿ BLAISE PASCAL
(1623–1662)
Man is neither angel or brute, and the unfortunate thing is that he who would act the angel acts the brute.

Pensées

✿ JOSEPH ADDISON
(1672–1719)
If the notion of a gradual rise in Beings from the meanest to the most High be not a vain imagination, it is not improbable that an Angel looks down upon a Man, as Man doeth upon a Creature which approaches the nearest to the rational Nature.

The Spectator, November 17, 1714

ALEXANDER POPE
(1688–1744)

Ambition . . . The glorious fault of angels and of gods.

Elegy to the Memory of an Unfortunate Lady

JOHN HENRY NEWMAN
(1801–1890)

On Thee the Angels look and are at peace; that is why they have perfect bliss. They never can lose their blessedness, for they never can lose Thee. They have no anxiety, no misgivings—because they love the Creator.

Meditations and Devotions

BENJAMIN DISRAELI
(1804–1881)

What is the question now placed before society with the glib assurance which to me is most astonishing? That question is this: is man an ape or an angel? I, my lord, I am on the side of the angels. I repudiate with indignation and abhorrence those new fangled theories.

Speech at meeting of the Society for Increasing Endowments of Small Livings in the Diocese of Oxford

HENRY WARD BEECHER
(1813–1887)

There's not much practical Christianity in the man who lives on better terms with angels and seraphs, than with his children, servants and neighbours.

Royal Truths

EDWIN BURNE-JONES
(1833–1898)

The more materialistic science becomes, the more angels shall I paint: their wings are my protest in favour of the immortality of the soul.

To Oscar Wilde

HYMNS ANCIENT AND MODERN
(1861)

Around the Throne of God a band
Of glorious Angels ever stand;
Bright things they see, sweet harps they
    hold,
And on their heads are crowns of gold.

Some wait around Him, ready still
To sing His praise and do His Will;
And some, when He commands them,
    go
To guard His servants here below.

Lord, give Thy Angels every day
Command to guide us on our way,
And bid them every evening keep
Their watch around us while we sleep.

So shall no wicked thing draw near,
To do us harm or cause us fear;
And we shall dwell, when life is past,
With Angels round Thy Throne at last.

❀ KAHLIL GIBRAN
(1883–1931)

Only the naked live in the sun. Only the artless ride the wind. And he alone who loses his way a thousand times shall have a homecoming.

The angels are tired of the clever. And it was but yesterday that an angel said to me: "We created hell for those who glitter. What else but fire can erase a shining surface and melt a thing at its core?"

The Garden of the Prophet

❀ ALAN WATTS
(1915–1973)

It is high time to ask whether it is really any scandal, any deplorable inconsistency, for a human being to be both angel and animal with equal devotion. . . . Not to cherish both the angel and the animal, both the spirit and the flesh, is to renounce the whole interest and greatness of being human, and it is really tragic that those in whom the two natures are equally strong should be made to feel in conflict with themselves. For the saint-sinner and the mystic-sensualist is always the most interesting type of human being because he is the most complete. When the two aspects are seen to be consistent with each other, there is a real sense in which spirit transforms nature: that is to say, the animality of the mystic is always richer, more refined, and more subtly sensuous than the animality of the merely animal man.

This Is IT and Other Essays on Zen and Spiritual Experience

❀ ANNIE LENNOX AND DAVID A. STEWART
(CONTEMPORARY)

No one on earth could feel like this,
I'm thrown and overblown with bliss
There must be an angel
Playing with my heart.

"There Must Be an Angel"

4

Beauty

❁ AMENHOTEP IV
(14TH CENTURY BCE)

Thy dawning is beautiful in the horizon
  of the sky,
O living Aton, Beginning of life!
When thou risest in the eastern
  horizon
Thou fillest every land with thy beauty.
Thou art beautiful, great, glittering,
  high above every land,
Thy rays, they encompass the lands,
  even all that thou hast made.
. . . .
Though thou art far away, thy rays are
  upon earth;
Though thou art on high, thy
  footprints are the day.

Hymn to Aton, the Creator

❁ BUDDHA
(563–483 BCE)

"Some people," said Buddha, the master,
"have accused me of uttering these words:

"When one attains the release called the
Beautiful, and abides therein, at such a
time he considers the whole universe as
ugly.

"But I never said these words. This is
what I do say:
When one attains the release called the
Beautiful, at such a time he knows in
truth what Beauty is."

The Samyuta

❁ ARISTOTLE
(384–322 BCE)

Beauty is the gift of God.

Quoted in Diogenes Laërtius,
Lives of Eminent Philosophers

❁ OLD TESTAMENT

He [God] hath made every thing
  beautiful in his time.

Ecclesiastes 3:11

Let the beauty of the Lord our God be
  upon us.

Psalms 90:1

⚙ PLOTINUS
(205–270)

Withdraw into yourself and look. And if you do not find yourself beautiful yet, act as does the creator of a statue that is to be made beautiful; he cuts away here, he smoothes there, he makes this line lighter, this other purer, until a lovely face has grown upon his work. So do you also; cut away all that is excessive, straighten all that is crooked, bring light to all that is in shadow; labour to make all one glow of beauty and never cease chiseling your statue until there shall shine out on you from it the godlike splendor of virtue, until you shall see the perfect Goodness established in the stainless shrine.

Enneads

⚙ ST. AUGUSTINE
(354–430)

Too late I loved you, O Beauty so ancient yet ever new! Too late I loved you! And, behold, you were within me, and I out of myself, and there I searched for you.

Confessions, X, 27

⚙ MURASAKI SHIKIBU
(974–1031?)

Beauty without color seems somehow to belong to another world.
(Of a snow covered landscape)

The Tale of Genji

⚙ JALAL AL-DIN RUMI
(1207–1273)

Know, son, that everything in the universe is a pitcher brimming with wisdom and beauty,

The universe is a drop of the Tigris of His beauty,
this beauty was a Hidden Treasure so full it burst open and made the earth more radiant than the heavens.

Mathnawi

⚙ JAMI
(1414–1492)

Do not begrudge me my ugly exterior, you who are lacking all virtue and fairness!
This body's a scabbard, the soul is the sabre:
in the sabre is action
—not in the scabbard.

The Abode of Spring

⚙ KABIR
(1440?–1518)

Do not go to the garden of flowers! O Friend! Go not there,
In your body is the garden of flowers.
Take your seat on the thousand petals of the lotus,
and there gaze on the Infinite Beauty.

One Hundred Poems of Kabir

⚙ MIRA BAI
(1450–1547)

Having beheld Thy beauty
I am caught and enmeshed.
My family members repeatedly try to restrain me,
But attachment to the Dancer with the Peacock Plume [Krishna]
Has now sunk deep.

Songs of Love, Devotional Poems

WILLIAM SHAKESPEARE
(1564–1616)

Beauty is a witch.

Much Ado About Nothing, II, i, 177

O, she doth teach the torches to burn
   bright!
It seems she hangs upon the cheek of
   night
As a rich jewel in an Ethiop's ear—
Beauty too rich for use, for earth too
   dear!

Romeo and Juliet, I, v, 46

She speaks, yet she says nothing.

Romeo and Juliet, II, ii, 12

From fairest creatures we desire
   increase,
That thereby beauty's rose might never
   die.

Sonnet 1

The ornament of beauty is suspect.

Sonnet 70

There's nothing ill can dwell in such a
   temple.
If the ill spirit have so fair a house,
Good things will strive to dwell with it.

The Tempest, I, ii, 458

JAKOB BÖHME
(1575–1624)

Now observe: if thou fixest thy thoughts concerning heaven, and wouldst willingly conceive in thy mind what it is and where it is and how it is, thou needst not to cast thy thoughts many thousand miles off, for that place, that heaven [above in the sky], is not thy heaven.

And though indeed that is united with thy heaven as one body, and so together is but the one body of God, yet thou art not become a creature in that very place which is above many hundred thousand miles off, but thou art in the heaven of this world, which contains also in it such a Deep as is not of any human numbering.

The true heaven is everywhere, even in that very place where thou standest and goest; and so when thy spirit presses through the astral and the fleshly, and apprehends the inmost moving of God, then it is clearly in heaven.

But that there is assuredly a pure glorious heaven in all the three movings aloft above the deep of this world, in which God's Being together with that of the holy angels springs up very purely, brightly, beauteously, and joyfully, is undeniable. And he is not born of God that denies it.

The Confessions

MARIE DE SÉVIGNÉ
(1626–1696)

There is nothing so lovely as to be beautiful. Beauty is a gift of God and we should cherish it as such.

*Letters of Madame de Sévigné to her
Daughter and Friends*

YOSA BUSON
(1716–1783)

In the rains of spring
An umbrella and raincoat
Pass by, conversing.

Haiku

❀ JOHN KEATS
(1795–1821)

Beauty is truth, truth beauty—that is all
   Ye know on earth, and all ye need
   to know.

Ode on a Grecian Urn

A thing of beauty is a joy for ever;
Its loveliness increases; it will never
Pass into nothingness; but still will
   keep
A bower quiet for us, and a sleep
Full of sweet dreams, and health,
and quiet breathing.

Endymion

❀ JOHN RUSKIN
(1819–1900)

Remember that the most beautiful things in the world are the most useless: peacocks and lilies, for instance.

The Stones of Venice

❀ CHARLES BAUDELAIRE
(1821–1867)

What do I care if you are good? Be
   beautiful! and be sad!

"Madrigal triste," in *Nouvelles Fleurs du mal*

❀ LEO TOLSTOY
(1828–1910)

It is amazing how complete is the delusion that beauty is goodness.

The Kreutzer Sonata

❀ WILLIAM MACCALL
(C. 1830)

Straight is the line of duty;
Curved is the line of beauty;

Follow the straight line, thou shalt see
The curved line ever follow thee.

Untitled

❀ ROBERT BRIDGES
(1844–1930)

For beauty being the best of all we know
Sums up the unsearchable and secret
   aims
Of nature.

The Growth of Love

❀ GERARD MANLEY HOPKINS
(1844–1889)

Come then, your ways and airs and looks, locks, maiden gear, gallantry and gaiety and grace,

Winning ways, airs innocent, maiden manners, sweet looks, loose locks, long locks, lovelocks, gaygear, going gallant, girl-grace—

Resign them, sign them, seal them, send them, motion them with breath,

And with sighs soaring, soaring sighs deliver

Them; beauty-in-the-ghost, deliver it, early now, long before death

Give beauty back, beauty, beauty, beauty, back to God, beauty's self and beauty's giver.

The Leaden Echo and the Golden Echo

❀ MARGARET HUNGERFORD
(1855–1897)

Beauty is in the eye of the beholder.

Molly Bawn

❀ THORSTEIN VEBLEN
(1857–1929)

The superior gratification derived from the use and contemplation of costly and supposedly beautiful products is, commonly, in great measure, a gratification of our sense of costliness masquerading under the name of beauty.

The Theory of the Leisure Class

❀ G. K. CHESTERTON
(1874–1936)

Every true artist does feel, consciously or unconsciously, that he is touching transcendental truths; that his images are shadows of things seen through the veil. In other words, the natural mystic does know that there is something *there*; something behind the clouds or within the trees; but he believes that the pursuit of beauty is the way to find it; that imagination is a sort of incantation that can call it up.

The Everlasting Man

❀ ISADORA DUNCAN
(1878–1927)

The artist is the only lover, he alone has the pure vision of beauty, and love is the vision of the soul when it is permitted to gaze upon immortal beauty.

My Life

❀ HAZRAT INAYAT KHAN
(1882–1927)

The purpose of creation is beauty. Nature in all its various aspects develops towards beauty, and therefore it is plain that the purpose of life is to evolve towards beauty.

The Sufi Message of Hazrat Inayat Khan: The Art of Personality

❀ VIRGINIA WOOLF
(1882–1941)

The beauty of the world which is soon to perish, has two edges, one of laughter, one of anguish, cutting the heart asunder.

A Room of One's Own

❀ D. H. LAWRENCE
(1885–1930)

Sex and beauty are inseparable, like life and consciousness.

Sex Versus Loneliness

❀ MARIANNE MOORE
(1887–1972)

Beauty is everlasting
And dust is for a time.

In Distrust of Merits

❀ DOROTHY PARKER
(1893–1967)

I might repeat to myself, slowly and
soothingly,
a list of quotations beautiful from
minds profound;
if I can remember any of the damn
things.

The Little Hours

❀ DYLAN THOMAS
(1914–1953)

Light breaks on secret lots . . .
Where logic die
The secret grows through the eye.

Untitled

✸ ANNE FRANK
(1929–1945)

Think of all the beauty still left around you and be happy.

Diary of a Young Girl

✸ OSHO
(1931–1990)

Whenever you say, "This is beautiful," you have brought ugliness into the world. Don't you see. Whenever you say, "I love," you have brought hatred into the world. Whenever you say, "You are my friend," you have brought enmity into the world. Whenever you say, "This is good, right, moral," you have brought immorality into the world, you have brought the devil into the world. In deep silence, when you don't know what is good and what is bad, you don't utter any labels and names, in that silence the duality disappears, the split disappears. The world becomes one.

Discourses

✸ JEAN KERR
(CONTEMPORARY)

I'm tired of all this business about beauty being only skin-deep. That's deep enough. What do you want—an adorable pancreas?

"Mirror, Mirror on the Wall," in
The Snake Has All the Lines

Belief and Doubt

❂ LAO-TZU

(C. 6TH CENTURY BCE)

When the highest type of men hear
   Tao,
They diligently practice it.
When the average type of men hear
   Tao,
They half believe in it.
When the lowest type of men hear Tao,
They laugh heartily at it.

Tao Te Ching

The Tao that can be told of is not the
   eternal Tao;
The name that can be named is not the
   eternal name.
The Nameless is the origin of Heaven
   and Earth;
The Named is the mother of all things.
Therefore let there always be non-
   being, so we may see their subtlety,
And let there always be being, so we
   may see their outcome.
The two are the same,
But after they are produced, they have
   different names.
They both may be called deep and
   profound
Deeper and more profound,
The door of all subtleties.

Tao Te Ching

❂ BUDDHA

(563–483 BCE)

Believe nothing, O monks, merely
because you have been told it . . . or
because it is traditional, or because you
yourselves have imagined it. Do not
believe what your teacher tells you
merely out of respect for the teacher.
But whatsoever, after due examination
and analysis, you find to be conducive to
the good, the benefit, the welfare of all
beings—that doctrine believe and cling
to, and take it as your guide.

The Dhammapada

❂ CONFUCIUS

(551–479 BCE)

Confucius said, "When you see a good
man, try to emulate his example, and
when you see a bad man, search yourself
for his faults."

The Aphorisms of Confucius: Wit and Wisdom

❂ THE BHAGAVAD GITA

(500? BCE)

Man is made by his belief. As he
believes, so he is.

❂ CHUANG TZU

(369–286 BCE)

Granting that you and I argue. If you get the better of me, and not I of you, are you necessarily right and I wrong? Or if I get the better of you and not you of me, am I necessarily right and you wrong? Or are we both partly right and partly wrong? Or are we both wholly right and wholly wrong? You and I cannot know this, and consequently we all live in darkness.

On Leveling All Things

❂ ASOKA

(C. 269–232 BCE)

It is forbidden to descry other sects; the true believer gives honor to whatever in them is worthy of honor.

Edicts

❂ NEW TESTAMENT

And in the fourth watch of the night Jesus went unto them, walking on the sea. And when the disciples saw him walking on the sea, they were troubled, saying, It is a spirit; and they cried out of fear. But straightway Jesus spake unto them, saying, Be of good cheer; it is I; be not afraid. And Peter answered him and said, Lord if it be thou, bid me come unto thee on the water. And he said, Come. And when Peter was come down out of the ship, he walked on the water, to go to Jesus. But when he saw the wind boisterous, he was afraid; and beginning to sink, he cried, saying, Lord, save me. And immediately Jesus stretched forth his hand, and caught him, and said unto him, O thou of little faith, wherefore didst thou doubt?

Matthew 14:25–31

❂ ST. JOHN CLIMACUS

(525–600)

Faith furnishes prayer with wings, without which it cannot soar to Heaven.

The Ladder of Divine Ascent

❂ MEDIEVAL LATIN SAYING

Believe, that you may understand.

❂ PETER ABELARD

(1079–1142)

The first key to wisdom is assiduous and frequent questioning. . . . For by doubting we come to inquiry, and by inquiry we arrive at truth.

Theologia

❂ HAKIM ABU' L-MAJD MAJDUD SANAI OF GHAZNA (HAKIM SANAI)

(12TH CENTURY)

The head has two ears;
love [of God] has just one:
this hears certitude,
whilst those hear doubt.

The Walled Garden of Truth

❂ FARID UD-DIN ATTAR

(1120?–1193?)

If disappointments darken all your days,
You need not grieve, for nothing
    worldly stays—
It is your passion for magnificence
That prompts your tears, not fancied
    indigence.

The Conference of the Birds

✹ JALAL AL-DIN RUMI
(1207–1273)

The wisdom of this world increases surmise and doubt; the wisdom of true religion soars beyond the sky.

I have put duality away, I have seen that the two worlds are one: one I seek, one I know, one I see, one I call. He is the first, he is the last. He is the outward, he is the inward.

Tales of the Masnavi

✹ FRANCIS BACON
(1561–1626)

Give to faith the things which belong to faith.

Advancement of Learning

If a man will begin with certainties, he shall end in doubts; but if he will be content to begin with doubts, he shall end in certainties.

Advancement of Learning

✹ RENÉ DESCARTES
(1596–1650)

If you would be a real seeker after truth, it is necessary that at least once in your life you doubt, as far as possible, all things.

Principles of Philosophy

✹ SIR THOMAS BROWNE
(1605–1682)

To believe only possibilities is not Faith, but mere Philosophy.

Religio Medici

✹ JOHN MILTON
(1608–1674)

A man may be heretic to the truth if he believes things only because his pastor says so, or the assembly so determines, without knowing other reason; though his belief be true, yet the very truth he holds becomes his heresy.

Aeropagitica

✹ MOLIÈRE
(1622–1673)

Doubts are more cruel than the worst of truths.

The Misanthrope

✹ BLAISE PASCAL
(1623–1662)

It is your own assent to yourself, and the constant voice of your own reason, and not of others, that should make you believe.

Pensées

✹ SAMUEL JOHNSON
(1709–1784)

Every man who attacks my belief diminishes in some degree my confidence in it, and therefore makes me uneasy, and I am angry with him who makes me uneasy.

Quoted in *Life of Johnson*, by James Boswell

✹ WILLIAM COWPER
(1731–1800)

Each man's belief is right in his own eyes.

Hope

❂ J. W. VON GOETHE
(1749–1832)

I believe in God—this is a fine, praiseworthy thing to say,
But to acknowledge God wherever and
  however He manifest
Himself, that in truth is heavenly bliss
  on earth.

Maxims and Reflections

Give me the benefit of your convictions,
if you have any, but keep your doubts to
yourself, for I have enough of my own.

Maxims and Reflections

❂ WILLIAM BLAKE
(1757–1827)

Every thing possible to be believ'd is an
  image of truth.
He who doubts from what he sees
Will ne'er believe, do what you please.
If the sun and moon should doubt,
They'd immediately go out.

Poems: Auguries of Innocence

❂ NAPOLEON BONAPARTE
(1791–1821)

All the scholastic scaffolding falls, as a
  ruined edifice, before one single
  word—faith.

Letter to Count Thibeaudeau, June 6, 1801

❂ THOMAS CARLYLE
(1795–1881)

No iron chain, or outward force of any
kind, could ever compel the soul of man
to believe or to disbelieve: it is his own
indefeasible light, that judgment of his;
he will reign and believe there by the
grace of God alone.

Heroes and Hero Worship

❂ JOHN KEATS
(1795–1821)

I am certain of nothing but of the holiness of the heart's affections, and the
truth of the Imagination.

Letter, November 22, 1817

❂ JOHN HENRY NEWMAN
(1801–1890)

It is as absurd to argue men, as to torture
them, into believing.

Apologia pro Vita Sua

❂ JEAN BAPTISTE LACORDAIRE
(1802–1861)

What takes place in us when we believe
is a phenomenon of intimate and
superhuman light.

Conferences de Notre Dame de Paris,
17th conference, 1850

❂ W. BERNARD ULLATHORNE
(1806–1889)

Nothing in this world is so marvelous as
the transformation that a soul undergoes
when the light of faith descends upon
the light of reason.

From Cabin-Boy to Archbishop

❂ ROBERT BROWNING
(1812–1889)

Who knows most, doubts most.

Motto

❂ SÖREN KIERKEGAARD
(1813–1855)

The method which begins by doubting
in order to philosophize is just as suited
to its purpose as making a solider lie

down in a heap in order to teach him to stand up straight.

Life

❁ WALT WHITMAN
(1819–1892)

Of the terrible doubt of appearances,
Of the uncertainty after all, that we
    may be deluded,
That may-be reliance and hope are but
    speculations after all,
That may-be identity beyond the grave
    is a beautiful fable only . . .

Of the Terrible Doubt of Appearances

❁ JAMES RUSSELL LOWELL
(1819–1891)

Toward no crimes have men shown themselves so cold-bloodedly cruel as in punishing differences in belief.

Witchcraft, vol. 2

❁ HENRI FRÉDÉRIC AMIEL
(1821–1881)

A belief is not true because it is useful.

Journal

❁ FYODOR DOSTOYEVSKY
(1821–1881)

Believe to the end, even if all men went astray and you were left the only one faithful; bring your offering even then and praise God in your loneliness.

The Brothers Karamazov

❁ THOMAS HENRY HUXLEY
(1825–1895)

What we call rational grounds for our beliefs are often extremely irrational attempts to justify our instincts.

On the Natural Inequality of Man

❁ THE SHIVAPURI BABA
(1826–1963)

If you believe in God, then your search must be for God; but even if you believe in nothing, you must still have some conviction that there is a meaning behind the visible world. You must be determined to seek out that meaning and understand it.

Quoted by J. G. Bennett in *Long Pilgrimage*

❁ EMILY DICKINSON
(1830–1886)

"Hope" is the thing with feathers—
That perches in the soul—
And sings the tune without the words—
And never stops—at all—

Poem no. 254

❁ HENRY GEORGE
(1839–1897)

In this tendency to accept what we find, to believe what we are told, is at once good and evil. It is this which makes social advance possible; it is this which makes it so slow and painful. It is thus tyranny is maintained and superstition perpetuated.

Social Problems

❋ VINCENT VAN GOGH
(1853–1890)

To believe in God for me is to feel that there is a God, not a dead one, or a stuffed one, but a living one, who with irresistible force urges us towards more loving.

Letters to Theo

❋ OSCAR WILDE
(1854–1900)

Man can believe the impossible, but man can never believe the improbable.

The Decay of Living

❋ HARRY EMERSON FOSDICK
(1878–1969)

It is cynicism and fear that freeze life; it is faith that thaws it out, releases it, sets it free.

The Hope of the World

❋ H. L. MENCKEN
(1880–1956)

Faith may be defined briefly as an illogical belief in the occurrence of the improbable.

Prejudices

❋ KAHLIL GIBRAN
(1883–1931)

Doubt is a pain too lonely to know that faith is his twin brother.

Doubt is a foundling unhappy and astray, and though his own mother who gave him birth should find him and enfold him, he would withdraw in caution and in fear.

Jesus, The Son of Man: His Words and
His Deeds as Told and Recorded by
Those Who Knew Him

❋ FRANÇOIS MAURIAC
(1885–1970)

Doubt is nothing but a trivial agitation on the surface of the soul, while deep down there is a calm certainty.

God and Mammon

❋ WALTER LIPPMAN
(1889–1974)

Many a time I have wanted to stop talking and find out what I really believed.

Observer, March 27, 1938

❋ J. KRISHNAMURTI
(1895–1986)

The constant assertion of belief is an indication of fear.

The Second Penguin Krishnamurti Reader

❋ ALAN WATTS
(1915–1973)

The attitude of faith must be basic—the final and fundamental attitude—and the attitude of doubt secondary and subordinate. This is another way of saying that toward the vast and all-encompassing background of human life, with which the philosopher as artist is concerned, there must be total affirmation and acceptance. Otherwise there is no basis at all for caution and control with respect to details in the foreground. But it is all too easy to become so absorbed in these details that all sense of proportion is lost, and for man to make himself mad by trying to bring everything under his control. We become insane, unsound, and without foundation when we lose consciousness of and faith in the uncontrolled and ungraspable background world which is ultimately what we ourselves are. And there is a very slight distinction, if any, between complete, conscious faith and love.

This Is IT and Other Essays on Zen and Spiritual Experience

Our society tolerates the full life, the love of both spirit and nature, only in the artist, but just because it does not take him seriously, because it regards him as an entertaining irrelevance. The man of deep spiritual wisdom is also irrelevant to this society, whether entertaining or otherwise. This has not just recently come to be so; it has been so for centuries, because—for centuries—society has consisted precisely of those human beings who are so deluded by the conventions of words and ideas as to believe that there is a real choice between the great opposites of life—between pleasure and pain, good and evil, God and Lucifer, spirit and nature.

This Is IT and Other Essays on Zen and Spiritual Experience

You know that if you get in the water and have nothing to hold on to, but try to behave as you would on dry land, you will drown. But if, on the other hand, you trust yourself to the water and let go, you will float. And this is exactly the situation of faith.

The Way of Liberation

☸ OSHO
(1931–1990)
Your personalities are nothing but dolls tied to your feet. I don't have to know your personal life, your personality. I don't have to be acquainted with you

personally, I know you essentially. By knowing myself, I have known you all. By dissolving my own problems I know your problems, and I know the key to how they can be dissolved.

Discourses

☸ DEEPAK CHOPRA
(CONTEMPORARY)
To find oneself living in an age of doubt is not such a curse. There is a kind of reverence in undertaking the quest for truth, even before the first scrap has been found.

Unconditional Life

☸ THEODORE M. HESBURGH
(CONTEMPORARY)
Faith is not an easy virtue but in the broad world of man's total voyage through time to eternity, faith is not only a gracious companion, but an essential guide.

The Way, June 1963

☸ CARTER HEYWOOD
(CONTEMPORARY)
But doubt is as crucial to faith as darkness is to light. Without one, the other has no context and is meaningless. Faith is, by definition, uncertainty. It is full of doubt, steeped in risk. It is about matters not of the known, but of the unknown.

A Priest Forever

⊛ U. G. KRISHNAMURTI
(CONTEMPORARY)

Your situation and prospects only seem hopeless because you have ideas of hope; knock off that hope and the crippling feelings of helplessness go with it. There is bound to be helplessness and overwhelming frustration as long as you exist in relationship with the hope for fulfilment, because there is no fulfilment at all.

Mind Is a Myth—Disquieting Conversations with a Man Called U. G.

⊛ FULTON J. SHEEN
(CONTEMPORARY)

An atheist is a man who has no invisible means of support.

Look magazine, December 14, 1955

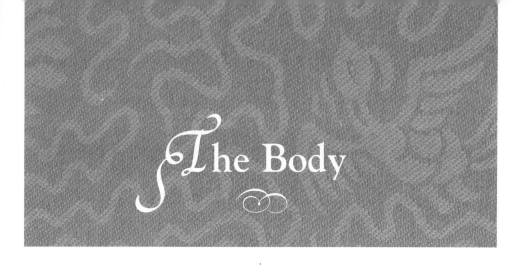

The Body

PROVERB

In thine eye be single, thy whole body
shall be full of light.

LAO-TZU
(C. 6TH CENTURY BCE)

A journey of a thousand miles must
begin with a single step.

The softest things in the world
overcome the hardest things in
the world.
Non-being penetrates that in which
there is no space.
Through this I know the advantage of
taking no action.

One may know the world without
going out of doors.
One may see the way of Heaven
without looking through the
windows.
The further one goes, the less one
knows.
Therefore the sage knows without
going about,
Understands without seeing,
And accomplishes without any action.

Tao Te Ching

BUDDHA
(563–483 BCE)

To keep the body in good health is a
duty, for otherwise we shall not be able
to trim the lamp of wisdom, and keep
our mind strong and clear. Water
surrounds the lotus flower, but does not
wet its petals.

The Dhammapada

THE BHAGAVAD GITA
(500? BCE)

These bodies are perishable; but the
dwellers in these bodies are eternal,
indestructible, and impenetrable.

MENCIUS
(372–289 BCE)

Is it only the mouth and belly which are
injured by hunger and thirst? Men's
minds are also injured by them.

Book VII

NEW TESTAMENT

Your body is the temple of the Holy
Ghost, which is in you, which ye have of
God, and ye are not your own.

I Corinthians 6:19

The Spirit indeed is willing, but the flesh is weak.

Matthew 26:41

❀ PETRONIUS
(D. 66)

From a man's face, I can read his character; if I can see him walk, I know his thoughts.

Satyricon

❀ EPICTETUS
(55–135)

It is more necessary for the soul to be healed than the body; for it is better to die than to live ill.

Discourses

He whose body is chained, and his soul unbound, is free.

Discourses

❀ JUVENAL
(55–127)

Our prayers should be for a sound mind in a healthy body.

The Satires

❀ SHANKARA
(788–820)

You never identify yourself with the shadow cast by your body, or with its reflection, or with the body you see in a dream or in your imagination. Therefore you should not identify yourself with this living body, either.

Crest-Jewel of Discrimination

One's body may be handsome, wife beautiful, fame excellent and varied, and wealth like unto Mount Meru; but if one's mind be not attached to the lotus feet of the *Guru* [teacher], what thence, what thence, what thence, what thence?

The Hymns of Shankara

Let there be births as a human being, as a god, as a mountain, or forest-animal, as a mosquito, cow or worm, as a bird or as any other. If the heart, here, is ever given to sporting in the flood of supreme bliss consisting of the contemplation of Thy lotus-feet, what does it matter in which body one is born?

Sivanandalahari

❀ JALAL AL-DIN RUMI
(1207–1273)

Know then that a fine and handsome exterior when paired with a bad character is not worth a sou; whereas if the exterior is unpleasing and contemptible but the disposition is good, you may gladly die at such a person's feet. Know that the external form passes away, whereas the world of inner truth abides eternally.

Tales of the Masnavi

God's wisdom in manifesting the world . . . is that which was known should come forth visibly. Until He made visible that which He knew, He did not impose upon the world the pains and throes of delivery. Not for a single moment can you sit inactive, without some evil or goodness issuing from you. These cravings for action were committed to you so that your secret heart might become visible. How should the reel, the body, ever be at rest seeing that the end of the thread, the mind, is always tugging it? The token of that tugging is your restlessness; to be inactive is for you like the agony of death. This world and the world beyond are forever giving birth; every cause is a mother, whereof the effect is the child. As soon as the effect is born it becomes a cause, so that other marvelous effects may be born of it. These causes mount back generation on generation, but it requires a very illumined eye to see the links.

Tales of the Masnavi

✸ MICHEL DE MONTAIGNE
(1533–1592)

Good looks are a possession of great value in human relations; they are the first means of establishing goodwill between men, and no one can be so barbarous or so surly as not to feel their attraction in some degree. The body enjoys a great share in our being, and has an eminent place in it. Its structure and composition, therefore, are worthy of proper consideration.

Essays

Those who would divide our two principal parts, and isolate one from the other, are in the wrong. On the contrary, we must reunite them and bring them together. We must command the soul not to draw aside and hold herself apart, not to scorn and abandon the body— which she can only do by some false pretense—but to ally herself with it, help control, advise, and correct it, and bring it back when it goes astray; in short, marry it and become its partner, so that their actions may not appear diverse and opposed, but harmonious and uniform. Christians have some particular instruction concerning this bond.

For they know that divine justice embraces the union and fellowship of body and soul, to the extent of making the body capable of eternal rewards; and that God regards the actions of the whole man, and wills him to receive as a whole his punishment or reward according to his deserts.

Essays

I, who am a very earthy person, loathe that inhuman teaching which would make us despise and dislike the care of the body. I consider it just as wrong to reject natural pleasures as to set too much store by them.

Essays

Our great, divine, and heavenly King, about whom every detail should be carefully, religiously, and reverently noticed, did not despise bodily superiority, for He was "fairer than the children of men" [Psalm 45:2]. And Plato desires beauty, as well as temperance and courage, in the guardians of his Republic.

Essays

We are all convention; convention carries us away, and we neglect the substance of things. We hold on to the branches, and let go the trunk and the body. We have taught ladies to blush at the mere mention of things they are not in the least afraid to do. We dare not call our parts by their right names, but are not afraid to use them for every sort of debauchery. Convention forbids us to express in words things that are lawful and natural; and we obey it. Reason forbids us to do what is unlawful or wicked, and no one obeys it.

Essays

❀ WILLIAM SHAKESPEARE
(1564–1616)

I have more flesh than another man,
    and therefore more frailty.

Henry IV Part I, III, iii

❀ JOHN DONNE
(1572–1631)

Love's mysteries in souls do grow,
But yet the body is his book.

The Ecstasy

❀ IZAAK WALTON
(1593–1683)

Look to your health; and if you have it,
praise God, and value it next to a good
conscience; for health is the second
blessing that we mortals are capable of; a
blessing that money cannot buy.

Compleat Angler

❀ JAMES THOMSON
(1700–1748)

But what avail the largest gifts of
    Heaven,
When drooping health and spirits go
    amiss?
How tasteless then whatever can be
    given!
Health is the vital principle of bliss.

Castle of Indolence

❀ HENRY WADSWORTH LONGFELLOW
(1807–1882)

How wonderful is the human voice! It is
indeed the organ of the soul! The intellect of man sits enthroned visibly upon
the forehead and in his eye; and the heart
of man is written upon his countenance.

But the soul reveals itself in the voice
only, as God revealed himself to the
prophet of old, in the "still, small voice,"
and in a voice from the burning bush.
The soul of man is audible, not visible. A
sound alone betrays the flowing of the
eternal fountain, invisible to man!

Quoted in *Elbert Hubbard's Scrapbook*,
by Elbert Hubbard

❀ ATTRIBUTED TO CHARLES READE
(1814–1884)

Sow an act, and you reap a habit.
Sow a habit, and you reap a character.
Sow a character, and you reap a destiny.

❀ WALT WHITMAN
(1819–1892)

If anything is sacred the human body is
    sacred.

I Sing the Body Electric

I sing the body electric,
The armies of those I love engirth me
    and I engirth them,
They will not let me off till I go with
    them, respond to them,
And discorrupt them, and charge them
    full with the charge of the soul.

I Sing the Body Electric

❀ THE SHIVAPURI BABA
(1826–1963)

Now, unless you live a disciplined life,
this meditation is not possible. There is
this body; you should know the
requirements of this body. You will have
to hear, you will have to see, you will
have to sleep, you will have to taste, you
will have to spit, you will have to breathe.

One thousand activities are there in this body. All these activities are to be controlled and commanded. How much to eat, how much to sleep, what to see, what to hear? All this should be controlled and commanded. This is one duty.

Another duty is towards home, society, nation, etc. Find out what we have to do.

Quoted by J. G. Bennett in *Long Pilgrimage*

MARGARET OLIPHANT
(1828–1897)

The first thing which I can record concerning myself is, that I was born. . . . These are wonderful words. This life, to which neither time nor eternity can bring diminution—this everlasting living soul, *began*. My mind loses itself in these depths.

Memoirs and Resolutions of Adam Graeme, of Mossgray

LEO TOLSTOY
(1828–1910)

A religious man is guided in his activity not by the consequences of his action, but by the consciousness of the destination of his life.

Confessions

FRIEDRICH WILHELM NIETZSCHE
(1844–1900)

Great health—a health such as one does not merely have but has continually to win because one has again and again to sacrifice it.

Ecce Homo

GEORGE SANTAYANA
(1863–1952)

For how are we to conceive that pre-existing consciousness should govern the formation of the body, move, warm, or guide it?

The Life of Reason

YOGASWAMI
(1872–1964)

Ill health is also a blessing.
The flesh and the ego are weakened
    and contemplation of God
    becomes easier.

Positive Thoughts for Daily Meditation

G. I. GURDJIEFF
(1877?–1949)

The sole means now for the saving of beings of the planet Earth would be to implant again into their presences a new organ . . . of such properties that every one of these unfortunates during the process of existence should constantly sense and be cognisant of the inevitability of his own death as well as the death of everyone upon whom his eyes or attention rests. Only such a sensation and such a cognisance can now destroy the egoism completely crystallised in them.

All and Everything

THE MOTHER
(1878–1990)

If you want to experience the body, you must live in the body! That's why the ancient sages and saints didn't know

23

what to do with their body: they left it and they meditated, so the body didn't participate at all.

Satprem, The Mind of the Cells

What the body is learning is this: to replace the mental rule of intelligence by the spiritual rule of consciousness (the other state). And that makes a tremendous difference (although it doesn't look like much, you can't notice anything,) to the point that it increases the body's capabilities a hundredfold. When the body follows certain rules, however broad they may be, it is a slave to those rules, and its possibilities are limited accordingly. But when it is governed by the spirit and consciousness (of the other state) its possibilities and flexibility become exceptional! And that's how it will acquire the capacity to extend its life at will.

Satprem, The Mind of the Cells

❀ MABEL DODGE

(1879–1962)

The strongest, surest way to the soul is through the flesh.

Lorenzo in Taos

❀ D. H. LAWRENCE

(1885–1930)

My great religion is a belief in the blood, the flesh, as being wiser than the intellect. We can go wrong in our minds. But what our blood feels and believes and says, is always true.

Letter to Ernest Collins, January 17, 1913, Collected Letters of D. H. Lawrence

❀ MIKHAIL NAIMY

(1889–1988)

Your breath upon the wind shall surely lodge within some breast. Ask not whose breast it is. See only that the breath itself be pure.

The Book of Mirdad—A Lighthouse and a Haven

❀ MARTHA GRAHAM

(1894–1991)

The body says what words cannot.

Interview, the New York Times, March 31, 1985

❀ LOUISE BOGAN

(1897–1970)

O remember
In your narrow dark hours
That more things move
Than blood in the heart.

Untitled

❀ ALBERT CAMUS

(1913–1960)

Alas, after a certain age, every man is responsible for his own face.

The Fall

❀ ALAN WATTS

(1915–1973)

Consider . . . that all your five senses are differing forms of one basic sense—something like touch. Seeing is highly sensitive touching. The eyes touch, or feel, light waves and so enable us to touch things out of reach of our hands. Similarly, the ears touch sound waves in the air, and the nose tiny particles of dust and gas.

The Book—On the Taboo Against Knowing Who You Are

✹ OSHO

(1931–1990)

The body has to be looked after: one has to be very caring about the body and very loving to the body. And then, its very spontaneity purifies it, makes it holy.

Discourses

✹ KATY BUTLER

(CONTEMPORARY)

For millennia, shamans and witch doctors . . . made no distinction between physical, emotional and spiritual healing. To them, all symptoms were signs of something awry in the individual's relationship with the larger universe of spirits and animal powers.

Family Therapy Networker

✹ MEINRAD CRAIGHEAD

(CONTEMPORARY)

I am born connected. I am born remembering rivers flowing from my mother's body into my body. I pray at her Fountain of Life, saturated in her milk and blood, water and honey. She passes on to me the meaning of religion because she links me to our origin in God and Mother.

The Mother's Song

A woman sheds blood from her body and from her spirit. Memories stir and incubate; they are remembered, reformed and animated into imagery. Whether we are weaving tissue in the womb or imagery in the soul, our work is sexual: the work of conception, gestation and birth. Our spirituality should center on the affirmation of our female sexuality in its seasons of cyclic change. Our feminine existence is connected to the metamorphoses of nature; the pure potential of water, the transformative power of blood, the seasonal rhythms of the earth, the cycles of lunar dark and light.

The Feminist Mystic

✹ DA FREE JOHN (ADIDA)

(CONTEMPORARY)

If the design of man is examined he is revealed to be a composite of all previous creatures, environments and experiences. His body below the brows is a machine of animals and elemental cycles. . . . He is not truly unique below the brows. He is rather a summation of all that came before him and everything he already knows. But man is also a new stage in the event of time. His newness or uniqueness is hidden in the brain. His lower, or vital, brain including his rudimentary speech and thought, is part of the summary and reflection of the past.

The Enlightenment of the Whole Body

✹ SHEILA FERGUSON

(CONTEMPORARY)

When you taste good soul food then it'll take ahold of your soul and hang your unsuspecting innards out to dry.

Soul Food

✱ JAMAKE HIGHWATER

(CONTEMPORARY)

"But here" Patu murmured, grazing at her fingers, "here in the skin of our fingertips we see the trail of the wind." And then she made a circular motion to indicate the whirlwind that had left its imprint in the whorl at the tips of the human finger. "It shows where the wind blew life into my ancestors when they were first made. It was in the legend days when these lines happened. It was in the legend days when the first people were given the breath of life."

Quoted in *Native American Wisdom*

✱ U. G. KRISHNAMURTI

(CONTEMPORARY)

The body is affected by everything that is happening around you; it is not separate from what is happening around you. Whatever is happening there, is also happening here—there is only the physical response. This is affection.

Conversations with a Man Called U. G.

✱ IDRIS PARRY

(CONTEMPORARY)

What evidence is there that the five senses, taken together, do cover the whole of possible existence? They cover simply our actual experience, our human knowledge of facts and events. There are gaps between the fingers; there are gaps between the senses. In these gaps is the darkness which hides the connection between things. . . . This darkness is the source of our vague fears and anxieties, but also the home of our gods. They alone see the connections, the total relevance of everything that happens; that which now comes to us in bits and pieces, the "accidents" which exist only in our heads, in our limited perceptions.

"Kafka, Rilke and Rumpelstiltskin," on *The Listener,* BBC, December 2, 1965

✱ PAUL JORDAN SMITH

(CONTEMPORARY)

It happened once that a group of physicians were in their cups and had fallen to quarreling about which part of the body was most important for life. As they could not agree among themselves, they decided to consult the rabbi.

"Of course it is the heart and blood vessels that are most important," said the first physician, "for on them the whole life of a man depends."

"Not at all," said the second physician. "It is the brain and nerves which are most vital, for without them, even the heart would not beat."

The third physician said, "You are both wrong. It is the stomach and the digestive passages which are important, for without the proper digestion of food, the body will die."

"The lungs are most important," declared the fourth, "for a man without air will surely die."

"You are all wrong," said the rabbi. "There are two vessels of the body only that are important, but you have no knowledge of them."

"What are they, then?" asked the physician.

The rabbi replied, "The channel that runs from the ear to the soul, and the one that runs from the soul to the tongue."

Adaptation from *Parabola*, vol. 3

❊ ALICE WALKER
(CONTEMPORARY)

The inner voice—the human compulsion when deeply distressed to seek healing counsel within ourselves, and the capacity within ourselves both to create this counsel and to receive it.

You Can't Keep a Good Woman Down

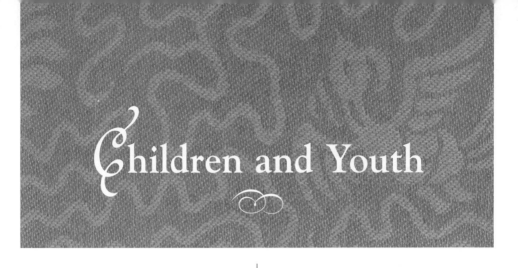

Children and Youth

☸ MENCIUS
(372–289 BCE)

Mencius said, "All men have a mind which cannot bear (to see the sufferings of) others. . . . The ground on which I say [this] is this:—Even nowadays, when men suddenly see a child about to fall into a well, they will all experience a feeling of alarm and distress. They will feel so not that they may thereon gain the favor of the child's parents; nor that they may seek the praise of their neighbors and friends; nor from a dislike to the reputation of (being unmoved by) such a thing. . . . That feeling of distress is the principle of benevolence; the feeling of shame and dislike is the principle of righteousness; the feeling of modesty and complaisance is the principle of propriety; and the feeling of approving and disapproving is the principle of knowledge.

"Men have these four principles just as they have their four limbs."

Book I

A great man is one who has not lost the child's heart.

Book I

☸ VIRGIL
(70–19 BCE)

Your descendants shall gather your fruits.

Eclogues

☸ SHANKARA
(788–820)

It is hard for any living creature to achieve birth in a human form.

Crest-Jewel of Discrimination

☸ WILLIAM WORDSWORTH
(1770–1850)

My heart leaps up when I behold
A rainbow in the sky:
So was it when my life began;
So is it now I am a man;
So be it when I shall grow old,
Or let me die!
The Child is father of the Man;
And I could wish my days to be
Bound each to each by natural
    piety.

My Heart Leaps

PERCY BYSSHE SHELLEY
(1792–1822)

Know ye what it is to be a child? . . . It is to have a spirit yet streaming from the waters of baptism; it is to believe in love, to believe in loveliness, to believe in belief.

Letters

HARRIET BEECHER STOWE
(1811–1896)

"Do you know who made you?" "Nobody, as I knows on," said the child, with a short laugh. The idea appeared to amuse her considerably; for her eyes twinkled, and she added—

"I 'spect I grow'd. Don't think nobody never made me."

Uncle Tom's Cabin

H. B. BLAVATSKY
(1831–1891)

Can you remember what you were or did when a baby? Have you preserved the smallest recollection of your life, thoughts or deeds, or that you lived at all during the first eighteen months or two years of your existence?

The Key to Theosophy

OSCAR WILDE
(1854–1900)

Children begin by loving their parents; after a time they judge them; rarely, if ever, do they forgive them.

A Woman of No Importance

RABINDRANATH TAGORE
(1861–1941)

The child who is decked with prince's robes and who has jewelled chains round his neck loses all pleasure in his play; his dress hampers him at every step.

In fear that it may be frayed, or stained with dust, he keeps himself from the world and is afraid ever to move.

Mother, it is no gain, thy bondage of finery, if it keep one shut off from the healthful dust of the earth, if it rob one of the right of entrance to the great fair of common human life.

Gitanjali (Song Offering)

HAZRAT INAYAT KHAN
(1882–1927)

The soul of an infant is like a photographic plate which has never been exposed before, and whatever impression falls on that photographic plate covers it; no other impressions which come afterwards have the same effect.

The Sufi Message of Hazrat Inayat Khan: The Art of Personality

The soul that has come from above is received and is reared and taken care of by the mother; and therefore the mother is its best friend. If there is anything that the father can do, it is to help the mother or the guardian to educate the child. If the child in its infancy were given entirely into the hand of the father, there would be little hope that it would come out right; because a man is a child all his life, and the help that is needed in the life of an infant is that of the mother. Nevertheless, later in the life of a child there comes a time when the father's influence is equally needed; but that time is not in infancy. As the Brahmin says, the first Guru is the mother, the second Guru is the father, and the third Guru is the teacher.

The Sufi Message of Hazrat Inayat Khan:
The Art of Personality

It is the will that has brought the child to the earth, otherwise it would not have come. It comes by its own will and it stays by its own will. The will is like the steam that makes the engine go forward. If the child wishes to go back, that depends upon its wish. It is always by the will of the soul. And therefore in the child you see the will in the form in which it has come. But often during childhood the will is broken, and then it remains broken all through life. If in childhood the parents took good care that the will was not broken, then the will would manifest itself in wonders. The child would do wonderful things in life if its will was sustained, if it was cherished.

The Sufi Message of Hazrat Inayat Khan:
The Art of Personality

The story of Adam's exile from the Garden of Eden shows that there is a certain time in a man's life when he is in the Garden of Eden, and after that time he is exiled from there and no longer experiences that joy and happiness and freedom that once the soul possessed. There is not one soul in this world who has not experienced the Garden of Eden, and that Garden of Eden is babyhood.

The Sufi Message of Hazrat Inayat Khan:
The Art of Personality

A child one day came to its guardian very perplexed because a boy had said to it, "Do you believe in Santa Claus? If you do then it is not right, because there never was such a being as Santa Claus." This child was very disappointed, because it had just written a letter to Santa Claus before Christmas. And in its great despair it came to the guardian to ask, "Is it true that Santa Claus exists, or is it not true?" Now suppose the guardian had said, "It is true," then in four or five years' time the child would have come and said, "No, it is not true;" and if he had said, "No, it is not true," then all the child's belief would have been totally destroyed. . . . But the guardian said to it, "Remember, all that the mind can conceive exists. If it does not exist on the physical plane, it exists in the sphere of the mind. So never say it does not exist. To the one who says that it does not exist, say that it exists in the sphere of mind;" and the child was very impressed by this answer.

A child can remember such an answer all its life.

The Sufi Message of Hazrat Inayat Khan:
The Art of Personality

❋ KAHLIL GIBRAN
(1883–1931)

And a woman who held a babe against
   her bosom said,
Speak to us of Children.
And he said:
Your children are not your children,
They are the sons and daughters of
   Life's longing for itself.
They come through you but not from
   you,

31

And though they are with you, yet they
  belong not to you.
You may give them your love but not
  your thoughts.
For they have their own thoughts.
You may house their bodies but not
  their souls,
For their souls dwell in the house of
  tomorrow,
which you cannot visit, not even in
  your dreams.
You may strive to be like them, but seek
  not
to make them like you.
For life goes not backward nor tarries
  with yesterday.
You are the bows from which your
  children
as living arrows are sent forth.
The archer sees the mark upon the
  path of the infinite,
and He bends you with His might
that His arrows may go swift and far.
Let your bending in the archer's hand
  be for gladness;
For even as he loves the arrow that
  flies,
so He loves the bow that is stable.

The Prophet

⊛ OSHO
(1931–1990)

The innocence of the child is his wisdom,
the simplicity of the child is his egoless-
ness. The freshness of the child is the freshness of your consciousness, which never
becomes old, which always remains young.

Discourses

⊛ ROBERT BLY
(CONTEMPORARY)

Our own father, through his cowardice
or fears, may have arranged our disasters
before we were born.

Iron John

⊛ CARLOS CASTANEDA
(CONTEMPORARY)

The fact of the matter is that many
children *see*. . . . Most of those who *see*
are considered to be oddballs and every
effort is made to correct them.

The Fire Within

⊛ DA FREE JOHN (ADIDA)
(CONTEMPORARY)

As a baby I remember crawling around
inquisitively with an incredible sense of
joy, light, and freedom in the middle of
my head that was bathed in energies
moving freely down from above, up,
around and down through my body and
my heart. It was an expanding sphere of
joy from the heart. And I was a radiant
form, a source of energy, bliss and light.
And I was the power of Reality, a direct
enjoyment and communication. I was
the Heart, who lightens the mind and all
things. I was the same as everyone and
everything, except it became clear that
others were unaware of the thing itself.

The Enlightenment of the Whole Body

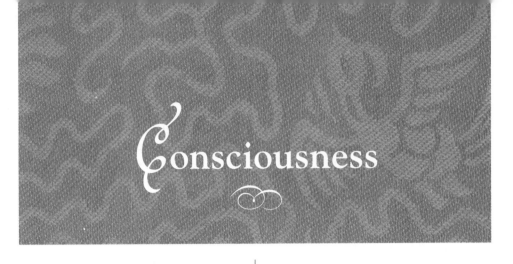

Consciousness

⊛ THE UPANISHADS

(C. 900–600 BCE)

It is not outer awareness
It is not inner awareness
Nor is it suspension of awareness
It is not knowing
It is not unknowing
Nor is it knowingness itself
It can neither be seen nor understood
It cannot be given boundaries
It is ineffable and beyond thought
It is indefinable
It is known only through becoming it.

Mandukya

⊛ THE DHAMMAPADA

(3RD CENTURY BCE)

Watchfulness is the path of immortality:
watchfulness is the path of death. Those
who are watchful never die: those who
do not watch are already as dead.

Translated by Juan Mascaro

⊛ SHANKARA

(788–820)

Who is thy wife? Who is thy son?
The ways of this world are strange
    indeed.
Whose art thou? When art thou come?
Vast is thy ignorance, my beloved.

Therefore ponder these things and
    worship the Lord.

The Shattering of Illusion

A clear vision of Reality may be obtained
only through our own eyes, when they
have been opened by spiritual insight—
never through the eyes of some other
seer. Through our own eyes we learn
what the moon looks like: how could
we learn this through the eyes of
others?

Crest-Jewel of Discrimination

I am the soul of the universe. I am all
things, and above all things. I am one
without a second. I am pure consciousness, single and universal. I am joy. I am
life everlasting.

Crest-Jewel of Discrimination

⊛ JUDAH BEN SAMUEL OF
REGENSBURG

(12TH CENTURY)

One must beware of saying what he does
not mean; instead he must speak what is
in his heart—one must match his speech
with what he believes. One must not
deceive anyone. . . . Even a single word
of deception is forbidden.

Sefer Hasidim

❂ JALAL AL-DIN RUMI
(1207–1273)

When you have seen your own
    cunning,
follow it back to its origin.
What is below comes from above.
Come on, turn your eyes to the
    heights.

> *Mathnawi*, translated by Camille
> and Kabir Helminski

Learn to recognize the false dawn from
the true; distinguish the color of the wine
from the color of the cup. Then it may
be that patience and time may produce,
out of the spectrum-viewing sight, true
vision, and you will behold colors other
than these mortal hues, you will see
pearls instead of stones. Pearls, did I
say? Nay more, you will become a sea,
you will become a sun traveling the sky.

> *Tales of the Masnavi*, translated by A. R. Arberry

Know that every bad habit is a
    thornbush.
After all, how often have you stepped
    on its thorns?

> *Mathnawi*, translated by Camille
> and Kabir Helminski

❂ JAMI
(1414–1492)

From the solitary Desert
Up to Baghdad came a simple
    Arab; there amid the rout
Grew bewilder'd of the countless
People, hither, thither, running,
Coming, going, meeting, parting,
Clamour, clatter and confusion,
    All about Him and about.
Travel-wearied, hubbub-dizzy,
Would the simple Arab fain
Get to sleep—But then, on waking,

"How," quoth he, "amid so many
    "Waking know Myself again?"
So, to make the matter certain,
Strung a gourd about his ankle,
And, into a corner creeping,
Baghdad and Himself and People
    Soon were blotted from his brain.
    But one that heard him and divined
His purpose, slyly crept behind;
From the Sleeper's ankle slipping,
    Round his own the pumpkin tied,
    And laid him down to sleep beside.
By and by the Arab waking
Looks directly for his Signal—
Sees it on another's Ankle—
Cries aloud, "Oh Good-for-nothing
Rascal to perplex me so!
That by you I am bewilder'd,
Whether I be *I* or no!
If *I*—the Pumpkin why on YOU?
If YOU—then Where am I, and WHO?"

> *Salaman and Absal*

❂ JOHN KEATS
(1795–1821)

When I have fears that I may cease to be
Before my pen has glean'd my teeming
    brain,
Before high-piled books, in charactery,
Hold like rich garners the full ripen'd
    grain;
When I behold, upon the night's starr'd
    face,
Huge cloudy symbols of a high
    romance,
And think that I may never live to trace
Their shadow, with the magic hand of
    chance;
And when I feel, fair creature of an
    hour,
That I shall never look upon thee
    more,
Never have relish in the faery power

Of unreflecting love;—then on the
    shore
Of the wide world I stand alone, and
    think
Till love and fame to nothingness do
    sink.

Sonnets VII

✸ SIGMUND FREUD
(1856–1939)

Conscience is the internal perception of
the rejection of a particular wish operating within us.

Totem and Taboo

✸ GEORGE SANTAYANA
(1863–1952)

Consciousness is the inner light kindled
in the soul . . . a music, strident or sweet,
made by the friction of existence.

The Realm of Trust

✸ SRI AUROBINDO
(1872–1950)

All eyes that look on me are my sole eyes;
The one heart that beats within all
    breasts is mine.
The world's happiness flows through
    me like wine,
Its million sorrows are my agonies.

Yet all its acts are only waves that pass
Upon my surface; only for ever still
Unborn I set, timeless, intangible:
All things are shadows in my tranquil
    glass.

My vast transcendence holds the
    cosmic whirl;
I am hid in it as in the sea a pearl.

Sonnets of Cosmic Consciousness

I have thrown from me the whirling
    dance of mind
And stand now in the spirit's silence free;
Timeless and deathless beyond
    creaturekind,
The center of my own eternity.

My mind is hushed in a wide and
    endless light,
My heart a solitude of delight and
    peace,
My sense ensnared by touch and sound
    and sight,
My body a point in white infinities.

I am the one Being's sole immobile Bliss:
No one I am, I who am all that is.

Sonnets of Cosmic Consciousness

✸ YOGASWAMI
(1872–1964)

Why do you want to open the outside
door when there is an inside door?
Everything is within.

Positive Thoughts for Daily Meditation

✸ G. K. CHESTERTON
(1874–1936)

Suppose somebody in a story says "Pluck
this flower and a princess will die in a
castle beyond the sea," we do not know
why something stirs in the subconscious,
or why what is impossible seems also
inevitable. . . . We do not know why the
imagination has accepted that image
before the reason can reject it; or why
such correspondences seem really to
correspond to something in the soul. Very
deep things in our nature, some dim sense
of the dependence of great things upon
small, some dark suggestion that the
things nearest to us stretch far beyond

our power, some sacramental feeling of the magic in material substances, and many more emotions past finding out, are in an idea like that of the external soul.

The Everlasting Man

The truth is that the thing most present to the mind of man is not the economic machinery necessary to his existence, but rather that existence itself; the world which he sees when he wakes every morning and the nature of his general position in it. There is something that is nearer to him than livelihood and that is life. For once that he remembers exactly what work produces his wages and exactly what wages produce his meals, he reflects ten times that it is a fine day or it is a queer world, or wonders whether life is worth living, or wonders whether marriage is a failure, or is pleased and puzzled with his own children, or remembers his own youth, or in any such fashion vaguely reviews the mysterious lot of man. This is true of the majority even of the wage-slaves of our morbid modern industrialism, which by its hideousness and inhumanity has really forced the economic issue to the front.

The Everlasting Man

✺ G. I. GURDJIEFF
(1877?–1949)

In speaking of evolution it is necessary to understand from the outset that no mechanical evolution is possible. The evolution of man is the evolution of consciousness and "consciousness" cannot evolve unconsciously. The evolution of man is the evolution of his will and "will" cannot evolve involuntarily. The evolution of man is the evolution of his

power of doing, and "doing" cannot be the result of things which "happen."

Letter to Ouspensky

✺ THE MOTHER
(1878–1990)

The ordinary consciousness lives in a constant state of fidgeting, it's frightening when you realize it! As long as you are not aware of it, it's perfectly natural, but when you become aware of it, you wonder how people don't go crazy, it's a grace! It is a kind of microscopic trepidation. Oh, how horrible!

And it's the same for everything: for world events and natural cataclysms and mankind, for earthquakes and tidal waves, for volcanic eruptions, floods and wars, for revolutions and people who take their own lives without even knowing why—everywhere, they are all impelled by something; behind that "fidgeting," there's a will for disorder seeking to prevent the establishment of harmony. It's in each individual in each group and in Nature.

Satprem, The Mind of the Cells

✺ PIERRE TEILHARD DE CHARDIN
(1881–1955)

My education and my religion had always led me obediently to accept—without much reflection, it is true—a fundamental heterogeneity between Matter and Spirit, between Body and Soul, between Unconscious and Conscious. These were to me two "substances" that differed in nature, . . . and it was important, I was told, to maintain at all cost that the first of these two (my divine Matter!) was no more than the humble servant of the second, if not, indeed, its enemy. Thus the second of the two (Spirit) was by that very fact henceforth reduced for me to being no more than a Shadow. In principle, it is true, I was compelled to venerate this shadow but, emotionally and intellectually speaking, I did not in fact have any live interest in it. You can well imagine, accordingly, how strong was my inner feeling of release and expansion when I took my first still hesitant steps into an 'evolutive' Universe, and saw that the dualism in which I had hitherto been enclosed was disappearing like the mist before the rising sun. Matter and Spirit: these were no longer two things but two *states* or two aspects of one and the same cosmic Stuff.

The Heart of the Matter

From the critical moment when I rejected many of the old moulds in which my family life and my religion had formed me and began to wake up and express myself in terms that were really my own, I have experienced no form of self-development without some feminine eye turned on me, some feminine influence at work.

The Heart of the Matter

✸ D. H. LAWRENCE
(1885–1930)

He had made a passionate study of education, only to come, gradually, to the knowledge that education is nothing but the process of building up, gradually, a complete unit of consciousness. And each unit of consciousness is the living unit of that great social, religious, philosophic idea towards which mankind, like an organism seeking its final form, is laboriously growing.

Phoenix II

✸ ERWIN SCHRÖDINGER
(1887–1961)

It is possible that this unity of knowledge feeling and choice which you call *your own* should have sprung into being from nothingness at a given moment not so long ago; rather this knowledge, feeling and choice are essentially and unchangeably and numerically *one* in all men, nay in all sensitive beings. But not in *this* sense—that *you* are a part, a piece, of an eternal, infinite being, an aspect or modification of it, as in Spinoza's pantheism. For we should have the same baffling question: which part, which aspect are you? What objectively differentiates it from the others? No, but inconceivably as it seems to ordinary reason, you—and all other conscious beings as such—are all in all. Hence this life of yours which you are living is not merely a piece of the entire existence, but is in a certain sense the whole; only this whole is not so constituted that it can be surveyed in one single glance.

My View of the World

✸ LUDGWIG WITTGENSTEIN
(1889–1951)

The aspects of things that are most important for us are hidden because of their simplicity and familiarity.

Lectures on Religious Belief

✸ WEI WU WEI (TERENCE GRAY)
(1895–1986)

I don't believe that there is anyone to wake up! Sentient beings are not *there* at all as such—as the Buddha pointed out in the Diamond Sutra, so how can they wake up? And *what* is there to wake up?

Open Secret

All I am is "see*ing*" when I see,
All I am is "hear*ing*" when I hear,
All I am is "sentience" when I feel,
All I am is understand*ing* when I know.

Open Secret

Pure Thought is seeing things as they appear—without arguing (thinking) about them, just "seeing, seeing, seeing," as Rumi said. Above all, without *inference*.

Open Secret

What do you have to do?

Pack your bags,
Go to the station without them,
Catch the train,
And leave your self behind.

Quite so: the only practice—and once.

Open Secret

We are all part of the party: the party goes on even if we fall asleep, but our falling asleep is also part of the party.

Open Secret

⊛ ANANDAMAYI MA
(1896–1982)

There is little to tell. My consciousness has never associated itself with this temporary body. Before I came on the earth, "I was the same." As a little girl, "I was the same." I grew into womanhood, but still "I was the same." When the family in which I had been born make arrangements to gave this body married, "I was the same." . . . And in front of you now, "I am the same." Ever afterwards, though the dance of creation change around me, "I shall be the same." Now and always one with That, "I am the same."

Autobiography of a Yogi

⊛ E. RECÉJAC
(D. 1899)

When mystical activity is at its height, we find consciousness possessed by a sense of a being at once *excessive and identical* with the self: great enough to be God; interior enough to be me.

Essay on the Being of the Mystical Knowledge

⊛ THOMAS MERTON
(1915–1968)

We stumble and fall constantly even when we are most enlightened. But when we are in true spiritual darkness, we do not even know that we have fallen.

Quoted in *The Soul: An Archeology*,
Claudia Setzer

⊛ ALAN WATTS
(1915–1973)

As the fish doesn't know water, man is ignorant of space. Consciousness is concerned only with changing and varying details; it ignores constants—especially constant backgrounds. Thus only very exceptional people are aware of what is basic to everything.

*Cloud-Hidden, Whereabouts Unknown—
A Mountain Journal*

The spiritual is not to be separated from the material, nor the wonderful from the ordinary. We need, above all, to disentangle ourselves from habits of speech and thought which set the two apart, making it impossible for us to see that *this*—the immediate, everyday, and present experience—is IT, the entire and ultimate point of the existence of the universe. But the recognition that the two are one comes to pass in an elusive, though relatively common, state of consciousness. . . . I believe that if this state of consciousness could become more universal, the pretentious nonsense which passes for the serious business of the world would dissolve in laughter. We should see at once that the high ideals for which we are killing and regimenting each other are empty and abstract substitutes for the unheeded miracles that surround us—not only in the obvious wonders of nature but also in the overwhelmingly uncanny fact of mere existence.

This Is IT and Other Essays on Zen and Spiritual Experience

If . . . consciousness ceases to ignore itself and becomes fully self-conscious, it discovers two things: (1) that it controls itself only very slightly, and is thoroughly dependent on other things—father and mother, external nature, biological processes, God or what you will, and (2) that there is no little man inside, no "I" who owns this consciousness. And if that is so, if I do not own my consciousness, and if there is even no "me" to own it, to receive it, or to put up with it, who on earth is there to be either the victim of fate or the master of nature? "What is troubling us," said Wittgenstein, "is the tendency to believe that the mind is like a little man within."

This Is IT and Other Essays on Zen and Spiritual Experience

The words which one might be tempted to use for a silent and wide-open mind are mostly terms of abuse—thoughtless, mindless, unthinking, empty-headed, and vague. Perhaps this is some measure of an innate fear of releasing the chronic cramp of consciousness by which we grasp the facts of life and manage the world. It is only to be expected that the idea of an awareness which is something other than sharp and selective fills us with considerable disquiet. We are perfectly sure that it would mean going back to the supposedly confused sensitivity of infants and animals, that we should be unable to distinguish up from down, and that we should certainly be run over by a car the first time we went out on the street.

Does It Matter?

⊛ ROBERTO ASSAGIOLI
(CONTEMPORARY)

Truly religious music . . . awakens and stimulates the spiritual "germs" which exist in every one of us, waiting to come to life. It lifts us above the level of everyday consciousness, up into those higher realms where light, love and joy ever reign.

Psychosynthesis: A Manual of Principles and Techniques

⊛ CARLOS CASTANEDA
(CONTEMPORARY)

This indeed is the mystery of awareness. Human beings reek of that mystery; we reek of darkness, of things which are inexplicable. To regard ourselves in any other terms is madness. So don't demean the mystery of man in you by feeling sorry for yourself or by trying to rationalize it. Demean the stupidity of man in you by understanding it. But don't apologize for either; both are needed.

The Fire Within

⊛ U. G. KRISHNAMURTI
(CONTEMPORARY)

All that you do makes it impossible for what already is there to express itself.

Conversations with a Man Called U. G.

✴ MARION MILNER
(CONTEMPORARY)

I tried to learn, not from reason but from my senses. But as soon as I began to study my perception, to look at my own experience, I found that there were different facts. There was a narrow focus which meant seeing life as if from blinkers and with the centre of awareness in my head; and there was a wide focus which meant knowing with the whole of my body, a way of looking which quite altered my perception of whatever I saw. And I found that the narrow focus way was the way of reason. If one was in the habit of arguing about life it was very difficult not to approach sensation with the same concentrated attention and so shut out its width and depth and height. But it was the wide focus way that made me happy.

A Life of One's Own

Those flickering leaf-shadows playing over the heap of cut grass. The shadows are blue or green, I don't know which, but I feel them in my bones. Down into the shadows of the gully, across it through glistening space, space that hangs suspended filling the gully, so that sounds wander there, lose themselves and are drowned; beyond, there's a splash of sunlight leaping out against the darkness of forest, the gold in it flows richly in my eyes, flows through my brain in still pools of light. That pine, my eye is led up and down the straightness of its trunk, my muscles feel its roots spreading wide to hold it so upright against the hill. The air is full of sounds, sighs of wind in the trees, sighs which fade back into the overhanging silence. A bee passes, a golden ripple in the quiet air.

A Life of One's Own

✴ SOGYAL RINPOCHE
(CONTEMPORARY)

All the buddhas, bodhisattvas, and enlightened beings are present at all moments to help us, and it is through the presence of the master that all of their blessings are focused directly at us. . . . All we need to do to receive direct help is to ask.

The Tibetan Book of Living and Dying

Compassion is a far greater and nobler thing than pity. Pity has its roots in fear, and a sense of arrogance and condescension, sometimes even a smug feeling of "I'm glad it's not me." . . . To train in compassion, then, is to know all beings are the same and suffer in similar ways, to honor all those who suffer, and to know you are neither separate from nor superior to anyone.

The Tibetan Book of Living and Dying

✴ YATRI
(CONTEMPORARY)

When the Void looks into the mirror
It sees us.
When we look into the Void we see the
   mirror.
When we look in the mirror
We see the Void.
When the mirror looks into the
   mirror . . .
It laughs.

Unknown Man

Creation

❀ INDIAN CREATION MYTH
(RECORDED 300?–500)

The world is created, destroyed, and re-created in an eternally repetitive series of cycles. It continuously moves from one Maha Yuga (Great Age) to the next, with each lasting for 4,320,000 years. Each Maha Yuga consists of a series of four shorter yugas, or ages, each of which is morally worse and of shorter duration than the age that preceded it. . . . At the end of 1,000 Maha Yugas (Great Ages), which is one day of the life of the world, the great god Vishnu will adopt the form of Shiva-Rudra and will destroy all life on earth. He will usher in one night in the life of the world, a period lasting as long as the day. . . . At the end of the long night of 1,000 Maha Yugas, Vishnu will awaken. A marvellous lotus flower will emerge from his navel, and Vishnu will emerge from the lotus flower in his creative form of Brahma, creator of life on earth. The lotus will become the foundation of the three worlds. . . . First Brahma the creator will bring forth water, fire, air, wind, sky, and earth, with mountains and trees upon the earth. Then he will create the forms of time, as a way of organizing the universe.

Soon thereafter, Brahma will concentrate upon creating gods, demons, and human beings. First he will bring forth the demons from his buttocks. He will then cast off his body, creating the darkness we call night, which belongs to the enemies of the gods. Taking a second body, Brahma will bring forth the gods from his face. He will cast off this body as well, creating the lightness we call day, which belongs to the gods. From successive bodies, Brahma's powers of concentration will bring forth human beings and Rakshasas, snakes and birds. Then Brahma will bring forth goats, buffalo, camels, donkeys, elephants, and other animals from his arms and legs, horses from his feet, and plant life from the hair on his body.

World Mythology, Donna Rosenberg

❀ JAPANESE CREATION MYTH
(DATE OF ORIGIN UNKNOWN,
FIRST KNOWN RECORD 712)

In the beginning, heaven and earth were one unformed mass, similar to a shapeless egg. The lighter, clearer part remained above and in time, became heaven. More slowly, the heavier, denser part sank below and became earth. At first, pieces of land floated about in the void as a fish floats on the surface of the sea. A detached object, shaped like a reed-shoot when it first emerges from the mud, floated in the void between heaven and earth as a cloud floats over the sea. This became the first god.

World Mythology, Donna Rosenberg

⊛ MAYAN CREATION MYTH
(DATE OF ORIGIN UNKNOWN,
FIRST KNOWN RECORD 1553–1558)

In the beginning, only the sky above and the sea below existed in the eternal darkness, and they were calm and silent, for nothing existed that could move or make noise. The surface of the earth had yet to rise forth from the waters. Grass and trees, stones, caves and ravines, birds and fish, crabs, animals, and human beings had yet to be created. Nothing could roar or rumble; nothing could sing or squeak; nothing could run or shake, for there was nothing but the vacant sky above and the tranquil sea below.

Hidden in the water under green and blue feathers were the Creators. These great thinkers talked quietly together in the water, alone in the universe, alone in the darkness of the eternal night. Together they decided what would be. Together they decided when the earth would rise from the waters, when the first human beings and all other forms of life would be born, what these living things would eat in order to survive, and when dawn would first flood the world with pale light. . . . And so they created it.

World Mythology, Donna Rosenberg

⊛ THE RIG VEDA
(C. 1200–900 BCE)

There was neither non-existence nor existence then; there was neither the realm of space nor the sky which is beyond. What stirred? Where? In whose protection? Was there water, bottomless deep?

There was neither death nor immortality then. There was no distinguishing sign of night or day. That one breathed, windless, by its own impulse. Other than that there was nothing beyond.

Darkness was hidden by darkness in the beginning; with no distinguishing sign, all this was water. The life force that was covered with emptiness, that one arose through the power of heat.

Desire came upon that one in the beginning; that was the first seed of mind. Poets seeking in their heart with wisdom found the bond of existence in non-existence.

Their cord was extended across. Was there below? Was there above? There were seedplacers; there were powers. There was impulse beneath; there was giving-forth above.

Who really knows? Who will here proclaim it? Whence was it produced? Whence is this creation? The gods came afterwards, with the creation of this universe. Who then knows whence it has arisen?

Whence this creation has arisen— perhaps it formed itself, or perhaps it did not—the one who looks down on it, in the highest heaven, only he knows—or perhaps he does not know.

Creation Hymn (Nasadiya)

There then was neither Aught nor
　　Nought,
No air nor sky beyond.
What covered all? Where rested all?
In watery gulf profound?

Nor death was there, nor deathlessness,
Nor change of night and day.
That One breathed calmly, self-
　　sustained:
Nor else beyond It lay.

Gloom hid in gloom existed first—
One sea eluding view.
That One, a void in chaos wrapt,
By inward fervour grew.

Within It first arose desire,
The primal germ of mind,
Which nothing with existence links,
As sages searching find.

The kindling ray that shot across
The dark and drear abyss,—
Was it beneath? Or high aloft?
What bard can answer this?

There fecundating powers were found,
and mighty forces strove,
A self-supporting mass beneath,
And energy above.

Who knows, whoe'er hath told, from
　　whence
This vast creation rose?
No gods had then been born, who then
　　can
e'er the truth disclose?

Whence sprang this world, and
　　whether framed
By hand divine or no,
Its lord in heaven alone can tell,—
If even he can show.

Hymn 129

❁ THE UPANISHADS
(C. 900–600 BCE)

Just as a spider voids its body by a thread, just as tiny sparks go forth from a fire, even so from this Self all the organs, all the worlds, all the gods, all things go forth.

Brhad Upanishad

As its web a spider emits and draws in, just as plants arise on the earth and wither, just as hair develops on living persons, even so this world from the Self arises.

Mundaka Upanishad

❁ LAO-TZU
(6TH CENTURY BCE)

"One who has a man's wings
And a woman's also
Is in himself a womb of the world"
And, being a womb of the world,
Continuously, endlessly,
Gives birth;
One who, preferring light,
Prefers darkness also
Is in himself an image of the world
And, being an image of the world,
Is continuously, endlessly
The dwelling of creation.

The Way of Life

❋ CHUANG TZU
(369–286 BCE)

If there was a beginning, then there was a time before that beginning, and a time before the time which was before the time of that beginning. If there is existence, there must have been non-existence. And if there was a time when nothing existed, then there must have been a time when even nothing did not exist. All of a sudden, nothing came into existence. Could one then really say whether it belongs to the category of existence or of non-existence? Even the very words I have just now uttered,—I cannot say whether they say something or not.

On Leveling All Things

Before heaven and earth were, Tao existed by itself from all time. It gave the spirits and rulers their spiritual powers, and gave Heaven and Earth their birth. To Tao, the zenith is not high, nor the nadir low; no point in time is long ago, nor by the lapse of ages has it grown old.

The Great Supreme

❋ HUAI-NAN TZU
(1ST CENTURY BCE)

Before heaven and earth had taken vague form all was vague and amorphous. Therefore it was called The Great Beginning. The Great Beginning produced emptiness and emptiness produced the universe. . . . The combined essences of heaven and earth became the yin and yang, the concentrated essences of the yin and yang became the four seasons, and the scattered essences of the four seasons became the myriad creatures of the world.

Sources of Chinese Tradition

❋ VIRGIL
(70–19 BCE)

With Jove I begin.

Eclogues

❋ OLD TESTAMENT

In the beginning God created the heaven and the earth. And the earth was without form, and void; and darkness was upon the face of the deep. And the Spirit of God moved upon the face of the waters. And God said, Let there be light; and there was light.

Genesis 11:3

❋ NEW TESTAMENT

In the beginning was the Word and the Word was with God, and the Word was God.

The same was in the beginning with God.

All things were made by him; and without him was not any thing made that was made.

In him was life; and the life was the light of men.

And the light shineth in darkness; and the darkness comprehended it not.

John 1:1–5

❋ SOLOMON BEN JUDAH IBN-GABIROL
(C. 1021–1070)

It is impossible to describe the Will. One may only approximate its definition by saying that it is a divine Power, creating matter and form and holding them together, and that it is diffused from the highest to the lowest. . . . It is this Power which moves and directs everything.

Fountain of Life

⚛ HAKIM ADU' L-MAJD MAJDUD SANAI OF GHAZNA (HAKIM SANAI)
(12TH CENTURY)

Your intellect is just a hotch-potch
of guesswork and thought,
limping over the face of the earth;
wherever they are, he [God] is not;
they are contained within his creation.
Man and his reason are just the latest
ripening plants in his garden.
Whatever you assert about his nature,
you are bound to be out of your depth,
like a blind man trying to describe
the appearance of his own mother.
While reason is still tracking down the
    secret,
you end your quest on the open field of
    love.

The Walled Garden of Truth

⚛ MOSES DE LEON
(1250–1305)

In the beginning, when the Will of the King began to take effect, He became imbued into the heavenly sphere. Within the Most Hidden, the *En Sof*, the Infinite, a dark flame issued forth, like a fog forming in the Unformed. Forming the concentric ring of that sphere, neither white nor black, neither red nor green, of no colour whatever. Only after this flame began to assume size and dimension, did it produce radiant colours. From the innermost center of the flame gushed forth a host

of colours which spread on everything beneath. Concealed within all was the hidden mystery of *En Sof*.

The Zohar

⚛ RALPH WALDO EMERSON
(1803–1882)

All I have seen teaches me to trust the Creator for all I have not seen.

The Best of Ralph Waldo Emerson

⚛ GUSTAVE FLAUBERT
(1821–1880)

The artist must be in his work as God is in creation, invisible and all-powerful; his presence should be felt everywhere, but he should never be seen.

Madam Bovary

⚛ PAUL VALÉRY
(1871–1945)

God made everything out of nothing. But the nothingness shows through.

Mauvaises Pensées et Autres

⚛ G. K. CHESTERTON
(1874–1936)

In a hundred forms we are told that heaven and earth were once lovers, or were once at one, when some upstart thing, often some undutiful child, thrust them apart; and the world was built on an abyss; upon a division and a parting. . . . One of its most charming versions was that . . . a little pepper-plant grew taller and taller and lifted the whole sky like a lid.

The Everlasting Man

⊛ SRI RAMANA MAHARSHI
(1879–1950)

There is neither creation nor
    destruction,
Neither destiny nor free will,
Neither path nor achievement;
This is the final truth.

Collected Works

⊛ HAZRAT INAYAT KHAN
(1882–1927)

Music is the basis of the whole creation.
In reality the whole of creation is music,
and what we call music is simply a
miniature of the original music, which is
creation itself, expressed in tone and
rhythm.

*The Sufi Message of Hazrat Inayat Khan:
The Art of Personality*

⊛ D. H. LAWRENCE
(1885–1930)

Cosmology, however, considers only
the creation of the material universe,
and according to the scientific idea life
itself is but a product of reactions in the
material universe. This is palpably
wrong.

When we repeat that on the First Day of
Creation God made Heaven and Earth
we do not suggest that God disappeared
between the two great valves of the
cosmos once these were created. Yet this
is the modern, scientific attitude.
Science supposes that once the first
force was in existence, and the first
motion set up, the universe produced
itself automatically, throwing off life as a
by-product, at a certain stage.

It is such an idea which has brought
about the materialization and emptiness
of life. When God made Heaven and
Earth, that is, in the beginning when the
unthinkable living cosmos divided itself,
God did not disappear. . . . There is a
mysterious duality, life divides itself, and
yet life is indivisible. When life divides
itself, there is no division in life. It is
a new life-state, a new being which
appears. So it is when an egg divides.
There is no split in life. Only a new
life-state is created. This is the eternal
oneness and magnificence of life, that it
moves creatively on in progressive being,
each state of being whole, integral,
complete.

Phoenix II

⊛ NIKOS KAZANTZAKIS
(1885–1957)

This, I thought, is how great visionaries
and poets see everything—as if for the
first time. Each morning they see a new
world before their eyes; they do not
really see it, they create it.

Zorba the Greek

The Australian aborigines . . . have a
story about a giant frog who had swal-
lowed the sea and all the waters of the
world; and who was only forced to spill
them by being made to laugh. All the
animals with all their antics passed
before him and, like Queen Victoria, he
was not amused. He collapsed at last
before an eel who stood delicately bal-
anced on the tip of its tail, doubtless
with a rather desperate dignity. Any
amount of fine fantastic literature might
be made out of that fable. There is
philosophy in that laughter.

The Everlasting Man

❀ SARVEPALLI RADHAKRISHNAN
(1888–1975)

The world process with its order and creativity requires for its explanation a creative power. For however far we may travel backwards in space or time, we cannot jump out of space or time, and we cannot account for space-time structure. The rationality of the universe suggests that the creative power is mind or spirit. There is no reason why we should identify it with vital force or life, as Bergson suggests, and not with spirit, for spirit is the highest we know. . . . The Indian figure of lila makes the creation of the universe an act of playfulness. Play is generally the expression of ideal possibilities. It is its own end and its own continuous reward. . . . Though the creation of the world is an incident in the neverending activity of the Absolute, it satisfies a deep want in God.

An Idealist View of Life

❀ ROBERT GRAVES
(1895–1985)

In the beginning, Eurynome, the Goddess of All Things, rose naked from Chaos, but found nothing substantial for her feet to rest upon, and therefore divided the sea from the sky, dancing lonely upon its waves. She danced towards the south, and the wind set in motion behind her seemed something new and apart with which to begin a work of creation. Wheeling about, she caught hold of this north wind, rubbed it between her hands, and behold! the great serpent Ophion. Eurynome danced to warm herself, wildly and more wildly, until Ophion, grown lustful, coiled about those divine limbs and was moved to couple with her. . . . Next, she

assumed the form of a dove, brooding on the waves and, in due process of time, laid the Universal Egg. At her bidding, Ophion coiled seven times about this egg, until it hatched and split in two. Out tumbled all things that exist, her children: sun, moon, planets, stars, the earth with its mountains and rivers, its trees, herbs, and living creatures.

Pelasgian creation myth, *The Greek Myths*

❀ OSHO
(1931–1990)

There has been no creation. How can there be "the beginning?" The creation is continuous; it is creativity. Back you move, you will not find the beginning, ahead you go, you will not find the end. It is beginningless, endless creative energy. So in the first place there was no beginning. God never created the world—there is no God.

Discourses

❀ LEO BOOTH
(CONTEMPORARY)

We are co-creators with God, not puppets on a string waiting for something to happen.

Creation Spirituality

❀ PAUL DAVIES
(CONTEMPORARY)

These days most cosmologists and astronomers back the theory that there was indeed a creation, about eighteen billion years ago, when the physical universe burst into existence in an awesome explosion popularly know as the 'big bang'.

God and the New Physics

✳ WILLIAM GERBER
(CONTEMPORARY)

[A basic tenet of Indian thought is] that the cosmos originated as the play or sport or whimsical willing ("*lila*") of a creator who molded available matter into an order which he himself designed. . . . Of the belief that God made and rules the world through sport or whim, a strain runs through Western thought from Plato, who asserted that man is God's plaything, and other Greek thinkers, who held that τυχη (chance, contingency, caprice) is a component of the world, through Descartes, who said that God could have made the laws of nature entirely different from what they are, and Peirce, who said that the cosmos originated in sport. Other Western thinkers, however, from Aristotle to Einstein, disagree.

The Mind of India

✳ JOHN A. O'BRIEN
(CONTEMPORARY)

As the tiny mountain rivulet as well as the majestic lake and river, after many windings and turnings, all trace their course at last down to the ocean's might shore, so all things and all living creatures, all trace their origin and existence back to God, their Creator.

The Origin of Man

✳ MARIE-LOUISE VON FRANZ
(CONTEMPORARY)

And the God laughed seven times. The God laughed seven times: Ha-Ha-Ha-Ha-Ha-Ha-Ha. God laughed, and from these seven laughs seven Gods sprang up which embraced the whole universe; those were the first Gods.

When he first laughed, light appeared and its splendor shone through the whole universe. The God of the cosmos and of the fire . . .

He laughed for the second time and everything was water; the earth heard the sound and heard the light and was astonished and moved . . .

When the God wanted to laugh for the third time, bitterness came up in his mind and in his heart and it was called Hermes, through whom the whole universe is made manifest. . .

Then the God laughed for the fifth time and while he was laughing he became sad and Moira (fate) appeared, holding the scales in her hand, showing that in her was justice. So you see justice comes from a state between laughing and sadness. . .

When the God laughed for the sixth time, he was terribly pleased and Chronos appeared with his scepter, the sign of power, and God said to him that he should have the glory and the light, the scepter of the ruler, and that everything present and future, would be submitted to him.

Then he laughed for the seventh time, drawing breath, and while he was laughing he cried, and thus the soul came into being. And God said, "Thou shall move everything, and everything will be made happier through you. Hermes will lead you." When God said this, everything was set in motion and filled with breath.

Patterns of Creativity

Death

⊛ THE EGYPTIAN BOOK OF THE DEAD
(C. 3000 BCE)

God is One and alone, and none other exists with Him; God is the One, the One who has made all things.

He is eternal and infinite; He has endured for countless ages, and He shall endure to all eternity.

God is a spirit, a hidden spirit, the Spirit of spirits, the Divine Spirit.

He is a mystery to His creatures, and no man knows how to know Him. His names are innumerable; they are manifold, and no one knows their number.

God has made the universe, and He has created all that is in it; He has stretched out the heavens and founded the earth. What His heart conceived came to pass straightway, and when He had spoken His word came to pass, and it shall endure forever.

⊛ THE EPIC OF GILGAMESH
(3RD MILLENNIUM BCE)

There is no permanence. Do we build a house to stand for ever, do we seal a contract to hold for all time? Do brothers divide an inheritance to keep for ever, does the flood-time of rivers endure? . . . From the days of old there is no permanence. The sleeping and the dead, how alike they are, they are like a painted death. What is there between the master and the servant when both have fulfilled their doom? When the Anunnaki, the judges [of the dead], come together, and Mammetun, the mother of destinies, together they decree the fates of men. Life and death they allot but the day of death they do not disclose.

⊛ THE BHAGAVAD GITA
(500? BCE)

He who, at the time of death, thinking of Me alone, goes forth, leaving the body, he attains unto my Being.

Quoted in *The Soul: An Archeology*, Claudia Setzer

⊛ THE DHAMMAPADA
(3RD CENTURY BCE)

All beings tremble before danger, all fear death. When a man considers this, he does not kill or cause to kill.

The Path of Perfection

When a man considers this world as a bubble of froth, and as the illusion of an appearance, then the king of death has no power of him.

The Path of Perfection

One who knows the Self puts death to death.

The Path of Perfection

The body dies, but the spirit is not entombed.

Quoted in *The Soul: An Archeology*, Claudia Setzer

❀ SAPPHO

(C. 610–635 BCE)

Death is an evil; the gods have so judged; had it been good, they would die.

Fragment

❀ MAHABHARATA XII

(4TH–5TH CENTURY BCE)

Possessed by delusion, a man toils for his wife and child; but whether he fulfills his purpose or not, he must surrender the enjoyment thereof. When one is blessed with children and flocks and his heart is clinging to them, Death carries him away as doth a tiger a sleeping deer.

❀ SOCRATES

(469–399 BCE)

You too, gentlemen of the jury, must look forward to death with confidence, and fix your minds on this one belief, which is certain: that nothing can harm a good man either in life or after death, and his fortunes are not a matter of indifference to the gods. This present experience of mine has not come about accidentally; I am quite clear that the time had come when it was better for me to die and be released from my distractions. That is why my sign (guiding spirit) never turned me back.

Plato's *Apology*

❀ CHUANG TZU

(369–286 BCE)

How do I know that the love of life is not a delusion; and that the dislike of death is not like a child that is lost and does not know the way home?

Texts of Taoism

When Lao Tse died, Ch'in Yi went to the funeral. He uttered three yells and departed. A disciple asked him saying, "Were you not our Master's friend?"

"I was," replied Ch'in Yi.

"And if so, do you consider that a sufficient expression of grief at his death?" added the disciple.

"I do," said Ch'in Yi. "I had thought he was a [mortal] man, but now I know that he was not. . . . The Master came, because it was his time to be born; he went, because it was his time to go away. Those who accept the natural course and sequence of things and live in obedience to it are beyond joy and sorrow.

The Preservation of Life

❀ MENANDER

(C. 342–292 BCE)

Whom the Gods love dies young.

The Double Deceiver

EPICURUS
(341–270 BCE)

Death is nothing to us, since when we are, death has not come, and when death has come, we are not.

From Diogenes Laërtius, book 10, sec. 125

LUCRETIUS
(99–55 BCE)

Why shed tears that thou must die? For if thy past life has been one of enjoyment, and if all thy pleasures have not passed through thy mind, as through a sieve, and vanished, leaving not a rack behind, why then dost thou not, like a thankful guest, rise cheerfully from life's feast, and with a quiet mind go take thy rest.

De rerum natura

VIRGIL
(70–19 BCE)

Naked in death upon an unknown shore.

Aeneid

SENECA
(C. 4 BCE–65 CE)

That day, which you fear as being the end of all things, is the birthday of your eternity.

Letters of Lucilius

OLD TESTAMENT

How dieth the wise man? as the fool.

Ecclesiastes 2:16

Man does not know his time.

Ecclesiastes 9:12 RSV

Death is better than bitter life or continual sickness.

Ecclesiastes 30:17

MARCUS AURELIUS
(121–180)

The act of dying is also one of the acts of life.

Meditations

And as for death, if there be any gods, it is no grievous thing to leave the society of men. The gods will do thee no hurt, thou mayest be sure. But if it be so that there be no gods, or that they take no care of the world, why should I desire to live in a world void of gods, and of all divine providence.

Meditations

OTOMO NO TABITO
(665–731)

Because it is the case that
Every living man
In the end dies,
While we are in the world
Let us be merry!

Japanese Poetry: The UTA, Arthur Waley

WANG WEI
(699–761)

White hairs will never be transformed
That elixir is beyond creation
To eliminate decrepitude
Study the absolute.

"Sitting alone on an autumn night,"
in *The Poems of Wang Wei*

✸ HUSAYN IBN MANSUR AL HALLAJ
(858–922)

My life is in my death, and my death is in my life.

Diwan

✸ LADY SARASHINA
(1008–?)

That smoke we watched above her pyre
Has vanished utterly.
How can she have hoped to find the grave
Among the bamboo grasses of the plain?

As I Crossed a Bridge of Dreams

✸ MILAREPA
(1040–1123)

Death is like a shadow cast by the sun;
I have never seen it prevented.

The Message of Milarepa, translated
by Sir Humphrey Clarke

✸ AL-GHAZZALI
(B. 1058)

The meaning of death is not the annihilation of the spirit, but its separation from the body, and that the resurrection and day of assembly do not mean a return to a new existence after annihilation, but the bestowal of a new form or frame to the spirit.

The Revival of Religious Sciences

The first sign of love to God is not to be afraid of death, and to be always waiting for it. For death unites the friend to his friend—the seeker to the object which he seeks.

The Revival of Religious Sciences

✸ RABELAIS
(1494?–1553)

Je vais querir un grand peut-être. . . .
Tirez le rideau, la farce est joué (I am going to seek a great perhaps. . . . Pull down the curtain, the farce is ended.)

By tradition, his last words

✸ MICHEL DE MONTAIGNE
(1533–1592)

If you do not know how to die, never mind. Nature will give you full and adequate instruction on the spot. She will do this job for you neatly; do not worry yourself with the thought.

Essays

If we have known how to live steadfastly and calmly, we shall know how to die in the same way. They may boast as much as they please, that "a philosopher's whole life is a contemplation of death." It seems to me, however, that it is indeed the end but the not the aim of life; it is its conclusion, its extreme point, yet not its object. Life should contain its own aim, its own purposes.

Essays

✸ FRANCIS BACON
(1561–1626)

The world's a bubble, and the life of
man less than a span.

The World

Who then to frail mortality shall trust
But limns on water, or but writes in dust.

The World

It is as natural to die as to be born; and to a little infant, perhaps the one is as painful as the other.

Essays

❀ WILLIAM SHAKESPEARE
(1564–1616)

Fear no more the heat of the sun
Nor the furious winter's rages;
Thou thy worldly task hast done,
Home art gone and ta'en thy wages.
Golden lads and girls all must,
As chimney-sweepers, come to dust.

Cymbeline, IV, 2 258

All that live must die, Passing through
    nature to eternity.

Hamlet, I, 2

❀ JOHN DONNE
(1572–1631)

Death be not proud, though some have
    called thee
Mighty and dreadful, for, thou art not
    so,
For, those, whom thou think'st thou
    dost overthrow,
Die not, poor death, nor yet can'st thou
    kill me.

Death Be Not Proud

❀ ROBERT BURTON
(1577–1640)

The fear of death is worse than
    death.

Anatomy of Melancholy

❀ TALES FROM THE THOUSAND AND ONE NIGHTS
(18TH CENTURY)

[The King] reigned through many joyful years, until he was visited by the Destroyer of all earthly pleasures, the Leveller of mighty kings and humble peasants.

The Tale of Ma'Aruf, The Cobbler

❀ HENRY FIELDING
(1707–1754)

It hath often been said that it is not death but dying that is terrible.

Amelia

❀ SAMUEL JOHNSON
(1709–1784)

Depend upon it, Sir, when a man knows he is to be hanged in a fortnight, it concentrates his mind wonderfully.

Quoted in *Life of Johnson*, James Boswell

❀ CHIEF SEATTLE
(1786–1866)

There is no death. Only a change of worlds.

Quoted in *The Spiritual Legacy of the American Indian*, Joseph Epes Brown

❀ PERCY BYSSHE SHELLEY
(1792–1822)

Life, like a dome of many-coloured
    glass,
Stains the white radiance of Eternity.
Until death tramples it to fragments.

Adonais

HENRY WADSWORTH LONGFELLOW
(1807–1882)

The grave is but a covered bridge leading from light to light, through a brief darkness.

A Covered Bridge at Lucerne

EMILY DICKINSON
(1830–1886)

Because I could not stop for Death
He kindly stopped for me
The Carriage held but just Ourselves
And Immortality.

Poem no. 712

CHRISTINA ROSSETTI
(1830–1894)

When I am dead, my dearest, Sing no sad songs for me.

Song

PHILLIPS BROOKS
(1835–1893)

Death is the enlightener. The essential thing concerning it must be that it opens the closed eyes, draws down the veil of blinding mortality, and lets the man see spiritual things.

Perennials

JOHN MUIR
(1838–1914)

Let children walk with Nature, let them see the beautiful blendings and communions of death and life, their joyous inseparable unity, as taught in woods and meadows . . . and they will learn that death is stingless indeed, and as beautiful as life.

A Thousand-Mile Walk to the Gulf

HENRY VAN DYKE
(1852–1933)

Some people are so afraid to die that they never begin to live.

Letters

CECIL RHODES
(1853–1902)

So little done, so much to do.

Dying words

DORA CARRINGTON
(1872–1941)

If this is death I don't think much of it.

Last words

W. SOMERSET MAUGHAM
(1874–1965)

Dying is a very dull, dreary affair. And my advice to you is to have nothing whatever to do with it.

A Writer's Notebook

THOMAS MANN
(1875–1955)

The only religious way to think of death is as part and parcel of life.

The Magic Mountain

ELIZABETH ARDEN
(1878–1966)

Death not merely ends life, it also bestows upon it a silent completeness, snatched from the hazardous flux to which all things human are subject.

The Life of the Mind

⊛ NIKOS KAZANTZAKIS
(1885–1957)

Luckless man has raised what he thinks is an impassable barrier round his poor little existence. He takes refuge there and tries to bring a little order and security into his life. A little happiness. Everything must follow the beaten track, the sacrosanct routine, and comply with safe and simple rules. Inside this enclosure, fortified against the fierce attacks of the unknown, his petty certainties, crawling about like centipedes, go unchallenged. There is only one formidable enemy, mortally feared and hated: the Great Certainty [death].

Zorba the Greek

⊛ D. H. LAWRENCE
(1885–1930)

I live and I die. I ask no other. Whatever proceeds from me lives and dies. I am glad, too. God is eternal, but my idea of Him is my own, and perishable. Everything human, human knowledge, human faith, human emotions, all perishes. And that is very good; if it were not so everything would turn to cast-iron. . . . It is the cycle of all things created, thank God. Because, given courage, it saves even eternity from staleness.

Phoenix II

⊛ DOROTHY PARKER
(1893–1967)

It costs me never a stab nor squirm
To tread by chance upon a worm.
"Aha, my little dear," I say,
"Your clan will pay me back one day."

Thoughts for a Sunshiny Morning

⊛ SYLVIA PLATH
(1932–1963)

Dying is an art, like everything else.

Lady Lazarus

⊛ MORRIS B. ABRAM
(CONTEMPORARY)

A painting on a canvas of infinite size, worked on eternally, would be without focus, meaning and probably without beauty. A painting, as life, needs limits. While I have an almost insatiable craving for knowledge, I believe death to be the final and perhaps greatest teacher—the one that provides the key to the ultimate questions life has never answered. In my darkest hours I have been consoled by the thought that death at least is a payment for the answer of life's haunting secrets.

The Wall Street Journal

⊛ WOODY ALLEN
(CONTEMPORARY)

It's not that I'm afraid to die. I just don't want to be there when it happens.

Without Feathers, "Death"

⊛ CARLOS CASTANEDA
(CONTEMPORARY)

An immense amount of pettiness is dropped if your death makes a gesture to you, or if you catch a glimpse of it, or if you just have the feeling that your companion is there watching you. . . . Death is the only wise adviser that we have. Whenever you feel . . . that everything is going wrong and you're about to be annihilated, turn to your death and ask if that is so. Your death will tell you that you're wrong; that nothing really matters outside its touch. Your death will tell you, "I haven't touched you yet."

Journey to Ixtlan

❂ ELISABETH KÜBLER-ROSS
(CONTEMPORARY)

It is those who have not really lived—who have left issues unsettled, dreams unfulfilled, hopes shattered, and who have let the real things in life (loving and being loved by others, contributing in a positive way to other people's happiness and welfare, finding out what things are *really* you) pass them by—who are most reluctant to die.

In *Weavers of Wisdom*, Anne Bancroft

❂ PETER LORIE
(CONTEMPORARY)

If I lie down one day and die in my
    sleep,
How will I know if I still dream,
A dream of death in life or a dream of
    life in death.
That maybe I will wake again a child
    still dreaming.
And how will I know which life I have
    left before sleep,
And which life I have come to on
    waking?
Would I dream of dying or die of
    dreaming?
And is there a difference?

Untitled

❂ G. S. MERRIAM
(CONTEMPORARY)

No one who is fit to live need fear to die. . . . To us here, death is the most terrible word we know. But when we have tasted its reality, it will mean to us birth, deliverance, a new creation of ourselves.

A Living Faith

❂ NORMAN O'BROWN
(CONTEMPORARY)

This incapacity to die, ironically but inevitably, throws mankind out of the actuality of living, which for all normal animals is at the same time dying; the result is the denial of life (repression). The incapacity to accept death turns the death instinct into its destructively human and distinctly morbid form. The distraction of human life to the war against death, by the same inevitable irony, results in death's dominion over life.

Life Against Death: The Psychoanalytic Meaning of History

❂ SOGYAL RINPOCHE
(CONTEMPORARY)

In the Buddhist approach, life and death are seen as one whole, where death is the beginning of another chapter of life. Death is a mirror in which the entire meaning of life is reflected.

The Tibetan Book of Living and Dying

❂ ANTONIN SERTILLAGES
(CONTEMPORARY)

When death is spoken of as a tearing asunder, we forget that it tears especially the veil of appearances and of deceptions which conceal from our view the depth of reality and of others and ourselves.

Recollections

Dream and Illusion

☸ TIBETAN BUDDHIST PRAYER

When the state of dreaming has
    dawned,
Do not lie in ignorance like a corpse,
Enter the natural sphere of unwavering
    attentiveness.
Recognize your dreams and transform
    illusion into luminosity.
Do not sleep like an animal.
Do the practice which mixes sleep and
    reality.

☸ THE BHAGAVAD GITA

(C. 500 BCE)

Never the spirit was born; the spirit
    shall cease to be never;
Never was time it was not; End and
    Beginning are dreams!
Birthless and deathless and changeless
    remaineth the spirit for ever;

☸ CHUANG TZU

(369–286 BCE)

I do not know whether I was then a man
dreaming I was a butterfly, or whether I
am now a butterfly dreaming I am a
man.

On Leveling All Things

☸ MURASAKI SHIKIBU

(974–1031?)

A night of endless dreams, inconsequent
and wild, is this my life; none more
worth telling than the rest.

The Tale of Genji

☸ ATISA (DIPANKARA)

(982–1054)

Think that all phenomena are like
    dreams.

Seven Points of Mind Training

☸ TIBETAN BUDDHIST TREATISE

(11TH CENTURY)

All is like a dream or a magic show.

☸ HAKIM ABU' L-MAJD MAJDUD SANAI OF GHAZNA (HAKIM SANAI)

(12TH CENTURY)

All mankind is asleep,
living in a desolate world;
the desire to transcend this
is mere habit and custom,
not religion—idle fairy tales.

The Walled Garden of Truth

⊛ SAIGYO HOSHI
(1118–1190)

Since I am convinced
That Reality is in no way
Real,
How am I to admit
That dreams are dreams?

Japanese Poetry: The UTA, Arthur Waley

⊛ OSCAR WILDE
(1854–1900)

A dreamer is one who can only find his way by moonlight, and his punishment is that he sees the dawn before the rest of the world.

The Critic As Artist

⊛ WILLIAM BUTLER YEATS
(1865–1939)

I have spread my dreams under your feet;
Tread softly, because you tread on my dreams.

He Wishes for the Clothes of Heaven

⊛ HERMANN HESSE
(1877–1962)

When anyone reads anything which he wishes to study, he does not despise the letters and punctuation marks, and call them illusion, chance and worthless shells, but he reads them, he studies and loves them, letter by letter. But I, who wished to read the book of the world and the book of my own nature, did presume to despise the letters and signs. I called the world of appearances, illusion. I called my eyes and tongue, chance. Now it is over; I have awakened.

I have indeed awakened and have only been born today.

Siddhartha

⊛ ALAN WATTS
(1915–1973)

This is more or less what I would do if I had the power to dream every night of anything I wanted. Some months I would probably fulfill all the more obvious wishes. There might be palaces and banquets, players and dancing girls, fabulous bouts of love, and sunlit gardens beside lakes, with mountains beyond. There would next be long conversations with sages, contemplation of supreme works of art, hearing and playing music, voyages to foreign lands, flying out into space to see the galaxies, and delving into the atom to watch the wiggling wavicles. But the night would come when I might want to add a little spice of adventure—perhaps a dream of dangerous mountain climbing, of rescuing a princess from a dragon, or, better, an unpredictable dream in which I do not know what will happen. Once this has started, I might get still more daring. I would wish to dream whole lifetimes, packing seventy years into a single night. I would dream that I am not dreaming at all, that I will never wake up, that I have completely lost myself somewhere down the tangled corridors of the mind, and, finally, that I am in such excruciating agony that when I wake up, it will be better than all possible dreams.

The Book

⊛ OSHO
(1931–1990)

I don't think you have two hours in a day without dreams, because if you have two hours without dreams, fully awake, those two hours will become your meditation. They will reveal immensely valuable secrets to you.

Discourses

⊛ CARLOS CASTANEDA
(CONTEMPORARY)

"And what is real?" don Juan asked me very calmly.

"This, what we're looking at, is real," I said, pointing to the surroundings.

"But so was the bridge you saw last night, and so was the forest and everything else."

"But if they are real, where are they now?"

"They are right here. If you had enough power you could call them back. Right now, you cannot do that because you think it is very helpful to keep on doubting and nagging. It isn't, my friend, it isn't. There are worlds upon worlds, right here in front of us."

The Power of Dreaming

⊛ U. G. KRISHNAMURTI
(CONTEMPORARY)

You want to change yourself into something and at the same time find you cannot change at all. This "change" you talk of is really just more romantic fancy-stuff for you. You never change,

only think about changing. As long as you want to change, for some reason or the other, so long will you insist upon changing the whole world. You want a different world so that you can be happy in it. That is your only interest. You can talk of mankind, concern for mankind, compassion for mankind, but it is all bullshit, horseshit. . . . Since you are determined to bring about change—a notion put into you by your culture—you remain discontent and want the world to be different. When your inner demand to be something different than what in fact you are comes to an end, then the neurotic demand to change your society ceases. Then you cannot be in conflict with society; you are in perfect harmony with society, including its brutalities and miseries. All your attempts to change this brutal society only add momentum to it.

Mind Is a Myth—Disquieting Conversations with a Man Called U. G.

⊛ ROBERT LAWLOR
(CONTEMPORARY)

The higher the initiation, the more an individual lives in the awareness of this Dreamtime reality and the stronger the ancestral soul will be at the time of death.

Voices of the First Day

⊛ LLEWELYN POWYS
(CONTEMPORARY)

It is the stupidity of our minds that prevents us from seeing existence as a mystery wilder than the dreams of Devil or God.

Earth Memories

KEITH THOMPSON
(CONTEMPORARY)

The way you would whimper and tremble during dreams. The deep breezy soul-breath that came each time we reached for you. Your animal warmth joining ours.

Quoted in *The Soul: An Archeology*, Claudia Setzer

Emotion

THE UPANISHADS
(900–600 BCE)

A man whose mind wanders among desires, and is longing for objects of desire, goes again to life and death according to his desires. But he who possesses the End of all longing, and whose self has found fulfillment, even in this life his desires will fade away.

Mandaka Upanishad

SAPPHO
(C. 610–635 BCE)

When anger spreads through the breast, guard thy tongue from barking idly.

Untitled fragment

ARISTOTLE
(384–322 BCE)

It is the nature of desire not to be satisfied, and most men live only for the gratification of it. The beginning of reform is not so much to equalise property as to train the noble sort of natures not to desire more, and to prevent the lower from getting more.

Politics

OLD TESTAMENT

He who is slow to anger is better than the mighty, and he who rules his spirit than he who takes a city.

Proverbs 16:32

SHANTIDEVA
(8TH CENTURY)

If things were brought into being by
   choice,
Then since no one wishes to suffer,
Suffering would not occur.

A Guide to the Bodhisattva's Way of Life

SHANKARA
(788–820)

In the cave of my heart dwells the Lord . . . who killed the Elephant-demon (which can destroy elephants), who destroyed the ferocious Tiger-demon (which can overcome even tigers), who has on him dead animals, and who has a white form (which has a majestic appearance). Whence is there fear for me!

Sivanandalahari

❁ MILAREPA
(1040–1123)

All worldly pursuits have but one unavoidable and inevitable end, which is sorrow; acquisitions end in dispersion; buildings in destruction; meetings in separation; births in death. Knowing this, one should, from the very first, renounce acquisitions and storing-up, and building, and meeting; and, faithful to the commands of an eminent Guru, set about realising the Truth. That alone is the best of religious observances.

The Message of Milarepa

❁ KABIR
(1440?–1518)

The lock of error shuts the gate, open
  it with the key of love:
Thus, by opening the door thou shalt
  wake the Beloved.
Kabir says: "O brother! Do not pass by
  such good fortune as this."

One Hundred Poems of Kabir

❁ ST. JOHN OF THE CROSS
(1542–1591)

To reach satisfaction in all, desire its possession in nothing. To come to possess all, desire the possession of nothing. To arrive at being all, desire to be nothing. To come to the knowledge of all, desire the knowledge of nothing.

The Ascent of Mount Carmel

❁ EDITH CAVELL
(1865–1915)

Standing, as I do, in the view of God and eternity I realise that patriotism is not enough. I must have no hatred or bitterness towards anyone.

Last words, as quoted in the *Times* newspaper (London)

❁ MOHANDAS K. GANDHI
(1869–1948)

I have learnt through bitter experience the one supreme lesson to conserve my anger, and as heat conserved is transmuted into energy, even so our anger controlled can be transmuted into a power which can move the world.

Quoted in *The Soul: An Archeology*, Claudia Setzer

❁ H. L. MENCKEN
(1880–1956)

Fear of death and fear of life both become piety.

Minority Report

❁ NIKOS KAZANTZAKIS
(1885–1957)

Once when I was a kid—this'll show you—I was mad on cherries. I had no money, so I couldn't buy many at a time, and when I'd eaten all I could buy I still wanted more. Day and night I thought of nothing but cherries. I foamed at the mouth; it was torture! But one day I got mad, or ashamed, I don't know which. Anyway, I just felt cherries were doing what they liked with me and it was ludicrous. So what did I do? I got up one night, searched my father's pockets and found a silver mejidie and pinched it. I was up early the next morning, went to the market-gardener and bought a basket o' cherries. I settled down in a ditch and began eating. I stuffed and stuffed till I was all swollen out. My stomach began to ache and I was sick. Yes, boss, I was thoroughly sick, and from that day to this I've never wanted a cherry. I couldn't bear the sight of them. I was saved. I could say to any cherry: I don't need you any more. And I did the same thing later with wine and tobacco. I still drink and smoke, but at any second, if I want to, whoop! I can cut it out. I'm not ruled by passion.

Zorba the Greek

⊛ D. H. LAWRENCE
(1885–1930)

A man cannot create desire in himself, nor cease at will from desiring. Desire, in any shape or form, is primal, whereas the will is secondary, derived. The will can destroy, but it cannot create.

Phoenix II

⊛ C. S. LEWIS
(1898–1963)

If I find I have a desire which no experience in this world can satisfy, the most probable explanation is that I was made for another world.

Quoted in *The Soul: An Archeology*, Claudia Setzer

⊛ ALBERT CAMUS
(1913–1960)

Like great works, deep feelings always mean more than they are conscious of saying. The regularity of an impulse or a repulsion in a soul is encountered again in habits of doing or thinking, is reproduced in consequences of which the soul itself knows nothing. Great feelings take with them their own universe, splendid or abject. They light up with their passion an exclusive world in which they recognise their climate. There is a universe of jealousy, or ambition, of selfishness or of generosity. A universe—in other words a metaphysic and an attitude of mind. What is true of already specialised feelings will be even more so of emotions basically as indeterminate, simultaneously as vague and as "definite," as remote and as "present" as those furnished us by beauty or aroused by absurdity.

The Myth of Sisyphus

⊛ ALAN WATTS
(1915–1973)

It is surely obvious that how you do things depends crucially upon how you feel. If you feel inwardly isolated from the natural world, your dealings with it will tend to be hostile and aggressive. It is not so much a matter of what you do as of how you do it, not so much the content as the style of action adopted. It is easy enough to see this in leading or persuading other people, for one and the same communication may have quite opposite results according to the style or feeling with which it is given. Yet this is equally true in dealing with inanimate nature and with our own inner nature—with our instincts and appetites. They will yield to intelligence much more agreeably to the extent that we feel ourselves to be one with them, or, to put it in another way, to be in relationship to them, to have the unity of mutual interdependence.

This Is IT and Other Essays on Zen and Spiritual Experience

✹ OSHO

(1931–1990)

Life up to now has been corrupted by ambition. There is no other poison which is more potent than ambition because it kills you and yet keeps you breathing. Ambition turns you into vegetables, and the lure of ambition is given to every child with the mother's milk. From the very first moment, his whole life is being based on principles of destructiveness. Nothing destroys more than ambitiousness.

Discourses

✹ SIDNEY GREENBERG

(CONTEMPORARY)

For all the unkind things said about envy, it would only be fair to acknowledge that not all envy is destructive. If envy leads us to work hard and to improve our skills, it becomes a stimulant to self-improvement. God has given us no quality that cannot be used for good.

Say Yes to Life

✹ DESMOND TUTU

(CONTEMPORARY)

A jealous person is doubly unhappy—over what he has, which is judged inferior, and over what he has not, which is judged superior. Such a person is doubly removed from knowing the true blessing of creation.

An African Prayer Book

Enlightenment

❀ THE UPANISHADS

(900–600 BCE)

Then Usata Akrayana asked him:
"O Yajnavalkya!" he said.
"Explain to me what is the
Brahman, immediate and direct,
which is the Self within all."
"It is your Self within all."
"O Yajnavalkya! Which of the Selves is
it that is within all?"
"It is your Self within all which
breathes in by your breathing in."
. . . You cannot see the Seer of seeing;
you cannot hear the Hearer of hearing;
you cannot think the Thinker of
thinking;
you cannot know the Knower of
knowing.
That is your Self within all.

Brhad Upanishad

As pure water becomes the same
when into water pure it flows,
So of the sage, O Gautama,
the Self becomes who Brahman
knows.

Katha Upanishad

As rivers flow into the sea and in so
doing lose name and form, even so the
wise man freed from name and form,
attains the Supreme Being, the Self-
luminous, the Infinite.

Mandaka Upanishad

❀ LAO-TZU

(C. 6TH CENTURY BCE)

He who knows others is wise;
He knows himself is enlightened.

Tao Te Ching

Whosoever stands on tiptoe does not
stand firmly. Whosoever stands with
legs astride will not advance. Whosoever
wants to shine will not be enlightened.
Whosoever wants to be someone will
not become resplendent. Whosoever
glorifies himself does not accomplish
works. Whosoever boasts of himself will
not be exalted. For Tao he is like kitchen
refuse and a festering sore. And all the
creatures loathe him. Therefore: whosoever has Tao does not linger with these.

Tao Te Ching

Going back to the origin is called peace;
it means reversion to destiny. Reversion
to destiny is called eternity. He who
knows eternity is called enlightened.

Tao Te Ching

❈ THE BHAGAVAD GITA
(500? BCE)

In this world, aspirants may find enlightenment by two different paths. For the contemplative is the path of knowledge; for the active is the path of selfless action.

❈ THE GOLDEN MEAN OF TSESZE
(4TH? CENTURY BCE)

The moral man conforms himself to his life circumstances; he does not desire anything outside of his position. Finding himself in a position of wealth and honour, he lives as becomes one living in a position of wealth and honour. Finding himself in a position of poverty and humble circumstances, he lives as becomes one living in a position of poverty and humble circumstances. Finding himself in uncivilised countries, he lives as becomes one living in uncivilised countries. Finding himself in circumstances of danger and difficulty. He acts according to what is required of a man under such circumstances. In one word, the moral man can find himself in no situation in life in which he is not master of himself.

The Humanistic Standard

❈ HERACLITUS
(C. 4TH CENTURY BCE)

Everything flows, nothing stays still.

Cratylus

❈ CHUANG TZU
(369–286 BCE)

To have been cast in this human form is to us already a source of joy. How much greater joy beyond our conception to know that that which is now in human form may undergo countless transitions, with only the infinite to look forward to? Therefore it is that the Sage rejoices in that which can never be lost, but endures always. For if we emulate those who can accept graciously long age or short life and the vicissitudes of events, how much more that which informs all creation on which all changing phenomena depend?

The Great Supreme

For all men strive to grasp what they do not know, while none strive to grasp what they already know; and all strive to discredit what they do not excel in, while none strive to discredit what they do excel in. This is why there is chaos.

Opening Trunks

❈ THE FIRST BOOK OF ENOCH
(3RD CENTURY BCE–3RD CENTURY CE)

Hear child, from the time when the Lord anointed me with the ointment of his glory, there has been no food in me and my soul remembers not earthly enjoyment, neither do I want anything earthly.

The Lost Books of the Bible and The Forgotten Books of Eden

❈ BHAGWAN SHREE PATANJALI
(2ND? CENTURY BCE)

This Samadhi completes the transformation and fulfils the purpose of evolution. Now the process by which evolution unfolds through time is understood. This is Enlightenment.

Yoga Sutras

✿ SOSAN (SENG-S'TAN) THE THIRD ZEN PATRIARCH

One in All,
All in One—
If only this is realized,
No more worry about your not being
perfect.

On Believing in Mind

✿ DEVARA DASIMAYYA

(10TH CENTURY)

If they see
breasts and long hair coming
they call it woman,

if beard and whiskers
they call it man:

but, look, the self that hovers
in between
is neither man
nor woman.

O Ramanatha: Speaking of Siva

✿ MARIE DE FRANCE

(1160?–1215?)

You have to endure what you can't
change.

The Lais of Marie de France

✿ ANNE BOLEYN

(1507–1536)

What will be, will be, grumble who
    may.

Motto embroidered on servants' livery

✿ MATSUO BASHO

(1644–1694)

Do not seek to follow in the footsteps of
the men of old; seek what they sought.

The Narrow Road to the Deep North

✿ WILLIAM BLAKE

(1757–1827)

To see a world in a grain of sand
And a heaven in a wild flower,
Hold infinity in the palm of your hand
And eternity in an hour.

Auguries of Innocence

✿ FYODOR DOSTOYEVSKY

(1821–1881)

Reality is infinitely various when compared to the deductions of abstract thought, even those that are most cunning, and it will not tolerate rigid, hard-and-fast distinctions. Reality strives for diversification.

The House of the Dead

✿ THOMAS HENRY HUXLEY

(1825–1895)

Education is the instruction of the intellect in the laws of Nature, under which name I include not merely things and their forces, but men and their ways; and the fashioning of the affections and of the will into an earnest and loving desire to move in harmony with those laws.

On the Natural Inequality of Man

SHRI RAMAKRISHNA
(1836–1886)

The Vedanta speaks of seven planes in which the mind moves and works. The ordinary man's mind moves only in the three lower centers and is content with satisfying itself through the common appetites: eating, drinking, sleeping and begetting. But when it reaches the fourth center opposite the heart, man sees divine effulgence. From this state, however, he often lapses back to the three lower centers. When the mind comes to the fifth center opposite the throat the spiritual aspirant cannot speak of anything but God. . . . Even from this state a man may slip down; he should therefore be very watchful. But he need not have any fear of a fall when the mind reaches the sixth center, level with the junction of the eyebrows. He gets the vision of the "Paramatman" (Oversoul) and remains always in "Samadhi." His mind, however, is not really merged in the "Paramatman" for there is a thin transparent veil between the sixth center and the "Sahasrar," the highest center.

Spiritual Teachings

SRI AUROBINDO
(1872–1950)

The soul and mind and life are powers of living and can grow, but cannot be cut out or made. . . . One can indeed help the being to grow . . . but even so, the growth must still come from within.

The Life Divine

YOGASWAMI
(1872–1964)

Running water will run faster if you remove an obstruction here and there. You need not do much more.

Positive Thoughts for Daily Meditation

D. H. LAWRENCE
(1885–1930)

Never to be able to love spontaneously, never to be moved by a power greater than oneself, but always to be within one's own control, deliberate, having the choice, this was horrifying, more deadly than death. Yet how was one to escape? How could a man escape from being deliberate and unloving, except a greater power, an impersonal, imperative love should take hold of him? And if the greater power should not take hold of him, what could he do but continue in his deliberateness, without any fundamental spontaneity?

Phoenix II

WEI WU WEI (TERENCE GRAY)
(1895–1986)

If you have the basic understanding that the primal Buddha-nature is that of all sentient beings, it follows that anyone who thinks that any *action* can lead to his "enlightenment" is turning his back on the truth: he is thinking that there is a "he" there to be "enlightened," whereas "enlightenment" is a name for the state wherein there is no separate individual at all, and which is that of all sentient beings, a name for what they are, but which cannot be recognized by anyone who believes himself to be an autonomous individual.

Open Secret

JEAN DUBUFFET
(1901–1985)

Unless one says good-bye to what one loves, and unless one travels to completely new territories, one can expect merely a long wearing away of oneself and an eventual extinction.

Quoted in the *New York Times*, obituary, May 15, 1985

ORSON WELLES
(1915–1985)

In Italy for thirty years under the Borgias they had warfare, terror, murder, bloodshed—they produced Michelangelo, Leonardo da Vinci and the Renaissance. In Switzerland they had brotherly love, five hundred years of democracy and peace, and what did they produce . . . ? The cuckoo clock.

The Third Man

OSHO
(1931–1990)

For seven days I lived in a very hopeless and helpless state, but at the same time something was arising. There was no ground underneath; I was in an abyss, a bottomless abyss, but there was no fear because there was nothing to protect. There was no fear because there was nobody to be afraid. Those seven days were of tremendous transformation, total transformation.

And on the last day, the presence of a totally new energy, a new light and a new delight, became so intense that it was almost unbearable. It was as if I was exploding, as if I was going mad with blissfulness.

The Discipline of Transcendence

The blind with a little courage gather around themselves the blind with less courage.

Discourses

PAUL BRUNTON
(CONTEMPORARY)

When camphor burns no residue is left. The mind is the camphor, when it has resolved itself into the self without leaving the slightest trace, it is Realization.

Quoted in *The Soul: An Archeology*, Claudia Setzer

NORMAN COUSINS
(CONTEMPORARY)

Education tends to be diagrammatic and categorical, opening up no sluices in the human imagination on the wonder of beauty of their unique estate in the cosmos. Little wonder that it becomes so easy for our young to regard human hurt casually or to be uninspired by the magic of sensitivity.

Saturday Review

JOHN W. GARDINER
(CONTEMPORARY)

I think that all human systems require continuous renewal. They rigidify. They get stiff in the joints. They forget what they cared about. The forces against it are nostalgia and the enormous appeal of having things the way they have always been, appeals to a supposedly happy past. But we've got to move on.

The *New York Times*, July 21, 1989

❁ D. S. SARMA
(CONTEMPORARY)

The ultimate aim of man is liberation; liberation not only from the bondage of the flesh, but also from the limitation of a finite being. In other words, *moksha* means becoming a perfect spirit like the Supreme Spirit. . . . But the law of *Karma* postulates that every individual has to pass through a series of lives either on earth or somewhere else before he attains *moksha* or liberation.

The Religion of the Hindus

❁ THICH NHAT HANH
(CONTEMPORARY)

There is no enlightenment outside of daily life.

Zen Keys

Liberation and enlightenment do not exist outside of your own self. We need only open our eyes to see that we ourselves are the very essence of liberation and enlightenment. All dharmas, all beings, contain the nature of full enlightenment within themselves. Don't look for it outside yourself. If you shine the light of awareness on your own self, you will realize enlightenment immediately. Bhikkhus, nothing in the universe exists independently of your own consciousness, not even nirvana or liberation. Don't search for them elsewhere. Remember that the object of consciousness cannot exist independently from consciousness. Don't chase after any dharma, including Brahma, nirvana, and liberation. That is the meaning of aimlessness. You already are what you are searching for. Aimlessness is a wondrous gate that leads to freedom.

Old Path White Clouds: The Life Story of the Buddha

❁ ANONYMOUS

What's a Hindu?
Lay eggs!

Source unknown

Freedom

PROVERB
Lean liberty is better than fat slavery.

THE BHAGAVAD GITA
(500? BCE)
He whose joy is within, whose pleasure is within, and whose light is within, that de-votee, being well established in the Supreme, attains to absolute freedom.

Book of Daily Thoughts and Prayers

CHUANG TZU
(369–286 BCE)
A thousand ounces of silver would be a great gain to me, and to be a high noble-man and minister is a most honourable position. But have you not seen the victim-ox for the ceremonial sacrifice? It is carefully fed for several years, and robed with rich embroidery that it may be fit to enter the Grand Temple. Then, when the time comes for it to do so, it would prefer to be a little pig, but it cannot get to be so. So, go away, and do not soil me with your presence. I would rather amuse and enjoy myself in the midst of a filthy ditch than be subject to the rules and restrictions in the court of a king. I have determined never to take such an office, but prefer the enjoyment of my own free will.

Opening Trunks

HAKIM ABU' L-MAJD MAJDUD SANAI OF GHAZNA (HAKIM SANAI)
(12TH CENTURY)
No one knows how far it is
from nothingness to God.
As long as you cling to your self
you will wander right and left,
day and night, for thousands of years;
and when, after all that effort,
you finally open your eyes,
you will see your self, through inherent
    defects,
wandering round itself like the ox in a
    mill;
but, if, once freed from your self,
you finally get down to work,
this door will open to you within two
    minutes.

The Walled Garden of Truth

❁ DESIDERIUS ERASMUS
(1466?–1536)

God commands us to pray without ceasing, to watch, to struggle and to contend for the reward of eternal life. Why does He wish to be prayed to endlessly for that which He has already decreed to grant or not to grant, since being immutable He cannot change His decrees?

Of Free Will

❁ WALT WHITMAN
(1819–1892)

What do you suppose will satisfy the soul, except to walk free and own no superior?

Source unknown

❁ MIKHAIL NAIMY
(1889–1988)

Happy are the staffless
They stumble not.
Happy are the homeless,
They are at home.
The stumblers only—like ourselves,
Need walk with staffs.
The home-chained only—like
    ourselves,
Must have a home.

The Book of Mirdad—A Lighthouse and a Haven

MIRDAD—This is the way to freedom
    from care and pain:
So think as if your every thought were
    to be etched in fire upon the sky
    for all and everything to see. For
    so, in truth it is.
So speak as if the world entire were but
    a single ear intent on bearing what
    you say. And so, in truth, it is.

So do as if your every deed were to
    recoil upon your heads. And so, in
    truth, it does.
So wish as if you were the wish. And so,
    in truth, you are.
So live as if your God Himself had
    need of you His life to live. And so,
    in truth, He does.

The Book of Mirdad—A Lighthouse and a Haven

True freedom is won and lost in the
    heart.

The Book of Mirdad—A Lighthouse and a Haven

❁ J. KRISHNAMURTI
(1895–1986)

I have only one purpose: to make man free, to urge him towards freedom; to help him to break away from all limitations, for that alone will give him eternal happiness, will give him the unconditional realisation of Self.

Because I am free, unconditioned, whole—not the part, not the relative but the whole Truth that is eternal—I desire those who seek to understand me to be free, not to follow me, not to make out of me a cage which will become a religion, a sect. Rather should they be free from all fears—from the fear of religion, from the fear of salvation, from the fear of death, from the fear of life itself. My purpose is to make man unconditionally free, for I maintain that the only spirituality is the incorruptibility of the Self which is eternal, is the harmony between reason and love.

This is the absolute, unconditioned Truth which is life itself. I want therefore to set man free, rejoicing as the bird in the clear sky, unburdened, independent, ecstatic in that freedom.

Quoted in Papul Jayakar, *Krishnamurti—
A Biography*

✹ ALAN WATTS
(1915–1973)

The student of Zen is confronted by a master who has himself experienced awakening, and is in the best sense of the expression a completely natural man. For the adept in Zen is one who manages to be human with the same artless grace and absence of inner conflict with which a tree is a tree. Such a man is likened to a ball in a mountain stream, which is to say that he cannot be blocked, stopped, or embarrassed in any situation. He never wobbles or dithers in his mind, for though he may pause in overt action to think a problem out, the stream of his consciousness always moves straight ahead without being caught in the vicious circles of anxiety or indecisive doubt, wherein thought whirls wildly around without issue. He is not precipitate or hurried in action, but simply continuous. This is what Zen means by being detached—not being without emotion or feeling, but being one in whom feeling is not sticky or blocked, and through whom the experiences of the world pass like the reflections of birds flying over water. Although possessed of complete inner freedom, he is not, like the libertine, in revolt against social standards, nor, like the self-righteous, trying to justify himself. He is all of a piece with himself and with the natural world, and in his presence you feel that without strain or artifice he is completely "all here"—sure of himself

without the slightest trace of aggression. He is thus the *grand seigneur*, the spiritual aristocrat who is so sure of the position given to him by birth that he has no need to condescend or put on airs.

*This Is IT and Other Essays on Zen and
Spiritual Experience*

✹ MEINRAD CRAIGHEAD
(CONTEMPORARY)

I began to feel that freedom should beget freedom. But it didn't work. In a way, the reverse happened, and the more involved I got in my painting, which subsequently led to many outside contracts and a lot of visitors and the writing of books, the less that I was liked in the community. The more I was different, the more I was rejected. And I finally had to realize that they were not interested in freedom. They were interested only in the survival of the Benedictine Order and in particular in the survival of the Abbey. So the kind of person they accepted became more and more the kind of person who would fit into the frame they allowed.

The Feminine Mystic

Friendship

✹ FRENCH PROVERB
Hatred watches while friendship sleeps.

✹ CONFUCIUS
(551–479 BC)

Have no friends not equal to yourself.

Analects

✹ OLD TESTAMENT
Forsake not an old friend; for the new is not comparable to him; a new friend is as new wine.

Ecclesiastes 9:10

✹ HAKIM ABU' L-MAJD MAJDUD SANAI OF GHAZNA (HAKIM SANAI)
(12TH CENTURY)

When he [God] admits you to his
    presence
ask from him nothing other than
    himself.
When he has chosen you for a friend,
you have seen all that there is to see.
There's no duality in the world of love:
what's all this talk of "you" and "me"?
How can you fill a cup that's full
    already?

The Walled Garden of Truth

✹ FARID UD-DIN ATTAR
(1120?–1193?)

This was no friendship, to forsake your
    friend,
To promise your support and at the end
Abandon him—this was sheer
    treachery.
Friend follows friend to hell and
    blasphemy—
When sorrows come a man's true
    friends are found;
In times of joy ten thousand gather
    round.

The Conference of the Birds

✹ COSIMO DE' MEDICI
(1389–1464)

We read that we ought to forgive our enemies; but we do not read that we ought to forgive our friends.

Letters

✸ KABIR
(1440?–1518)

When my friend is away from me, I am
    depressed;
Nothing in the daylight delights me,
Sleep at night gives no rest
Who can I tell about this?

The night is dark, and long . . . hours
    go by . . .
because I am alone, I sit up suddenly,
fear goes through me . . .

Kabir says: Listen, my friend
there is one thing in the world that
    satisfies,
and that is a meeting with the Guest.

The Fish in the Sea Is Not Thirsty

✸ WILLIAM SHAKESPEARE
(1564–1616)

To me, fair friend, you never can be
    old.

Sonnet 104

✸ BEN JONSON
(1573?–1637)

True happiness consists not in the multitude of friends, but in the worth and choice.

Volpone

✸ SARMAD
(17TH CENTURY)

The friendship of the worldly persons
    developed in me
A love for endless chatter, and for
    women and for wine.
But our talks were never satisfying,
And my friends all ran away,

When the Wine-flask Divine appeared
    on the scene.

Rubaiyats of Sarmad 12

✸ LA ROCHEFOUCAULD
(1613–1680)

A true friend is the most precious of all possessions and the one we take the least thought about acquiring.

Maxims

✸ EARL OF CHESTERFIELD
(1694–1773)

There is a Spanish proverb, which says very justly, Tell me whom you live with, and I will tell you who you are.

Letter to his son, October 9, 1747

✸ SAMUEL JOHNSON
(1709–1784)

If a man does not make new acquaintances as he advances through life, he will soon find himself left alone.

Quoted in Life of Johnson, James Boswell

✸ J. C. FRIEDRICH VON SCHILLER
(1759–1805)

The zeal of friends it is that knocks me down, and not the hate of enemies.

Wallenstein's Death

✸ RALPH WALDO EMERSON
(1803–1882)

A friend is a person with whom I may be sincere. Before him, I may think aloud.

Friendship

A friend may well be reckoned the masterpiece of nature.

Friendship

✺ MARK TWAIN
(1835–1910)

The holy passion of friendship is so sweet and steady and loyal and enduring in nature that it will last through a whole lifetime, if not asked to lend money.

"Pudd'nhead Wilson's Calendar,"
in *Pudd'nhead Wilson*

✺ HENRY BROOKS ADAMS
(1838–1913)

Friends are born, not made.

The Education of Henry Adams

One friend in a life is much, two are many, three are hardly possible.

The Education of Henry Adams

✺ COLETTE
(1873–1954)

My true friends have always given me that supreme proof of devotion, a spontaneous aversion for the man I loved.

Break of Day

✺ E. M. FORSTER
(1879–1970)

If I had to choose between betraying my country and betraying my friend, I hope I should have the guts to betray my country.

"What I Believe," in *Two Cheers for Democracy*

✺ E. B. WHITE
(1899–1985)

It is not often that someone comes along who is a true friend and a good writer.

Charlotte's Web

✺ DAG HAMMARSKJÖLD
(1905–1961)

Friendship needs no words—it is solitude delivered from the anguish of loneliness.

Markings

God

☸ ANONYMOUS

When God invented man, she was only joking.

How can we be certain that God is dead? We're not even sure about Elvis.

I am all that has been, and that is, and that shall remain, and no one unworthy has ever unraveled, loosened, or even touched the surface of my woven veil.

> Carving on an ancient statue of
> Pallas Athena, cited in
> Plutarch's "Lives"

God is not dead but alive and well and working on a much less ambitious project.

> Graffiti, published in *The Guardian*,
> November 27, 1975

☸ SUMERIAN TEXT

Oh my Queen, Queen of the Universe, the Queen who encompasses the universe, may he the King, enjoy long days at your holy lap.

Who is supreme in heaven? Thou alone art supreme. Who is supreme on earth?

Thou alone art supreme. Thy will is made known in heaven and the spirits thereof bow low before thee. Thy will is made known upon earth and the spirits thereof kiss the ground before thee. . . . Thy mighty word createth right and ordaineth justice for mankind, and thy powerful ordinance reacheth unto the uttermost parts of heaven and earth. Who can know thy will and who can dispute it? . . . O thou king of kings whose judgments are inscrutable and whose divinity is unsurpassed.

> Prayer to the Moon-God from an
> Assyrian translation inscribed on
> a tablet in the Nineveh gallery at
> the British Museum in London,
> quoted in *Sacred Books of the
> World*, A. C. Bouquet

☸ THE PURVA-MIMAMSA

Wherefore God? The world itself suffices for itself.

> Prior investigation of the Vedanta

❁ JEWISH PRAYER

Throughout all generations we will
    render thanks unto Thee
And declare Thy praise,
Evening, morning, and noon,
For our lives which are in Thy care,
For our souls which are in Thy keeping
For Thy miracles which we witness
    daily,
And for Thy wondrous deeds and
    blessings towards us at all times.

*Jewish Sabbath Evening Service in
Prayers for the Pilgrim Festivals*

❁ THE UPANISHADS

(900–600 BCE)

He who consists of the mind, whose
body is breath, whose form is the light of
Consciousness, whose resolve is true,
whose Self is space, containing all actions,
containing all desires, containing all odors,
containing all tastes, pervading this whole
world, the unspeaking, the unconcerned;
this my Self within the heart is smaller
than a grain of rice, or a barley-corn, or
a mustard-seed, or a grain of millet, or
the kernel of a grain of millet; this my
Self within the heart is larger than the
earth, larger than the sky, larger than the
heavens, larger than all these words.

Chandogya Upanishad

This shining, immortal Person who is in
the heart, and, with reference to oneself,
this shining, immortal Person—who is
in the body—he, indeed, is just this Soul,
this Immortal, this Brahma, this All.

Brhadaranyaka Upanishad

The Self of all creatures, the One
    Controller,
who makes his one form into many
    objects,

Is seen by the wise to exist inside them;
such men and no others have Bliss
    Eternal.

Katha Upanishad

Brahman is supreme; he is self-luminous,
he is beyond all thought. Subtler than
the subtlest is he, farther than the farthest, nearer than the nearest. He
resides in the heart of every being.

Chandogya Upanishad

He burns as fire, shines as the sun
Falls as bountiful rain, blows as the wind;
Matter He, and earth, and god,
both false and true
is He, immortal too.
One god there is hidden in every
creature, the Self of all creatures, and all
pervading, abiding in all, overseer of
Karma, sole Witness, Overseer, beyond
the Gunas.

Sueta Upanishad

Verily there are two modes of Brahman—
that with form and the formless, the
mortal and the immortal, the fixed and
the moving, the actual and the beyond.

Brhad Upanishad

He desired, Would that I were many; let
me procreate myself. He underwent
religious austerity. Having undergone
austerity. He projected all this, whatever
there is here. Having projected that, He
entered into it. Having entered into it.
He became the actual and the beyond.

Taittisiya Upanishad

Formless is the Person bright,
Within and yet outside the soul;
Anterior to both life and mind,
unborn, the Transcendental Goal.

Mundaka Upanishad

Neither grasped by sight nor the other
   senses, not by speech nor penance
   nor sacrifices,
But made pure by brightness or
   understanding, then may one
   perceive It in meditation.

Mundaka Upanishad

This Being primeval pervades all
   quarters, the first to be born, in the
   womb subsisting.
Of old He was born, will be born in
   future, indwelling His offspring in
   every region.

Suetas Upanishad

❀ XENOPHANES

(570–475 BCE)

God is one, greatest among gods and
men, in no way like mortals, having
neither body nor mind. He sees as a
Whole, perceives as a Whole, hears as a
Whole. . . . He remains ever stationary,
unmoving; for there is no necessity for
Him to go here and there on different
occasions. Without acting, He makes all
things vibrate by the impulse of His
Mind.

Fragment

❀ CONFUCIUS

(551–479 BCE)

Do not take liberties with the gods, or
weary them.

The Book of Rites

❀ EMPEDOCLES

(490–430 BCE)

God is a circle whose center is everywhere
and whose circumference is nowhere.

Fragment

❀ PLATO

(C. 428–348 BCE)

He was a wise man who invented God.

Sisyphus

❀ OVID

(43 BCE–17 CE)

It is convenient that there be gods, and,
as it is convenient, let us believe there are.

Ars amatoria

❀ SENECA

(C. 4 BCE–65 CE)

He worships God who knows him.

Letters to Lucilius

❀ OLD TESTAMENT

God is no respecter of persons.

Acts 10:34

And God said unto Moses, I AM THAT
I AM.

Exodus 3:14

Hear, O Israel: The Lord our God is
one Lord.

And thou shalt love the Lord thy God
with all thine heart, and with all thy
soul, and with all thy might.

And these words, which I command thee
this day, shall be in thine heart:

And thou shalt teach them diligently
unto thy children, and shalt talk of them
when thou sittest in thine house, and
when thou walkest by the way, and when
thou liest down, and when thou risest
up.

Deuteronomy 6:4–7

Man doth not live by bread only, but by every word that proceedeth out of the mouth of the Lord doth man live.

Deuteronomy 8:3

❀ THE APOCRYPHA

(OLD TESTAMENT TEXTS NOT INCLUDED IN THE BIBLE)

For in wisdom there is a spirit intelligent and holy, unique in its kind yet made up of many parts, subtle, free-moving, lucid, spotless, clear, invulnerable, loving what is good, eager, unhindered, benefi-cent, kindly towards men, steadfast, un-erring, untouched by care, all-powerful, all-surveying, and permeating all intel-ligent, pure, and delicate spirits. For wisdom moves more easily than motion itself, she pervades and permeates all things because she is so pure. Like a fine mist she rises from the power of God, a pure effluence from the glory of the Almighty; nothing defiled can enter into her by stealth. She is the brightness that streams from everlasting light, the flaw-less mirror of the active power of God and the image of his goodness. She is but one, yet can do everything; herself unchanging, she makes all things new; age after age she enters into holy souls, and makes them God's friends and prophets, for nothing is acceptable to God but the man who makes his home with wisdom. She is more radiant than the sun, and surpasses every constel-lation; compared with the light of day, she is found to excel; for day gives place to night, but against wisdom no evil can prevail. She spans the world in power from end to end, and orders all things benignly.

The Wisdom of Solomon

❀ NEW TESTAMENT

I am Alpha and Omega, the beginning and the end, the first and the last.

Revelations 22:13

He that loveth not knoweth not God, for God is love.

I John 4:8

❀ EULOGY

(2ND CENTURY)

Holy Goddess Tell us,
Mother of Living Nature,
The food of life
Thou meter out in eternal loyalty
And, when life has left us,
We take our refuge in Thee.
Thus everything Thou dolest out
Returns into Thy womb.
Rightly Thou art called Mother of the
    Gods
Because by Thy loyalty
Thou hast conquered the power of the
    Gods.
Verily Thou art also the Mother
Of the peoples and the Gods,
Without Thee nothing can thrive
    nor be;
Thou art powerful, of the Gods Thou
    art
The Queen and also the Goddess.
Thee, Goddess, and Thy power I now
    invoke;
Thou canst easily grant all that I ask,
And in exchange I will give Thee,
    Goddess, sincere thanks.

❀ PLUTARCH

(c. 46–120)

There is one divine Mind which keeps the universe in order and one providence which governs it. The names given to this supreme God differ; he is worshipped in different ways in different religions; the religious symbols used in them vary, and their qualities are different; sometimes they are rather vague, and sometimes more distinct.

Lives

✿ ORIGEN
(185–254)

The man who was made in God's image is the inner man, the incorporeal, incorruptible immortal one.

Hexapla

✿ RAB
(3RD CENTURY)

The name of the forty-two letters [that constitute God's name and were used for mystical reflection] can only be entrusted by us to a person who is modest and meek, in the midway of life, not easily provoked to anger, temperate, and free from vengeful feelings. Whoever understands it, is cautious with it, keeps it in purity, is loved above and is liked here below. He is revered by his fellows; he is heir to two worlds—this world and the world to come.

The Talmud

✿ PLOTINUS
(205–270)

We may think of the Divine as a fire whose outgoing warmth pervades the Universe.

Enneads

✿ ST. AUGUSTINE
(354–430)

We do not walk to God with the feet of our body, nor would wings, if we had them, carry us to Him, but we go to Him, by the affections of our soul.

Confessions

✿ THE BOOK OF COMMON PRAYER
(1549)

Praise him upon the well-tuned cymbals: praise him upon the loud cymbals.

Let every thing that hath breath: praise the Lord.

Psalm 51

✿ THE KORAN
(7TH CENTURY)

How can you deny God? Did He not give you life when you were dead, and will He not cause you to die and then restore you to life? Will you not return to Him at last? He created for you all that the earth contains; then, ascending to the sky, He fashioned it into seven heavens. He has knowledge of all things.

God is the East and the West, and wherever ye turn, there is God's face.

He is the first and the last, the manifest and the hidden: and He knoweth all things.

✿ ST. JOHN OF DAMASCUS
(C. 700–760)

God is a sea of infinite substance.

Common definition of Christ during the Middle Ages

❋ RABI'A AL-ADAWIYYA
(717–809)

I love God: I have no time left
In which to hate the devil.

Doorkeeper of the Heart—Versions of Rabi'a

May God steal from you
All that steals you from Him.

Doorkeeper of the Heart—Versions of Rabi'a

❋ ST. ANSELM
(C. 1033–1109)

God is that, the greater than which
cannot be conceived.

Poslogian

❋ AL-GHAZZALI
(B. 1058)

Know that all that is other than God
veils you from Him. . . . If it were not for
your alienation, you would look upon
Him face to face.

Al-Ghazzali

❋ HILDEGARD OF BINGEN
(1098–1179)

Divinity is in its omniscience and omnipotence like a wheel, a circle, a whole,
that can neither be understood, nor
divined, nor begun nor ended.

The marvels of God are not brought
forth from one's self. Rather, it is more
like a chord, a sound that is played. The
tone does not come out of the chord
itself, but rather, through the touch of
the musician. I am, of course, the lyre
and harp of God's kindness.

Meditations

❋ MAHADEVI
(12TH CENTURY)

Like
treasure hidden in the ground
taste in the fruit
gold in the rock
oil in the seed

the Absolute hidden away
in the heart

no one can know
the ways of our lord

white as jasmine.

Speaking of Siva

Sunlight made visible
the whole length of a sky,
movement of wind,
leaf, flower, all six colours
on tree, bush and creeper:
      all this
is the day's worship.

The light of moon, star and fire,
lightnings and all things
that go by the name of light
are the night's worship.

      Night and day
      in your worship
      I forget myself

O lord white as jasmine.

Speaking of Siva

❋ HAKIM ABU' L-MAJD MAJDUD SANAI OF GHAZNA (HAKIM SANAI)
(12TH CENTURY)

In the name of God, the merciful, the
compassionate.

O Thou who nurturest the mind, who adornest the body,

O Thou who givest wisdom, who showest mercy on the foolish, Creator and Sustainer of Earth and time, Guardian and Defender of dweller and dwelling: dwelling and dweller, all is of thy creation; time and earth, all under the control of Thy omnipotence, O Thou the Ineffable.

The first lines of The Walled Garden of Truth

You cannot distinguish
the good from the bad.
He [God] treasures you more
than you do yourself.

The Walled Garden of Truth

He [God] knows what is in your heart;
for he made your heart along with your
    clay [body];
but if you think that he knows
in the same way that you do,
then you are stuck like a donkey
in your own mud.

The Walled Garden of Truth

❀ FARID UD-DIN ATTAR
(1120?–1193?)

No one can bear His beauty face to
    face,
And for this reason, of His perfect
    grace,
He makes a mirror in our hearts—
    look there
To see Him, search your hearts with
    anxious care.

The Conference of the Birds

❀ MUHI 'I-DIN IBN ARABI-AL-FUTU HAT AL-MAKKIYYA
(1165–1240)

God made the creatures as veils. He who knows them to be such is led back to Him, but he who takes them as real is barred from His Presence.

Sufis of Andalusia

❀ ELEAZAR BEN JUDAH OF WORMS
(C. 1165–1230)

"Let a man always be subtle in the fear of God." This means that a person should reflect on the subtleties and the glories of the world: how, for example, a mortal king commands his soldiers to engage in battle. Even though they know they may be killed, they are afraid of him and obey him even though they know that the fear of him is not everlasting, because he will eventually die and perish and they can escape to another country. How much more so, therefore, should men fear the King of the King of Kings, the Holy One, blessed be he, and walk in his ways, since he is everywhere and gazes at the wicked as well as the good.

The Secret of Secrets

❀ MECHTILD OF MAGDEBURG
(1207–1249)

Lord, you are my lover,
My longing,
My flowing stream,
My sun,
And I am your reflection.

The Flowing Light of the Godhead

❂ JALAL AL-DIN RUMI
(1207–1273)

The spirit came from God and will
    return to God.
The present life is only a moment in
    between.

Mathnawi

Never be without remembrance of Him,
for His remembrance gives strength and
wings to the bird of the Spirit. If that
objective of yours is fully realized, that is
"Light upon Light." But at the very
least, by practicing God's remembrance
your inner being will be illumined little
by little and you will achieve some
measure of detachment from the world.

Fih ma fih

❂ MEISTER ECKHART
(1260–1327)

God
    loves the soul so deeply
    that were anyone to take away from
    God
    the divine love of the soul,
that person would kill God.

If you were to let a horse
    run about in a green meadow,
the horse would want to pour forth its
    whole strength
    in leaping about the meadow.

So too
it is a joy to God
    to have poured out
    the divine nature and being
    completely into us

    who are divine images.

Meditations with Meister Eckhart

❂ JULIANA OF NORWICH
(C. 1342–1417?)

He said not, "thou shalt not be troubled,
thou shalt not be travailed, thou shalt
not be diseased;" but He said, "Thou
shalt not be overcome."

Revelations of Divine Love

❂ KABIR
(1440?–1518)

I laugh when I hear that the fish in the
    water is thirsty:
Why so impatient, my heart?
He who watches over the birds, beasts
    and insects,
He who cared for you whilst you were
    yet in your mother's womb,
Shall he not care for you now that you
    have come forth?
O my heart, how could you turn from
    the smile of your Lord and wander
    so far from Him?
You have left your beloved and are
    thinking of others:
And this is why all your work is in vain.

One Hundred Poems of Kabir

❂ CATHERINE OF GENOA
(1447–1510)

I am so washed in the tide of His measureless love that I seem to be below the
surface of a sea and cannot touch or see or
feel anything around me except its water.

La Vita della B. Caterina Fiesca,
Adorna Dama Genouese

❂ GURU NANAK
(1469–1539)

Were I given a hundred thousand
    tongues instead of one,

And the hundred thousand multiplied
    twentyfold,
A hundred thousand times would I say,
    and say again,
The Lord of all the worlds is one.

Hymns of Guru Nanak

Numerous worlds there be in regions
    beyond the skies and below,
Research-weary scholars have delved
    but do not know.
He is boundless the Vedas [Hindu
    scriptures] proclaim
He is in eighteen hundred worlds the
    Muslim texts say,
The Reality behind forms is one and
    the same.

Hymns of Guru Nanak

There is One Reality, the Unmanifest-
Manifested. Ever-existent, He is Naam
[Conscious Spirit], the Creator; pervad-
ing all.

Without fear; without enmity; the
Timeless; the Unborn and the Self-
existent; complete within Itself.

Through the favor of His true Servant,
the Guru, He may be realized.

He was when there was nothing; He was
before all ages began; He existeth now,
O Nanak, and shall exist forevermore.
. . . .
All things are manifestations of His Will;
but His Will is beyond description.

By His Will is matter quickened into
life; by His Will is greatness obtained;
by His Will some are born high and
others low. By His Will are men's joys
and sorrows ordained; by His Will the
pious obtain salvation; by His Will the
impious wander in endless transmigration.
All exist under His Will and nothing
stands outside.

One attuned with His Will, O Nanak, is
wholly freed from ego.

Psalms and Devotions

God is the Master, God is Truth,
His name spelleth love divine.

Hymns of Guru Nanak

✸ MARGUERITE OF NAVARRE
(1492–1549)
God always helps madmen, lovers, and
    drunkards.

The Heptameron; or, Novels of the Queen of Navarre

✸ MIRA BAI
(1450–1547)
Hari is an ocean.
my eyes touch him.
Mira is an ocean of joy.
She takes him inside.

Devotional Poems

✸ ST. TERESA OF AVILA
(1515–1582)
Be not perplexed,
Be not afraid,
Everything passes,
God does not change.
Patience wins all things.
He who has God lacks nothing;
God alone suffices.

Untitled

❁ ARJUN
(1563–1606)

God is in thy heart, yet thou searchest for Him in the wilderness.

❁ JOHANNES KEPLER
(1571–1630)

My greatest desire is that I may perceive the God whom I find everywhere in the external world, in like manner also within and inside myself.

Letters

❁ MATSUO BASHO
(1644–1694)

God of this mountain,
May you be kind enough
To show me your face
Among the dawning blossoms?

Koan

❁ ALEXANDER POPE
(1688–1744)

Lo, the poor Indian! whose untutored
  mind
Sees God in clouds, or hears him in the
  wind;
His soul proud science never taught to
  stray
Far as the solar walk, or milky way.

Essay on Man

❁ CHARLES, BARON DE MONTESQUIEU
(1689–1755)

There is a very good saying that if triangles invented a god, they would make him three-sided.

Lettres persanes

❁ VOLTAIRE
(1694–1778)

If god did not exist, it would be necessary to invent him.

Letters

❁ THOMAS JEFFERSON
(1743–1826)

It does me no injury for my neighbor to say there are twenty Gods, or no God.

Notes on the State of Virginia

❁ CHIEF SEATTLE
(1786–1866)

Your religion was written on tablets of stone by the iron finger of an angry God. . .

Our religion is the tradition of our ancestors—the dreams of our old men, given to them in the solemn hours of the night by the Great Spirit—and it is written in the hearts of our people.

His address, 1853

❁ HEINRICH HEINE
(1797–1856)

God will forgive me, it is his business.

Last words, attributed in many sources, including the *Goncourt* Journals

❁ JOHN HENRY NEWMAN
(1801–1890)

[On Christ] I see the figure of a man, whether young or old I cannot tell. He may be fifty or He may be thirty. Sometimes He looks one, sometimes the other. There is something inexpressible about His face which I cannot solve. Perhaps, as he bears *all* burdens, He bears that of old age too. But so it is; His face is at once most venerable, yet most childlike, most calm, most sweet, most modest, beaming with sanctity and with loving-kindness. His eyes rivet me and move my heart. His breath is all fragrant, and transports me out of myself. Oh, I will look upon that face for ever, and will not cease.

Meditations and Devotions

⊛ RALPH WALDO EMERSON
(1803–1882)

All Spiritual being is in man. A wise old proverb says, "God comes to see us without bell": that is, as there is no screen or ceiling between our heads and the infinite heavens, so is there no bar or wall in the soul where man, the effect, ceases, and God, the cause, begins.

"The Over-Soul" in *Essays*

⊛ BENJAMIN JOWETT
(1817–1893)

My dear child, you must believe in God despite what the clergy tell you.

Quoted by Margot Asquith, *Autobiography*

⊛ THE SHIVAPURI BABA
(1826–1963)

The sole purpose of this human life is nothing but the realization of God. Meditate on Him with as much reverence and love as you can. . . . Forget all except Him. Speak to Him, "O God, bless me." Speak, cry, laugh, dance, do anything, let flow your ecstatic tears.

From Him is this all. Without Him there is nothing. . . . Then a time will come when you will actually see Him before you. Your joy will know no bounds. Your ignorance, all this pleasure and pain will vanish. Your whole outlook will be changed.

Quoted by J. G. Bennett in *Long Pilgrimage*

⊛ EMILY DICKINSON
(1830–1886)

They say that God is everywhere, and yet we always think of Him as somewhat of a recluse.

Letters

⊛ ROBERT G. INGERSOLL
(1833–1899)

An honest God's the noblest work of man.

The Gods

⊛ WILLIAM JAMES
(1842–1910)

The prince of darkness may be gentleman, as we are told he is, but whatever the God of earth and heaven is, He can surely be no gentleman. His menial services are needed in the dust of our human trials, even more than his dignity is needed in the empyrean.

The Varieties of Religious Experience

⊛ GERARD MANLEY HOPKINS
(1844–1889)

The world is charged with the grandeur of God.

God's Grandeur

❋ FRIEDRICH WILHELM NIETZSCHE
(1844–1900)

God is dead: but considering the state the species Man is in, there will perhaps be caves, for ages yet, in which his shadow will be shown.

Joyful Wisdom

❋ ELLEN KEY
(1849–1926)

I wrote in the sand, "God is dead." In doing so I thought, If there is a God, He will kill me now with a thunderbolt. But since the sun continued to shine, the question was answered for the time being; but it soon turned up again.

The Century of the Child

❋ SIGMUND FREUD
(1856–1939)

At bottom God is nothing more than an exalted father.

Totem and Taboo

❋ CLARENCE DARROW
(1857–1938)

In spite of all the yearnings of men, no one can produce a single fact or reason to support the belief in God and in personal immortality.

Sign magazine, May 1938

❋ HYMNS ANCIENT AND MODERN
(1861)

God be in my head,
And in my understanding;

God be in my eyes,
and in my looking;

God be in my mouth,
And in my speaking;

God be in my heart,
And in my thinking;

God be at my end,
And at my departing.

❋ HYMNS ANCIENT AND MODERN
(1861)

Praise, my soul, the King of Heaven,
To His feet thy tribute bring;
Ransom'd, heal'd, restored, forgiven,
Evermore His praises sing;
Alleluia! Alleluia!
Praise the everlasting King.

Praise Him for His grace and favor
To our fathers in distress;
Praise Him still the same as ever,
Slow to chide, and swift to bless;
Alleluia! Alleluia!
Glorious in His faithfulness.

Father-like, He tends and spares us,
Well our feeble frame He knows;
In His hands He gently bears us,
Rescues us from all our foes;
Alleluia! Alleluia!
Widely yet His mercy flows.

Angels in the height, adore Him;
Ye behold Him face to face;
Saints triumphant, bow before Him,
Gathers in from every race;
Alleluia! Alleluia!
Praise with us the God of grace.

GEORGE SANTAYANA
(1863–1952)

My atheism . . . is true piety towards the universe and denies only gods fashioned by men in their own image, to be servants of their human interests.

On My Friendly Critics

SWAMI VIVEKANANDA
(1863–1902)

Vedanta [Hindu] says there is nothing that is not God. . . . The living God is within you. . . . The only God to worship is the human soul in the human body.

Speech in *Yoga and Other Works*

Man is to become divine by realizing the divine. Idols or temples, or churches or books are only the supports, the help of his spiritual childhood.

Address, Parliament of World Religions

MOHANDAS K. GANDHI
(1869–1948)

[God] is the greatest democrat the world knows, for He leaves us "unfettered" to make our own choice between evil and good. He is the greatest tyrant ever known, for He often dashes the cup from our lips and under cover of free will leaves us a margin so wholly inadequate as to provide only mirth for Himself at our expense. Therefore it is that Hinduism calls it all His sport (Lila), or calls it all an illusion (Maya). We are not, He alone Is. And if we will be, we must eternally sing His praise and do His will. Let us dance to the tune of his bansi (flute), and all would be well.

"Statements on the Nature of God," published in *Young India*

ANDRÉ GIDE
(1869–1951)

God lies ahead. . . . He depends on us. It is through us that God is achieved.

Journals

Toward what should we aim if not toward God?

Th,s,e

SRI AUROBINDO
(1872–1950)

The divine Nature, free and perfect and blissful, must be manifested in the individual in order that it may manifest in the world.

Synthesis of Yoga

BERTRAND RUSSELL
(1872–1970)

I believe that when I die I shall rot, and nothing of my ego will survive. . . . But I should scorn to shiver with terror at the thought of annihilation. Happiness is nonetheless true happiness because it must come to an end, nor do thought and love lose their value because they are not everlasting.

What I Believe

YOGASWAMI
(1872–1964)

God is within you, but we place Him outside and worship Him.

Clever is the person who sees God both inside and outside.

Positive Thoughts for Daily Meditation

⊛ W. SOMERSET MAUGHAM
(1874–1965)

What mean and cruel things men do for the love of God.

A Writer's Notebook

⊛ HARRY EMERSON FOSDICK
(1878–1969)

Divinity is not something supernatural that ever and again invades the natural order in a crashing miracle. Divinity is not in some remote heaven, seated on a throne. Divinity is love. . . . Wherever goodness, beauty, truth, love, are—there is the divine.

The Hope of the World

⊛ ALBERT EINSTEIN
(1879–1955)

Raffiniert ist der Herr Gott, aber boshaft ist er nicht. (God is subtle, but he is not malicious.)

Inscription in Fine Hall, Princeton University

⊛ H. L. MENCKEN
(1880–1956)

It takes a long while for a naturally trustful person to reconcile himself to the idea that after all God will not help him.

Minority Report

⊛ NIKOS KAZANTZAKIS
(1885–1957)

I think of God as being exactly like me. Only bigger, stronger, crazier. And immortal, into the bargain. He's sitting on a pile of soft sheep-skins and his hut's the sky. It isn't made out of old petrol-cans, like ours is, but clouds. In his right hand he's holding not a knife or a pair of scales—those damned instruments are meant for butchers and grocers—no, he's holding a large sponge full of water, like a rain-cloud. On his right is Paradise, on his left Hell. Here comes a soul; the poor little thing's quite naked, because it's lost its cloak—its body, I mean—and it's shivering. God looks at it, laughing up his sleeve, but he plays the bogy man: "Come here," he roars, "come here, you miserable wretch!"

And he begins his questioning. The naked soul throws itself at God's feet. "Mercy!" it cries. "I have sinned." And away it goes reciting its sins. It recites a whole rigmarole and there's no end to it. God thinks this is too much of a good thing. He yawns. "For heaven's sake stop!" he shouts. "I've heard enough of all that!" Flap! Slap! a wipe of the sponge, and he washes out all the sins. "Away with you, clear out, run off to Paradise!" he says to the soul. "Peterkin, let this poor little creature in, too!"

Because God, you know, is a great lord, and that's what being a lord means: to forgive!

Zorba the Greek

Have you noticed . . . everything good in this world is an invention of the devil? Pretty women, spring, roast suckling, wine—the devil made them all! God made monks, fasting, camomile-tea and ugly women . . . pooh!

Zorba the Greek

⊛ CESAR VALLEJO
(1892–1938)

Well, on the day I was born, God was sick.

Savage Story

❋ CÉLINE
(1894–1961)
God is under repair.

The School for Corpses

❋ JEAN ROSTAND
(1894–1977)
Kill a man and you are a murderer. Kill millions of men, and you are a conqueror. Kill everyone, and you are a god.

Pensées biologiste

❋ R. BUCKMINSTER FULLER
(1895–1983)
God, to me, it seems, is a verb.

No More Secondhand God

❋ WILHELM REICH
(1897–1957)
I am not a Christian or a Jew or a Mohammedan, a Mormon, Polygamist, Homosexual, Anarchist or Boxer. . . . I do not believe that, in order to be religious in the good and genuine sense of the word, one has to ruin one's love life and has to become rigid and shrunken in body and soul.

I know that what you call "God" actually exists, but in a different way from what you think: as the primal cosmic energy in the universe, as your love in your body, as your honesty and your feeling of nature in you and around you.

Listen, Little Man!

❋ LUIS BUÑUEL
(1900–1983)
I am an atheist still, thank God.

Quoted in *Luis Buñuel*, Ado Kyrou

❋ JOSEPH CAMPBELL
(1904–1987)
The known God cannot endure. Whereas formerly, for generations, life so held to established norms that the lifetime of a deity could be reckoned in millenniums, today all norms are in flux, so that the individual is thrown, willy-nilly, back upon himself, into the inward sphere of his own becoming, his forest adventurous without way or path, to come through his own integrity in experience to his own intelligible Castle of the Grail—integrity and courage, in experience, in love, in loyalty, and in act. And to this end the guiding myths can no longer be of any ethnic norms. No sooner learned, these are outdated, out of place, washed away. There are today no horizons, no mythogenetic zones. Or rather, the mythogenetic zone is the individual heart. Individualism and spontaneous pluralism—the free association of men and women of like spirit, under protection of a secular, rational state with no pretensions to divinity—are in the modern world the only honest possibilities: each the creative center of authority for himself, in Cusanus's circle without circumference whose center is everywhere, and where each is the focus of God's gaze.

Creative Mythology: The Masks of God

❋ PHYLLIS MCGINLEY
(1905–1978)
Benevolent, stormy, patient, or out of sorts. God knows which God is the God God recognizes.

The Day After Sunday

⊛ SIMONE WEIL
(1909–1943)

Christ himself came down and took possession of me . . . I had never foreseen the possibility of that, of a real contact, person to person, here below, between a human being and God . . . in this sudden possession of me by Christ, neither my sense nor my imagination had any part: I only felt in the midst of my suffering the presence of a love.

Waiting on God

⊛ OSHO
(1931–1990)

God is not yet finished with creation.

Come, Come, Yet Again Come

⊛ DA FREE JOHN (ADIDA)
(CONTEMPORARY)

This is the Spiritual Domain. This is the Spirit World. This is the world of God. God is not merely invisible and inside us. *This* is the manifestation of God. There are many other manifestations of God as well, but we must not deny this manifestation.

The Fire Gospel

Spiritual life is a matter of literally consorting with God, submission to God literally, Who is a Person with Whom we are ultimately Identified and relative to Whom we are in Play in this world.

The Fire Gospel

⊛ KATHLEEN RAINE
(CONTEMPORARY)

When I say "God," I explain it in this way. I see the divine Self—that which is—as a person. Not in the sense of a personified God or a deified man in the sense of Jesus, but because the eternal and everlasting Self has consciousness, has knowledge of all things, one speaks of a person rather than of a life-force or anything of that kind; because mind, consciousness, sat-chit-ananda is a living being or spirit, you see, and so I do believe in a divine being. One cannot speak of mind or consciousness without speaking of God as not *a* person but *the* person of the universe.

Weavers of Wisdom, Women Mystics of the Twentieth Century—Ann Bancroft—Quoted in an interview with Kathleen Raine

⊛ J. D. SALINGER
(CONTEMPORARY)

"I was six when I saw that everything was God, and my hair stood up, and all," Teddy said. "It was on a Sunday, I remember. My sister was only a tiny child then, and she was drinking her milk, and all of a sudden I saw that she was God and the milk was God. I mean, all she was doing was pouring God into God, if you know what I mean."

Teddy

⊛ FULTON J. SHEEN
(CONTEMPORARY)

An atheist is a man who has no invisible means of support.

Look magazine, December 14, 1955

Good and Evil

LAO-TZU
(6TH CENTURY BCE)

I find good people good
And I find bad people good
If I am good enough.

The Way of Life

MENCIUS
(372–289 BCE)

Mencius said, "In good years the children of the people are most of them good, and in bad years they are most of them evil. It is not owing to their natural endowments conferred by Heaven, that they are thus different. It is owing to the circumstances in which they allow their minds to be ensnared and devoured that they appear so (as in the latter case).

Book 6

OLD TESTAMENT

Woe to those who call evil good and good evil, who put darkness for light and light for darkness, who put bitter for sweet and sweet for bitter!

Isaiah 5:20

How art thou fallen from heaven, O Lucifer, son of the morning!

Isaiah 14:12

NEW TESTAMENT

Be sober, be vigilant; because your adversary the devil, as a roaring lion, walketh about, seeking whom he may devour.

I Peter 5:8

Resist the devil, and he will flee from you.

James 4:7

JUVENAL
(55–127)

No evil man is happy.

Satires

THE MISHNA
(C. 200)

Rabbi Jannai said: "It is beyond our power to explain either the prosperity of the wicked or the afflictions of the righteous."

The Talmud, quoted in *The World's Great Scriptures*, Lewis Browne

THE KORAN
(7TH CENTURY)

If God afflicts you with evil, none can remove it but He; and if He blesses you with good fortune, know that He has power over all things.

We created man from dry clay, from black moulded loam, and before him Satan from smokeless fire. Your Lord said to the angels: "I am creating man from dry clay, from black moulded loam. When I have fashioned him and breathed of My spirit into him, kneel down and prostrate yourselves before him."

The angels, one and all, prostrated themselves, except Satan. He refused to prostrate himself with the others.

"Satan," said God, "Why do you not prostrate yourself?"

He replied: "I will not bow to a mortal whom You created of dry clay, of black moulded loam."

"Begone," said God, "you are accursed. My curse shall be on you till Judgement-day."

"Lord," said Satan, "reprieve me till the Day of Resurrection."

He answered: "You are reprieved till the Appointed Day."

"Lord," said Satan, "since You have thus seduced me, I will tempt mankind on earth: I will seduce them all, except those of them who are your faithful servants."

He replied: "This is My straight path. You shall have no power over My servants, only the sinners who follow you."

❂ FARID UD-DIN ATTAR
(1120?–1193?)

God said to Moses one: "Go out and find
The secret truth that haunts the devil's
    mind."

When Moses met the devil that same
    day
He asked for his advice and heard him
    say:
"Remember this, repeat it constantly,
Don't speak of 'me,' or you will be like
    me."

The Conference of the Birds

❂ ST. THOMAS AQUINAS
(1224/5–1274)

Every prudent man tolerates a lesser evil for fear of preventing a greater good.

De Veritate

❂ JAMI
(1414–1492)

Souzani
I am a thousand times more evil
than anything you know of evil:
in this no one knows me
as I know myself.
Outwardly I am evil,
but inwardly I am even more so.
God and I, we know
my exterior and my interior.
Satan may be my guide
in the occasional venial sin;
but in a hundred deadly sins
I show Satan the way.

The Abode of Spring

❂ THOMAS LODGE
(1558?–1625)

Devils are not so black as they are painted.

Rosalynde

WILLIAM SHAKESPEARE

(1564–1616)

This is the foul fiend Flibbertigibbet. He begins at curfew, and walks till the first cock. He gives the web and the pin, squints the eye, and makes the harelip; mildews the white wheat, and hurts the poor creature of earth.

King Lear, III, 4, 116

The Prince of Darkness is a gentleman.

King Lear, III, 4, 146

MR. TUT-TUT

(17TH? CENTURY)

Who does evil and is afraid of letting it be known has still a seed of good in his evil; who does good and is anxious to have it known has still a root of evil in his good.

One Hundred Proverbs

Of the things that are good, only study is good without accompanying evil; the love of mountains and rivers is good without accompanying evil; taking pleasure in the moon, the breeze, flowers and bamboos is good without accompanying evil; sitting in upright posture in silence is good without accompanying evil [practicing meditation].

One Hundred Proverbs

SAMUEL BUTLER

(1612–1680)

An apology for the Devil: It must be remembered that we have only heard one side of the case. God has written all the books.

"Higgledy-Piggledy," in *Notebooks*

BLAISE PASCAL

(1623–1662)

Men never do evil so completely and cheerfully as when they do it from religious conviction.

Pensées

DANIEL DEFOE

(1661?–1731)

Wherever God erects a house of prayer, The Devil always builds a chapel there, And 'twill be found upon examination, The latter has the largest congregation.

The True-Born Englishman

EDMUND BURKE

(1729–1797)

All that is necessary for the triumph of evil is that good men do nothing.

Speech

JOHN HENRY NEWMAN

(1801–1890)

If Thou sendest evil upon us, it is in love. All the evils of the physical world are intended for the good of Thy creatures, or are the unavoidable attendants on that good. And Thou turnest that evil into good. Thou visitest men with evil to bring them to repentance, to increase their virtue to gain for them greater good hereafter. Nothing is done in vain, but has its gracious end. Thou dost punish, yet in wrath Thou dost remember mercy.

Meditations and Devotions

❂ SHRI RAMAKRISHNA
(1836–1886)

Know that God resides in all things animate and inanimate. Hence everything is an object of worship, be it men, beasts or birds, plants or minerals. In our relation with men all that we can do is to take heed to ourselves that we mix with good people and avoid bad company. It is true, however, that God resides in bad people also, yes, even in a tiger; but surely it does not follow that we should embrace a tiger. It may be asked: Why should we run away from a tiger when God is dwelling in that form? To this the answer is that God abiding in our hearts directs us to run away from the tiger. Why should we not obey His will? . . .

A person living in society should have a little Tamas [the spirit of resisting evil] for purposes of self-protection. But this is necessary only for outward show, its object being to prevent the wicked from doing harm to you. At the same time you should not do actual injury to another on the ground that he has done injury to you. . . . Resist not evil by causing evil in return.

Spiritual Teachings

❂ ELLEN KEY
(1849–1926)

All philanthropy—no age has seen more of it than our own—is only a savoury fumigation burning at the mouth of a sewer. This incense offering makes the air more endurable to passersby, but it does not hinder the infection in the sewer from spreading.

The Century of the Child

❂ MARGOT ASQUITH
(1864–1945)

Riches are overestimated in the Old Testament: the good and successful man received too many animals, wives, apes, she-goats and peacocks.

The Autobiography of Margot Asquith

❂ G. K. CHESTERTON
(1874–1936)

If I had been a Heathen,
I'd have praised the purple vine,
My slaves would dig the vineyards,
And I would drink the wine;
But Higgins is a Heathen,
And his slaves grow lean and grey,
That he may drink some tepid milk
Exactly twice a day.

The Song of the Strange Ascetic

❂ FRANZ KAFKA
(1883–1924)

There is nothing beside a spiritual work: what we call the world of the senses is Evil in the spiritual world, and what we call evil is only the necessity of a moment in our eternal evolution.

Reflections

❂ MIKHAIL NAIMY
(1889–1988)

What you dislike and cast away as evil is surely liked and picked up by someone, or something as good. Can one thing be at once two self-excluding things? Neither is it the one, nor the other, excepting that *your* I has made it evil; another *I* has made it good.

The Book of Mirdad—A Lighthouse and a Haven

⊛ ALBERT CAMUS

(1913–1960)

I have seen people behave badly with great morality and I note every day that integrity has no need of rules.

The Myth of Sisyphus

⊛ ALAN WATTS

(1915–1973)

At the roots of Chinese life there is a trust in the good-and-evil of one's own nature which is peculiarly foreign to those brought up with the chronic uneasy conscience of the Hebrew-Christian cultures. Yet it was always obvious to the Chinese that a man who mistrusts himself cannot even trust his mistrust, and must therefore be hopelessly confused.

This Is IT and Other Essays on Zen and Spiritual Experience

⊛ HUBERT BENOIT

(CONTEMPORARY)

"God" is conceived as a perfect anthropomorphic positivity, he is just, good, beautiful, affirming, constructive. "Satan" is conceived as a perfect anthropomorphic negativity, he is unjust, wicked, ugly, negating, destructive. Since this dualism of the principles contradicts the intuition that man has, in other respects, of a Unique Principle which unifies everything, the existence of "Evil," of "Satan," opposed to 'God', poses to man a problem that is practically insoluble and forces him into philosophical acrobatics.

The Supreme Doctrine

As soon as you have good and evil
Confusion follows and the mind is lost.

The Supreme Doctrine

Heaven and Hell

❂ ANONYMOUS

Everyone wants to go to heaven, but no one wants to die.

❂ THE SUMERIAN UNDERWORLD

It is a house that separates the wicked and the good; this is a house from out of which
no one escapes, but just men need not fear before its judge,
For in this river of spent souls the good shall never die although the wicked perish.

> Sumerian text (date unknown, but probably 2nd millennium BCE)

❂ JEWISH PSALM

The heavens declare the glory of God,
The skies proclaim His handiwork.
Day unto day utters a message,
Night unto night reveals knowledge.
There is no speech, there are no words,
Neither is their voice heard.
Yet their eloquence resounds
    throughout all the earth,
And their testimony to the end of the world.
A tent in the heavens has He set for the sun,
Which goes forth as a bridegroom
    from his chamber,
And rejoices as a hero to run his course.
From one end of the heaven it goes forth;
It moves round to the ends of it,
    missing nothing with its heat.

> *Psalm XIX*

❂ MOTSE
(C. 468–401 BCE)

Now, what does Heaven desire and what does it abominate? Heaven desires righteousness and abominates unrighteousness. . . . But how do we know Heaven desires righteousness and abominates unrighteousness? For, with righteousness the world lives and without it the world dies; with it the world becomes rich and without it the world becomes poor; with it the world becomes orderly and without it the world becomes chaotic. And Heaven likes to have the world live and dislikes to have it die, likes to have it rich and dislikes to have it poor, and likes to have it orderly and dislikes to have it disorderly. Therefore we know Heaven desires righteousness and abominates unrighteousness.

> *The Will of Heaven*

❀ LUCRETIUS
(99–55 BCE)

I know that men often speak of sickness or of shameful life as more to be dreaded than the terrors of Hell. . . . But all this talk is based more on a desire to show off than on actual proof, as you may infer from their conduct. These same men, though they may be exiled from home, banished far from the sight of their fellows, soiled with some filthy crime, a prey to every torment, still cling to life.

On the Nature of Things

❀ VIRGIL
(70–19 BCE)

Each of us bears his own hell.

Aeneid

❀ ST. AUGUSTINE
(354–430)

But by what means did you make heaven and earth? What tool did you use for this vast work? You did not work as a human craftsman does, making one thing out of something else as his mind directs. His mind can impose upon his material whatever form it perceives within itself by its inner eye. But how could his mind do this unless it was because you had made it?

Confessions

❀ THE KORAN
(7TH CENTURY)

But the true servants of God shall be well provided for, feasting on fruit, and honored in the gardens of delight. Reclining face to face upon soft couches, they shall be served with a goblet filled at a gushing fountain, white, and delicious to those who drink it. It will neither dull their senses nor befuddle them. They shall sit with bashful, dark-eyed virgins, as chaste as the sheltered eggs of ostriches.

❀ SOSAN (SENG-S'TAN) THE THIRD ZEN PATRIARCH
(C. 600)

The perfect Tao knows no difficulties;
It only refuses to make preferences.
When freed from hate and love,
It reveals Itself fully and without
disguise.

A tenth of an inch's difference,
And heaven and earth are set apart;
If you want to see It manifest,
Take no thought either for or against it.

On Believing in Mind

❀ ARGULA VON GRUMBACK
(1492–1563?)

I have even heard some say, "if my father and mother were in hell, I wouldn't want to be in heaven." Not me, not if all my friends were down there.

Letter to her cousin, Adam von Torring

❀ PARACELSUS
(1493–1541)

In every human being there is a special heaven whole and unbroken.

Essential Writings

❀ JAKOB BÖHME
(1575–1624)

Where will you seek for God? Seek him in your soul that is proceeded out of the eternal nature, the living fountain of forces wherein the divine working stands.

Oh that I had but the pen of a man, and were able therewith to write down the spirit of knowledge! I can but stammer of great mysteries like a child that is beginning to speak; so very little can the earthly tongue express of that which the spirit comprehends. Yet I will venture to try whether I may incline some to seek the pearl of true knowledge, and myself labour in the works of God in my paradisical garden of roses; for the longing of the eternal nature-mother drives me on to write and to exercise myself in this my knowledge.

No money, nor goods, nor art, nor power can bring you to the eternal rest of the eternal paradise, but only the knowledge in which you may steep your soul. That is the pearl which no thief can steal away; seek after it and you will find the noble treasure. . . . O beloved man, paradise is the divine Joy. It is the divine and angelical Joy, yet it is not outside the place of this world. When I speak of the fountain and joy of paradise, and of its substance, what it is, I have no similitude for it in this world; I stand in need of angelical speech and knowledge to express it; and though I had them yet I could never express it with this tongue.

The Confessions

If we will enter into the kingdom of heaven we must be children, and not cunning and wise in the understanding of this world; we must depart from our earthly reason and enter into obedience to our eternal first Mother. So we shall receive the spirit and live of our Mother, and then also we shall know her habitation.

The Confessions

⚙ JOHN MILTON
(1608–1674)

The mind is its own place, and in it self
Can make a Heav'n of Hell, a Hell of
   Heav'n.

Paradise Lost

Here we may reign secure, and in my
   choice
To reign is worth ambition though in
   hell:
Better to reign in hell, than serve in
   heav'n.

Paradise Lost

⚙ ROBERT BROWNING
(1812–1889)

Ah, but a man's reach should exceed his grasp, Or what's a heaven for?

Andrea del Sarto

⚙ EMILY BRONTË
(1818–1848)

No coward soul is mine,
No trembler in the world's storm-
   troubled sphere:
I see heaven's glories shine,
And faith shines equal, arming me from
   fear.

"No Coward Soul Is Mine"

✸ FRIEDRICH WILHELM NIETZSCHE
(1844–1900)

In heaven all the interesting people are missing.

Thus Spake Zarathustra

✸ NIKOS KAZANTZAKIS
(1885–1957)

My boy, if a woman calls you to share her bed and you don't go, your soul will be destroyed! That woman will sigh before God on judgement day, and that woman's sigh, whoever you may be and whatever your fine deeds, will cast you into Hell!

Zorba the Greek

✸ EVELYN WAUGH
(1903–1966)

It is a curious thing that every creed promises a paradise which will be absolutely uninhabitable for anyone of civilised taste.

Letters

✸ JEAN-PAUL SARTRE
(1905–1980)

So that's what Hell is. I'd never have believed it. . . . Do you remember, brimstone, the stake, the gridiron? . . . What a joke! No need of a gridiron, Hell is other people.

In Camera

✸ HUBERT BENOIT
(CONTEMPORARY)

Everything happens in me as if I believed myself exiled from a paradise which exists somewhere and as if I saw, in such and such a modification of the outside world or of my-self, the key capable of opening the door of this lost paradise. And I live in the quest of this key.

While waiting I kill time as I may.

The Supreme Doctrine

✸ PAT CONROY
(CONTEMPORARY)

"You think heaven's prettier than Venice?" she asked, looking around us. "Too much to ask," I said.

Beach Music

✸ SANGHARAKSHITA
(CONTEMPORARY)

Heaven, the ultimate goal of so many faiths, since it is a mode of contingent and hence of transitory existence, is accounted no more than a pleasant interlude in a pilgrimage fundamentally of more serious import.

The Three Jewels

Ideals

CONFUCIUS
(551–479 BCE)

To be able to practice five things every-where under heaven constitutes perfect virtue . . . gravity, generosity of soul, sincerity, earnestness, and kindness.

Analects

Confucius said, "The superior man goes through his life without any one pre-conceived course of action or any taboo. He merely decides for the moment what is the right thing to do."

The Aphorisms of Confucius, VII, "The Superior Man and The Inferior Man"

ARISTOTLE
(384–322 BCE)

So far as in us lies, we must play the immortal and do all in our power to live by the best element in our nature.

On Interpretation

OVID
(43 BCE–17 CE)

Thy destiny is only that of man, but thy aspirations may be those of a god.

Ars Amatoria

HSUEH-TOU
(950–1052)

What life can compare to this?
Sitting quietly by the window,
I watch the leaves fall and the flowers
    bloom,
As the seasons come and go.

Untitled

HAKIM ABU' L-MAJD MAJDUD SANAI OF GHAZNA (HAKIM SANAI)
(12TH CENTURY)

When the eye is pure
it sees purity.

The Walled Garden of Truth

MR. TUT-TUT
(17TH? CENTURY)

The sun and moon shoot past like a bullet in our floating life; only sleep affords a little extension of our span of life. Business affairs fly about like thick dust to belabor our lives; only sleep affords a little reprieve. Gorging oneself with fish and meat morning and night besmirches our taste; only sleep gives opportunity for a short fast. Contention and strife disturb our peace; only sleep restores for us a short Golden Age. As for seeing novel things in our sleep—traveling abroad and being able to walk without legs and fly without wings—it provides us also with a little fairyland.

One Hundred Proverbs

CHARLOTTE LENNOX
(1720–1804)

I believe there is an intelligent cause which governs the world by physical rules. As for moral attributes, there is no such thing; it is impious and absurd to suppose it.

Henrietta

VICTOR HUGO
(1802–1885)

The human soul has still greater need of the ideal than of the real. It is by the real that we exist; it is by the ideal that we live.

William Shakespeare

ROBERT BROWNING
(1812–1889)

Ah, but a man's reach should exceed his grasp,
Or, what's heaven for?

Letters

HENRY WARD BEECHER
(1813–1887)

We are not to make the ideas of contentment and aspiration quarrel, for God made them fast friends. A man may aspire, and yet be quite content until it is time to rise; and both flying and resting are but parts of one contentment. The very fruit of the gospel is aspiration. It is

to the heart what spring is to the earth, making every root, and bud, and bough desire to be more.

Royal Truths

CARL SCHURZ
(1829–1906)

Ideals are like stars: you will not succeed in touching them with your hands. But like the seafaring man on the desert waters, you choose them as your guides, and, following them you will reach your destiny.

Speech

PIERRE TEILHARD DE CHARDIN
(1881–1955)

The whole of Evolution being reduced to a process of union [communion] with God, it becomes, in its totality, loving and loveable in the innermost and most ultimate of its developments.

My Intellectual Position

It will not be long before the human mass closes in upon itself and groups all its mem-bers in a definitively realised unity. Respect for one and the same law, one and the same orientation, one and the same spirit, are tending to overlay the permanent diversity of individuals and nations. Wait but a little longer, and we shall form but one solid block. The cement is *setting*.

Already, in the silence of the night, I can hear through this world of tumult a confused rustling as of crystalline needles forming themselves into a pattern or of birds huddling closer together in their nest—a deep murmur of distress, of discomfort, of well-being, of triumph, rising up from the Unity which is reaching its fulfilment.

The Great Monad

✸ HAZRAT INAYAT KHAN
(1882–1927)

The man who has never had an ideal may hope to find one; he is in a better state than the man who allows the circumstances of life to break his ideal. To fall beneath one's ideal is to lose one's track in life; then confusion rises in the mind, and that light which one should hold high becomes covered and obscured, so that it cannot shine out to light one's path.

The Sufi Message of Hazrat Inayat Khan: The Art of Personality

✸ ROBERT BLY
(CONTEMPORARY)

We could say that New Age people in general are addicted to harmony.

Iron John

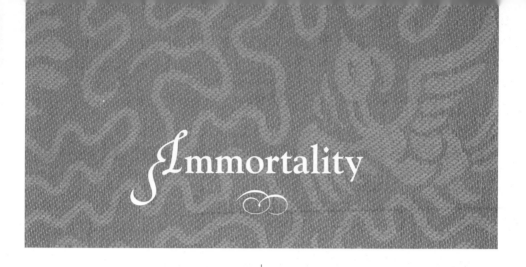

Immortality

☸ THE VEDAS

The gods lived constantly in dread of
    death—
the might Ender—so with toilsome
    rites
They worshipped and performed
    religious acts
Till they became immortal. Then the
    Ender
Said to the gods, "As ye have made
    yourselves
Imperishable, so will men endeavor
To free themselves from me; what
    portion then
Shall I possess in man?" The gods
    replied,
"Henceforth no being shall become
    immortal
In his own body; this his mortal frame
Shalt thou still seize; this shall remain
    thy own.
He who through knowledge or
    religious works
Henceforth attains to immortality
Shall first present his body, Death, to
    thee."

Satapatha Brahmana

Hail to thee, mighty Lord, all-potent
    Vishnu!

Soul of the universe, unchangeable,
Holy, eternal, always one in nature,
Whether revealed as Brahma, Hari,
    Siva—
Creator or Preserver or Destroyer—
Thou art the cause of final liberation;
Whose form is one, yet manifold;
    whose essence
Is one, yet diverse; tenuous, yet vast;
Discernible, yet indiscernible;
Root of the world, yet of the world
    composed;
Prop of the universe, yet more minute
Than earth's minutest particles; abiding
In every creature, yet without
    defilement,
Imperishable, one with perfect wisdom.

Vishnu Purana, Indian Wisdom

☸ THE RIG VEDA
(C. 1200–900 BCE)

See how the dawns have set up their
banner in the eastern half of the sky,
adorning and anointing themselves with
sunlight for balm. Unleashing themselves like impetuous heroes unsheath-
ing their weapons, the tawny cows, the
mothers . . .

⊛ THE UPANISHADS
(900–600 BCE)

Above the senses is the mind. Above the mind is the intellect. Above the intellect is the ego. Above the ego is the unmanifested seed, the Primal Cause. And verily beyond the unmanifested seed is the self, the unconditioned knowing whom one attains to freedom and achieves immortality.

Katha Upanishad

That which dwelling within all things is yet other than all things, which all things do not know whose body is all things, which controls all things from within, He is your own Self, The Inner Controller, the Immortal.

Brhad Upanishad

His form isn't set up where one can see it;
no one can perceive that One through
   the senses.
But He is revealed by the understanding
   and feelings.
Who knows this becomes immortal.

Katha Upanishad

⊛ LAO-TZU
(C. 6TH CENTURY BCE)

Going back to the origin is called peace; it means reversion to destiny. Reversion to destiny is called eternity. He who knows eternity is called enlightened.

Tao Te Ching

Can you hold the door of your tent
Wide to the firmament?
Can you, with the simple stature
Of a child, breathing nature,
Become, notwithstanding,
A man?

The Way of Life

⊛ HERACLITUS
(C. 4TH CENTURY BCE)

Greater dooms bring greater destinies.

Speech

⊛ PLATO
(428–348 BCE)

When the soul returns into itself and reflects, it passes into . . . the region of that which is pure and everlasting, immortal and unchangeable.

Phaedo

⊛ CHUANG TZU
(369–286 BCE)

Life and Death, existence and non-existence, success and non-success, poverty and wealth, virtue and vice, good and evil report, hunger and thirst, warmth and cold—these all revolve upon the changing wheel of Destiny.

⊛ CICERO
(106–43 BCE)

Whatever that which feels, which has knowledge, which wills, which has the power of growth, it is celestial and divine, and for that reason must of necessity be eternal.

Tusculanae Disputationes

⊛ VIRGIL
(70–19 BCE)

The great cycle of the ages is renewed. Now the Maiden returns, returns the Gold Age; a new generation now descends from heaven.

Eclogues

⊛ THE KADDISH

The living God we praise, exalt, adore;
He was; He is; He will be evermore.
No unity like unto His can be;
Eternal, inconceivable is He.
No form or shape has the incorporeal
  One,
Most holy, beyond comparison.
He was ere aught was made in heaven
  or earth;
But His existence has no date or birth.

Prayers for the Pilgrim Festivals

⊛ THE APOCRYPHA

(OLD TESTAMENT TEXTS NOT INCLUDED IN THE BIBLE)

Wisdom shines bright and never fades; she is easily discerned by those who love her, and by those who seek her she is found. She is quick to make herself known to those who desire knowledge of her; the man who rises early in search of her will not grow weary in the quest, for he will find her seated at his door. To set all one's thoughts on her is prudence in its perfect shape, and to lie wakeful in her cause is the short way to peace of mind. For she herself ranges in search of those who are worthy of her; on their daily path she appears to them with kindly intent, and in all their purposes meets them half-way. The true beginning of wisdom is the desire to learn, and a concern for learning means love towards her; the love of her means the keeping of her laws; to keep her laws is a warrant of immortality; and immortality brings a man near to God. Thus the desire of wisdom leads to kingly stature.

The Wisdom of Solomon

⊛ NEW TESTAMENT

Except a man be born again, he cannot see the kingdom of God.

John 3:3

Except a man be born of water and of the Spirit, he cannot enter into the kingdom of God.

John 3:5

Ye must be born again.

John 3:7

⊛ SHANKARA

(788–820)

He who has become liberated in this life gains liberation in death and is eternally united with Brahman, The Absolute Reality. Such a seer will never be reborn.

Crest-Jewel of Discrimination

⊛ NAROPA

(1016–1100)

The bird of the Five Buddhas has risen
In the vastness of the ultimate,
It holds the jewel of a universal
  monarch.
The human line has faded like a flower,
The Dharma has become a river.
Samsara's wave, that dazzling picture
Of desire, of its own has passed away.

The Songs of Naropa

⊛ HAKIM ABU' L-MAJD MAJDUD SANAI OF GHAZNA (HAKIM SANAI)

(12TH CENTURY)

Slave that you are
of fame and shame,
what is eternity to you?

The Walled Garden of Truth

⊛ FARID UD-DIN ATTAR
(1120?–1193?)

The paths of God are intricate and
    strange—
What can you do? Accept what will not
    change!

The Conference of the Birds

⊛ MEISTER ECKHART
(1260–1327)

The soul is created in a place between
Time and Eternity: with its highest
powers it touches Eternity, with its
lower Time.

⊛ GURU NANAK
(1469–1539)

. . . Few, some very few,
From this havoc return home,
And others inquire of them
About their lost dear ones.
Many are lost forever,
And weeping and anguish are the lot of
    those who survive.
Ah, Nanak, how completely helpless
    mere men are!
It is God's will that is done, for ever
    and ever.

Hymns of Guru Nanak

⊛ JAKOB BÖHME
(1575–1624)

I declare unto you that the eternal
Being, and also this world, is like man.
Eternity bringeth to birth nothing but
that which is like itself; as you find man
to be, just so is eternity. Consider man in
body and soul, in good and evil, in joy
and sorrow, in light and darkness, in
power and weakness, in life and death:
all is in man, both heaven and the earth,
stars, and elements; also the threefold
God.

The Confessions

⊛ HENRY VAUGHAN
(1622–1695)

I saw Eternity the other night,
Like a great ring of pure and endless
    light,
All calm, as it was bright;
And round beneath it, Time in hours,
    days, years,
Driv'n by the spheres
Like a vast shadow mov'd; in which the
    world
And all her train were hurl'd.

"I Saw Eternity the Other Night"

⊛ BARUCH SPINOZA
(1632–1677)

It is not possible that we should remember that we existed before our body,
for our body can bear no trace of such
existence, neither can eternity be defined
in terms of time or have any relation to
time. But notwithstanding, we feel and
know that we are eternal.

Tractatus Politicus

⊛ THOMAS TRAHERNE
(1637–1674)

Death cannot kill what never dies.

Centuries of Meditation

⊛ CHARLOTTE SMITH
(1749–1806)

When the imagination soars into those
regions, where the planets pursue each
its destined course, in the immensity of
space—every planet, probably, containing

creatures adapted by the Almighty, to the residence he has placed them in; and when we reflect, that the smallest of these is of as much consequence in the universe, as this world of ours; how puerile and ridiculous do those pursuits appear in which we are so anxiously busied; and how insignificant the trifles we toil to obtain, or fear to lose.

Desmond

✸ WILLIAM BLAKE
(1757–1827)

If the doors of perception were cleansed every thing would appear to man as it is, infinite.

The Marriage of Heaven and Hell

✸ FRANÇOIS GUIZOT
(1787–1874)

Neither experience nor science has given man the idea of immortality. . . . The idea of immortality rises from the very depths of his soul—he feels, he sees, he knows that he is immortal.

General History of Civilization

✸ JOHN HENRY NEWMAN
(1801–1890)

If we have but once seen any child of Adam, we have seen an immortal soul. It has not passed away, as a breeze or sunshine, but it lives; it lives at this moment in one of those many places, whether in bliss or misery in which all souls are reserved until the end.

Parochial and Plain Sermons

Whatever be my age, whatever the number of my years, I am ever narrowing the interval between time and eternity. I am ever changing in myself. Youth is not like age; and I am continually changing, as I pass along out of youth towards the end of life. O my God, I am crumbling away, as I go on! I am already dissolving into my first elements. My soul indeed cannot die, for Thou hast made it immortal; but my bodily frame is continually resolving into that dust out of which it was taken. All below heaven changes: spring, summer, autumn, each has its turn. The fortunes of the world change; what was high lies low; what was low rises high. Riches take wings and flee away; bereavements happen. Friends become enemies, and enemies friends. Our wishes, aims, and plans change. There is nothing stable but Thou, O my God.

Meditations and Devotions

✸ PHILLIPS BROOKS
(1835–1893)

The ideal life is in our blood, and never will be still. We feel the thing we ought to be beating through the thing we are.

Perennials

✸ SHRI RAMAKRISHNA
(1836–1886)

Infinite is the number of ways leading to the sea of immortality.

It is immaterial how thou gettest into this sea. Suppose there is a reservoir of nectar. It is open to thee to walk slowly down the sloping bank from any point, get to the nectar and have a drink. Thou gettest immortal in any case.

Again, what doth it signify if one throwest oneself into the reservoir or is pushed into it by somebody? The result in either case is the same. Thou tasteth the nectar—the water of life—in either case. Thou becomest immortal.

Hidden Treasure of the Gospel of Sri Ramakrishna, Sri Surath

❀ FRIEDRICH WILHELM NIETZSCHE
(1844–1900)

All things return eternally, and ourselves with them; we have already existed in times without number, and all things with us.

Quoted in *The Soul: An Archeology,* Claudia Setzer

❀ I. I. METCHNIKOFF
(1845–1916)

Buddhism . . . is so persuaded of survival after death as being the rule, that it grants only to rare and elect souls the privilege of at length laying down the burden of continuous life.

The Nature of Man

❀ KNUT HAMSUN
(1859–1952)

When good befalls a man he calls it Providence, when evil, Fate.

❀ CHARLOTTE PERKINS GILMAN
(1860–1935)

Eternity is not something that begins after you are dead. It is going on all the time. We are in it now.

The Forerunner

❀ J. KRISHNAMURTI
(1895–1986)

To the alone, life is eternal; to the alone there is no death. The alone can never cease to be.

Commentaries on Living—From the Notebooks of J. Krishnamurti

❀ JOHN ELOF BOODIN
(CONTEMPORARY)

We are material in the hands of the Genius of the universe for a still larger destiny that we cannot see in the everlasting rhythm of worlds.

Cosmic Evolution

❀ CARLOS CASTANEDA
(CONTEMPORARY)

There is nothing more lonely than eternity. And nothing is more cozy for us than to be a human being. This indeed is another contradiction—how can man keep the bonds of his humanness and still venture gladly and purposefully into the absolute loneliness of eternity?

The Fire Within

❀ NORMAN COUSINS
(CONTEMPORARY)

If something comes to life in others because of you, then you have made an approach to immortality.

Quoted in *The Soul: An Archeology,* Claudia Setzer

❀ WILLIAM GERBER
(CONTEMPORARY)

Thinkers west of India who have entertained at least the idea of the cycle of births and deaths (usually referred to as "the transmigration of souls")—if not also the idea of the breaking of the chain when one achieves *moksha* [an enduring and blissful state of union with "the all"]—include Pythagoras, Empedocles, Plato, Cicero, Jesus (who said that John the Baptist was a reincarnation of Elijah; Matthew, xvii, 12–13), Plutarch, Origen, Plotinus, Bruno, Hume, Goethe, Novalis, Kant, Fichte, Schopenhauer, Wordsworth ("Our birth is but a sleep and a forgetting"), Emerson, Thoreau, Nietzsche, Tolstoy, Charles Renouvier, C. D. Broad, and C. J. Ducasse.

The Mind of India

JACOB NEUSNER
(CONTEMPORARY)

The idea of life after death is clearly an embarrassment to modern thinking—most major philosophers have ridiculed it—but it is just as clearly the touchstone of all religion. Religion says that being human has eternal meaning. If religion announces that life is over at the grave, then it is not talking about what people expect religion to discuss.

Newsweek, March 27, 1989

D. T. SUZUKI
(CONTEMPORARY)

To Zen, time and eternity are one.

Zen Buddhism

SPEAKER UNKNOWN

If there is such a thing as reincarnation, knowing my luck, I'll come back as me.

British television program, *Video Nation: Life, Death, God and Everything*, shown on BBC2 February 1996 in which the members of the public used camcorders to record their lives and opinions.

Joy and Despair

❂ THE EPIC OF GILGAMESH
(3RD MILLENNIUM BCE)

When the gods created man they allotted to him death, but life they retained in their own keeping. As for you, Gilgamesh, fill your belly with good things; day and night, night and day, dance and be merry, feast and rejoice. Let your clothes be fresh, bathe yourself in water, cherish the little child that holds your hand, and make your wife happy in your embrace; for this too is the lot of man.

❂ BUDDHA
(563–483 BCE)

Happy is he who has overcome his ego; happy is he who has attained peace; happy is he who has found the Truth.

Anguttara-Nikaya

It remains a fact and the fixed and necessary constitution of being, that all of its constituents are misery.

Anguttara-Nikaya

He who recognizes the existence of suffering, its cause, its remedy, and its cessation, has fathomed the four noble truths. He will walk in the right path.

Anguttara-Nikaya

❂ THE BHAGAVAD GITA
(500? BCE)

For certain is death for the born,
And certain is birth for the dead;
Therefore over the inevitable
Thou shouldst not grieve.

Chapter 2, section 27

❂ TRIPITAKA (BUDDHIST SCRIPTURES)
(500 BCE–1 CE)

All the foolish common people take delight in the senses and their objects, are impressed by them, are attached to them. In that way they are carried away by the flood, and are not set free from birth, old age, and death, from grief, lamentation, pain sadness, and despair— they are, I say, not set free from suffering. But the well-informed holy disciples do not take delight in the senses and their objects, are not impressed by them, are not attached to them, and in consequence their craving ceases; the cessation of craving leads successively to that of grasping, of becoming, of birth, of old age and death, of grief, lamentation, pain, sadness, and despair—that is to say to the cessation of all this mass of ill. It is thus that cessation is Nirvana.

Questions of King Milina

117

THE DHAMMAPADA
(3RD CENTURY BCE)

O let us live in joy, in love amongst those who hate! Among men who hate, let us live in love.

O let us live in joy, in health amongst those who are ill! Among men who are ill, let us live in health.

The Path of Perfection

ARISTOTLE
(384–322 BCE)

True happiness flows from the possession of wisdom and virtue and not from the possession of external goods.

Politics

MENCIUS
(372–289 BCE)

There is no greater delight than to be conscious of sincerity on self-examination.

Book VII

When Heaven is about to confer a great office on any man, it first exercises his mind with suffering, and his sinews and bones with toil.

Book VI

MENANDER
(C. 342–292 BCE)

Health and intellect are the two blessings of life.

Monostikoi

EPICURUS
(341–270 BCE)

It is impossible to live pleasurably without living wisely, well and justly, and impossible to live wisely, well and justly without living pleasurably.

Diogenes Laërtius

GOTAMA AKSAPADA
(2ND CENTURY BCE)

Misapprehension, faults, activity, birth and pain, these in their uninterrupted course constitute the "world." Release, which consists in the soul's getting rid of the world, is the condition of supreme felicity marked by perfect tranquillity and not tainted by any defilement. A person, by the true knowledge of the sixteen categories is able to remove his misapprehension. When this is done, his faults, viz., affection, aversion and stupidity, disappear. He is then no longer subject to any activity and is consequently freed from transmigration and pains. This is the way in which his release is effected and supreme felicity secured.

The Nyaya Sutras

SHANTIDEVA
(8TH CENTURY)

Having patience I should develop
   enthusiasm;
For Awakening will dwell only in those
   who exert themselves.

. . . .

What is enthusiasm? It is finding joy in
   what is wholesome.

A Guide to the Bodhisattva's Way of Life

P'ANG-YUN
(C. 800)

How wondrously supernatural,
And how miraculous this!
I carry water, and I carry fuel.

Haiku

ZIYAD B. AL-ARABI
(9TH CENTURY)

The beginning of ecstasy is the lifting of the veil and the vision of the Divine Guardian, and the presence of understanding, and the contemplation of the invisible, and the discoursing on secret things and perceiving the non-existent, and it means that you pass away from where you are.

Writings

HROSWITHA OF GANDERSHEIM
(C. 935–1000)

Better far that my body should suffer outrage than my soul.

Untitled

MILAREPA
(1040–1123)

I, the sage, am the holy one among men.
I am Milarepa.
I am he who goes his own way;
I am he who has counsel for every circumstance;
I am the sage who has no fixed abode.
I am he who is unaffected whatever befall;
I am the alms-seeker who has no food;
I am the naked man who has no clothes;
I am the beggar who has no possessions.
I am he who takes no thought for the morrow;
I am he who has no house here nor dwelling there;
I am the victor who has known consummation.

I am the madman who counts death happiness;
I am he who has naught and needs naught

The Message of Milarepa

HÉLOISE
(C. 1098–1164)

The blessings promised us by Christ were not promised to those alone who were priests; woe unto the world, indeed, if all that deserved the name of virtue were shut up in a cloister.

Letters

ELEAZAR BEN JUDAH OF WORMS
(C. 1165–1230)

The soul is filled with love [of God], bound with the bonds of love in great joy. This joy chases away all bodily pleasure and worldly delight from his heart. The powerful joy of love seizes his heart so that he continually thinks, "How can I do God's will?" . . . The love of heaven in his heart is like the flame attached to the coal. He does not gaze at women; he does not engage in frivolous talk, but he concerns himself only to do God's will, and he sings songs in order to become filled with joy in the love of God.

The Secret of Secrets

JALAL AL-DIN RUMI
(1207–1273)

"Shaikh," he cried, "now is the time for compassion and pity. I am in despair; now is the hour for loving kindness."

"Declare the reason for your despair," said the shaikh. "What is the object of your quest? What do you seek?"

"The emperor," said the envoy, "chose me out to search for a certain well-branched tree. For there is a tree, unique in all the world, whose fruit is the substance of the Water of Life. Many years I have searched, but I have seen no sign of it, save the banter and ridicule of those merry-makers."

"Simpleton," the shaikh laughed, "this tree is the tree of knowledge in the learned man, very high, very huge, very wide-spreading—Water of Life from the Ocean Divine. You have gone after the form only, and have gone astray; you have abandoned the reality, and therefore cannot find it. Sometimes it is named 'tree' and sometimes 'sun;' sometimes it is named 'sea' and sometimes 'cloud.' It is that one Thing from which effects multitudinous arise, and its least effects are life everlasting. Though it is single, it has a thousand effects; names innumerable are proper to that one. One person may be father to you, but son in regard to someone else, wrath and foe to another, to another loving kindness and good. Hundreds of thousands of names he has, yet is one man; even he who possesses his every quality is blind to his quality. Whoever searches after the name only, though a man of trust, like you falls into despair and distraction. Why do you stick to this name 'tree,' so that you remain with bitterness in your mouth, utterly luckless? Pass on from the Names and contemplate the Attributes, that haply the Attributes may guide you to the Essence."

Tales of the Masnavi

How should a friend run away from the pain inflicted by his friend? Pain is the kernel; friendship is only as the husk to it. The sign of true friendship is joy in affliction, calamity and suffering. A friend is as gold, and affliction is like the fire; pure gold rejoices in the heart of the fire.

Tales of the Masnavi

✸ KABIR
(1440?–1518)
Dance, my heart! Dance today with joy.
The strains of love fill the days and the
    nights with music, and the world is
    listening to its melodies:
Mad with joy, life and death dance to
    the rhythm of this music. The hills
    and the sea and the earth dance.
The world of man dances in laughter
    and tears.
Why put on the robe of the monk, and
    live aloof from the world in lonely
    pride?
Behold! My heart dances in the delight
    of a hundred arts; and the Creator
    is well pleased.

One Hundred Poems of Kabir

✸ MICHEL DE MONTAIGNE
(1533–1592)
There is indeed a certain sense of gratification when we do a good deed that gives us inward satisfaction, and a generous pride that accompanies a good conscience. A resolutely wicked soul may perhaps arm itself with some assurance, but it cannot provide itself with this contentment and satisfaction. . . . These testimonies of a good conscience are pleasant; and such a natural pleasure

120

is very beneficial to us; it is the only payment that can never fail.

Essays

⊛ FRANCIS BACON
(1561–1626)

What then remains but that we still
   should cry
For being born, and, being born to die?

The World

⊛ IZAAK WALTON
(1593–1683)

Affliction is a divine diet which though it be not pleasing to mankind, yet almighty God hath often imposed it as a good, though bitter, physic, to those children whose souls are dearest to him.

The Complete Angler

⊛ MR. TUT-TUT
(17TH? CENTURY)

Poverty is not a disgrace; disgrace lies in poverty without ambition. A mean position is not a cause for contempt; contempt belongs to one in a mean position without ability. Old age is no cause for regret; regret that one is old, having lived in vain. Death is no cause for sorrow; sorrow that one dies without benefit to the world.

One Hundred Proverbs

Who does not enjoy his happy moments cannot after all be called lucky; who feels happy in extremities is the real cultivated scholar.

One Hundred Proverbs

To be elated at success and disappointed at failure is to be the child of circumstances; how can such a one be called master of himself?

One Hundred Proverbs

All people are in financial troubles sometimes. The failure to realize the meaning of poverty must be also considered a fault of the wealthy and successful. Moreover, there are heroes among the poor: the right thing is to open your eyes and broaden your chest.

One Hundred Proverbs

⊛ JOHN LOCKE
(1632–1704)

The necessity of pursuing true happiness is the foundation of all liberty—Happiness, in its full extent, is the utmost pleasure we are capable of.

Letters

⊛ MATSUO BASHO
(1644–1694)

The passing spring,
Birds mourn,
Fishes weep
With tearful eyes.

Haiku

⊛ MATTHEW HENRY
(1662–1714)

Extraordinary afflictions are not always the punishment of extraordinary sins, but sometimes the trial of extraordinary graces—Sanctified afflictions are spiritual promotions.

Letters

❀ MARIE ANNE DU DEFFAND
(1697–1780)

I remember thinking in my youth that no one was happy but madmen, drunkards, and lovers.

Correspondance inédite

❀ JANET GRAHAM
(1723?–1789)

If the Supreme Creator had meant us to be gloomy, he would, it seems to me, have clothed the earth in black, not in that lively green, which is the livery of cheerfulness and joy.

The History of Emily Montague

❀ MARTHA WASHINGTON
(1731–1802)

The greater part of our happiness or misery depends on our dispositions, and not on our circumstances. We carry the seeds of the one or the other about with us in our minds wherever we go.

Letters

❀ THE DECLARATION
OF INDEPENDENCE
(JULY 4, 1776)

We hold these truths to be self-evident: that all men are created equal; that they are endowed by their Creator with certain inalienable Rights; that among these are Life, Liberty and the pursuit of Happiness.

❀ ARTHUR SCHOPENHAUER
(1788–1860)

The happiness which we receive from ourselves is greater than that which we obtain from our surroundings. . . . The world in which a man lives shapes itself chiefly by the way in which he looks at it.

The World As Will and Idea

❀ JOHN HENRY NEWMAN
(1801–1890)

God has created all things for good; all things for their greatest good; everything for its own good. What is the good of one is not the good of another; what makes one man happy would make another unhappy. God has determined, unless I interfere with His plan, that I should reach that which will be my greatest happiness. He looks on me individually, He calls me by my name, He knows what I can do, what I can best be, what is my greatest happiness, and He means to give it me.

God knows what is my greatest happiness, but I do not. There is no rule about what is happy and good; what suits one would not suit another. And the ways by which perfection is reached vary very much; the medicines necessary for our souls are very different from each other. Thus God leads us by strange ways; we know He wills our happiness, but we neither know what our happiness is, nor the way. We are blind; left to ourselves we should take the wrong way; we must leave it to Him.

Meditations and Devotions

❀ VICTOR HUGO
(1802–1885)

The supreme happiness of life is the conviction that we are loved.

Lés Misérables

RALPH WALDO EMERSON
(1803–1882)

Nothing can bring you peace but
yourself.

The Best of Ralph Waldo Emerson

CHARLES DICKENS
(1812–1870)

Reflect upon your present blessings, of
which every man has many; not on your
past misfortunes, of which all men have
some.

Oliver Twist

ROBERT LOUIS STEVENSON
(1850–1894)

There is no duty we so much under-rate
as the duty of being happy.

Letters

ARTHUR RIMBAUD
(1854–1891)

J'ai tendu des cordes de clocher à clocher;
des guirlandes de fenêtre à fenêtre; des
chaînes d'or d'ètoile à étoile, et je danse.

(I stretched out ropes from spire to
spire; garlands from window to window;
golden chains from star to star, and I
dance.)

Les Illuminations

GEORGE BERNARD SHAW
(1856–1950)

A lifetime of happiness! No man
alive could bear it: it would be hell on
earth.

Man and Superman

W. B. YEATS
(1865–1939)

I am content to follow to its source
Every event in action or in thought;
Measure the lot; forgive myself the lot!
When such as I cast out remorse
So great a sweetness flows into the
    breast
We must laugh and we must sing,
We are blest by everything,
Everything we look upon is blessed.

A Dialogue of Self and Soul

YOGASWAMI
(1872–1964)

If you are a king,
Will you have contentment?
If you are a beggar,
Will you have contentment?
Whatever your walk in life may be,
You will only have contentment
    through
Knowing yourself by yourself.

Positive Thoughts for Daily Meditation

Happiness and sorrow are twins let
    them come and go like clouds.

Positive Thoughts for Daily Meditation

WINSTON CHURCHILL
(1874–1965)

I am easily satisfied with the very best.

Speech

POPE PIUS XII
(1876–1958)

Our Savior has nowhere promised
to make us infallibly happy in this
world.

Letters

❁ HAZRAT INAYAT KHAN
(1882–1927)

Mankind is interdependent, and the happiness of each depends upon the happiness of all, and it is this lesson that humanity has to learn today as the first and the last lesson.

The Sufi Message of Hazrat Inayat Khan:
The Art of Personality

❁ ROBERT LYND
(1892–1970)

I am a confirmed believer in blessings in disguise. I prefer them undisguised when I myself happen to be the person blessed; in fact I can hardly recognize a blessing in disguise except when it is bestowed upon someone else.

Middletown

❁ J. KRISHNAMURTI
(1895–1986)

There is great happiness in not wanting, in not being something, in not going somewhere.

Commentaries on Living—from the
Notebooks of J. Krishnamurti

To seek fulfilment is to invite frustration.

Commentaries on Living—from the
Notebooks of J. Krishnamurti

❁ LILLIAN HELLMAN
(1905–1984)

I am suspicious of guilt in myself and in other people; it is usually a way of not thinking, or of announcing one's own fine sensibilities the better to be rid of them fast.

Letters

❁ ALBERT CAMUS
(1913–1960)

For the first time, the first, I laid my heart open to the benign indifference of the universe. To feel it so like myself, indeed so brotherly, made me realize that I'd been happy, and that I was happy still.

The Myth of Sisyphus

❁ ALAN WATTS
(1915–1973)

Not only the anxiety but also the sheer stalemate and paralysis which often attend strictly intelligent and noninstinctual action are the most important causes of anti-intellectual movements in our society. It is through impatience and exasperation with such snarls that democracies vote themselves into dictatorships. It is in protest against the laborious unmanageability of vast technical knowledge in literature, painting, and music that writers and artists go berserk and break every rule in the name of sheer instinctual exuberance. It is in revolt against the insufferable heaps of unproductive paperwork that small businesses sell out to big corporations, and independent professional men take routine salaried jobs without responsibility. It is in disgust with the complex organization of the omnipotent registrar's office and the unimaginative pedantry of the Ph.D. course that people of real genius or creative ability are increasingly unable to work in our universities. It is also in despair of being able to understand or make any productive contribution to the highly organized chaos of our politico-economic system that large numbers of people simply abandon political and social commitments. They just let society be taken over by a pattern of organization which is as self-proliferative as a weed, and whose ends and values are neither human nor instinctual but mechanical. And we should note that a self-contradictory system of action breeds forms of revolt which are contradictory among themselves.

This Is IT and Other Essays on Zen and Spiritual Experience

❀ OSHO
(1931–1990)

And the miracle is: if you can go into your suffering as a meditation, watching, to the deepest roots of it, just through watching, it disappears. You don't have to do anything more than watching. If you have found the authentic cause by your watching, the suffering will disappear.

Discourses

❀ WILLIAM BENNETT
(CONTEMPORARY)

Happiness is like a cat. If you try to coax it or call it, it will avoid you, it will never come. But if you pay no attention to it and go about your business, you'll find it rubbing against your legs and jumping into your lap.

Quoted from *The Soul: An Archeology*, Claudia Setzer

❀ CARLOS CASTANEDA
(CONTEMPORARY)

Modern man has left the realm of the unknown and the mysterious, and has settled down in the realm of the functional. He has turned his back to the world of the foreboding and the exulting and has welcomed the world of boredom.

The Fire Within

❀ RABBI HAROLD KUSHNER
(CONTEMPORARY)

When your life is filled with the desire to see the holiness in everyday life, something magical happens: ordinary life becomes extraordinary, and the very process of life begins to nourish your soul!

God's Fingerprints on the Soul, Handbook for the Soul, eds. Richard Carlson and Benjamin Shield

❀ BERNARD LEVIN
(CONTEMPORARY)

Countries like ours are full of people who have all of the material comforts they desire, yet lead lives of quiet (and at times noisy) desperation, understanding nothing but the fact that there is a hole inside them and that however much food and drink they pour into it, however many motorcars and television sets they stuff it with, however many well-balanced children and loyal friends they parade around the edges of it . . . it aches!

The *Times* (London), 1968

❀ SOGYAL RINPOCHE
(CONTEMPORARY)

May the vision that so many mystic masters of all traditions have had, of a future world free of cruelty and horror, where humanity can live in the ultimate happiness of the nature of mind, come, through all our efforts, to be realized.

The Tibetan Book of Living and Dying

❀ ROSEMARY RADFORD RUETHER
(CONTEMPORARY)

A reencounter with original blessing is experienced as a leap to a new state of being that breaks the hold of false power upon our spirit. In this sense, it is psychologically experienced as something beyond our present state of existence. But . . . we know it to be the most natural thing in the world, since, when we encounter original blessing, we immediately recognize it as our true selves— something with which we are already gifted, not something we have to strive to achieve.

Quoted from *The Soul: An Archeology*, Claudia Setzer

❀ SANGHARAKSHITA
(CONTEMPORARY)

In reality Buddhism is neither pessimistic nor optimistic. If compelled to label it in thisway at all we should borrow a word from George Eliot and call it melioristic, for though asserting that conditioned existence is suffering it also maintains, as the Third Aryan Truth teaches, that suffering can be transcended.

The Three Jewels

❀ BERNIE SIEGEL
(CONTEMPORARY)

Every day is my best day; this is my life; I'm not going to have this moment again.

Love: The Work of the Soul, Handbook for the Soul, eds. Richard Carlson and Benjamin Shield

❀ D. T. SUZUKI
(CONTEMPORARY)

The ultimate standpoint of Zen . . . is that we have been led astray through ignorance to find a split in our own being, that there was from the very beginning no need for a struggle between the finite and the infinite, that the peace we are seeking so eagerly after has been there all the time.

Quoted from *The Soul: An Archeology*, Claudia Setzer

❀ THOMAS SZASZ
(CONTEMPORARY)

Happiness is an imaginary condition formerly often attributed by the living to the dead, now usually attributed by adults to children, and by children to adults.

"Emotions" in *The Second Sin*

❀ THICH NHAT HANH
(CONTEMPORARY)

Lay disciples living in the world can follow the principles of the [Buddha's] teaching to foster true happiness. First of all, do not let a desire for wealth cause you to become so consumed by your work that you prevent happiness for yourself and your family in the present moment. Happiness is foremost. A look filled with understanding, an accepting smile, a loving word, a meal shared in warmth and awareness are the things which create happiness in the present moment. By nourishing awareness in the present moment, you can avoid causing suffering to yourself and those around you. The way you look at others, your smile, and your small acts of caring can create happiness. True happiness does not depend on wealth or fame.

Old Path White Clouds: The Life Story of the Buddha

The Buddha explained that the source of true happiness is living in ease and freedom, fully experiencing the wonders of life. Happiness is being aware of what is going on in the present moment, free from both clinging and aversion. A happy person cherishes the wonders taking place in the present moment—a cool breeze, the morning sky, a golden flower, a violet bamboo tree, the smile of a child. A happy person can appreciate these things without being bound by them. Understanding all dharmas as impermanent and without a separate self, a happy person does not become consumed even by such worry and fear. Because he understands that a flower will soon wilt, he is not sad when it does. A happy person understands the nature of birth and death of all dharmas. His happiness is true happiness, and he does not even worry about or fear his own death.

Old Path White Clouds: The Life Story of the Buddha

Knowledge

⊛ **ATTRIBUTED TO VARIOUS**
Know thyself.

⊛ **CONFUCIUS**
(551–479 BCE)
Confucius said, "To know what you know and know what you don't know is the characteristic of one who knows."

The Aphorisms of Confucius, V, "Wit and Wisdom"

Confucius said, "The young people should be good sons at home, polite and respectful in society; they should be careful in their conduct and faithful, love the people, and associate themselves with the kind people. If after learning all this, they still have energy left, let them read books."

The Aphorisms of Confucius, X, "On Education, Ritual and Poetry"

⊛ **CHUANG TZU**
(369–286 BCE)
For we can only know that we know nothing, and a little knowledge is a dangerous thing.

Quoted in *The Soul: An Archeology,* Claudia Setzer

Cherish that which is within you, and shut off that which is without; for much knowledge is a curse.

On Tolerance

Human life is limited, but knowledge is limitless. To drive the limited in pursuit of the limitless is fatal; and to presume that one really knows is fatal indeed!

The Preservation of Life

⊛ **THE APOCRYPHA**
(OLD TESTAMENT TEXTS NOT INCLUDED IN THE BIBLE)
A scholar's wisdom comes of ample
 leisure;
if a man is to be wise he must be
 relieved of other tasks.

Ecclesiasticus

⊛ **HUANG-PO**
(800–850)
Regarding this Zen Doctrine of ours, since it was first transmitted, it has never taught that men should seek for learning or form concepts. "Studying the way" is just a figure of speech. It is a method of arousing people's interest in the early

stages of their development. In fact, the Way is not something which can be studied. Study leads to the retention of concepts and so the Way is entirely misunderstood. Moreover, the Way is not something specially existing; it is called the Mahayana Mind—Mind which is not to be found inside, outside or in the middle. Truly it is not located anywhere. The first step is to refrain from knowledge-based concepts. This implies that if you were to follow the empirical method to the utmost limit, on reaching that limit you would still be unable to locate Mind. The way is spiritual Truth and was originally without name or title. It was only because people ignorantly sought for it empirically that the Buddhas appeared and taught them to eradicate this method of approach. Fearing that nobody would understand, they selected the name "Way." You must not allow this name to lead you into forming a mental concept of a road. So it is said "When the fish is caught we pay no more attention to the trap." When body and mind achieve spontaneity, the Way is reached and Mind is understood.

The Zen Teaching of Huang-po

⊛ HAKIM ABU' L-MAJD MAJDUD SANAI OF GHAZNA (HAKIM SANAI)
(12TH CENTURY)

But how will you ever know him [God], as long as you are unable to know
    yourself?

The Walled Garden of Truth

He doesn't know his own self:
how should he know the self of
    another?

The Walled Garden of Truth

If you know your own worth,
what need you care about
the acceptance or rejection of others?

The Walled Garden of Truth

Knowing what you know,
be serene also, like a mountain;
and do not be distressed by misfortune.
Knowledge without serenity
is an unlit candle;
together they are honey-comb;
honey without wax is a noble thing;
wax without honey is only fit for
    burning.

The Walled Garden of Truth

⊛ FARID UD-DIN ATTAR
(1120?–1193?)

You cannot carve your way to heaven's
    throne
If you sit locked in vanity alone.
You need a skilful guide; you cannot
    start
This ocean-voyage with blindness in
    your heart.

The Conference of the Birds

⊛ MICHEL DE MONTAIGNE
(1533–1592)

The active pursuit of truth is our proper business. We have no excuse for conducting it badly or unfittingly. But failure to capture our prey is another matter. For we are born to quest after it; to possess it belongs to a greater power. Truth is not, as Democritus said, hidden in the depths of the abyss, but situated rather at an infinite height in the divine understanding. The world is but a school of inquiry.

Essays

It once pleased me to see, in one place or another, men who had, in the name of religion, made vows of ignorance as well as of chastity, poverty, and penitence. This too is a gelding of our unruly appetites, a blunting of that cupidity which drives us on to the study of books, and a ridding of the mind of that luxuriant complacency which tickles us with the belief in our learning. And it is a rich fulfilment of the view of worldly poverty to add to it poverty of mind. We need hardly any knowledge to live happily.

Essays

⊛ FRANCIS BACON
(1561–1626)
Knowledge is power.

Meditationes Sacrae De Haeresibus

⊛ ALFRED, LORD TENNYSON
(1809–1892)
Knowledge comes, but wisdom lingers.

Motto

⊛ THE SHIVAPURI BABA
(1826–1963)
There is a vast difference in knowing a thing and in having it. Knowledge of a thing is not necessarily the realisation of it. For instance, we know that there is such a country as England which is so and so. But this knowledge itself it not the realisation of it. Likewise, for a real aspirant after truth, the simple knowledge gained of it alone can do no good. Such a knowledge we can have from the writings of the great thinkers of the world, the Vedas and the Upanishads. Suppose we have gone through all of them and gained knowledge of the truth,

does this mean that we have realised it? Yes, we have done what we can to gain the knowledge. But with simply this we do not get satisfied. We can still assume that there is something beyond and there is a longing for that.

Quoted by J. G. Bennett in *Long Pilgrimage*

⊛ MARY COLERIDGE
(1861–1907)
The fruits of the tree of knowledge are various; he must be strong indeed who can digest all of them.

Gathered Leaves for the Prose of Mary E. Coleridge

⊛ HERMANN HESSE
(1877–1962)
Knowledge can be communicated, but not wisdom. One can find it, live it, be fortified by it, do wonders through it, but one cannot communicate and teach it.

Siddhartha

⊛ LILLIAN SMITH
(1897–1966)
To believe in something not yet proved and to underwrite it without lives: it is the only way we can keep the future open. Man, surrounded by facts, permitting himself no surprise, no intuitive flash, no great hypothesis, no risk, is in a locked cell. Ignorance cannot seal the mind and imagination more securely.

The Journey

⊛ OSHO
(1931–1990)
Knowledge is always borrowed. It is not a flower that grows in your soul, it is something plastic that been imposed upon you.

Discourses

131

✸ CARLOS CASTANEDA
(CONTEMPORARY)

In the face of the unknown, man is adventurous. It is a quality of the unknown to give us a sense of hope and happiness. Man feels robust, exhilarated. Even the apprehension that it arouses is very fulfilling. . . . [But] whenever what is taken to be the unknown turns out to be the unknowable the results are disastrous . . . for the unknowable has no energizing effects whatsoever. It is not within human reach; therefore, it should not be intruded upon foolishly or even prudently.

The Fire Within

✸ THICH NHAT HANH
(CONTEMPORARY)

My teaching is not a philosophy. It is the result of direct experience. The things I say come from my own experience. You can confirm them all by your own experience. I teach that all things are impermanent and without a separate self. This I have learned from my own direct experience. You can too. I teach that all things depend on all other things to arise, develop, and pass away. Nothing is created from a single, original source. I have directly experienced this truth, and you can also. My goal is not to explain the universe, but to help guide others to have a direct experience of reality. Words cannot describe reality. Only direct experience enables us to see the true face of reality.

Old Path White Clouds: The Life Story of the Buddha

Life

☸ THE CHĀRVĀKA, FROM THE BRHASPATI-SUTRA

While life is yours, live joyously;
None can escape Death's searching eye:
When once this frame of ours they burn,
How shall it e'er again return?

A Source Book in Indian Philosophy, S.
Radhakrishna and Charles A. Moore

☸ LAO-TZU
(C. 6TH CENTURY BCE)

Existence is beyond the power of words
To define:
Terms may be used
But are none of them absolute.

The Way of Life

Fatalism is acceptance of destiny
And to accept destiny is to face life with
    open eyes,
Whereas not to accept destiny is to face
    death blindfolded.

The Way of Life

The way to use life is to do nothing
    through acting,
The way to use life is to do everything
    through being.

The Way of Life

Let life ripen and then fall.
Will is not the way at all:
Deny the way of life and you are
    dead.

The Way of Life

☸ THE GOLDEN MEAN OF TSESZE
(4TH? CENTURY BCE)

Confucius remarked: "There are men
who seek for the abstruse and strange
and live a singular life in order that they
may leave a name to posterity. This is
what I never would do. There are again
good men who try to live in conformity
with the moral law, but who, when they
have gone halfway, throw it up. I never
could give it up. Lastly, there are truly
moral men who unconsciously live a life
in entire harmony with the universal moral order and who live unknown
to the world and unnoticed of men
without any concern. It is only men of
holy, divine natures who are capable of
this."

The Golden Mean

❋ THE DHAMMAPADA
(3RD CENTURY BCE)

Look upon the man who tells thee thy faults as if he told thee of a hidden treasure, the wise man who shows thee the dangers of life. Follow that man: he who follows him will see good and not evil.

The Path of Perfection

What is life but the flower or the fruit which falls when ripe, but yet which ever fears the untimely frost?

The Path of Perfection

❋ BHAGWAN SHREE PATANJALI
(2ND? CENTURY BCE)

Yoga consists in the (intentional) stoppage of the spontaneous activities of the life-stuff.

Yoga Sutras

❋ NEW TESTAMENT

Strait is the gate, and narrow is the way, which leadeth unto life, and few there be that find it.

Matthew 7:14

❋ WANG WEI
(699–761)

The world's affairs and the floating
    clouds—
        why question them?
You had best take life easily—
        and have a good dinner.

"Giving P'ei Ti a Drink," in
The Poems of Wang Wei

❋ OMAR KHAYYAM
(D. 1123)

For in and out, above, about, below,
'Tis nothing but a Magic Shadow-show,
Play'd in a Box whose Candle is the
    Sun,
Round which we Phantom Figures
        come and go.

Rubaiyat

❋ HILDEGARDE OF BINGEN
(1098–1179)

I am that supreme and fiery force that sends forth all living sparks. Death hath no part in me, yet I bestow death, wherefore I am girt about with wisdom as with wings. I am that living and fiery essence of the divine substance that glows in the beauty of the fields, and in the shining water, and in the burning sun and the moon and the stars, and in the force of the invisible wind, the breath of all living things, I breathe in the green grass and in the flowers, and in the living waters. . . . All these live and do not die because I am in them. . . . I am the source of the thundered word by which all creatures were made, I permeate all things that they may not die. I am life.

Meditations

❋ JALAL AL-DIN RUMI
(1207–1273)

The breath of the flute player,
does it belong to the flute?

Mathnawi

MIRA BAI
(1450–1547)

How can one come to meet the
    Lord?
For fifteen hours one is busy,
And the remaining nine one sleeps.
Having received the priceless gift
Of a human birth,
We remain asleep and it is wasted.

The World: Devotional Poems

GURU NANAK
(1469–1539)

Were life's span extended to the four
    ages
And ten times more,
Were one known over the nine
    shores
Ever in humanity's fore,
Were one to achieve greatness
With a name noised over the earth,
If one found not favor with the lord
What would it all be worth?

Hymns of Guru Nanak

MICHEL DE MONTAIGNE
(1533–1592)

Our life, like the harmony of the world,
is composed of contrarieties, also of varying tones, sweet and harsh, sharp and
flat, soft and loud. If a musician liked
one sort only, what effect would he
make? He must be able to employ them
together and blend them. And we too
must accept the good and evil that are
consubstantial with our life. Our existence is impossible without this mixture,
and one side is no less necessary to us
than the other.

Essays

FRANCIS BACON
(1561–1626)

But men must know that in this theater
of man's life, it is reserved only for God
and angels to be lookers on.

The Advancement of Learning

JOHN DONNE
(1572–1631)

Though our natural life were no life, but
rather a continual dying, yet we have two
lives besides that, an eternal life reserved
for heaven, but yet a heavenly life too, a
spiritual life, even in this world.

Quoted from *The Soul: An Archeology*,
Claudia Setzer

JAKOB BÖHME
(1575–1624)

The law of God and also the way to life
is written in our hearts; it lies in no man's
supposing, nor in any historical opinion,
but in a good will and well doing.

The Confessions

MR. TUT-TUT
(17TH? CENTURY)

To see through fame and wealth is to
gain a little rest; to see through life and
death is to gain a big rest.

One Hundred Proverbs

SIR THOMAS BROWNE
(1605–1682)

Life is a pure flame, and we live by an
invisible sun within us.

Quoted in *The Soul: An Archeology*,
Claudia Setzer

❀ WILLIAM BLAKE
(1757–1827)

For man has closed himself up, 'till he sees all things thro' the chinks of his cavern.

The Portable Blake

❀ JOHN STUART MILL
(1806–1873)

Human existence is girt round with mystery: the narrow region of our experience is a small island in the midst of a boundless sea.

Three Essays on Religion

❀ MARY BAKER EDDY
(1821–1910)

To live and let live, without clamor for distinction of recognition; to wait on divine Love; to write truth first on the tablet of one's own heart—this is the sanity and perfection of living, and my human ideal.

Message to The Mother Church

❀ THE SHIVAPURI BABA
(1826–1963)

J.G.B.: All that you have said so far amounts to this: that man should live on the earth a normal, well-balanced life in accordance with all natural laws. I take it that this is just a foundation: what is to be built upon the foundation?

S.B.: No. It is separate in itself. This right life should be lived for its own sake. When all this is done, one will have a very healthy body, one will have useful friends to help, and one will have sufficient wealth and material to live on. And life will be very pleasant.

J.G.B.: But man does not live for pleasure.

S.B.: One should not live for pleasure; but, if it comes, it should not be rejected also. Pleasure will give satisfaction if it is accepted without being sought for.

J.G.B.: After these duties, what prepares in man the necessary qualification to come to the spiritual life?

S.B.: That is to be separately studied.

J.G.B.: There are some things which you, Babaji [a term of respect], must be able to see from your vision which you cannot speak about. Even if you wanted to, you could not tell us.

S.B.: I cannot. Words cannot reach this. Words cannot reach.

J.G.B.: Therefore, if we wish to know what you know, we have to come by the same path that you have come by.

S.B.: Experience alone will teach you— experience is beyond explanation.

J.G.B.: We have been here eight days, and we never saw Himal. We thought we would go away without seeing the snow mountains. Today, it became clear, and we saw the mountains; and we were saying, as were coming, the mountains have been there every day, but only on the last day we saw them. It is like that with God.

S.B.: It is like that.

Recorded by J. G. Bennett in *Long Pilgrimage*

✹ ANNIE BESANT
(1847–1933)

We are part of one great Life, which knows no failure, no loss of effort or strength, which "mightily and sweetly ordering all things" bears the worlds onwards to their goal.

Quoted from *The Soul: An Archeology*, Claudia Setzer

✹ VINCENT VAN GOGH
(1853–1890)

First of all the twinkling stars vibrated, but remained motionless in space, then all the celestial globes were united into one series of movements. . . . Firmament and planets both disappeared, but the mighty breath which gives lives to all things and in which all is bound up remained.

Letters

✹ GEORGE SANTAYANA
(1863–1952)

There is no cure for birth and death save to enjoy the interval.

✹ NATSUME SOSEKI
(1867–1916)

What a long spring day!
Catching yawns from one another
We go each our way.

Koan

✹ WILLIAM HENRY DAVIES
(1871–1940)

What is this life if, full of care,
We have no time to stand and stare?

Collected Poems

✹ G. I. GURDJIEFF
(1877?–1949)

Each of them (our inner selves) is a caliph for an hour, does what he likes regardless of everything, and, later on, the others have to pay for it. And there is no order among them whatever. Whoever gets the upper hand is master. He whips everyone on all sides and takes heed of nothing. But the next moment another sees the whip and beats him. Imagine a country where everyone can be king for five minutes and do during these five minutes just what he likes with the whole kingdom. That is our life.

In Search of the Miraculous: Fragments of an Unknown Teaching, P. D. Ouspensky

✹ HERMANN HESSE
(1877–1962)

It is harder to kill something that is spiritually alive than it is to bring the dead back to life.

Siddhartha

✹ THE MOTHER
(1878–1990)

The number of suggestions one could call "defeatist" within the earth's atmosphere is simply overwhelming! It's so surprising that everything isn't crushed to death. . . . Everyone is constantly creating disasters; expecting the worst, seeing the worst, observing only the worst. . . . And it's down to the smallest things, you know (the body observes everything). When people react harmoniously, everything goes well; when there is the reaction which I now call defeatist: if the person picks up an object, he drops it. It happens all the time, without any reason whatsoever; it's the presence of that defeatist consciousness. And I've seen this: all the wills or vibrations (for in the end, it all boils down to qualities of vibration) that bring about everything, from little nuisances to the greatest disasters, all have that same quality!

Satprem, The Mind of the Cells

⊛ PIERRE TEILHARD DE CHARDIN
(1881–1955)

And then there is the man who picks himself up, covered in dust but unharmed, after a five-nine has exploded uncomfortably close to him: whence comes this joyful expansion of the heart, this alacrity of the will, this new savour in life—things that we do not experience if we have just missed being run over by a train or shot by a bullet from a carelessly handled revolver? Is it solely the joy of 'staying alive' that so fills the soul of survivors in war-time and gives new youth to their world? For my part, I believe that the completely fresh flavour added to living after a narrow escape derives above all from this deep-seated intuition that the existence we have found again, consecrated by danger, is a new existence. The physical well-being which at that moment spreads over the soul is a sign of the higher Life into which the survivor has just been baptised. The man who has passed through the fire is another species of man among men.

Nostalgia for the Front

⊛ P. G. WODEHOUSE
(1881–1975)

I spent the afternoon musing on Life. If you come to think of it, what a queer thing Life is! So unlike anything else, don't you know, if you see what I mean.

My Man Jeeves

⊛ KAHLIL GIBRAN
(1883–1931)

My kingdom is not of the earth. My kingdom shall be where two or three of you shall meet in love, and in wonder at the loveliness of life, and in good cheer, and in remembrance of me.

Jesus, The Son of Man: His Words and His Deeds As Told and Recorded by Those Who Knew Him

⊛ D. H. LAWRENCE
(1885–1930)

For man, the vast marvel is to be alive. For man, as for flower and beast and bird, the supreme triumph is to be most vividly, most perfectly alive. Whatever the unborn and the dead may know, they cannot know the beauty, the marvel of being alive in the flesh. The dead may look after the afterwards. But the magnificent here and now of life in the flesh is ours, and ours alone and ours only for a time. We ought to dance with rapture that we should be alive and in the flesh, and part of the living incarnate cosmos. I am part of the sun as my eyes is part of me. That I am part of the earth my feet know perfectly, and my blood is part of the sea. My soul knows that I am part of the human race, my soul is an organic part of the great human soul, as my spirit is part of my nation. In my very own self, I am part of my family. There is nothing of me that is alone and absolute except my mind, and we shall find that the mind has no existence by itself, it is only the glitter of the sun on the surface of the waters.

Apocalypse

I know that man cannot live by his own will alone. With his soul, he must search for the sources of the power of life. It is life we want.

Phoenix II

What is alive, and open, and active, is good. All that makes for inertia, lifeless-ness, dreariness, is bad. This is the essence of morality.

Phoenix II

◉ PAUL TILLICH
(1886–1965)
We are separated from the mystery, the depth, and the greatness of our exist-ence. We hear the voice of that depth; but our ears are closed.

The Shaking of the Foundations

◉ T. S. ELIOT
(1888–1965)
Let us go, through certain half-deserted streets,

The muttering retreats
Of restless nights in one-night cheap hotels
And sawdust restaurants with oyster shells:
Streets that follow like a tedious argument
Of insidious intent
. . . .
In the room the women come and go
Talking of Michelangelo

The Love Song of J. Alfred Prufrock

◉ EUGENE O'NEILL
(1888–1953)
Life is perhaps best regarded as a bad dream between two awakenings.

Quoted from *The Soul: An Archeology*,
Claudia Setzer

◉ MIKHAIL NAIMY
(1889–1988)
Die to live, or live to die.

The Book of Mirdad

Let things alone and labor not to change them. For they seem what they seem only because you seem what you seem. They neither see nor speak except you lend them sight and speech.

The Book of Mirdad

◉ ALBERT CAMUS
(1913–1960)
I see many people die because they judge that life is not worth living. I see others paradoxically getting killed for the ideas or illusions that give them a reason for living (what is called a reason for living is also an excellent reason for

dying). I therefore conclude that the meaning of life is the most urgent of questions.

The Myth of Sisyphus

But the point is to live.

The Myth of Sisyphus

If any art is devoid of lessons, it is certainly music. It is too closely related to mathematics not to have borrowed their gratuitousness. That game the mind plays with itself according to set and measured laws takes place in the sonorous compass that belongs us and beyond which the vibrations nevertheless meet in an inhuman universe. There is no purer sensation.

The Myth of Sisyphus

✸ ALAN WATTS
(1915–1973)

To be a Tathagata is to dance the day instead of working it. The "curse of work" that came from the Fall was the supposition that one "must" live.

The Book—On the Taboo Against Knowing Who You Are

A bird is one egg's way of becoming other eggs.

The Book—On the Taboo Against Knowing Who You Are

✸ R. D. LAING
(1927–1989)

We are born into a world where alienation awaits us. We are potentially men, but are in an alienated state and this state is not simply a natural system. Alienation as our present destiny is achieved only by outrageous violence perpetrated by humans beings on human beings.

The relevance of Freud to our time is largely his insight and to a very considerable extent his demonstration that the ordinary person is a shriveled, desiccated fragment of what a person can be. As adults, we have forgotten most of our childhood, not only its contents, but its flavor. As men, we hardly remember our dreams and make little sense of them when we do. As for our bodies we retain just sufficient proprioceptive sensations to coordinate our movements and to ensure the minimal requirements for bio-social survival—to register fatigue, signals for food, sex, defecation, sleep: beyond that . . . little or nothing.

Our capacity to think, except in the service of what we are dangerously deluded in supposing is our self interest, and in conformity with common sense, is pitifully limited: our capacity even to see, hear, touch, taste and smell is so shrouded in veils of mystification that an intensive discipline of unlearning is necessary for anyone before one can begin to experience the world afresh, with innocence, truth and love.

The Politics of Experience and the Bird of Paradise

Life is a sexually transmitted disease with a hundred percent mortality.

Spoken

✸ OSHO
(1931–1990)

Life is not short; life is eternal, so there is no question of any hurry. By hurrying you can only miss. In existence do you see any hurry? Seasons come in their time, flowers come in their time, trees are not running to grow fast because life is short. It seems as if the whole existence is aware of the eternity of life.

We have been here always, and we will be here always—of course not in the same forms, and not in the same bodies. Life goes on evolving, reaching to higher stages. But there is no end anywhere, and there has been no beginning anywhere either.

Discourses

The first thing to be done is laughter, because that sets the trend for the whole day. If you wake up laughing, you will soon begin to feel how absurd life is. Nothing is serious: even your disappointments are laughable, even your pain is laughable, even you are laughable.

The Orange Book

❀ ALAN BENNETT
(CONTEMPORARY)
You know life . . . it's rather like opening a tin of sardines. We are all of us looking for the key.

Beyond the Fringe

❀ FR. ALFRED D'SOUZA
(CONTEMPORARY)
For a long time it seemed to me that life was about to begin—real life. But there was always some obstacle in the way, something to be got through first, some unfinished business, time still to be served, a debt to be paid. Then life

would begin. At last it dawned on me that these obstacles were my life.

❀ T. GEORGE HARRIS
(CONTEMPORARY)
The social hierarchies of the past, where some boss above you always punished any error, conditioned men to feel a chain of harsh authority reaching all the way "up there." We don't even have, since Dr. Spock, many Jehovah-like fathers in the human family. So the average unconscious no longer learns to seek forgiveness from the wrathful God alone.

Our generation knows a cold hell, solitary confinement in this life, without a God to damn or save it. Until man figures out the trap and hunts . . . "the Ultimate Ground of Being," he has no reason at all for his existence. Empty, finite, he knows only that he will soon die. Since this life has no meaning, and he sees no future life, he is not really a person but a victim of self-extinction.

"The Battle of the Bible," in *Look* magazine, July 1965.

❀ SAM KEEN
(CONTEMPORARY)
Once we abandon the age-old quest for consistency, for forging a single identity, for a unifying vision we are left with no guiding principle except to follow the dictates of the moment.

Fire in the Belly

❀ U. G. KRISHNAMURTI
(CONTEMPORARY)
The natural state is not the state of self-realised or God-realised man, it is

not a thing to be achieved or attained, it is not a thing to be willed into existence; it is there—it is the living state. This state is just the functional activity of life. By "life" I do not mean something abstract; it is the life of the senses, functioning naturally without the interference of thought. Thought is an interloper, which thrusts itself into the affairs of the senses. It has a profound motive; thought directs the activity of the senses "to get something out of them," and uses them to give continuity to itself. This constant demand to experience everything is because if we don't, we come to an end—that is, the "we" as we know ourselves and we don't want that at all. What we want is the continuity.

The Mystique of Enlightenment—The Unrational Ideas of a Man Called U. G.

◉ LEONARD LAUDER
(CONTEMPORARY)

When a person with experience meets a person with money, the person with experience will get the money. And the person with the money will get some experience.

A speech on the early years of the Estee Lauder company, Woman's Economic Development Corporation, February 1985

◉ RUPERT SHELDRAKE
(CONTEMPORARY)

Spoken softly, the possibility is open that the phenomenon of "life" depends upon laws and factors which have not been recognized so far by scientists.

A New Science of Life

◉ MARION WOODMAN
(CONTEMPORARY)

We all experience "soul moments" in life—when we see a magnificent sunrise, hear the call of a loon, see the wrinkles in our mother's hands, or smell the sweetness of a bay. During these moments, our body, as well as our brain, resonates as we experience the glory of being a human being.

Quoted in *Soul Moments: Handbook for the Soul,* eds. Richard Carlson and Benjamin Shield

◉ GARY ZUKAV
(CONTEMPORARY)

As the human species awakens to itself as a collection of immortal souls learning together, caring for the environment and the earth will become a matter of the heart, the natural response of souls moving toward their full potential.

Evolution and Business

Love

⊛ ANONYMOUS
The heart that loves is always young.

Greek proverb

Love teaches even asses to dance.

French proverb

⊛ THE GUHYASAMAJATANTRA
"Tantra" is continuity, and this is
　　threefold:
Ground, Actuality, and Inalienableness.
"Actuality" is immanent causality,
　　"Inalienableness" is the effect,
"Ground" is the process.

⊛ LAO-TZU
(C. 6TH CENTURY BCE)
He who loves the world as his body may
be entrusted with the empire.

Tao Te Ching

⊛ BUDDHA
(563–483 BCE)
Let a man overcome anger by kindness,
　　evil by good. . . .

Victory breeds hatred, for the
　　conquered is unhappy. . . .

Never in the world does hatred cease
　　by hatred; hatred ceases by love.

Samyuta

⊛ CONFUCIUS
(551–479 BCE)
Can there be a love which does not
make demands on its object?

Analects

⊛ SOPHOCLES
(496?–406 BCE)
One word frees us of all the weight and
pain of life: That word is love.

Oedipus at Colonus

⊛ EURIPIDES
(485?–406? BCE)
Love is all we have, the only way that
each can help the other.

Orestes

⊛ PLATO
(C. 428–348 BCE)
[Love is] the joy of the good, the wonder of the wise, the amazement of the
gods.

The Symposium

✹ THE DHAMMAPADA

(3RD CENTURY BCE)

"This man abused me: he beat me and
  conquered,
Conquered and plundered." Wrapped
  up in such thoughts,
Never appeased is the hatred of such
  men.

"This man abused me, he beat me and
  conquered,
Conquered and plundered." Stripped
  bare of such thoughts,
Quickly appeased is the hatred of such
  men.

Never by hatred is hatred appeased,
Nay! but by not-hate: that's the old-
  time Law.

✹ MENANDER

(C. 342–292 BCE)

Love blinds all men alike, both the
reasonable and the foolish.

Andria

✹ LUCRETIUS

(99–55 BCE)

Love is a product of habit.

De rerum natura

✹ VIRGIL

(70–19 BCE)

Love conquers all: and let us too surrender to love.

Eclogues

✹ OVID

(43 BCE–17 CE)

Love is a kind of warfare.

Ars amatoria

✹ OLD TESTAMENT

Hatred stirs up strife, but love covers
  all offenses.

Proverbs 10:12, RSV

Thou shalt love thy neighbor as thyself.

Leviticus 19:18

✹ NEW TESTAMENT

I may have all knowledge and
  understand all secrets; I may have
  all the faith needed
to move mountains—but if I have no
  love, I am nothing.

I Corinthians, 13, ii

Be kindly affectioned one to another
  with brotherly love: in honor
  preferring one another.

Romans 12:10

✹ TACITUS

(C. 55–117)

It is human to hate those whom we have
injured.

Life of Agricola

✹ EPICTETUS

(55–135)

The universe is but one great city, full of
beloved ones, divine and human by
nature, endeared to each other.

Manual

✹ THE MISHNA

(C. 200)

Ben Azai used to say: "Despise no man,
and consider nothing impossible, for

every man has his hour and everything its place."

The Talmud quoted in *The World's Great Scriptures,* Lewis Browne

❀ ANONYMOUS 4TH CENTURY GNOSTIC

Gradually the soul recognizes her
    beloved
and she rejoices once more,
yet weeping before him
as she remembers the disgrace of her
    former widowhood.
She adorns herself still more,
so that he might be pleased to stay with
    her.
He requires her to turn to face from
    her people
and the multitude of her adulterers
in whose midst she once was,
To devote herself only to her kind, her
    real lord,
and to forget the house of the earthly
    father
where things went so badly with her
But to remember her Father who is in
    heaven.
And the prophet said in the Psalms:
"Hear, my daughter, and see, then
    incline your ear,
Forget your people and your father's
    house
for the king has desired your beauty; he
    is your lord."

The Exegesis of the Soul,
Nag Hammadi Gospels

❀ ST. AUGUSTINE
(354–430)

There is no one in the whole human family to whom kindly affection is not due by reason of the bond of a common humanity, although it may not be due on the ground of reciprocal love.

To Proba

❀ BOETHIUS
(470?–524)

Who can give law to lovers? Love is a greater law to itself.

De consolatione philosophiae

❀ THE KORAN
(7TH CENTURY)

To be charitable in public is good, but to give alms to the poor in private is better and will atone for some of your sins. God has knowledge of all your actions.

Fight for the sake of God those that fight against you, but do not attack them first. God does not love the aggressors.

❀ SHANTIDEVA
(8TH CENTURY)

There is no evil like hatred,
And no fortitude like patience.

A Guide to the Bodhisattva's Way of Life

❀ RABI'A AL-ADAWIYYA
(717–809)

I set up house for You in my heart
As a friend that I could talk with.
I gave my body to someone else
Who wanted to embrace it.
This body, all in all, is good enough for
    embracing—
But the Friend who lives in my house
Is the lover of my heart.
I have two ways of loving You:

A selfish one
And another way that is worthy of You.
In my selfish love, I remember You and
    You alone.
In that other love, You lift the Veil
And let me feast my eyes on Your living
    Face.
That I remember You always, or that I
    see You face-to-face—
No credit to me in either:
The credit is to You in both.
If you hadn't singled me out to suffer
    your love,
I never would've brought you
All these lovers—
(Lord Remember!)

Doorkeeper of the Heart

Marriage has to do with being—
But where can this being be found?
I should belong to you?
What makes you think
I even belong to myself?
I am His—His!

Doorkeeper of the Heart

⊛ MILAREPA
(1040–1123)

Wealth is like the dew on a blade of
    grass,
so give alms without covetousness.

The Message of Milarepa

⊛ AL-GHAZZALI
(B. 1058)

Love for God is the farthest reach of all
stations, the sun of the highest degrees,
and there is no station after that of love,
except its fruit and its consequences.

Quoted from The Soul: An Archeology,
Claudia Setzer

⊛ HAKIM ABU' L-MAJD MAJDUD SANAI OF GHAZNA (HAKIM SANAI)
(12TH CENTURY)

Whilst in this land
of fruitless pursuits,
you are always unbalanced, always
either all back or all front;
but once the seeking soul has progressed
just a few paces beyond this state,
loves seizes the reins.

The Walled Garden of Truth

Love's conqueror is he
whom love conquers.

The Walled Garden of Truth

⊛ FARID UD-DIN ATTAR
(1120?–1193?)

A man whose eyes love opens risks his
    soul—
His dancing breaks beyond the mind's
    control.

The Conference of the Birds

⊛ MECHTILD OF MAGDEBURG
(1207–1249)

Those who would know much, and love
little, will ever remain at but the beginning of a godly life.

The Flowing Light of the Godhead

⊛ JALAL AL-DIN RUMI
(1207–1273)

Love makes bitter things sweet; love
converts base copper to gold. By love
dregs become clear; by love pains become
healing. By love the dead are brought to
life; by love a king is made a slave.

Tales of the Masnavi

I have ordained for every man a manner of conduct; I have given to every man his own way of expression. In regard to him it is praiseworthy, in regard to you it is blameworthy; in regard to him it is honey, in regard to you it is poison. I am independent of all purity and uncleanness; I am far above all sloth and alacrity. I made not any commandment that I might make profit, but I might be bountiful to My servants. To Indians the usage of Hind is praiseworthy, to Sindians the usage of Sind is praiseworthy; I am not sanctified by their magnificats, it is they who are sanctified so that they scatter pearls. I do not regard the tongue and the speech; I regard the inward soul and the spirit's state. I look into the heart, whether it be humble even though the words spoken be far from humble. For the heart is the substance; speech is only the accident; therefore the accident is adventitious, the substance is the true object. How many more of these phrases, these concepts, these metaphors? What I want is burning, burning; attune yourself to burning! Kindle a fire of love in your soul, burn utterly all thought and expression!

Tales of the Masnavi

The lover and the letter, on complete absorption:

A lover, being admitted to sit beside his beloved, thereupon drew out a letter and read it to her. The letter, which was in verse, told over her praises together with much lamentation, misery and supplication.

"If all this is for my sake," said the beloved, "to read this now you are with me is a sheer waste of time. Here I am beside you, and you read a letter! This is certainly not the sign of a true lover."

"True, you are here with me," the lover replied. "All the same, I am not enjoying myself as well as I should. Though we are united now, I am not experiencing what I did last year on your account. I have drunk limpid water from this foundation, I have refreshed my eyes and my heart. I still see the fountain, but there is no water; perchance some footpad has cut off my water!"

"Then," said his lady, "I am not your beloved. I am in Tartary, while your desire is in Cathay. You are in love with me and with a certain emotion together, and the emotion eludes your grasp, young man. So I am not the entire object of your quest; at this moment I am only a part of your aim. I am the dwelling-place of the beloved, not the beloved herself. True love is fixed on the gold and not on the coffer."

Tales of the Masnavi

⊛ **GEOFFREY CHAUCER**
(1340?–1400)
Love is blind.

"The Merchant's Tale," in
The Canterbury Tales

⊛ **CATHERINE OF SIENA**
(1347–1380)
If thou wish to reach the perfection of love, it befits thee to set thy life in order.

Letter to Monna alessa dei Saracini

✺ THOMAS À KEMPIS
(1380–1471)

Love is swift, sincere, pious, pleasant, generous, strong, patient, faithful, prudent, long-suffering, manly, and never seeking her own; for wheresoever a man seeketh his own, there he falleth from love.

Imitation of Christ

✺ JAMI
(1414–1492)

Two sages had taken up the topic of love.

One declared: "The hallmarks of love are misfortune and suffering. Incessantly the lover experiences torment and affliction."

The other replied, "Enough! I suppose you have never seen peace follow war, or tasted the delight of union after separation! None in the world are more delightful than those who, with a pure heart, give themselves to love; and none cruder than those insensitive beings who remain aloof from such cares!"

The Abode of Spring

✺ KABIR
(1440?–1518)

Knowing nothing shuts the iron gates; the new love opens them.

The sound of the gates opening wakes the beautiful woman asleep.

Kabir says: Fantastic! Don't let a chance like this go by!

The Fish in the Sea Is Not Thirsty

✺ MIRA BAI
(1450–1547)

I am mad with love
And no one understands my plight.
Only the wounded
Understand the agonies of the
    wounded,
When a fire rages in the heart.

Hymns of Praise: Devotional Poems

✺ MARINA DE GUEVARA
(c. 1510–1559)

To bring the heart into tune with God is better than audible prayer.

Letters

✺ ST. JOHN OF THE CROSS
(1542–1591)

The very fire of love which afterwards is united with the soul, glorifying it, is that which previously assails it by purging it, just as the fire that penetrates a log of wood is the same that first makes an assault upon it, wounding it with its flame, drying it out, and stripping it of its unsightly qualities until it is so disposed that it can be penetrated and transformed into the fire.

The Ascent of Mount Carmel

✺ THE BOOK OF COMMON PRAYER
(1549)

With this Ring I thee wed, with my body I thee worship, and with all my worldly goods I thee endow.

The Wedding

JOHN LYLY
(1554?–1606)

Love knoweth no laws.

Euphues

FRANCIS BACON
(1561–1626)

It is impossible to love and be wise.

Of Love

CHRISTOPHER MARLOWE
(1564–1593)

Who ever loved that loved not at first sight?

Hero and Leander

WILLIAM SHAKESPEARE
(1564–1616)

Let me not to the marriage of true
  minds
Admit impediments.
Love is not love
Which alters when it alteration finds,
Or bends with the remover to remove.
Oh no! It is an ever-fixed mark
That looks on tempests and is never
  shaken.
It is the star to every wandering bark,
Whose worth's unknown, although his
  height be taken.

Sonnet 116

Love is a familiar. Love is a devil.
  There is no evil angel but Love.

Love's Labour's Lost, I, 2

But love is blind, and lovers cannot
  see
The pretty follies that themselves
  commit.

The Merchant of Venice, II, 6

The course of true love never did run
  smooth.

A Midsummer Night's Dream, I, 1

Speak of me as I am . . . one that loved
  not wisely but too well.

Othello, V, 2

They do not love that do not show
  their love.

The Two Gentlemen of Verona, I, 2

JOHN DONNE
(1572–1631)

Love, all alike, no season knows, nor
clime, Nor hours, days, months, which
are the rags of time.

The Sun Rising

BEN JONSON
(1573?–1637)

Who falls for love of God shall rise a
star.

Letters

JAKOB BÖHME
(1575–1624)

O gracious amiable Blessedness and
great Love, how sweet art thou! How
friendly and courteous art thou! How
pleasant and lovely is thy relish and
taste! How ravishing sweetly dost thou
smell! O noble Light, and bright Glory,
who can apprehend thy exceeding
beauty? How comely adorned is thy
love! How curious and excellent are thy
colours! And all this eternally. Who can
express it?

Or why and what do I write, whose tongue does but stammer like a child which is learning to speak? With what shall I compare it? Or to what shall I liken it? Shall I compare it with the love of this world? No, that is but a mere dark valley to it.

O immense Greatness! I cannot compare thee with any thing, but only with the resurrection from the dead; there will the Love-Fire rise up again in us, and rekindle again our astringent, bitter, and cold, dark and dead powers, and embrace us most courteously and friendly.

O gracious, amiable, blessed Love and clear bright Light, tarry with us, I pray thee, for the evening is at hand.

The Confessions

☉ THOMAS FULLER
(1608–1661)
Malice drinketh up the greater part of its own poison.

☉ LA ROCHEFOUCAULD
(1613–1680)
There is no disguise which can hide love for long where it exists, or simulate it where it does not.

Maxims

If one judges love by the majority of its effects, it is more like hatred than friendship.

Maxims

In their first passion, women love their lovers; in all the others, they love love.

Maxims

☉ MOLIÈRE
(1622–1673)
We are easily duped by those we love.

Tartuffe

☉ JOHN DRYDEN
(1631–1700)
For heaven be thanked, we live in such an age, When no man dies for love, but on the stage.

Epilogue to *Mithridates*

☉ WILLIAM CONGREVE
(1670–1729)
Heaven has no rage like love to hatred turned,
Nor hell a fury like a woman scorned.

The Mourning Bride

Love and murder will out.

The Double Dealer

☉ JOHN GAY
(1685–1732)
She who has never loved has never lived.

Captives

☉ VOLTAIRE
(1694–1778)
Love those who love you.

Letter to d'Alembert, November 28, 1762

☉ BA'AL SHEM TOV
(1700–1760)
From every human being there rises a light that reaches straight to heaven, and when two souls that are destined to be together find each other, the streams

of light flow together and a single
brighter light goes forth from that
united being.

Prayer

❀ SAMUEL JOHNSON
(1709–1784)

I am willing to love all mankind, "except
an American."

James Boswell, *Life of Johnson*

❀ PIERRE-AUGUSTIN
DE BEAUMARCHAIS
(1732–1799)

Where love is concerned, too much is
not even enough.

The Marriage of Figaro

❀ SÉBASTIEN R. N. CHAMFORT
(1740–1794)

Love, such as it is in society, is only the
exchange of two fantasies, and the
contact of two bodies.

Maximes et pensées

❀ WILLIAM BLAKE
(1757–1827)

Love seeketh not itself to please,
Nor for itself hath any care,
But for another gives its ease,
And builds a Heaven in Hell's despair.

Untitled

Love seeketh only Self to please,
To bind another to its delight,
Joys in another's loss of ease,
And builds a Hell in Heaven's despite.

Untitled

❀ J. C. FRIEDRICH VON SCHILLER
(1759–1805)

What is life without the radiance of love?

Wallenstein's Death

❀ GERMAINE DE STAËL
(1766–1817)

Love, supreme power of the heart,
mysterious enthusiasm that
encloses in itself all poetry, all
heroism, all religion!

Delphine

Between God and love, I recognise no
mediator but my conscience.

Delphine

❀ WILLIAM HAZLITT
(1778–1830)

We can scarcely hate anyone that we
know.

On Criticism

Violent antipathies are always suspicious,
and betray a secret affinity.

Table Talk

❀ THOMAS MOORE
(1779–1852)

No, there's nothing half so sweet in life
As love's young dream.

Love's Young Dream

❀ LORD BYRON
(1788–1824)

Now hatred is by far the longest
pleasure;
Men love in haste, but they detest at
leisure.

Don Juan

151

Man's love is of man's life a thing apart,
'Tis woman's whole existence.

Don Juan

⚙ PERCY BYSSHE SHELLEY
(1792–1822)

Familiar acts are beautiful through
love.

Prometheus Unbound

All love is sweet, Given or returned.
Common as light is love, And its familiar
voice wearies not ever.

Prometheus Unbound

⚙ T. H. BAYLY
(1797–1839)

Absence makes the heart grow fonder.

Isle of Beauty

⚙ RALPH WALDO EMERSON
(1803–1882)

All mankind loves a lover.

Love

⚙ HENRY WADSWORTH LONGFELLOW
(1807–1882)

All your strength is in your union;
All your danger in discord
Therefore be at peace henceforward
And as brothers live together.

Untitled

⚙ ALFRED, LORD TENNYSON
(1809–1892)

'Tis better to have loved and lost Than
never to have loved at all.

In Memoriam

O, tell her, brief is life but love is long.

The Princess

⚙ FRANCIS EDWARD SMEDLEY
(1818–1864)

All's fair in love and war.

Frank Fairlegh

⚙ LEO TOLSTOY
(1828–1910)

All, everything that I understand, I understand only because I love.

War and Peace

⚙ WILLIAM MORRIS
(1834–1896)

Fellowship is heaven, and lack of fellowship is hell; fellowship is life, and lack of
fellowship is death; and the deeds that ye
do upon the earth, it is for fellowship's
sake that ye do them.

Untitled

⚙ W. S. GILBERT
(1836–1911)

It's love that makes the world go round!

Iolanthe

⚙ FRIEDRICH NIETZSCHE
(1844–1900)

This is the hardest of all: to close the
open hand out of love, and to keep modest as a giver.

Thus Spake Zarathustra

⊛ ELLEN KEY
(1849–1926)

Love is moral even without legal marriage, but marriage is immoral without love.

The Morality of Woman

⊛ RENÉ BAZIN
(1853–1932)

There is no need to go searching for a remedy for the evils of the time. The remedy already exists—it is the gift of one's self to those who have fallen so low that even hope fails them. Open wide your heart.

Redemption

⊛ ARTHUR RIMBAUD
(1854–1891)

Dress up, dance, laugh. I will never be able to throw Love out of the window.

Les Illuminations

⊛ GEORGE BERNARD SHAW
(1856–1950)

Hate is the coward's revenge for being humiliated.

Major Barbara

⊛ JEROME K. JEROME
(1859–1927)

Love is like the measles; we all have to go through it.

"On Being in Love," in
Idle Thoughts of an Idle Fellow

⊛ HYMNS ANCIENT AND MODERN
(1861)

New every morning is the love
Our wakening and uprising prove;
Through sleep and darkness safely
　　brought,
Restored to life, and power, and
　　thought.

New mercies, each returning day,
Hover around us while we pray;
New perils past, new sins forgiven,
New thoughts of God, new hopes of
　　Heaven.

If on our daily course our mind
Be set to hallow all we find,
New treasures still, of countless price,
God will provide for sacrifice.

The trivial round, the common task,
Will furnish all we need to ask,
Room to deny ourselves, a road
To bring us daily nearer God.

Only, O Lord, in They dear love
Fit us for perfect rest above;
And help us, this and every day,
To live more nearly as we pray.

⊛ RABINDRANATH TAGORE
(1861–1941)

It is said in one of the Upanishads: It is not that thou lovest thy son because thou desirest him, but thou lovest thy son because thou desirest thine own soul. The meaning of this is, that whomsoever we love, in him we find our own soul in the highest sense. The final truth of our existence lies in this. *Paramatma*, the supreme soul, is in me, as well as in my son, and my joy in my son is the realization of this truth. It has become quite a common-place fact, yet it is wonderful to think upon, that the joys and sorrows of our loved ones are joys and sorrows to us—nay, they are more. Why so? Because in them we have grown larger, in them we have touched that great truth which comprehends the whole universe.

Soul Consciousness

Life of my life, I shall ever try to keep my body pure, knowing that thy living touch is upon all my limbs. I shall ever try to keep all untruths out from my thoughts, knowing that thou art that which has kindled the light of reason in my mind.

I shall ever try to drive all evils away from my heart and keep my love in flower, knowing that thou has thy seat in the inmost shrine of my heart.

And it shall be my endeavour to reveal thee in my actions, knowing it is thy power gives me strength to act.

Gitanjali (Song Offering)

✿ SWAMI VIVEKANANDA
(1863–1902)

You are a part of the Infinite. This is your nature. Hence you are your brother's keeper.

Quoted in *The Soul: An Archeology*, Claudia Setzer

✿ RUDYARD KIPLING
(1865–1936)

A fool there was and he made his
prayer (Even as you and I!)
To a rag and a bone and a hank of hair
(We called her the woman who did not
care)
But the fool he called her his lady
fair—
Even as you and I.

The Vampire

✿ WILLIAM BUTLER YEATS
(1865–1939)

A pity beyond all telling
Is hid in the heart of love.

The Pity of Love

✿ WILLA CATHER
(1873–1947)

I tell you there is such a thing as
creative hate.

The Song of the Lark

✿ W. SOMERSET MAUGHAM
(1874–1965)

When you have loved as she has loved, you grow old beautifully.

The Circle

✿ THOMAS MANN
(1875–1955)

It is love, not reason, that is stronger than death.

The Magic Mountain

EVELYN UNDERHILL
(1875–1941)

The anonymous author of the "Mirror" writes, in one of his most daring passages, " 'I am God,' says Love, 'for Love is God, and God is Love. And this soul is God by condition of love: but I am God by Nature Divine, and this [state] is hers by righteousness of love, so that this precious beloved of me, is learned, and led of Me without her [working]. . . . This [soul] is the eagle that flies high, so right high and yet more high than doth any other bird; for she is feathered with fine love.' "

Mysticism

HAZRAT INAYAT KHAN
(1882–1927)

Many religions and philosophies have considered the sex-relationship to be most sacred, since it is thus that the spirit manifests itself. And for the same reason the sex-relationship may become most sinful, if this purpose of the spirit is lost to view. For to disregard this purpose of the spirit is a defiance of the law of the whole mechanism, which inevitably drags the structure to ruins.

The Sufi Message of Hazrat Inayat Khan: The Art of Personality

Love, like a flame, cannot fail to give out light.

The Sufi Message of Hazrat Inayat Khan: The Art of Personality

So far as human understanding can probe, it can discover nothing of greater purpose and value to the world than passion. Under that covering is hidden the hand of the creator.

The Sufi Message of Hazrat Inayat Khan: The Art of Personality

Religious man, wherever found and whatever teacher he followed, has . . . been prone to look at contact with woman with contempt, with the thought of there being something unholy in the passionate love of woman. Indeed it is a question whether the libertine has actually debased woman as much as the religious man, who believes that to hold himself aloof from any woman with contempt and to strangle his love within him, will be for his own spiritual benefit. And is it possible to debase woman and the position of woman in the scheme of life without debasing man and the whole of life?

The Sufi Message of Hazrat Inayat Khan: The Art of Personality

JAMES JOYCE
(1882–1941)

Her image had passed into his soul for ever and no word had broken the holy silence of his ecstasy.

Portrait of the Artist As a Young Man

COCO CHANEL
(1883–1971)

Great loves too must be endured.

Quoted in *Coco Chanel, Her Life, Her Secrets*, Marcel Haedrich

D. H. LAWRENCE
(1885–1930)

Some men want the path of love to run pleasantly between allotment-gardens stocked with cabbages and potatoes and an occasional sweet-William; some men want rose-avenues and trickling streams, and so scratch themselves and get gnat-bitten; some want to scale unheard-of heights, roped to some extraordinary female of their fancy. *Chacun à son gout.*

Phoenix II

GABRIELA MISTRAL
(1889–1957)

I dream of a vase of humble and simple
    clay,
to keep your ashes near my watchful
    eyes;
and for you my cheek will be the wall
    of the vase
and my soul and your soul will be
    satisfied.

I will not sift them into a vase of
    burning gold,
not into a pagan urn that mimics carnal
    lines;
I want only a vase of simple clay to hold
you humbly like a fold in this skirt of
    mine.

One of these afternoons I'll gather clay
by the river, and I'll shape it with
    trembling hand.
Women, bearing sheaves, will pass my
    way,
not guessing I fashion a bed for a
    husband.

The fistful of dust, I hold in my hands,
will noiseless pour, like a thread of
    tears.

I will seal this vase with an infinite kiss,
and I'll cover you only with my endless
    gaze!

"The Vase," in *Love Poems: From
Spain and Spanish America*

DOROTHY PARKER
(1893–1967)

Oh, life is a glorious cycle of song, A medley of extemporanea; And love is a thing that can never go wrong, And I am Marie of Roumania.

Comment

By the time you swear you're his
    shivering and sighing,
And he vows his passion is Infinite,
    undying—
Lady make a note of this: One of you is
    lying.

Unfortunate Coincidence

MEHER BABA
(1894–1969)

The Beloved is devoted to its lovers for how else can it be Belovedness? Each and every Lover is the beloved; each and every Beloved is the Lover. The Absolute Unity, which is the Absolute Beauty and Absolute Love, loves its Beloved so intensely it leaves not a trace of themselves. For in reality there is only the Beloved, only loving.

God Speaks—The Theme of Creation and Its Purpose

J. KRISHNAMURTI
(1895–1986)

Love is vulnerable, pliable, receptive; it is the highest form of sensitivity, and identification makes for insensitivity.

Identification and love do not go together, for the one destroys the other.

Commentaries on Living—from the Notebooks of J. Krishnamurti

Love admits no division. Either you love, or do not love. . .

Commentaries on Living—from the Notebooks of J. Krishnamurti

⊛ WEI WU WEI (TERENCE GRAY)
(1895–1986)

Unless you can hate you cannot
    possibly love.
And vice-versa.

Open Secret

⊛ JOSEPH CAMPBELL
(1904–1987)

In so far as love expresses itself, it is not expressing itself in terms of socially approved manners of life. That's why it is all so secret. Love has nothing to do with social order. It is a higher spiritual experience than that of socially organized marriage.

The Masks of God

⊛ PABLO NERUDA
(1904–1973)

Your breast is enough for my heart,
and my wings for your freedom.
What was sleeping above your soul will
    rise
out of your mouth to heaven.

In you is the illusion of each day.
You arrive like the dew to the cupped
    flowers.

You undermine the horizon with your
    absence.
Eternally in flight like the wave.

Twenty Love Poems and a Song of Despair

⊛ ALBERT CAMUS
(1913–1960)

When one has once had the good luck to love intensely, life is spent in trying to recapture that ardor and that illumination.

Return to Tipasa

⊛ OSHO
(1931–1990)

When I say, "Love yourself," this is for those who have never gone inside, because they can always. . . . They are bound to understand only a language of duality. Love yourself—that means you are dividing yourself into two, the lover and the loved. You may not have thought about it, but if you go inside you will not love yourself, you will be love.

Discourses

If I love someone, immediately my mind will start working on how to marry them, because marriage fixes things. Love is a flux, love cannot be predicted. No one knows where it will lead, or whether it will lead anywhere.

Discourses

The word hatred means the desire to destroy the other.

Discourses

❈ THE BEATLES
(CONTEMPORARY)

All you need is love.

Popular song

❈ LAWRENCE DURRELL
(CONTEMPORARY)

It is not love that is blind, but jealousy.

Justine

❈ GABRIEL GARCÍA MARQUEZ
(CONTEMPORARY)

The only regret I will have in dying is if it is not for love.

Love in the Time of Cholera

❈ JAVAD NURBAKHSH
(CONTEMPORARY)

I thought of You so often that I completely became You. Little by little You drew near, and slowly but slowly I passed away.

In the Tavern of Ruin

❈ ERICH SEGAL
(CONTEMPORARY)

Love means never having to say you're sorry.

Love Story

❈ 'UMAR AL-SUHRAWARDI
(CONTEMPORARY)

Music does not produce in the Heart anything which is not already there. Music arouses sensual desire in one whose inner self is attached to something other than God; but one who is inwardly attached to the love of God is moved, by hearing music, to do His will.

Awarif al-a'arif

❈ JANE WYMAN
(CONTEMPORARY)

The opportunity to practice brotherhood presents itself every time you meet a human being.

Spoken

Man and Womankind

☸ PROTAGORAS
(C. 481–411 BCE)

Man is the measure of all things

Concerning the Gods

☸ THE DHAMMAPADA
(3RD CENTURY BCE)

Let man be free from pleasure and let man be free from pain; for not to have pleasure is sorrow and to have pain is also sorrow. From pleasure arises sorrow and from pleasure arises fear. If a man is free from pleasure, he is free from fear and sorrow.

There never was, there never will be, nor is there now, a man whom men always blame, or a man whom they always praise.

☸ MARCUS TULLIUS CICERO
(106–43 BCE)

No man was ever great without divine inspiration.

De Natura Deorum

☸ VIRGIL
(70–19 BCE)

We are not all capable of everything.

Eclogues

☸ PLOTINUS
(205–270)

Man as he now is has ceased to be the All. When he ceases to be a separate individual, he raises himself again and penetrates the whole world.

Enneads

☸ HAKIM ABU' L-MAJD MAJDUD SANAI OF GHAZNA (HAKIM SANAI)
(12TH CENTURY)

It is your [God's] part to hand out
forgiveness and mercy;
mine to falter and fall.
Fool that I am, take me,
stumbling drunk that I am,
take my hand.

The Walled Garden of Truth

☸ MAHMUD SHABISTARI
(1250–1320)

Non-being is a mirror, the world an image and man is the eye of the image in which the person is hidden. You are the eye of the image and the light of the eye. Who has ever seen the eye through which all things are seen? The world has become a man and man a world. There is no clearer explanation than this.

When you look well into the root of the matter He is at once seen, both seeing eye and thing seen.

The Garden of Mystery

❀ MARIE ANNE DU DEFFAND
(1697–1780)

I do not know why Diogenes [a Greek philosopher] went looking for a man: nothing could happen to him worse than finding one.

Correspondance inédite

❀ CHIEF SEATTLE
(1786–1866)

This we know. The Earth does not belong to man; man belongs to the Earth. This we know. All things are connected like blood which unites one family. All things are connected.

Whatever befalls the Earth befalls the sons of the Earth. Man did not weave the web of life; he is merely a strand in it. Whatever he does to the web, he does to himself.

His address, 1853

❀ FYODOR DOSTOYEVSKY
(1821–1881)

Man is a creature that can get used to anything, and I think that is the best definition of him.

The House of the Dead

It sometimes happened that you might be familiar with a man for several years thinking he was a wild animal, and you would regard him with contempt. And then suddenly a moment would arrive when some uncontrollable impulse would lay his soul bare, and you would behold in it such riches, such sensitivity and warmth, such a vivid awareness of its own suffering and the suffering of others, that the scales would fall from your eyes and at first you would hardly be able to believe what you had seen and heard. The reverse also happens.

The House of the Dead

❀ THE SHIVAPURI BABA
(1826–1963)

Apart from the physiological and psychological distinctions there is no other fundamental distinction between man and woman. A woman like a man can also realize the Truth, if she follows the path of Right Life and Meditation. A woman has, however, some special duties to perform.

Quoted by J. G. Bennett in *Long Pilgrimage*

❀ ELLEN KEY
(1849–1926)

Woman . . . as the bearer and guardian of the new lives, has everywhere greater respect for life than man, who for centuries, as hunter and warrior, learned that the taking of lives may be not only allowed, but honourable.

The Renaissance of Motherhood

❀ ROBERT LOUIS STEVENSON
(1850–1894)

Every man is his own doctor of divinity, in the last resort.

An Inland Voyage, Noyon

OSCAR WILDE
(1854–1900)

I think that God in creating man somewhat overestimated his ability.

The Critic As Artist

HAVELOCK ELLIS
(1859–1939)

Civilized men arrive in the Pacific, armed with alcohol, syphilis, trousers, and the Bible.

The Dance of Life

MARGOT ASQUITH
(1864–1945)

The spirit of man is an inward flame, a lamp the world blows upon but never puts out.

Autobiography

MARIA MONTESSORI
(1870–1952)

Humanity is still far from that stage of maturity needed for the realisation of its aspirations, for the construction, that is, of a harmonious and peaceful society and the elimination of wars. Men are not yet ready to shape their own destinies, to control and direct world events, of which—instead—they become the victims.

The Absorbent Mind

THE MOTHER
(1878–1990)

I am sure the movement has begun. . . . How long it will take to arrive at a concrete, visible and organized reality I don't know. Something has begun. It seems it's going to be the onrush of the new species, the new creation, or at any rate a new creation. A reorganization of the earth and a new creation . . . but even today, the, overwhelming majority of people and intellectuals are perfectly content with taking care of themselves and their little rounds of progress. They don't even want anything else! Which means that the advent of the next being may well go unnoticed, or be misunderstood. It's hard to tell since there is no precedent to compare it with; but more than likely, if one of the great apes ever ran into the first man, it must simply have felt that that being was a little . . . strange. That's all. Men are used to thinking that anything higher than they has to be . . . divine beings— that is, without a body—who appear in a burst of light. In other words, all the gods as they are conceived—but it isn't like that at all. It is almost as if a new mind is being formed And the body is learning its lesson—all bodies, all bodies.

Satprem—The Mind of the Cell

PIERRE TEILHARD DE CHARDIN
(1881–1955)

Everywhere on Earth, at this moment, in the new spiritual atmosphere created by the idea of evolution, there float, in a state of extreme mutual sensitivity, love of God and faith in a new world: the two essential components of the ultra human. These two components are everywhere in the air. . . . Sooner or later there will be a chain reaction.

The Phenomenon of Man

Shatter, my God, through the daring of your revelation the childishly timid outlook that can conceive of nothing greater or more vital in the world than the pitiable perfection of our human organism.

The Mass on the World

❋ NIKOS KAZANTZAKIS
(1885–1957)

Every one follows his own bent. Man is like a tree. You've never quarreled with a fig tree because it doesn't bear cherries, have you?

Zorba the Greek

Every man has his folly, but the greatest folly of all . . . is not to have one.

Zorba the Greek

❋ IMAJAT KHAN
(1889–1988)

The difference between human language and divine words is this—that a human word is a pebble; it exists, but there is nothing further; the divine word is a living word, just like a grain of corn. . . .

In the grain there is an essence which is always multiplying and which will show perfection in itself.

The Flower Garden of Imajat Khan

❋ MIKHAIL NAIMY
(1889–1988)

I say to you, there is not God *and* man. But there is God-Man or Man-God. There is the One. However multiplied, however divided, it is forever One.

Is not the sea—though vast and deep—
   a single drop?
Is not the Earth—though flung so far—
   a single sphere?
Are not the spheres—though
   numberless—a single universe?
Likewise is mankind but a single
   Man—likewise is Man, with all his
   worlds, a singleness complete.

The Book of Mirdad—A Lighthouse and a Haven

❋ J. KRISHNAMURTI
(1895–1986)

Inequality is a fact, and no revolution can do away with it.

Commentaries on Living—from the Notebooks of J. Krishnamurti

❋ ALAN WATTS
(1915–1973)

The Highest to which man can attain is wonder; and if the prime phenomenon makes him wonder, let him be content; nothing higher can it give him, and nothing further should he seek for behind it; there is the limit.

The Book

❋ OSHO
(1931–1990)

Remove God and put man in his place, and you will have a totally different world. The suffering is absolutely un-wanted. The anguish is our stupidity. Man can live a tremendously rich, bliss-ful, ecstatic life. But the first thing is, he has to accept his responsibility.

Discourses

Man is upset when he cannot show that he carries a big load on his back, so another interesting feature emerges: he generally boasts a bigger load than he actually has.

Discourses

⊛ CARLOS CASTANEDA
(CONTEMPORARY)

I care so much for my fellow man . . . that I don't do anything for him. I wouldn't know what to do. And I would always have the nagging sense that I was imposing my will on him with my gifts.

The Fire Within

⊛ DA FREE JOHN (ADIDA)
(CONTEMPORARY)

Man is only a brief design in the numberless evolutionary stages of the World. And the individual human being is only a moment, a specimen, a partial realization of Man. The individual is not made for his own sake, but to be sacrificed toward Man—so that Man may fulfill his evolutionary destiny. And Man is not made for his own sake, but to be sacrificed toward the ultimate evolutionary process of the World. And the World is not made for its own sake, but to be sacrificed to the unqualified and Eternal Divine.

The Enlightenment of the Whole Body

⊛ ADRIEN-EMMANUEL ROQUETTE
(CONTEMPORARY)

Man is the medium between spirit and matter; he is between the visible and the invisible world. He sums them up in his person, as in a universal center.

⊛ MORRIS WEST
(CONTEMPORARY)

Man is the only significant link between the physical order and the spiritual one. Without man the universe is a howling wasteland contemplated by an unseen Deity.

The Shoes of the Fisherman

Meditation

THE UPANISHADS
(C. 900–600 BCE)

Where the channels are brought
   together
Like the spokes in the hub of a wheel—
Therein he moves about,
Becoming manifold.
Om!—Thus meditate upon the Soul.
Success to you in crossing to the
      farther shore beyond darkness!

He who is all-knowing, all wise,
Whose is this greatness on the earth—
He is in the divine Brahma city
And in the heaven established! The Soul!
Consisting of mind, leader of the life-
      breaths and of the body,
He is established on food, controlling
      the heart.
By this knowledge the wise perceive
The blissful Immortal that gleams forth.

The Second Khanda

BUDDHA
(563–483 BCE)

Great becomes the fruit, great the advantage of earnest contemplation, when
it is set round with upright conduct.

Great becomes the fruit, great the advantage of intellect when it is set round
with earnest contemplation.

The Dialogues

THE BHAGAVAD GITA
(500? BCE)

He who is ever content and meditative,
self-subjugated and possessed with firm
conviction, with mind and heart dedi-
cated to Me, he who is thus consecrated
to Me is dear to Me.

Book of Daily Thoughts and Prayers

SARAHA
(1ST OR 2ND CENTURY)

This world of appearance has from its
      radiant beginning
Never come to be; unpatterned it has
      discarded patterning.
As such it is continuous and unique
      meditation;
It is non meditation, stainless
      contemplation, and nonmind.

The Royal Song of Saraha

MILAREPA
(1040–1123)

If there is joy in meditation upon the
      sun and moon,
the planets and fixed stars are the magic
      creation of the sun and moon;
make thyself like unto the sun and
      moon themselves.

If there is joy in meditation upon the
mountain,
the fruit-trees are the magic creation of
the mountain;
make thy self like the mountain itself.
. . . .
If there is joy in meditation upon thine
own mind,
distinctive thought is the magic
creation of the mind;
make thyself like unto the mind itself.

The Message of Milarepa

✹ ISAAC OF ACCO
(13TH–14TH CENTURY)

A sage once came to one of the medi-
tators and asked that he be accepted
into their society. The other replied,
"My son, blessed are you to God. Your
intentions are good. But tell me, have
you attained stoicism?" The sage
said, "Master, explain your words." The
meditator said, "If one man is praising
you and another is insulting you, are the
two equal in your eyes or not?" He
replied, "No, my master, I have pleasure
from those who praise me, and pain
from those who degrade me. But I do
not take revenge or bear a grudge." The
other said, "Go in peace my son. You
have not attained stoicism. You have not
reached a level where your soul does not
feel the praise of one who honours you,
nor the degradation of one who insults
you. You are not prepared for your
thoughts to bound on high, that you
should come and meditate. Go and
increase the humbleness of your heart,
and learn to treat everything equally
until you have become stoic. Only then
will you be able to meditate."

The Light of the Eyes

✹ ABRAHAM BEN SAMUEL ABULAFIA
(1240–AFTER 1292)

Those who are called prophets in this
sense [as practitioners of Jewish mysti-
cism] meditate in their hearts on the
changing substance of their thoughts, and
their deliberations are purely subjective.
The light of God illumines some of their
thoughts, sometimes with a tiny light.
They themselves recognise that this em-
anates from outside themselves, but they
receive no verbalised message that they
should recognise as speech—it is only
light. . . . From this stage they rise from
light to light, through meditation on the
ramification of their thoughts, which are
rendered sweet by their fusion with the
divine realm. Through the enhancement
of their merit they approach the highest
distinction to a point where the speech
they hear within themselves is linked
with the fountain from which all speech
derives. They ascend from speech to
speech until their inner speech is potent
in itself and becomes ready to receive
the divine speech, whether it be the
form of the speech, or the contents of
the speech itself. These are the true
prophets, in justice and in righteousness.

Sefer ha-Ot

✹ MICHEL DE MONTAIGNE
(1533–1592)

Meditation is a rich and powerful
method of study for anyone who knows
how to examine his mind, and to employ
it vigorously. I would rather shape my
soul than furnish it. There is no exercise
that is either feebler or more strenuous,
according to the nature of the mind
concerned, than that of conversing with

one's own thoughts. The greatest men make it their vocation, "those for whom to live is to think" [a quotation from Cicero]. Moreover, nature has favoured it with this privilege, that there is nothing we can do for so long at a time, nor any action to which we can apply ourselves more frequently and easily. It is the occupation of the gods, says Aristotle, the source from which comes their beatitude and ours.

Essays

⊛ THE SHIVAPURI BABA
(1826–1963)

Meditation is profound thinking. It makes our health better, gives extremely helpful ideas, and is quite essential for our spiritual progress. Meditation is a mad man's business.

Quoted by J. G. Bennett in *Long Pilgrimage*

Only if our life is exactly regulated, will we have the time and energy required for meditation. Right meditation cannot be based upon a disordered life.

Quoted by J. G. Bennett in *Long Pilgrimage*

⊛ YOGASWAMI
(1872–1964)

When you have entirely surrendered, everything you do will be meditation.

Positive Thoughts for Daily Meditation

Meditate in the morning and evening and at night before you go to bed. Sit quietly for about two minutes. You will find everything in your life falling into place and your prayers answered.

Positive Thoughts for Daily Meditation

⊛ PIERRE TEILHARD DE CHARDIN
(1881–1955)

Lord, lock me up in the deepest depths of your heart; and then, holding me there, burn me, purify me, set me on fire, sublimate me, till I become utterly what you would have me be, through the utter annihilation of my ego.

The Mass on the World

⊛ J. KRISHNAMURTI
(1895–1986)

Meditation is not the means to an end. It is both the means and the end.

The Second Penguin Krishnamurti Reader

Any form of conscious meditation is not the real thing: it can never be. Deliberate attempt to meditate is not meditation. It must happen; it cannot be invited. Meditation is not the play of the mind nor of desire and pleasure. All attempt to meditate is the very denial of it. Only be aware of what you are thinking and doing and nothing else. The seeing, the hearing, is the doing, without reward and punishment.

The Second Penguin Krishnamurti Reader

Meditation is danger for it destroys everything, nothing whatsoever is left, not even a whisper of desire, and in this vast, unfathomable emptiness there is creation and love.

The Second Penguin Krishnamurti Reader

The flower is the form, the scent, the color and the beauty that is the whole of it. Tear it to pieces actually or verbally, then there is not the flower, only the remembrance of what it was, which is never the flower. Meditation is the whole flower in its beauty, withering and living.

The Second Penguin Krishnamurti Reader

Meditation is the freeing of energy in abundance; and control, discipline and suppression spoil the purity of that energy.

The Second Penguin Krishnamurti Reader

❀ WEI WU WEI (TERENCE GRAY)
(1895–1986)

The practice of meditation is represented by the three famous monkeys, who cover their eyes, ears and mouths so as to avoid the . . . world. The practice of non-meditation is ceasing to be the see-er, hearer or speaker while eyes, ears and mouths are fulfilling their function in daily life.

Open Secret

❀ OSHO
(1931–1990)

Meditation is pure space, undisturbed by knowledge.

Discourses

Meditation is nothing but coming back home, just to have a little rest inside. It is not the chanting of a mantra, it is not even a prayer, it is just coming back home and having a little rest.

Discourses

❀ SOGYAL RINPOCHE
(CONTEMPORARY)

Fortunately we live in a time when all over the world many people are becoming familiar with meditation. It is being increasingly accepted as a practice that cuts through and soars above cultural and religious barriers, and enables those who pursue it to establish a direct contact with the truth of their being. It is a practice that at once transcends the dogma of religions and is the essence of religions.

The Tibetan Book of Living and Dying

❀ ELIEZER SHORE
(CONTEMPORARY)

The contemplative is to the community what the soul is to the body.

Parabola

Mind

❁ THE UPANISHADS
(C. 900–600 BCE)

Moved by whom does thinking attain
    its object?
Who directs the function of vital
    breathing?
Moved by whom do people engage in
    speaking?
Say what force directs both the sight
    and hearing,
He, the hearing's Hearer, the thinking's
    Thinker,
speaking's Speaker, even the breathing's
    Breather.
Eye of eye. The wise by renouncing
    find Him;
parting from this World they become
    immortal.

Kena Upanishad

❁ THE BHAGAVAD GITA
(500? BCE)

The mind is indeed restless, Arjuna: it is
indeed hard to train. But by constant
practice and by freedom from passions
the mind in truth can be trained.

When the mind is not in harmony, this
divine communion is hard to attain; but
the man whose mind is in harmony
attains it, if he knows and if he strives.

❁ THE DHAMMAPADA
(3RD CENTURY BCE)

What we are today comes from our
thoughts of yesterday, and our present
thoughts build our life of tomorrow: our
life is the creation of our mind.

If a man speaks or acts with an impure
mind, suffering follows him as the wheel
of the cart follows the beast that draws
the cart.

If a man speaks or acts with a pure mind,
joy follows him as his own shadow.

The Path to Perfection

Make haste and do what is good; keep
your mind away from evil. If a man is
slow in doing good, his mind finds
pleasure in evil.

The Path of Perfection

❁ WEI LANG
(80? BCE)

The capacity of the mind is as great as
that of space. It is infinite, neither round
nor square, neither great nor small,
neither green nor yellow, neither red
nor white, neither above nor below,
neither long nor short, neither angry
nor happy, neither right nor wrong,

neither good nor evil, neither first nor last. . . . Intrinsically our transcendental nature is void and not a single Dharma [Truth] can be attained. It is the same with the Essence of Mind, which is a state of "Absolute Void" (i.e. the voidness of non-void).

Learned Audience, when you hear me talk about the Void, do not at once fall into the idea of vacuity, (Because this involves the heresy of the doctrine of annihilation.) It is of the utmost importance that we should not fall into this idea, because when a man sits quietly and keeps his mind blank he will abide in a state of "Voidness of Indifference."

Learned Audience, the illimitable Void of the universe is capable of holding myriads of things of various shape and form, such as the sun, the moon, stars, mountains, rivers, worlds, springs, rivulets, bushes, woods, good men, bad men, Dharmas [teachings leading to the truth] pertaining to goodness or badness . . . hells, great oceans. . . . Space takes in all these, and so does the voidness of our nature. We say that the Essence of Mind is great because it embraces all things, since all things are within our nature. When we see the goodness or the badness of other people we are not attracted by it, nor repelled by it, nor attached to it; so that our attitude of mind is as void as space. In this way we say our mind is great. . . .

It is of itself that the divine thought thinks (since it is the most excellent of things), and its thinking is a thinking on thinking.

Metaphysics, book 1, chapter 9

Learned Audience, you should know that the mind is very great in capacity, since it pervades the whole Dharmadhatu (the sphere of the Law, i.e. the Universe). When we use it, we can know something of everything, and when we use it to its full capacity we shall know all. All in one and one in all.

The Sutra

Our Essence of Mind is intrinsically pure; all things are only its manifestations, and good deeds and evil deeds are only the result of good thoughts and evil thoughts respectively. This, within the Essence of Mind all things (are intrinsically pure), like the azure of the sky and the radiance of the sun and the moon, which, when obscured by passing clouds, may appear as if their brightness had been dimmed; but as soon as the clouds are blown away, brightness reappears and all objects are fully illuminated. Learned Audience, our evil habits may be likened unto the clouds; while sagacity and wisdom (Prajna), are the sun and the moon respectively. When Mind is clouded by wanton thoughts which prevent our Sagacity and Wisdom from sending forth their light.

The Sutra

⊛ **VIRGIL**
(70–19 BCE)
Practice and thought might gradually forge many an art.

Georges I

Happy the man who could search out the causes of things.

Georges I

THE GOSPEL OF MARY
(C. 100)

"I," she said, "I saw the Lord in a vision and I said to him, 'Lord, I saw you to-day in a vision.' He answered and said to me, 'Blessed are you, since you did not waver at the sight of me. For where the mind is, there is your countenance.' I said to him, 'Lord, the mind which sees the vision, does it see it through the soul or through the spirit?' The Savior answered and said, 'It sees neither through the soul nor through the spirit, but the mind, which is between the two, which sees the vision.'"

Attributed to Mary Magdalene, from *Gnosticism: A Sourcebook of Heretical Writings*, Robert Grant

ST. AUGUSTINE
(354–430)

For I remember the kind of man I was, O Lord, and it is a sweet task to confess how you tamed me by pricking my heart with your goad; how you bridged every valley, levelled every mountain and hill of my thoughts; how you cut straight through their windings, paved their rough paths.

Confessions

LANKAVATARA SUTRA
(4TH CENTURY CE)

It is like an image reflected in a mirror, it is seen but it is not real; the one Mind is seen as a duality by the ignorant when it is reflected in the mirror constructed by our memory . . . the existence of the entire universe is due to memory that has been accumulated since the beginningless past but wrongly interpreted.

HUI HAI
(750–810)

Q: Do you make efforts in the practice of the Way, Master?
Master: Yes, I do.
Q: How?
Master: When hungry, I eat; when tired, I sleep.
Q: And does everybody make the same efforts as you do, Master?
Master: When they are eating, they think of a hundred kinds of necessities, and when they are going to sleep they ponder over affairs of a thousand different kinds. That is how they differ from me.

The Zen Teachings of Hui Hai

SHANKARA
(788–820)

The Self never undergoes change; the intellect never possesses consciousness. But when one sees all this world, he is deluded into thinking "I am the seer, I am the knower." Mistaking one's Self for the individual entity, like the rope mistaken for the snake, one is overcome with fear. If one knows oneself not as the individual but as the supreme Self, one becomes free from fear.

Meditations

HUANG-PO
(800–850)

Q: From all you have just said, Mind is the Buddha; but it is not clear as to what sort of mind is meant by this "Mind which is the Buddha."
A: How many minds have you got?
Q: But is the Buddha the ordinary mind or the Enlightened mind?

A: Where on earth do you keep your "ordinary mind" and your "Enlightened mind?"

Q: In the teaching of the Three Vehicles it is stated that there are both. Why does Your Reverence deny it?

A: In the teaching of the Three Vehicles it is clearly explained that the ordinary and Enlightened minds are illusions. You don't understand. All this clinging to the idea of things existing is to mistake vacuity for the truth. How can such conceptions not be illusory? Being illusory, they hide Mind from you. If you would only rid yourselves of the concepts of ordinary and Enlightened, you would find that there is no other Buddha than the Buddha in your own Mind. When Bodhidharma came from the West, he just pointed out that the substance of which all men are composed is the Buddha. You people go on misunderstanding; you hold to concepts such as "ordinary" and "Enlightened," directing your thoughts outwards where they gallop about like horses! All this amounts to beclouding your own minds! So I tell you Mind is the Buddha. As soon as thought or sensation arises, you fall into dualism. Beginningless time and the present moment are the same. There is no this and no that. To understand this truth is called complete and unexcelled Enlightenment.

The Zen Teaching of Huang-po

If you look upon the Buddha as presenting a pure, bright or enlightened appearance, or upon sentient beings as presenting a foul, dark or mortal-seeming appearance, these conceptions resulting from attachment to form will keep you from supreme knowledge, even after the passing of as many eons as there are sands in the Ganges. There is only the One Mind and not a particle of anything else on which to lay hold, for this Mind is the Buddha.

The Zen Teaching of Huang-po

Were you now to practise keeping your minds motionless at all times, whether walking, standing, sitting or lying; concentrating entirely upon the goal of no thought-creation, no duality, no reliance on others and no attachments; just allowing all things to take their course the whole day long, as though you were too ill to bother; unknown to the world; innocent of any urge to be known or unknown to others; with your minds like blocks of stone that mend no holes—then all the Dharmas [Laws of Existence or Universal Laws] would penetrate your understanding through and through. In a little while you would find yourselves firmly unattached. Thus, for the first time in your lives, you would discover your reactions to phenomena decreasing and, ultimately, you would pass beyond the Triple World; and people would say that a Buddha had appeared in the world.

The Zen Teaching of Huang-po

❁ MILAREPA
(1040–1123)

I have already fully realised that all beings and all phenomena are of one's own mind. The mind itself is a transparency of Voidness. What, therefore, is the use of

172

all this, and how foolish I am to try to dispel these manifestations physically.

The Hundred Thousand Songs of Milarepa

✿ HAKIM ABU' L-MAJD MAJDUD SANAI OF GHAZNA (HAKIM SANAI)
(12TH CENTURY)

The self is a servant in his [God's]
  cavalcade;
reason a new boy in his school.
What is reason in this guesthouse,
but a crooked scrawling
of God's handwriting?

The Walled Garden of Truth

✿ ST. THOMAS AQUINAS
(1224/5–1274)

Reason in man is rather like God in the
  world.

Opuscule II, De Regno

✿ MIRA BAI
(1450–1547)

What is beyond the mind,
has no boundary,
In it our senses end.

Devotional Poems

✿ MICHEL DE MONTAIGNE
(1533–1592)

I imagine virtue to be both something else and something nobler than the propensity towards goodness that is born in us. The well-disposed and naturally well-controlled mind follows the same course as the virtuous, and presents the same appearance in its actions. But virtue sounds like some greater and more active thing than merely to let oneself be led by a happy disposition quietly and peaceably along the path of reason. One who out of natural mildness and good-nature overlooks injuries received performs a very fine and praiseworthy action; but another who, though provoked and stung to anger by an insult, takes up the weapons of reason against his furious desire for revenge, and after hard battle finally masters it, is undoubtedly doing a great deal more. The first man is behaving well, the second virtuously; the first action might be called goodness, the second virtue. For the word virtue, I think, presupposes difficulty and struggle, and something that cannot be practiced without an adversary. This is perhaps why we call God good, mighty, liberal, and just, but do not call Him virtuous; His workings are all natural and effortless.

Essays

✿ WILLIAM SHAKESPEARE
(1564–1616)

There is nothing either good or bad
  but thinking makes it so.

Hamlet, II, 2, 253

✿ JOHN DONNE
(1572–1631)

Reason is our soul's left hand, Faith her
  right,
By these we reach divinity.

To the Countess of Bedford

173

❂ ELIZABETH CLINTON
(1574–1630?)

Whatsoever things are true, whatsoever things are honest . . . whatsoever things are just, whatsoever things are pure, whatsoever things are of good report . . . think on these things; these things do, and the God of peace shall be with you.

Letters

❂ SARMAD
(17TH CENTURY)

O my friend! Remain in solitude with a
    passion to meet the Lord;
Rid thyself of all grief and be happy.
Be not like the whirlwind; be not
    baffled or perplexed.
Centre thy mind on one point, and be
    free from all thought.

Rubaiyats of Sarmad 226

❂ MR. TUT-TUT
(17TH? CENTURY)

The proud spirit, the chivalric spirit and the beautiful spirit suffuse fragrance even when their bones are dead; words of cool detachment, witty words and words of charm carry weight though their volume be small.

One Hundred Proverbs

❂ WALT WHITMAN
(1819–1892)

Do I contradict myself? Very well then I contradict myself, (I am large, I contain multitudes.)

"Song of Myself," in *Leaves of Grass*

❂ THE SHIVAPURI BABA
(1826–1963)

One should have no liking, one should have no disliking. Reason must prevail.

Lectures

Suppose you like me: you will give me everything. Suppose you hate me: you will give me nothing. This is under the influence of like and disliking. Under the influence of reason, what will you do? You will see if I deserve or not. Suppose I am your enemy; still, if I deserve, you will give me. Suppose I am your friend, if I do not deserve, you will not give me.

This is the direction of reason. This reason must always prevail. Liking and disliking must perish.

Quoted by J. G. Bennett in *Long Pilgrimage*

In normal times we generally live our lives quite happily, giving as much attention as is necessary to our daily run of duties. We have our fixed principles and fixed ideas, and with them we keep up our balance of mind. We are not disturbed by anything whatsoever, and so we go on smoothly with our normal course, with the result that peace and happiness is ever flowing in our mind. As long as we are following our ordinary course of living, we never expect any change in our circumstances that might disturb our mental equipoise.

But no. It is simply our blindness to World-nature. Anything may happen to us at any time quite unexpectedly. Abnormal circumstances come to us at times and we are thrown out from our seats. We become helpless and have to succumb to such overwhelming force from the external. The result is that our peace of mind is disturbed and so we lose our previous position. All our structures in the form of routines and principles tumble down and we are thrown into a state which is new and foreign to us. What happens? We generally get stupefied and cannot easily recover our mental balance. We become like a fish out of water. . . . What do we do? We try to regain our previous position, thinking that this is the only course left open to us in order to preserve that peace of mind we were enjoying previously. Here, we are mistaken. We overlook the fact that our effort to regain our previous status is quite futile because in this ever-changing world what has happened will never return. Instead, if we are wise we should try to adjust ourselves to the new status in which we find ourselves. New schemes and projects we must introduce which are adaptable to the present conditions and build anew. To look back and bemoan the loss of our previous status is death to us.

Quoted by J. G. Bennett in *Long Pilgrimage*

⊛ SIGMUND FREUD
(1856–1939)

The voice of the intellect is a soft one, but it does not rest until it has gained a hearing. Ultimately, after endless repeated rebuffs, it succeeds. This is one of the few points in which one may be optimistic about the future of mankind, but in itself it signifies not a little.

Future of an Illusion

⊛ BERNARD BERENSON
(1865–1959)

Consistency requires you to be as ignorant today as you were a year ago.

Notebook, 1892

⊛ YOGASWAMI
(1872–1964)

One method is to stop all thought. Another method is to remain simply as a witness, allowing thoughts to come and go. As one becomes more and more mature in this practice, thoughts will begin to come from the inner silence. Be very attentive to these thoughts.

Positive Thoughts for Daily Meditation

If you try to stop the mind, it will only become more active. It is not necessary to stop it. You must ask it where it is going.

Positive Thoughts for Daily Meditation

If the chimney is full of smoke, how can the light be seen? If the mind is full of dirt, how can the soul shine?

Positive Thoughts for Daily Meditation

⊛ G. K. CHESTERTON
(1874–1936)

It is not natural to see man as a natural product. It is not common sense to call man a common object of the country or the sea-shore. It is not seeing straight to see him as an animal. It is not sane. . . . If we imagine that an inhuman or impersonal intelligence could have felt from the first the general nature of the non-human world sufficiently to see that things would evolve in whatever way they did evolve, there would have been nothing whatever in all that natural world to prepare such a mind for such an unnatural novelty. . . . Suppose that one bird out of a thousand birds began to do one of the thousand things that man had already done even in the morning of the world; and we can be quite certain that the onlooker would not regard such a bird as a mere evolutionary variety of the other birds; he would regard it as a very fearful wild-fowl indeed. . . . That bird would tell the augurs, not of something that would happen, but of something that had happened. That something would be the appearance of a mind with a new dimension of depth; a mind like that of man. If there be no God, no other mind could conceivably have foreseen it.

The Everlasting Man

⊛ RAMANA MAHARSHI
(1879–1950)

Have you not heard of the saying of Vivekananda, that if one but thinks a noble, selfless thought even in a cave, it sets up vibrations throughout the world and does what has to be done—what can be done?

Discourse

⊛ D. H. LAWRENCE
(1885–1930)

Emotions by themselves become just a nuisance. The mind by itself becomes just a sterile thing, making everything sterile. So what's to be done?

You've got to marry the pair of them. Apart, they are no good. The emotions that have not the approval and inspiration of the mind are just hysterics. The mind without the approval and inspiration of the emotions is just a dry stick, a dead tree, no good for anything unless to make a rod to beat and bully somebody with.

Phoenix II

Man is a thought-adventurer.

Which isn't the same as saying that man has intellect. . . . Real thought is an experience. It begins as a change in the blood, a slow convulsion and revolution in the body itself. It ends as a new piece of awareness, a new reality in mental consciousness.

On this account, thought is an adventure, and not a practice. In order to think, man must risk himself. He must risk himself doubly. First, he must go forth and meet life in the body. Then he must face the result in his mind.

Phoenix II

⊛ ERWIN SCHRÖDINGER
(1887–1961)

Mind is always now. There is really no before and after for mind. There is only a now that includes memories and expectations.

My Life

⊛ LUDGWIG WITTGENSTEIN
(1889–1951)

Suppose someone were a believer and said: "I believe in a Last Judgment," and I said: "Well, I'm not so sure. Possibly."

You would say that there is an enormous gulf between us. If he said "There is a German airplane overhead," and I said "Possibly. I'm not so sure," you'd say we were fairly near.

Lectures on Religious Belief

❁ J. KRISHNAMURTI
(1895–1986)

Freedom is emptying the mind of experience. When the brain ceases to nourish itself through experience, then its activity is not self-centered. It then has its nourishment that makes the mind religious.

The mind is the true ruler, the true helper, the true guide; but the mind is also the destroyer, if misused. The mind, when properly used, should be the guiding force for the majority of us. Though we may not be intellectual giants, we have ordinary intelligence, ordinary perception and the power to balance things. When you use the mind in this manner, you have a tremendous helper, a great power to build, to create.

The Pool of Wisdom

Thought creates a division between what *is* and what *should* be, and on this division morality is based; but neither the moral nor the immoral known love. This moral structure, created by the mind to hold social relationships together, is not love, but a hardening process like that of cement.

Commentaries on Living

The very activity of the mind is a barrier to its own understanding.

Commentaries on Living

❁ ALBERT CAMUS
(1913–1960)

The mind's deepest desire, even in its most elaborate operations, parallels man's unconscious feelings in the face of his universe: it is an insistence upon familiarity, an appetite for clarity. Understanding the world for a man is reducing it to the human, stamping it with his seal. . . . If man realized that the universe like him can love and suffer, he would be reconciled. If thought discovered in the shimmering mirrors of phenomena eternal relations capable of summing them up and summing themselves up in a single principle, then would be seen an intellectual joy of which the myth of the blessed would be but a ridiculous imitation.

The Myth of Sisyphus

All great deeds and all great thoughts have ridiculous beginnings. Great works are often born on a street-corner or in a restaurant's revolving door.

The Myth of Sisyphus

❁ OSHO
(1931–1990)

The Indian system of reasoning is not like investigating truth with the help of a lamp. It is like investigating the dark night in the dazzling brilliance of a lightning flash, where everything becomes visible simultaneously. Not that something—a part—is seen now, sometime later another part, later again something more, and so on; no the Indian way is not like that. In the Indian system of investigation, the revelation of truth takes place all at once; everything is discovered at one and the same time.

Discourses

Ideas create stupidity because the more the ideas are there, the more the mind is burdened. And how can a burdened mind know? The more ideas are there, the more it becomes just like dust which has gathered on a mirror. How can a mirror mirror? How can the mirror reflect? Your intelligence is just covered by opinions, the dust, and everyone who is opinionated is bound to be stupid and dull.

Discourses

The mind needs occupation. The mind needs that you should forget yourself and be occupied with something. This is an escape from the innate truth.

Discourses

⊛ ROBERTO ASSAGIOLI

(CONTEMPORARY)

We think that there is such a thing as the "unconscious will" of the higher Self which tends always to bring the personality in line with the over-all purpose of the spiritual Self.

Psychosynthesis: A Manual of Principles and Techniques

⊛ U. G. KRISHNAMURTI

(CONTEMPORARY)

Every time a thought is born, you are born. When the thought is gone, you are gone. But the "you" does not let the thought go, and what gives continuity to this "you" is thinking. Actually there's no permanent entity in you, no totality of all your thoughts and experiences. You think that there is "somebody" who is feeling your feelings—that's the

illusion. I can say it is an illusion but it is not an illusion to you.

The Mystique of Enlightenment—The Unrational Ideas of a Man Called U. G.

There is only one action possible for you: thinking. The birth of thought itself is action. The thinker who says he is looking at cause-and-effect is himself thought. Thought creates the space between the thinker and his thoughts, and then tells itself, "I am looking at my thoughts." Is it possible? Forgetting about what has happened in the past, try to look at your thoughts at this very moment. I am asking you to do something which is quite simple. If you will tell me how to look at thought I will be your student. I will be very grateful to you. Instead of looking at thought, you focus on me. If you repeat a mantra, that is thought. The repetition of the mantra is another thought. The idea that these repetitive thoughts have not succeeded in producing the state you want is another thought. The idea that you must find a new mantra or practice some technique that does work is another thought. What is thought other than this?

Mind Is a Myth—Disquieting Conversations with a Man Called U. G.

Where are the thoughts located? They are not in the brain. Thoughts are not manufactured by the brain. It is, rather, that the brain is like an antenna, picking up thoughts on a common wavelength, a common thought-sphere.

Mind Is a Myth—Disquieting Conversations with a Man Called U. G.

❀ EMERSON PUGH

(CONTEMPORARY)

If the human brain were so simple that
we could understand it, we would
be so simple that we wouldn't.

Untitled

❀ RAMTHA

(CONTEMPORARY CHANNELING)

All things are created by taking that
which has no speed—thought—and expanding it into that which does—light—
and then slowing the light down until
you create this and that and all that is
around you.

Ramtha: An Introduction, S. L. Weinberg

❀ ARTHUR WALEY

(CONTEMPORARY)

Thought grows out of environment.

Translator's introduction to
The Analects of Confucius

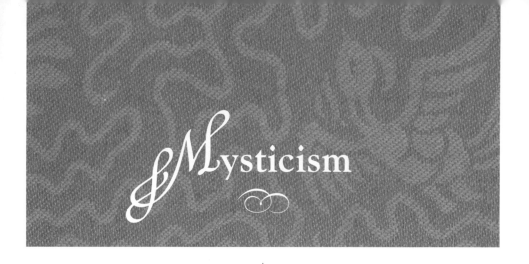

Mysticism

☸ LAO-TZU
(C. 6TH CENTURY BCE)

The Way is like an empty vessel that yet may be drawn from.

Tao Te Ching

The Way [Tao] that can be told is not the eternal way.

Tao Te Ching

☸ SHANKARA
(788–820)

The knower of the Atman [pure consciousness] does not identify himself with his body. He rests within it, as if within a carriage. If people provide him with comforts and luxuries, he enjoys them and plays with them like a child. He bears no outward mark of a holy man. He remains quite unattached to the things of this world.

He may wear costly clothing, or none. He may be dressed in deer or tiger skin or clothed in pure knowledge. He may seem like a madman, or like a child, or sometimes like an unclean spirit. Thus, he wanders the earth.

The man of contemplation walks alone. He lives desireless amidst the objects of desire. The Atman is his eternal satisfaction. He sees the Atman present in all things.

Sometimes he appears to be a fool, sometimes a wise man. Sometimes he seems splendid as a king, sometimes feeble-minded. Sometimes he is calm and silent. Sometimes he draws men to him, as a python attracts its prey.

Sometimes people honor him greatly, sometimes they insult him. Sometimes they ignore him. That is how the illumined soul lives, always absorbed in the highest bliss.

Crest-Jewel of Discrimination

☸ ST. JOHN OF THE CROSS
(1542–1591)

The dark night of the soul through which the soul passes on its way to the Divine Light.

The Ascent of Mount Carmel

☸ BENJAMIN WHICHCOTE
(1609–1683)

The more mysterious, the more imperfect: that which is mystically spoken is but half spoken.

Moral and Religious Aphorisms

✶ FLORENCE NIGHTINGALE
(1820–1910)

For what is Mysticism? Is it not the attempt to draw near to God, not by rites or ceremonies, but by inward disposition? Is it not merely a hard word for "The Kingdom of Heaven is within"? Heaven is neither a place nor a time.

Mysticism

✶ ANDRÉ GIDE
(1869–1951)

Without mysticism man can achieve nothing great.

The Counterfeiters

✶ BERTRAND RUSSELL
(1872–1970)

Mysticism is, in essence, little more than a certain intensity and depth of feeling in regard to what is believed about the universe.

Mysticism and Logic

✶ EVELYN UNDERHILL
(1875–1941)

Mysticism is the art of union with Reality. The mystic is a person who has attained that union in greater or less degree; or who aims at and believes in such attainment.

Practical Mysticism

✶ ALBERT EINSTEIN
(1879–1955)

The most beautiful thing we can experience is the mysterious. It is the source of all true art and science.

What I Believe

✶ MIKHAIL NAIMY
(1889–1988)

To pierce the veils you need an eye other than that shaded with lash, and lid and brow.

To break the seals you need a lip other than the familiar piece of flesh below the nose.

First see the eye itself aright, if you would see the other things aright. Not with the eye, but through it must you look that you may see all things beyond it.

The Book of Mirdad—A Lighthouse and a Haven

✶ WILHELM REICH
(1897–1957)

You have lost the feeling for the best that is in you. You have strangled it, and you murder it wherever you detect it in others, in your children, your wife, your husband, your father and your mother. You are little and you want to remain little. . . . True enough, you want to have 'geniuses' and you are willing to pay them homage. But you want a *good* genius, one with moderation and decorum, one without folly, in brief, a *seemly, measured and adjusted* genius, not an unruly, untamed genius which breaks down all your barriers and limitations. You want a limited, wing-clipped and dressed-up genius whom, without blushing, you can triumphantly parade through the street of your towns. . . . All you can do is to slay me, as you have slain so many others of your true friends: Jesus, Rathenau, Karl Liebknecht, Lincoln, and many others. . . . A great many great, courageous and lonely men have told you

182

long since what you should do. Again and again you have twisted their teachings, torn them apart and destroyed them. Again and again you tackled them from the *wrong* end, made the small error instead of the great truth the guiding line of your life, in Christianity, in the teaching of socialism, in the teaching of the sovereignty of the people, in absolutely everything you touched, Little Man.

Listen, Little Man!

❀ ALAN WATTS
(1915–1973)

Now if we examine the records of mystical experience . . . we shall find that time and time again, it is connected with "spiritual poverty"—that is to say with giving up the ownership of everything, including oneself or one's consciousness. It is the total abandonment of proprietorship on the external world of nature and the internal world of the human organism. . . . When it thus becomes clear that I own nothing, not even what I have called myself, it is as if, to use St. Paul's words, I had nothing but possessed all things.

This Is IT and Other Essays on Zen and Spiritual Experience

❀ R. D. LAING
(1927–1989)

Mystics and schizophrenics find themselves in the same ocean, but the mystics swim whereas the schizophrenics drown.

The Politics of Experience and the Bird of Paradise

❀ ROBERTO ASSAGIOLI
(CONTEMPORARY)

The true nature of mysticism cannot be considered as some investigators have maintained, to be merely a product or by-product of sex. On the one hand, one finds many people whose normal sexual life is inhibited yet who show no trace of mysticism; on the other hand, there are instances of people leading a normal sexual life, raising a family, etc., and having at the same time genuine mystical experiences.

Psychosynthesis: A Manual of Principles and Techniques

❀ JAMES BROUGHTON AND JOEL ANDREWS
(CONTEMPORARY)

This is It
and I am It
and You are It
and so is That
and He is It
and She is It
and It is It
and That is That.

The Bard and the Harper

❀ DA FREE JOHN (ADIDA)
(CONTEMPORARY)

The Adept . . . is a useful and remarkable Agency, a unique mechanism in nature, a hole in the universe through which the Transcendental Influence moves through to the world. Therefore, this remarkable Agency, when it occurs, should be used. It should be acknowledged and understood as it is. People should know how to relate to it, how to use it as a unique instrument of the Divine. Adepts appear to serve your Realization. Otherwise, as soon as someone entered into the sphere of Perfect Realization, he or she would be Translated, and that would be the end of it. Even if some Great Teaching appeared, there would never be the unique instrument of the Adept.

The Fire Gospel

Nature

⊛ ANONYMOUS

A fallen leaf returning to the branch?
    Butterfly.

⊛ ANONYMOUS
(CHINESE CHOU DYNASTY BCE)

Grant that this year abundant harvest
    reign,
And be our granaries piled with rice
    and grain.
Let sheaves in myriads and in millions
    fill
Our barns. From these sweet wine we
    will distil,
To pour as solemn offerings at the
    shrine
Of those, who, passed away, are now
    divine;
The sainted sires and mothers of our line.
Pleased with such sacrifice may they
    bestow
Unnumbered blessings on the folk
    below.

        Hymn for the Harvest/The Shih Ching

⊛ ANONYMOUS
(C. 1412 BCE)

Sole likeness, maker of what is,
Sole and only one, maker of what
    exists.
From whose eyes men issued,
From whose mouth the gods came
    forth,
Maker of herbs for the cattle,
And the tree of life for mankind.

        "Hymn to the Sun-god," in
        Sacred Books of the World,
        A. C. Bouquet

⊛ THE UPANISHADS
(C. 900–600 BCE)

My Son! Bees create honey by gathering
the sweet juices from different flowers,
and mixing all into a common juice.

And there is nothing in honey whereby
the juice of a particular flower can be
identified, so it is with the various creatures who merge in that Being, in deep
sleep or in death.

Whatever they may be, tiger, lion, wolf,
boar, worm, moth, gnat, mosquito, they
become aware of particular life when
they are born into it or awake.

That Being is the seed; all else but His
expression. He is truth. He is Self,
Shwetaketu! You are That.

        Chandogya Upanishad

✸ A Disciple of Buddha's?

(6TH? CENTURY BCE)

Like a lion which fears not noises, un-obstructed like the wind whistling through a net, not touching anything like the lotus-leaf untouched by water, let one walk alone like a rhinoceros.

. . . .

In fit time, observe kindness, impartiality, mercy, freedom from sin, and delight at the prosperity of others: un-opposed to the whole world, let one walk alone like a rhinoceros.

Having abandoned lust, malice, ignorance, having broken the bonds of transmigration, entertaining no fears for the loss of life, let one walk alone like a rhinoceros.

Men associate with and serve others for the sake of an object; friends who have no object in view are difficult to obtain. They are wise enough to gain some object for themselves. Men are not pure. Let one walk alone like a rhinoceros.

> The Khaggavisana Sutra (The Rhinoceros Discourse), translated in *The Sacred Books and Early Literature of the East*

✸ Lao-Tzu

(C. 6TH CENTURY BCE)

Nature is not human-hearted.

> *Tao Te Ching*

✸ Aesop

(C. 550 BCE)

A peacock taunted a Crane with the dullness of her plumage. "Look at my brilliant colours," said she, "and see how much finer they are than your poor feathers." "I am not denying," replied the Crane, "that yours are far gayer than mine; but when it comes to flying I can soar into the clouds, whereas you are confined to the Earth like any dunghill cock."

> *Aesop's Fables*

✸ The Bhagavad Gita

(500? BCE)

Even a wise man acts under the impulse of his nature: all beings follow nature. Of what use is restraint?

✸ Chuang Tzu

(369–286 BCE)

There is an original nature in things. Things in their original nature are curved without the help of arcs, straight without lines, round without compasses, and rectangular without squares; they are joined together without glue and hold together without cords. In this manner, all things live and grow from an inner urge and none can tell how they come to do so. They all have a place in the scheme of things and none can tell how they come to have their proper place. From time immemorial this has always been so, and it may not be tampered with.

> *Joined Toes*

✸ Zeno

(335–263 BCE)

The goal of your life is living in agreement with nature.

> *Diogenes Laërtius*, book 3, sec. 87

⊛ LUCRETIUS
(99–55 BCE)

Nature is free and uncontrolled by proud masters and runs the universe by herself without the aid of gods. For who—by the sacred hearts of the gods who pass their unruffled lives, their placid aeon, in calm and peace!—who can rule the sum total of the measureless? Who can hold in coercive hand the strong reins of the un-fathomable?

On the Nature of Things

⊛ OLD TESTAMENT

And the wolf shall dwell with the lamb,
And the leopard shall lie down with the
   kid;
And the calf and the young lion and the
   fatling shall be together;
And a little child shall lead them.
And the cow shall graze with the bear;
Their young ones shall lie down
   together;
And the lion shall eat straw like the ox.
And the sucking child shall play at the
   hole of the asp,
And the weaned child shall put his hand
   on the adder's den.
None shall hurt nor destroy in all My
   holy mountain;
For the earth shall be full of the
   knowledge of the Lord,
As the waters cover the sea.

Isaiah xi

I do set my bow in the cloud, and it shall be for a token of a covenant between me and the earth. And it shall come to pass, when I bring a cloud over the earth, that the bow shall be seen in the cloud. And I will remember my covenant, which is between me and you and every living creature of all flesh; and the waters shall no more become a flood to destroy all flesh.

Genesis 9:13–15

⊛ NEW TESTAMENT

And there arose a great storm of wind, and the waves beat into the ship, so that it was now full. And he was in the hinder part of the ship, asleep on a pillow: and they awake him, and say unto him, Master, carest thou not that we perish? And he arose, and rebuked the wind, and said unto the sea, Peace, be still. And the wind ceased, and there was a great calm. And he said unto them, Why are ye so fearful? How is it that ye have no faith? And they feared exceedingly, and said one to another, What manner of man is this, that even the wind and the sea obey him?

Mark 4:37–41

⊛ SARAHA
(1ST OR 2ND CENTURY)

Though the fragrance of a flower
   cannot
   be touched,
'Tis all pervasive and at once
   perceptible.
So by unpatterned being-in-itself
Recognize the round of mystic circles.

The Royal Song of Saraha

⊛ ORIGEN
(185–254)

Thou art a second world in miniature, the sun and moon are within thee, and also the stars.

Hexapla

❀ THE GEMARA
(c. 500)

Honi ha-Ma'aggel once saw on his travels an old man planting a carob tree. He asked him when he thought the tree would bear fruit. "After seventy years," was the reply.

"Does thou expect to live seventy years and eat the fruit of thy labor?"

"I did not find the world desolate when I entered it," said the old man, "and as my fathers planted for me before I was born, so do I plant for those who will come after me."

Ta'anit, 23a, The Talmud quoted in The World's Great Scriptures, Lewis Browne

❀ HUANG-PO
(800–850)

Your true nature is something never lost to you even in moments of delusion, nor is it gained at the moment of Enlightenment.

The Zen Teaching of Huang-po

❀ LADY SARASHINA
(1008–?)

Still no news of blossom time!
Has Spring not come this year,
Or did the flowers forget to bloom?

Diaries

❀ ST. BERNARD
(1091–1153)

What I know of the divine science and Holy Scripture I learnt in woods and fields.

Epistle 106

Listen to a man of experience: thou wilt learn more in the woods than in books.

Epistle 106

You will find something more in woods than in books. Trees and stones will teach you that which you can never learn from masters.

Epistle 106

❀ JALAL AL-DIN RUMI
(1207–1273)

I died a mineral, and became a plant.
I died a plant and rose an animal.
I died an animal and I was a man.
Why should I fear? When was I less by
    dying?
Yet once more I shall die as man, to
    soar
With the blessed angels; but even from
    angelhood
I must pass on. All except God
    perishes.
When I have sacrificed my angel soul,
I shall become that which no mind ever
    conceived.
O, let me not exist! for Non-Existence
    proclaims,
"To Him we shall return."

Untitled

❀ MECHTILD OF MAGDEBURG
(1207–1249)

The fish cannot drown in the water, the bird cannot sink in the air, gold cannot perish in the fire, where it gains its clear and shining worth. God has granted to each creature to cherish its own nature. How can I withstand my nature?

The Flowing Light of the Godhead

❀ JULIANA OF NORWICH
(1343–1417)

He showed me a little thing, the quantity of a hazel nut, lying in the palm of my hand. . . . I look thereupon and thought: "What may this be?" And I was answered . . . thus: "It is all that is made. . . . It lasts and ever shall last because God loves it, and hath allthings its being through the love of God."

Revelations of Divine Love

❀ GURU NANAK
(1469–1539)

Air, water and earth,
Of these are we made.
Air like the Guru [Nanak]'s word gives
    the breath of life
To the babe born to the great mother
    earth
Sired by the waters.
The day and night our nurses be
That watch over us in our infancy.
In their laps we play.
The world is our playground.

Hymns of Guru Nanak

❀ MARGUERITE OF NAVARRE
(1492–1549)

No one ever perfectly loved God who did not perfectly love some of His creatures in this world.

The Heptameron; or, Novels of the Queen of Navarre

❀ MICHEL DE MONTAIGNE
(1533–1592)

Every man carries in himself the complete pattern of human nature.

Essays

There is a certain consideration, and a general duty of humanity, that binds us not only to the animals, which have life and feeling, but even to the trees and plants. We owe justice to men, and kindness and benevolence to all other creatures who may be susceptible of it. There is some intercourse between them and us, and some mutual obligation.

Essays

When I dance, I dance; when I sleep, I sleep: Yes, and when I am walking by myself in a beautiful orchard, even if my thoughts dwell for part of the time on distant events, I bring them back for another part to the walk, the orchard the charm of this solitude, and to myself. Nature has with maternal care provided that the actions she has enjoined on us for our need shall give us pleasure; and she uses not only reason but appetite to attract us to them. It is wrong to infringe her rules.

Essays

❀ FRANCIS BACON
(1561–1626)

Nature to be commanded, must be obeyed.

"Aphorism 129," in *Novum Organum*

Nature is often hidden; sometimes overcome, seldom extinguished.

"Of Nature in Men," in *Essays*

❀ MR. TUT-TUT
(17TH? CENTURY)

Only watch how the flowers bloom, how the flowers fade; say not this man is right, that man is wrong.

One Hundred Proverbs

MATSUO BASHO
(1644–1694)

Lady butterfly
perfumes her wings
by floating
over the orchid

Haiku

Not a flaw there is
On the polished surface
Of the divine glass,
Chaste with flowers of snow.

Haiku

GOVIND-SINGH
(1666 OR 1675–1708)

Could I transform all the islands
Into paper;
Could I turn the seven oceans
Into ink—

Of all the trees grown on earth
I then would mould
A pen—

Bidding Sarasvati
Guardian of Knowledge
To write, to write—

But Thou, O highest Lord,
By all this praise, wouldst not be raised
To greater glory.

Mystic lyrics from the Indian Middle Ages

ISAAC WATTS
(1674–1748)

Let dogs delight to bark and bite,
For God hath made them so;
Let bears and lions growl and fight,
For 'tis their nature too.

Hymn

KOBAYASHI ISSA
(1763–1827)

With one another
Let's play; O sparrow
Who has no mother.

Haiku

WILLIAM WORDSWORTH
(1770–1850)

One impulse from a vernal wood
May teach you more of man,
Of moral evil and of good,
Than all the sages can.

Untitled

JOHN RUSKIN
(1819–1900)

There is no climate, no place, and
scarcely an hour, in which nature does
not exhibit color which no mortal effort
can imitate or approach. For all our
artificial pigments are, even when seen
under the same circumstances, dead
and lightless beside her living color;
nature exhibits her hues under an
intensity of sunlight which trebles their
brilliancy.

Modern Painters

WALT WHITMAN
(1819–1892)

I think I could turn and live with the
    animals, they are so placid and self-
    contain'd,
I stand and look at them long and
    long,
They do not sweat and whine about
    their condition,
They do not lie awake in the dark and
    weep for their sins,

They do not make me sick discussing
their duty to God,
Not one is dissatisfied, not one is
demented with the mania of
owning things,
Not one kneels to another, nor to his
kind that lived thousands of years
ago,
Not one is respectable or unhappy over
the whole earth.

Song of Myself

❀ HENRY BERGSON
(1859–1941)

The emotion felt by a man in the
presence of nature certainly counts for
something in the origin of religions.

The Two Sources of Morality and Religion

❀ HYMNS ANCIENT AND MODERN
(1861)

All things bright and beautiful,
All creatures great and small,
All things wise and wonderful,
The Lord God made them all.

Each little flower that opens,
Each little bird that sings,
He made their glowing colours,
He made their tiny wings.

The rich man in his castle,
The poor man at his gate, ·
God made them, high or lowly,
And order'd their estate.

The purple-headed mountain,
The river running by,
The sunset and the morning,
That brightens up the sky. . .

❀ HYMNS ANCIENT AND MODERN
(1861)

We plough the fields, and scatter
The good seed on the land,
But it is fed and water'd
By God's Almighty Hand;
He sends the snow in winter,
The warmth to swell the grain,
The breezes, and the sunshine,
And soft refreshing rain.
All good gifts around us
Are sent from Heav'n above,
Then thank the Lord, O thank the Lord,
For all His love.

He only is the Maker
Of all things near and far;
He paints the wayside flower,
He lights the evening star;
The winds and waves obey Him,
By Him the birds are fed;
Much more to us, His children,
He gives our daily bread.
All good gifts around us
Are sent from Heav'n above,
Then thank the Lord, O thank the Lord,
For all His love.

❀ NATSUME SOSEKI
(1867–1916)

Spring rain:
Come inside my nightgown,
You nightingale, too.

Haiku

❀ SRI AUROBINDO
(1872–1950)

The quest of man for God, which becomes
in the end the most ardent and enthral-
ling of all his quests, begins with the first
vague questioning of nature and a sense of
something unseen both in himself and her.

The Life Divine

❁ EVELYN UNDERHILL
(1875–1941)

Nothing in all nature is so lovely and so vigorous, so perfectly at home in its environment, as a fish in the sea. Its surroundings give to it a beauty, quality, and power which is not its own. We take it out, and at once a poor, limp, dull thing, fit for nothing, is gasping away its life. So the soul sunk in God, living the life of prayer, is supported, filled, transformed in beauty, by a vitality and a power which are not its own.

The Golden Sequence

❁ THE MOTHER
(1878–1990)

The sublime state is the natural state! It's you who are constantly in a state that is not natural, that is not normal, that is false, a deformation.

Satprem, The Mind of the Cells

❁ HAZRAT INAYAT KHAN
(1882–1927)

A soul who is not close to nature is far away from what is called spirituality. In order to be spiritual one must communicate, and especially one must communicate with nature; one must feel nature.

The Sufi Message of Hazrat Inayat Khan:
The Art of Personality

All the good qualities which help to fulfill the purpose of life are the natural inheritance that every soul brings to the earth; and almost all the bad traits that mankind shows in its nature are as a rule acquired after birth. This shows that goodness is natural and badness unnatural.

The Sufi Message of Hazrat Inayat Khan:
The Art of Personality

❁ D. H. LAWRENCE
(1885–1930)

Man fights for a new conception of life and God, as he fights to plant seeds in the spring: because he knows that is the only way to harvest. If after harvest there is winter again, what does it matter? It is just seasonable.

Phoenix II

❁ NIKOS KAZANTZAKIS
(1885–1957)

If only we know, boss, what the stones and rain and flowers say. Maybe they call—call us—and we don't hear them. When will people's ears open, boss? When shall we have our eyes open to see? When shall we open our arms to embrace everything—stones, rain, flowers, and men? What d'you think about that, boss? And what do your books have to say about it?

Zorba the Greek

I remembered one morning when I discovered a cocoon in the bark of a tree, just as the butterfly was making a hole in its case and preparing to come out. I waited a while, but it was too long appearing and I was impatient. I bent over it and breathed on it to warm it. I warmed it as quickly as I could and the miracle began to happen before my eyes, faster than life. The case opened, the butterfly started slowly crawling out and I shall never forget my horror when I saw how its wings were folded back and crumpled; the wretched butterfly tried with its whole trembling body to unfold them. Bending over it, I tried to help it with my breath. In vain. It needed to be hatched out patiently and the unfolding of the wings should be a gradual process in the sun. Now it was too late. My breath had forced the butterfly to appear, all crumpled, before its time. It struggled desperately and, a few seconds later, died in the palm of my hand.

That little body is, I do believe, the greatest weight I have on my conscience. For I realize today that it is a mortal sin to violate the great laws of nature. We should not hurry, we should not be impatient, but we should confidently obey the eternal rhythm.

Zorba the Greek

⊛ DALE CARNEGIE
(1888–1955)

Close your eyes. You might try saying . . . something like this: "The sun is shining overhead. The sky is blue and sparkling. Nature is calm and in control of the world—and I, as nature's child, am in tune with the Universe." Or—better still—pray!

Relaxation technique given in
How to Stop Worrying and Start Living

⊛ WILHELM REICH
(1897–1957)

Don't try to improve nature. Try, instead to understand and protect it. . . . And, most important, THINK COR-RECTLY, listen to your inner voice which nudges you gently. You have your life in your own hand. Do not entrust it to anybody else, least of all to the Führers you elected. BE YOURSELF! Many great men have told you so.

Listen, Little Man!

⊛ ORPINGALIK
(EARLY 20TH CENTURY)

Reindeer,
earth-louse,
long-legged,
large-eared,
bristly-neck,
don't run away
from me!
If I kill you,
I will offer
handsome presents
to your soul:
hides for kamiks,
moss for wicks.
Come happily,
towards me!
Come!

Eskimo Poems from Canada and Greenland

⊛ ALAN WATTS
(1915–1973)

Human purposes are pursued within an immense circling universe which does not seem to me to have purpose, in our sense, at all. Nature is much more playful that purposeful, and the probability that it has no special goals for the future need not strike one as a defect. On the contrary, the processes of nature as we see them both in the sur-rounding world and in the involuntary aspects of our own organisms are much more like art than like business, politics, or religion. They are especially like the arts of music and dancing, which unfold themselves without aiming at future destinations. No one imagines that a symphony is supposed to improve in quality as it goes along, or that the whole object of playing it is to reach the finale. The point of music is discovered in every moment of playing and listening to it. It is the same, I feel, with the greater part of our lives, and if we are unduly absorbed in improving them we may forget altogether to live them.

This Is IT and Other Essays on Zen and Spiritual Experience

❋ OSHO
(1931–1990)
Sitting silently,
Doing nothing,
Spring comes,
And the grass grows by itself.

Discourses

❋ CARLOS CASTANEDA
(CONTEMPORARY)
For don Juan, then, the reality of our day-to-day life consists of an endless flow of perceptual interpretations which we, the individuals who share a specific *membership*, have learned to make in common.

Journey to Ixtlan

❋ KENNETH TANEMURA
(CONTEMPORARY)
A single petal
Of the cherry blossom fell:
Mountain silence.

Haiku

❋ DAVI KOPENAWA TANOMAMI
(CONTEMPORARY)
We don't have poor people. Every one of us can use the land, can clear a garden, can hunt, fish. An Indian, when he needs to eat, kills just one or two tapirs.

He only cuts down a few trees to make his garden. He doesn't annihilate the animals and the forest. The whites do this. . .

Chief of a Brazilian Yanomami tribe

❋ PETER TOMPKINS AND CHRISTOPHER BIRD
(CONTEMPORARY)
In addition to souls which run and shriek and devour might there not be souls which bloom in stillness, exhale fragrance and satisfy their thirst with dew and their impulses by their burgeoning.

The Secret Life of Plants

❍neness

❋ THE UPANISHADS

(C. 900–600 BCE)

Know that the Self is the master,
the body is the car, 'tis plain;
Know the intellect as the driver
and the mind of course the rein.
The senses are the horses, sure,
the objects, roads that here, there wind;
The wise him call the enjoyer
combined with body, sense and mind.

Katha Upanishad

Everything here is Brahman: He is
      That
From which all things originate;
That which sustains all things;
That into which all things will be
      dissolved
so no one should meditate in
      tranquillity.

Chandogya Upanishad

❋ LAO-TZU

(C. 6TH CENTURY BCE)

Tao invariably takes no action, and yet
      there is nothing left undone.
Reversion is the action of Tao.
Weakness is the function of Tao.
All things in the world come from being.
And being comes from non-being.

Tao Te Ching

❋ THE BHAGAVAD GITA

(500? BCE)

Forsaking egoism, power, pride, lust,
anger and possession freed from the
notion of "mine" and tranquil; one is thus
fit to become one with the Supreme.
Becoming one with the Supreme, serene-
minded, he neither grieves nor desires;
alike to all beings, he attains supreme
devotion unto Me.

Book of Daily Thoughts and Prayers

He who is established and unshaken; he
who is alike in pleasure and pain, who is
the same in pleasant and unpleasant, in
praise and blame, and steady, he who is
alike in honor and dishonor, the same to
friend and foe, giving up all selfish
undertakings, he is said to have crossed
beyond the qualities of Nature. And
He who, crossing over these qualities,
serves Me with unwavering devotion,
becomes fit to attain oneness with the
Supreme.

Book of Daily Thoughts and Prayers

❋ CHUANG TZU
(369–286 BCE)

Take, for instance, a twig and a pillar or the ugly person and the great beauty and all the strange and monstrous transformation. These are all leveled together by Tao. Division is the same as creation; creation is the same as destruction.

On Levelling All Things

❋ SARAHA
(1ST OR 2ND CENTURY)

It arises as a thing and into no thing fades,
Having no essence when will it arise again?
Without end or beginning, that which links both is not found.
Stay! The gracious master speaks.

Look and listen, touch and eat,
Smell and wander, sit and stand,
Pass your time in easy talk,
Let mind go, move not from singleness.

The Royal Song of Saraha

❋ MARCUS AURELIUS
(121–180)

Being is as it were a torrent, in and out of which bodies pass, coalescing and cooperating with the whole, as the various parts in us so with one another.

Meditations

❋ HAKIM ABU' L-MAJD MAJDUD SANAI OF GHAZNA (HAKIM SANAI)
(12TH CENTURY)

Melt yourself down in this search [for God]:
venture your life and your soul in the path of sincerity;
strive to pass from nothingness to being,
and make yourself drunk with the wine of God.

The Walled Garden of Truth

❋ JALAL AL-DIN RUMI
(1207–1273)

I have put duality away, I have seen that the two worlds are one: one I seek, one I know, one I see, one I call. He is the first, he is the last. He is the outward, he is the inward.

Quoted from *The Soul: An Archeology*, Claudia Setzer

❋ JOHN DONNE
(1572–1631)

No man is an *Island*, entire of itself; every man is a piece of *Continent*, a part of the *main*, if a *clod* be washed away by the *sea*, *Europe* is the less, as well as if a *promontory* were, as well as if a *manor* or thy *friends* or of *thine own* were; any man's *death* diminishes *me*, because I am involved in *Mankind*.

Meditation

❋ RABINDRANATH TAGORE
(1861–1941)

Joy is the realization of oneness, the oneness of our soul with the world and of the world-soul with the supreme love.

Quoted from *The Soul: An Archeology*, Claudia Setzer

❋ ERWIN SCHRÖDINGER
(1887–1961)

Thus you can throw yourself flat on the ground, stretched out upon Mother

Earth, with the certain conviction that you are one with her and she with you. You are as firmly established, as invulnerable as she, indeed a thousand times firmer and more invulnerable. As surely as she will engulf you tomorrow, so surely will she bring you forth anew to new striving and suffering. And not merely "some day:" now, today, every day she is bringing you forth, *not once* but thousands of times, just as every day she engulfs you a thousand times over. For eternally and always there is only *now*, one and the same now; the present is the only thing that has no end.

My View of the World

✸ ALAN WATTS

(1915–1973)

Just as the study of natural history was first an elaborate classification of the separate species and only recently involved ecology, the study of the interrelation of species, so intelligence as a whole is at first no more than a division of the world into things and events. This overstresses the independence and separateness of things, and of ourselves from them, as things among things. It is the later task of intelligence to appreciate the inseparable relationships between the things so divided, and so to rediscover the universe as distinct from a mere multiverse. In so doing it will see its own limitations, see that intelligence alone is not enough—that it cannot operate, cannot *be* intelligence, without an approach to the world through instinctual feeling with its possibility of *knowing* relationship as you know when you drink it that water is cold.

This Is IT and Other Essays on Zen and Spiritual Experience

Prayer

HOMER
(C. 900 BCE)

Pray, for all men need the aid of the gods.

Odyssey

BUDDHA
(563–483 BCE)

To the Awakened One for Refuge I go,
To the Sangha for Refuge I go,
To the Dharma for refuge I go,

The Three Great Shelters

AESCHYLUS
(C. 525–456 BCE)

Ask the gods nothing excessive.

The Suppliant Women

THE BHAGAVAD GITA
(500? BCE)

Fill thy mind with Me, be thou My devotee, worship Me and bow down to Me; thus steadfastly uniting thy heart with Me alone and regarding Me as thy Supreme Goal, thou shalt come unto Me.

Book of Daily Thoughts and Prayers

PRAYER

Almighty God, who art the light of the world, grant us Thy heavenly blessing. May the radiance of these lights, kindled in honour of this Festival, illumine our hearts, and brighten our home with the spirit of faith and love. Let the light of thy Presence guide us, for in Thy light do we see light. Bless also with Thy spirit the homes of all Israel and all mankind, that happiness and peace may ever abide in them. Amen.

Prayer for Kindling the Lights in Prayers for the Pilgrim Festivals

BENEDICTINE ORDER
(ESTABLISHED APPROXIMATELY 540)

Orare est laborare, laborare est orare.

(To pray is to work, to work is to pray.)

Motto

HIPPOCRATES
(C. 460–357 BCE)

Prayer indeed is good, but while calling on the gods, a man should himself lend a hand.

Regimen

❋ OLD TESTAMENT

The heavens declare the glory of God;
 and the firmament sheweth his
 handywork.
Day unto day uttereth speech, and
 night unto night sheweth
 knowledge.
There is no speech nor language,
 where their voice is not heard.
The line is gone out through all the
 earth and their words to the end of
 the world. In them hath he set a
 tabernacle for the sun,
Which is as a bridegroom coming out
 of his chamber, and rejoiceth as a
 strong man to run a race.
His going forth is from the end of the
 heaven, and his circuit unto the
 ends of it: and there is nothing hid
 from the heat thereof.
The law of the Lord is perfect,
 converting the soul; the testimony
 of the Lord is sure, making wise
 the simple.
The statutes of the Lord are right,
 rejoicing the heart: the
 commandment of the Lord is pure,
 enlightening the eyes.
The fear of the Lord is clean, enduring
 for ever: the judgements of the
 Lord are true and righteous
 altogether.
More to be desired are they than god,
 yea, than much fine gold: sweeter
 also than honey and the
 honeycomb.
Moreover by them is thy servant
 warned: and in keeping of them
 there is great reward.
Who can understand his errors: cleanse
 thou me from secret faults.
Keep back thy servant also from
 presumptuous sins; let them not
have dominion over me: then shall
 I be upright, and I shall be
 innocent from the great
 transgression.
Let the words of my mouth, and the
 meditation of my heart, be
 acceptable in thy sight, O Lord, my
 strength, and my redeemer.

Psalm 19

❋ NEW TESTAMENT

When thou prayest, thou shalt not be as
the hypocrites are: for they love to pray
standing in the synagogues and in the
corners of the streets that they may be
seen of men. Verily I say unto you, they
have their reward.

Matthew 6:6

❋ CLEMENT OF ALEXANDRIA
 (150–211)
Prayer is conversation with God.

Stromateis

❋ THE GEMARA
 (c. 500)
Rabbi Johanan said: He who recounts
the praise of God more than is fitting
will be torn away from the world.

Eurbin, 65a, *The Talmud* quoted
in *The World's Great Scriptures*,
Lewis Browne

Rab said: He whose mind is not quieted
should not pray. Rabbi Hanina was wont
not to pray when he was irritated.

Eurbin, 65a, *The Talmud* quoted
in *The World's Great Scriptures*,
Lewis Browne

✸ HAKIM ABU' L-MAJD MAJDUD SANAI OF GHAZNA (HAKIM SANAI)
(12TH CENTURY)

When you sincerely enter into prayer,
you will come forth with all your
    prayers answered;
but a hundred prayers that lack
    sincerity
will leave you still the bungler that you
    are,
your work a failure; prayers said from
    habit
are like the dust that scatters in the
    wind.
The prayers that reach God's court are
    uttered by the soul;
the mimic remains a worthless, witless
    beggar,
who has chose the road to madness; on
    this path
prayer of the soul prevails, not barren
    mimicry.

The Walled Garden of Truth

✸ ATTRIBUTED TO MOSES BEN SHEM TOV
(13TH CENTURY)

Happy is the portion of whoever can penetrate into the mysteries of his master and become absorbed into him, as it were. Especially does a man achieve this when he offers up his prayer to his master in intense devotion, his will then becoming as the flame, inseparable from the coal, and his mind concentrated on the unity of the higher firmaments, and finally on the absorption of them all into the most high firmament. Whilst a man's mouth and lips are moving, his heart and will must soar to the height of heights, so as to acknowledge the unity of the whole, in virtue of the mystery of mysteries in which all ideas, all wills, and all thoughts, find their goal.

Zohar

✸ MECHTILD OF MAGDEBURG
(1207–1249)

A hungry man can do no deep study, and thus must god, through such default, lose the best prayers.

The Flowing Light of the Godhead

✸ MICHEL DE MONTAIGNE
(1533–1592)

There are few men who would dare publish to the world the prayers they make to almighty God.

Essays

✸ THE BOOK OF COMMON PRAYER
(1549)

Lighten our darkness, we beseech thee, O Lord; and by thy great mercy defend us from all perils and dangers of this night.

"Evening Prayer: Third Collect"

✸ JONATHAN SWIFT
(1667–1745)

Complaint is the largest tribute Heaven receives, and the sincerest part of our devotion.

Thoughts on Various Subjects

✸ GOTTHOLD EPHRAIM LESSING
(1729–1781)

A single grateful thought raised to heaven is the most perfect prayer.

Minna von Barnhelm

❀ SAMUEL TAYLOR COLERIDGE
(1772–1834)

He prayeth best, who loveth best
All things both great and small;
For the dear God who loveth us,
He made and loveth all.

The Rime of the Ancient Mariner

He prayeth well, who loveth well
Both man and bird and beast.

The Rime of the Ancient Mariner

❀ VICTOR HUGO
(1802–1885)

Certain thoughts are prayers. There are moments when, whatever be the attitude of the body, the soul is on its knees.

Les Misérables

❀ RALPH WALDO EMERSON
(1803–1882)

Prayer is the contemplation of the facts of life from the highest point of view.

Self-Reliance

❀ ALFRED, LORD TENNYSON
(1809–1892)

Pray for my soul.
More things are wrought by prayer
Than this world dreams of.

"The Passing of Arthur," in *Idylls of the King*

❀ IVAN TURGENEV
(1818–1883)

Whatever a man prays for, he prays for a miracle. Every prayer reduces itself to this: "Great God, grant that twice two be not four."

Prayer

❀ EMILY DICKINSON
(1830–1886)

Prayer is the little implement
Through which men reach
Where presence—is denied them.

Poem no. 437

❀ AMBROSE BIERCE
(1842–1914)

To ask that the rules of the universe be annulled on behalf of a single petitioner, confessedly unworthy.

The Devil's Dictionary

❀ KAHLIL GIBRAN
(1883–1931)

You pray in your distress and in your need: would that you might pray also in the fullness of your joy and in your days of abundance.

The Prophet

❀ ATTRIBUTED TO REINHOLD NIEBUHR
(1892–1971)

God grant me the serenity to accept the things I cannot change, the courage to change the things I can, and the wisdom to distinguish the one from the other.

Prayer adopted by Alcoholics Anonymous, attributed to but not accepted by Niebuhr

Religion

❂ JAPANESE PROVERB

Forgiving the unrepentant is like drawing pictures on water.

❂ PROVERB

Many bring their clothes to church rather than themselves.

❂ THE UPANISHADS
(C. 900–600 BCE)

Just as an embroiderer, taking off the loom a piece of embroidered cloth, weaves another newer and more beautiful form, so this Self, setting aside this body, causing it to become insensible, creates another newer and more beautiful form.

According to one's actions, according to one's conduct, so one becomes—the doer of good becomes good, the doer of evil becomes evil; a man becomes virtuous by virtuous action, sinful by sin.

Now they say further that this Person is made up of desire alone: as he desires so he resolves, as he resolves so he acts, as he acts so he becomes.

Brhad Upanishad

❂ ATTRIBUTED TO MAHAVIRA
(599–527 BCE)

A monk or a nun on a begging-tour should not accept food etc., which has been placed on a post or pillar or beam or scaffold or loft or platform or roof or some such-like elevated place; for such food fetched from above is impure and unacceptable.

Akaranga Sutra

❂ NEW TESTAMENT

[God] hath made us able ministers of the new testament; not of the letter, but of the spirit: for the letter killeth, but the spirit giveth life.

II Corinthians 3:6

Thou art Peter, and upon this rock I
    will build my church; and the gates
    of hell shall not prevail against it.

Matthew 16:18

Where two or three are gathered
    together in my name, there am I in
    the midst of them.

Matthew 18:20

Man shall not live by bread alone, but
    by every word that proceedeth out
    of the mouth of God.

Matthew 4:4

The kingdom of heaven is like unto a net, that was cast into the sea, and gathered of every kind.

Matthew 13:47

✹ THE KORAN
(7TH CENTURY)

Let there be no violence in religion.

✹ HUI HAI
(750–810)

Q: "Do Confucianism, Taoism and Buddhism really amount to one doctrine or to three?"

A: Master: "Employed by men of great capacity, they are the same. As understood by men of limited intellect, they differ. All of them spring forth from the functioning of the one self-nature. It is views involving differentiation which make them three. Whether a man remains deluded or gains Illumination depends upon himself, not upon differences or similarity of doctrine."

The Zen Teachings of Hui Hai

✹ JALAL AL-DIN RUMI
(1207–1273)

The prince of Tirmidh said one night to his court-jester Dalquak, "You have taken to wife a harlot in your haste. You should have mentioned the matter to me, then we might have married you to a respectable woman."

"I have already married nine respectable and virtuous women," said the jester. "They all became harlots, and I wasted away with grief. Now I have taken this harlot not knowing her previously so as to see how this one would turn out in the end. I have tried good sense often enough already; henceforward I intend to cultivate madness!"

Let safety go, and live dangerously; forsake good repute, be notorious and a scandal. I have made trial of provident good sense; hereafter I am going to make myself mad.

Tales of the Masnavi

✹ MARTIN LUTHER
(1483–1546)

It is impossible for the Christian and true church to subsist without the shedding of blood, for her adversary, the Devil, is a liar and murderer. The church grows and increases through blood; she is sprinkled with blood.

Table Talk

✹ KATHERINE ZELL
(1497/8–1562)

You remind me that the Apostle Paul told women to be silent in church. I would remind you of the world of this same apostle that in Christ there is no longer male nor female.

Entschuldigung Katharina Schutzinn

✹ FRANCIS BACON
(1561–1626)

The greatest vicissitude of things amongst men is the vicissitude of sects and religions.

Essays

All good moral philosophy is but the handmaid to religion.

The Advancement of Learning, book 2

⊛ GALILEO
(1564–1642)

The Bible shows the way to go to heaven, not the way the heavens go.

Fragment

⊛ WILLIAM SHAKESPEARE
(1564–1616)

The devil can cite Scripture for his purpose.

The Merchant of Venice, I, 3, 95

'Tis mad idolatry
To make the service greater than the god.

Troilus and Cressida, II, 2, 56

They should be good men, their affairs as righteous;
But all hoods make not monks.

Henry VIII, III, 1, 22

⊛ ROBERT BURTON
(1577–1640)

One religion is as true as another.

The Anatomy of Melancholy

⊛ GEORGE HERBERT
(1593–1633)

Kneeling ne'er spoiled silk stocking: quit thy state.
All equal are within the church's gate.

The Church-Porch

⊛ SARMAD
(17TH CENTURY)

O, my holy friends! How double-eyed you are!

You carry holy books and do unholy things
Like chessmen you seem to obey the rules,
But feuds rage wildly in your hearts.

Rubaiyats of Sarmad 75

Come, leave the worldly mud;
surrender thyself to the Master.
For worthless also is religion, and the world entire.

Rubaiyats of Sarmad 71

⊛ MR. TUT-TUT
(17TH? CENTURY)

If a scholar, being poor, cannot help people with money but will on occasions wake up a man from his folly or save a man from trouble with a word of advice, that is also a form of (religious) merit.

One Hundred Proverbs

⊛ BLAISE PASCAL
(1623–1662)

Men despise religion; they hate it, and they fear it is true.

Pensées

Religion is so great a thing that it is right that those who will not take the trouble to seek it if it be obscure, should be deprived of it.

Pensées

❀ MARY WORTLEY MONTAGU
(1689–1762)

Nobody can deny but religion is a comfort to the distressed, a cordial to the sick, and sometimes a restraint on the wicked; therefore, whoever would laugh or argue it out of the world, without giving some equivalent for it, ought to be treated as a common enemy.

Letter to Countess of Bute

❀ CHARLES, BARON DE MONTESQUIEU
(1689–1755)

No kingdom has ever had as many civil wars as the kingdom of Christ.

Lettres pesanes

❀ LAETITIA PILKINGTON
(1712–1750?)

Lying is an occupation
Used by all who mean to rise;
Politicians owe their station
But to well-concerted lies.

These to lovers give assistance
To ensnare the fair one's heart;
And the virgin's best resistance
Yields to this commanding art.

Study this superior science,
Would you rise in church or state;
Bid to truth a bold defiance,
'Tis the practice of the great.

Untitled

❀ JANET GRAHAM
(1723?–1789)

We have been saying, Lucy, that 'tis the strangest thing in the world people should quarrel about religion, since we undoubtedly all mean the same thing; all good minds in every religion aim at pleasing the Supreme Being; the means we take differ according to where we are born, and the prejudices we imbibe from education; a consideration which ought to inspire us with kindness and indulgence to each other.

The History of Emily Montague

❀ THOMAS PAINE
(1737–1809)

Any system of religion that has anything in it that shocks the mind of a child, cannot be a true system.

The Age of Reason

❀ NAPOLEON BONAPARTE
(1791–1821)

A nation must have a religion, and that religion must be under the control of the government.

Letter to Count Thibaudeau, June 6, 1801

❀ JOHN HENRY NEWMAN
(1801–1890)

Dogma has been the fundamental principle of my religion. . . . Religion, as mere sentiment, is to me a mockery.

Apologia pro Vita Sua

❀ VICTOR HUGO
(1802–1885)

I am for religion, against religions.

Les Misérables

❀ RALPH WALDO EMERSON
(1803–1882)

If I should go out of church whenever I hear a false sentiment I could never stay there five minutes. But why come out? The street is as false as the church.

Essays, Second Series: New England Reformers

God builds his temple in the heart on the ruins of churches and religions.

Worship

❂ KARL MARX
(1818–1883)

Religion is the sign of the oppressed creature, the sentiment of a heartless world, and the soul of soulless conditions. It is the opium of the people.

Criticism of Hegel's Philosophy of Right

❂ HERMAN MELVILLE
(1819–1891)

Better sleep with a sober cannibal than a drunken Christian.

Moby Dick

❂ ULYSSES S. GRANT
(1822–1885)

Leave the matter of religion to the family altar, the church, and the private school, supported entirely by private contributions. Keep the church and the State for ever separate.

Speech at Des Moines, Iowa

❂ AMBROSE BIERCE
(1842–1914)

Heathen, n. A benighted creature who has the folly to worship something that he can see and feel.

The Devil's Dictionary

❂ WILLIAM JAMES
(1842–1910)

Religion is a monumental chapter in the history of human egotism.

The Varieties of Religious Experience

❂ F. ADLER
(1851–1933)

The Bible . . . is the classical book of noble ethical sentiment. In it the mortal fear, the overflowing hope, the quivering longings of the human soul . . . have found their first, their freshest, their fittest utterance.

Creed and Deed

❂ SIGMUND FREUD
(1856–1939)

Religion is an illusion and it derives its strength from the fact that it falls in with our instinctual desires.

"A Philosophy of Life," in *New Introductory Lectures in Psychoanalysis*

If one wishes to form a true estimate of the full grandeur of religion, one must keep in mind what it undertakes to do for men. It gives them information about the source and origin of the universe, it assures them of protection and final happiness amid the changing vicissitudes of life, and it guides their thoughts and motions by means of precepts which are backed by the whole force of its authority.

"A Philosophy of Life," in *New Introductory Lectures on Psychoanalysis*

Religion is an illusion and it derives its strength from the fact that it falls in with our instinctual desires.

"A Philosophy of Life," in *New Introductory Lectures on Psychoanalysis*

✿ GEORGE SANTAYANA
(1863–1952)

The Bible is literature, not dogma.

The Ethics of Spinoza

Religion is the love of life in the consciousness of importance.

Winds of Doctrine

Each religion, by the help of more or less myth which it takes more or less seriously proposes some method of fortifying the human soul and enabling it to make its peace with its destiny.

Winds of Doctrine

✿ VIVEKANANDA
(1863–1902)

If there is ever to be a universal religion, it must be one which will have no location in place or time; which will be infinite, like the God it will preach, and whose sun will shine upon the followers of Krishna and of Christ, on saints and sinners alike; which will not be Brahminic or Buddhistic, Christian or Mohammedan, but the sum total of these, and still have infinite space for development; which in its catholicity will embrace in its infinite arms, and find a place for, every human being, from the lowest grovelling savage not far removed from the brute, to the highest man towering by the virtues of his head and heart almost above humanity, making society stand in awe of him and doubt his human nature. It will be a religion which will have no place for persecution or intolerance in its polity, which will recognise divinity in every man and woman, and whose whole scope, whose whole force, will be centered in aiding humanity to realise its own true, divine nature.

Offer such a religion and all the nations will follow you. . . .

May He who is the Brahman of the Hindus, the Ahura-Mazda of the Zoroastrians, the Buddha of the Buddhists, the Jehovah of the Jews, the Father in Heaven of the Christians, give strength to you to carry out your noble idea!

Hinduism

✿ BENJAMIN CARDOZO
(1870–1938)

The submergence of self in the pursuit of an ideal, the readiness to spend oneself without measure, prodigally, almost ecstatically, for something intuitively apprehended as great and noble, spend oneself one knows not why— some of us like to believe that this is what religion means.

Values

✿ CARL GUSTAV JUNG
(1875–1961)

During the past thirty years, people from all the civilised countries of the earth have consulted me. I have treated many hundreds of patients. Among all my patients in the second half of life— that is to say, over thirty-five—there has not been one whose problem in the last resort was not that of finding a religious outlook on life. It is safe to say that every one of them fell ill because he had lost that which the living religions of every age have given to their followers, and none of them has been really healed who did not regain his religious outlook.

Modern Man in Search of a Soul

RAINER MARIA RILKE
(1875–1926)

Religion is something infinitely simple, ingenuous. . . . In the infinite extent of the universe, it is a direction of the heart.

Letter to Ilse Blumenthal-Weiss,
December 28, 1921

ALBERT EINSTEIN
(1879–1955)

Science without religion is lame; religion without science is blind.

Quoted in Reader's Digest, November 1973

H. L. MENCKEN
(1880–1956)

We must respect the other fellow's religion, but only in the sense and to the extent that we respect his theory that his wife is beautiful and his children smart.

Minority Report

JAWAHARLAL NEHRU
(1889–1964)

I want nothing to do with any religion concerned with keeping the masses satisfied to live in hunger, filth, and ignorance.

Quoted in Journey to the Beginning, Edgar Snow

MEHER BABA
(1894–1969)

I am not come to establish any cult, society or organisation; nor even to establish a new religion. The religion that I shall give teaches the knowledge of the one behind the many. The book that I shall make people read is the book of the heart that holds the key to the mystery of life. I shall bring about a happy blending of the head and the heart. I shall revitalise all religions and cults, and bring them together like beads on one string.

God Speaks—The Theme of Creation
and Its Purpose

J. KRISHNAMURTI
(1895–1986)

Conversion is change from one belief or dogma to another, from one ceremony to a more gratifying one, and it does not open the door to reality. On the contrary, gratification is a hindrance to reality. And yet that is what organised religions and religious groups are attempting to do: to convert you to a more reasonable or less reasonable dogma, superstition or hope. They offer you a better cage.

Commentaries on Living—from the
Notebooks of J. Krishnamurti

WILHELM REICH
(1897–1957)

You had the choice between the majestic simplicity of Jesus and the celibacy of Paul for his priests and life-long compulsive marriage for yourself. You chose celibacy and compulsive marriage, forgetting about Jesus's simple mother who bore her child Christ out of love only.

Listen, Little Man!

JORGE LUIS BORGES
(1899–1986)

To die for a religion is easier than to live it absolutely.

"Deutsches Requiem," in Labyrinths

✹ SIR KENNETH CLARK
(1903–1983)

The all-male religions have produced no religious imagery. . . . The great religious art of the world is deeply involved with the female principle.

Civilization

✹ CYRIL CONNOLLY
(1903–1974)

In my religion, there would be no exclusive doctrine; all would be love, poetry, and doubt.

The Unquiet Grave

The true index of a man's character is the health of his wife.

The Unquiet Grave

✹ L. RONALD HUBBARD
(1911–1986)

Writing for a penny a word is ridiculous. If a man really wants to make a million dollars, the best way would be to start his own religion.

Lecture 1949, quoted in the *New York Times*, July 11, 1984

✹ ALAN WATTS
(1915–1973)

Irrevocable commitment to any religion is not only intellectual suicide; it is positive unfaith because it closes the mind to any new vision of the world. Faith is, above all, open-ness—an act of trust in the unknown.

The Book—On the Taboo Against Knowing Who You Are

✹ LENNY BRUCE
(1926–1966)

Every day, people are straying away from the church and going back to God.

The Essential Lenny Bruce

✹ MARTIN LUTHER KING, JR.
(1929–1968)

The church must be reminded that it is not the master or the servant of the state, but rather the conscience of the state.

Strength to Love

✹ OSHO
(1931–1990)

Moses went up the mountain. After a long time God appeared. "Hello, Moses. Good to see you. Sorry you had to wait, but I think you will feel it is worth it because I have something very special for you today."

Moses thought for a second and then said, "Oh, no, Lord, really. Thank you, but I don't need anything right now. Some other time perhaps."

"Moses, this is free," said the Lord.

"Then," said Moses, "give me ten!"

That's how the Jews got the Ten Commandments.

Discourses

All the religions have lied to you. . . . They say that if you give here, you will be rewarded in heaven. Neither do they have any evidence of heaven nor do they have any evidence from millions of people who have gone before—just a single letter, a postcard—that "Yes, what these priests are saying is right."

Discourses

❂ T. H. BRINDLEY
(CONTEMPORARY)

We need to find out, not a formula, but a temper—not a creed, but a Faith—which is common to all, and which underlies all, and supports all, and inspires all.

The Modern Churchman, September 1921

❂ LEWIS BROWNE
(CONTEMPORARY)

Men may differ grossly in what and how they worship, but not in why and how they believe they should behave. They may be divided by what their priests assert to be divine, but not by what their prophets prescribe as humane. See, for example, how is the Golden Rule. You find it in one form or another in the scriptures of *all* the major religions. Witness—

BRAHMANISM: "This is the sum of duty: Do naught unto other which would cause you pain if done to you."

Mahabharata, 5, 1517

BUDDHISM: "Hurt not others in ways that you yourself would find hurtful."

Udana-Varga 5, 18

CONFUCIANSIM: "Is there one maxim which ought to be acted upon throughout one's whole life?

Surely it is the maxim of loving-kindness: Do not unto others what you would not have them do unto you."

Analects 15, 23

TAOISM: "Regard your neighbor's gain as your own gain, and your neighbor's loss as your own loss."

T'ai Shang Kan Ying P'ien.

ZOROASTRIANISM: "That nature alone is good which refrains from doing unto another what-soever is not good for itself."

Dadistan-i-dinik, 94, 5

JUDAISM: "What is hateful to you, do not to your fellowman. That is the entire Law; all the rest is commentary."

Talmud, Shabbat 31a

CHRISTIANITY: "All things whatsoever ye would that men should do to you, do ye even so to them: for this is the Law and the Prophets.

Matthew 7, 12

ISLAM: "No one of you is a believer until he desires for his brother that which he desires for himself."

Sunnah

There are distinctions of phrasing in those eight quotations, but no difference in meaning. Though diverse, they are not at all divergent, and in this they typify the various ethical systems.

The World's Great Scriptures

⊛ **EDWIN GRANT COKLIN**
(CONTEMPORARY)

No religion that ministers only to the intellect and not also to the emotions can meet the needs of men, and this accounts in large measure of the failure of all essentially intellectual religions to gain popular favor.

Man, Real and Ideal

⊛ **SYDNEY J. HARRIS**
(CONTEMPORARY)

Scripture has been, and can be, the most dangerous weapon in the world unless it is carefully read and understood in full context.

Pieces of Eight

⊛ **BARON D' HOLBACH**
(CONTEMPORARY)

All religions are ancient monuments to superstitions, ignorance, ferocity; and modern religions are only ancient follies rejuvenated.

Le Bon Sens

⊛ **V. S. PRITCHETT**
(CONTEMPORARY)

The world would be poorer without the antics of clergymen.

"The Dean," in *My Good Books*

⊛ **ELTON TRUEBLOOD**
(CONTEMPORARY)

Religion is never devoid of emotion, any more than love is. It is not a defect of religion, but rather its glory, that it speaks always the language of feeling.

The Logic of Belief

⊛ **ANONYMOUS**

Q: Why does Granny read the Bible so much?

A: I think she's cramming for her finals.

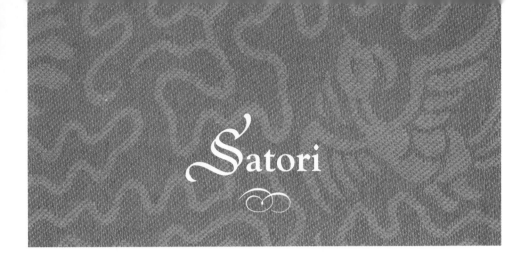

Satori

HUI HAI
(750–810)

When you sit contemplating your original nature, that is samadhi, for indeed that original nature is your eternal mind. By samadhi, you withdraw your minds from their surroundings, thereby making them impervious to the eight winds, that is to say, impervious to gain and loss, calumny and eulogy, praise and blame, sorrow and joy. By concentrating in this way, even ordinary people may enter the state of Buddhahood.

The Zen Teachings of Hui Hai

JULIANA OF NORWICH
(1342–1417?)

And then our good Lord opened my ghostly eye, and showed me my soul in the midst of my heart. I saw the soul so large as it were an endless world, and also as it were a blessed kingdom. And by the conditions that I saw therein, I understood that it is a worshipful city.

Revelations of Divine Love

BERNARD BERENSON
(1865–1959)

It was a morning in early summer. A silver haze shimmered and trembled over the lime trees. The air was laden with their fragrance. The temperature was like a caress. I remember—I need not recall—that I climbed up a tree and felt suddenly immersed in "Itness." I did not call it that name. I had no need for words. It and I were one.

Sketch for a Self Portrait

THE MOTHER
(1878–1990)

The entire body became a single, extremely rapid and intense vibration, but motionless. I don't know how to explain it because it wasn't moving in space, and yet it was a vibration (meaning it wasn't immobile), but it was motionless in space. It was in the body, as if each cell had a vibration and there was but a single block of vibrations.

Satprem, The Mind of the Cells

PIERRE TEILHARD DE CHARDIN
(1881–1955)

Starting from the point at which a spark was first struck, a point . . . was built into me congenitally, the World gradually caught fire for me, burst into flames; how this happened all *during* my life, and *as a result of* my whole life, until it formed a great luminous mass, lit from within, that surrounded me.

The Heart of the Matter

213

❂ MEHER BABA
(1894–1969)

And spontaneously there occurred a sort of eruption, disrupting the individual poise and the unconscious tranquillity of the Infinite Soul with a recoil or tremendous shock which impregnated the unconsciousness of its apparent separateness from the indivisible state.

God Speaks—The Theme of Creation and Its Purpose

❂ ALAN WATTS
(1915–1973)

There are occasions when this vision of the world takes us by surprise, the mind having slipped unconsciously into a receptive attitude. It is like the oft-recurring tale of coming upon an unexpected door in a familiar wall, a door that leads into an enchanted garden, or a cleft in a rock that gives entrance to a cavern of jewels. Yet when one comes back to the place again, looking for the entrance, it is no longer to be found. It was in just this way that late one afternoon my own garden became suddenly transfigured—for about half an hour, just at the beginning of twilight. The sky was in some way transparent, its blue quiet and clear, but more inwardly luminous than ever at high noon. The leaves of the trees and shrubs assumed qualities of green that were incandescent, and their clusterings were no longer shapeless daubs, but arabesques of marvelous complexity and clarity. The interlacing of branches against the sky suggested filigree or tracery, not in the sense of artificiality, but of distinctness and rhythm. Flowers—I remember especially fuchsias—were suddenly the lightest carvings of ivory and coral.

The Book

❂ ANNE BANCROFT
(CONTEMPORARY)

Moments of true consciousness, unconditioned by the self, are usually fleeting but indelible. We always remember them. They remain to us as moments out of time. It is a fallacy to believe that only the spiritually mature can experience such relations. They do not come because one is for many hours in meditation or prayer although, if that meditation softens and opens the hard core of self, they are there for the taking. But as gifts they are given to all—to young children as well as the very old, to the murderer as well as the monk, and for all we know to the animals—to accept or to ignore.

Weavers of Wisdom, Women Mystics of the Twentieth Century

❂ HUBERT BENOIT
(CONTEMPORARY)

He who would understand Zen should never lose sight of the fact that here it is essentially a question of the *sudden* doctrine. Zen, denying that man has any liberation to attain, or has to improve himself in any way, could not admit that his condition can improve little by little until it becomes normal at last. The satori-occurrence is only an instant between two periods of our temporal life; it may be likened to the line which separates a zone of shade from a zone of light, and it has no more real existence than this line. Either I do not see things as they are, or I see them; there is no period during which I should see little by little the Reality of the Universe.

The Supreme Doctrine

RICHARD BUCKE
(CONTEMPORARY)

All at once without any warning of any kind, I found myself wrapped in a flame-colored cloud. For an instant I thought of fire, an immense conflagration some-where close by in the great city; the next, I knew that the fire was within myself. Directly afterward there came upon me a sense of exultation, of immense joy-ousness accompanied or immediately followed by an intellectual illumination impossible to describe. Among other things, I did not merely come to believe, but I saw that the universe is not composed of dead matter, but is, on the contrary, a living Presence; I became conscious in myself of eternal life. It was not a conviction that I would have eter-nal life, but a consciousness that I pos-sessed eternal life then; I saw that all men are immortal; that the cosmic order is such that without any peradventure all things work together for the good of each and all; that the foundation prin-ciple of the world, of all worlds, is what we call love, and that happiness of each and all is in the long run absolutely cer-tain. The vision lasted a few seconds and was gone; but the memory of it and the sense of reality of what it taught has remained during the quarter of a cen-tury which has since elapsed.

Cosmic Consciousness

MEINRAD CRAIGHEAD
(CONTEMPORARY)

I think everything and everyone slept that afternoon in Little Rock. I sat with my dog in a cool place on the north side of my grandparents' clapboard home. Hydrangeas flourished there, shaded from the heat. The domed blue flowers were higher than our heads. I held the dog's head, stroking her into sleep. But she held my gaze. As I looked into her eyes I realized that I would never travel further than into this animal's eyes. At this particular moment I was allowed to see infinity through my dog's eyes, and I was old enough to know that. They were as deep, as bewildering, as unattainable as a night sky.

The Mother's Songs

DOUGLAS HARDING
(CONTEMPORARY)

The best day of my life—my rebirthday, so to speak—was when I found I had no head. This is not a literary gambit, a witticism designed to arouse interest at any cost. . . . What actually happened was something absurdly simple and unspectacular: just for the moment I stopped thinking. Reason and imagi-nation and all mental chatter died down. For once, words really failed me. I for-got my name, my humanness, my thingness, all that could be called me or mine. Past and future dropped away. It was as if I had been born that instant, brand new, mindless, innocent of all memories. There existed only the Now, that present moment and what was clearly given in it. To look was enough. And what I found was khaki trouser legs terminating downwards in a pair of brown shoes, khaki sleeves terminating sideways in a pair of pink hands, and a khaki shirtfront terminating upwards in—absolutely nothing whatever! Cer-tainly not in a head.

It took me no time at all to notice that this nothing, this hole where a head should have been, was no ordinary vacancy, no mere nothing. On the contrary, it was very much occupied. It was a vast emptiness vastly filled, a nothing that found room for everything—room for grass, trees, shadowy distant hills, and far about them snowpeaks like a row of angular clouds riding the blue sky, I had lost a head and gained a world. . . . It felt like a sudden waking from the sleep of ordinary life, an end to dreaming. . . . *It was the revelation, at long last, of the perfectly obvious.*

On Having No Head

☸ JOANNA MACY

(CONTEMPORARY)

I was sitting in a train when it happened, crossing the Punjab to Pathankot and reading a book on Buddhism. And sitting there in that crowded train, with all its heat and smell, suddenly it was utterly self-evident that I did not exist in the way I thought I did. And this realization brought with the experience which I can only describe as a kernel of popcorn popping. It was as though the inside came out on the outside and I looked with wonder and joy at everything. And the sense then was of unutterable relief, of "I don't need to do anything with the self, I don't need to improve it or make it good or sacrifice it or crucify it—I don't need to do

anything because it isn't even there. . . . There was an immense feeling of release, and with that release came at once, immediately, a feeling that it was release into action.

*Weavers of Wisdom, Women Mystics of the Twentieth Century—Anne Bancroft—*Quoted from an interview with Joanna Macy

☸ KATHLEEN RAINE

(CONTEMPORARY)

But here I had it, and sat like a bird on her nest, secure, unseen, part of the distance, with the world, day and night, wind and light, revolving round me in the sky. The distant and the near had no longer any difference between them, and I was in the whole, as far as my eyes could see, right to the sunset. The wind and the rain were like the boiling elements in a glass flask, that was the entire earth and sky held in my childish solipsist mind. The sun, the stratus clouds, the prevailing wind, the rustle of dry sedge, the western sky, were at one. Until the cold evening, or the rain, or the fear of the dark drove me to run home for safety to the less perfect, the human world, that I would enter, blinking as I came back into the light of a paraffin lamp in the kitchen.

Farewell Happy Fields

Science

FARID UD-DIN ATTAR
(1120–1193?)

Why exert to probe the essence of
God?

Why strain thyself by stretching thy
limitations?

When thou canst not catch even the
essence of an atom,

How canst thou claim to know the
essence of God Himself?

The Conference of the Birds

GERMAINE DE STAËL
(1766–1817)

Scientific progress makes moral progress a necessity; for if man's power is
increased, the checks that restrain him
from abusing it must be strengthened.

Influence of Literature upon Society

MARY BAKER EDDY
(1821–1910)

Jesus of Nazareth was the most scientific
man that ever trod the globe. He
plunged beneath the material surface of
things, and found the spiritual cause.

Science and Health, with Key to the Scriptures

THE SHIVAPURI BABA
(1826–1963)

There should be no conflict between
Science and Religion. They are comple-
mentary. Science has taken Religion to
be its enemy which it should not.
Practice of Right Life is a kind of
science. There is no harm if science is
able to bring any comfort to individuals
and society. But science should not
attempt to override Divine laws, nor
should it be used to gain material wealth
at the cost of social harmony.

Every religion is restricted by theories,
arguments, blind faith, unnecessary and
sometimes unwanted practices. Religion
may at times create an atmosphere for
good life, but it cannot fulfil the tasks
ordained by God, nor can it by itself lead
to God or Realization.

Quoted by J. G. Bennett in *Long Pilgrimage*

CARL GUSTAV JUNG
(1875–1961)

We must remember that the rationalistic
attitude of the West is not the only
possible one and is not all-embracing,

but is in many ways a prejudice and a bias that ought perhaps to be corrected. . . . Causality . . . acquired its importance only in the course of the last two centuries, thanks to the levelling influence of the statistical method on the one hand and the unparalleled success of the natural sciences on the other, which brought the metaphysical view of the world into disrepute.

"Synchronicity: An Acausal Connecting Principle," in *The Interpretation of Nature and the Psyche*

✸ ALBERT EINSTEIN
(1879–1955)

A conviction, akin to religious feeling, of the rationality or intelligibility of the world lies behind all scientific work of a higher order. This firm belief, a belief bound up with deep feeling, in a superior mind that reveals itself in the world of experience, represents my conception of God.

The American Weekly, 1948

✸ ALDOUS HUXLEY
(1894–1963)

Scientists simplify, they abstract, they eliminate all that, for their purposes, is irrelevant and ignore whatever they choose to regard as inessential; they impose a style, they compel the facts to verify a favorite hypothesis, they consign to the waste-paper basket all that, to their mind, falls short of perfection.

The Doors of Perception

✸ MARTIN LUTHER KING, JR.
(1929–1968)

Our scientific power has outrun our spiritual power. We have guided missiles and misguided men.

Strength to Love

✸ DAVID BOHM
(CONTEMPORARY)

The present state of theoretical physics implies that empty space has all this energy and that matter is a slight increase of that energy and therefore matter is like a small ripple on this tremendous ocean of energy, having some relative stability and being manifest.

Therefore my suggestion is that this implicate order implies a reality immensely beyond what we call matter. Matter itself is merely a ripple in this background.

Dialogues with Scientists and Sages: The Search for Unity, Renée Weber

✸ JACQUES COUSTEAU
(CONTEMPORARY)

Scientists in their quest for certitude and proof tend to reject the marvelous.

Quoted from *Unknown Man* by Yatri

✸ ARTHUR EDDINGTON
(CONTEMPORARY)

We see the atoms with their girdles of circulating electrons darting hither and thither, colliding and rebounding. Free electrons torn from the girdles hurry away and a hundred times faster, curving sharply round the atoms with side-slips and hairbreadth escapes. . . . The spectacle is so fascinating that we have perhaps forgotten that there was a time when we wanted to be told what an electron is. The question was never answered. . . . *Something unknown is doing we don't know what*—that is what our theory amounts to. It does not sound a particularly illuminating theory. I have read something like it elsewhere:

The Slithy toves Did gyre and gimble in the wabe. [Lewis Carroll, *Alice in Wonderland*]

There is the same suggestion of activity. There is the same indefiniteness as to the nature of the activity and of what it is that is acting.

The Nature of the Physical World

⊛ MARILYN FERGUSON
(CONTEMPORARY)

From science and from the spiritual experience of millions, we are discovering our capacity for endless awakenings in a universe of endless surprises.

The Aquarian Conspiracy

⊛ SOGYAL RINPOCHE
(CONTEMPORARY)

Over the years and over many meetings with scientists of all kinds, I have become increasingly struck by the richness of the parallels between the teachings of Buddha and the discoveries of modern physics. Fortunately many of the major philosophical and scientific pioneers of the West have also become aware of these parallels and are exploring them with tact and verve and a sense that from the dialogue between mysticism, the science of mind and consciousness, and the various sciences of matter, a new vision of the universe and our responsibility to it could very well emerge.

The Tibetan Book of Living and Dying

⊛ LYALL WATSON
(CONTEMPORARY)

As our knowledge grows there must be a million or more genes in our nuclei that we are just not using—we have enormous genetic deposit accounts on which we could presumably draw in times of need.

Life Tide

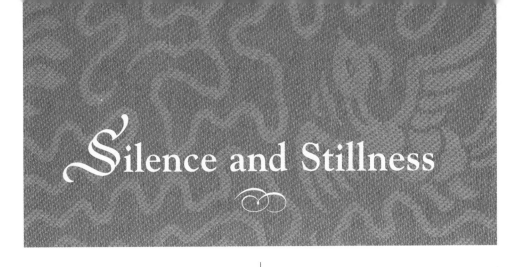

Silence and Stillness

⊛ **ANONYMOUS ZEN SAYING**

Soundless and without scent, heaven and earth are incessantly repeating unwritten sutras.

⊛ **THE UPANISHADS**
(C. 900–600 BCE)

Om. That is whole, and this also is
  whole,
For only the whole is born out of the
  whole;
and when the whole is taken from the
  whole,
behold, the remainder is whole.
Om. Peace, peace, peace.

Isavasya Upanishad

This is perfect. This is perfect. Perfect comes from perfect. Take perfect from perfect, the remainder is perfect.

May peace and peace and peace be everywhere.

Isha Upanishad

⊛ **LAO-TZU**
(C. 6TH CENTURY BCE)

He who knows does not speak.
He who speaks does not know.

Tao Te Ching

The Way is unimpeded harmony; its potential may never be fully exploited. It is as deep as the source of all things: it blunts the edges, resolves the complications, harmonises the light, assimilates to the world. Profoundly still, it seems to be there: I don't know whose child it is, before the creation of images.

The Essential Tao, Thomas Cleary

⊛ **THE BHAGAVAD GITA**
(500? BCE)

The man who, casting off all desires, lives free from attachment; who is free from egoism and from the feeling that this or that is mine, obtains tranquillity.

Book of Daily Thoughts and Prayers

That man attains peace who, abandoning all desires, moves about without attachment and longing, without the sense of "I" and "mine." This is the state of dwelling in God; having attained this, no one is ever deluded. Being established in this knowledge even at the end of life, one attains oneness with the Supreme.

Book of Daily Thoughts and Prayers

He who thus understands truly My Divine birth and action is not born again on leaving his body, but he attains unto Me. Freed from attachment, fear and anger, being absorbed in Me and taking refuge in Me, purified by the fire of wisdom, may have attained My Being.

Book of Daily Thoughts and Prayers

✸ DHAMMAPADA

(3RD CENTURY BCE)

All thy rafters are broken, thy ridge-pole is sundered; thy mind, approaching Nirvana, has attained to extinction all desires.

Quoted from *The Soul: An Archaeology,* Claudia Setzer

✸ SOSAN (SENG-S'TAN) THE THIRD ZEN PATRIARCH

Emptiness here, Emptiness there, but the infinite universe stands always before your eyes.

Discourses on the Faith Mind; or, *The Book of Nothing (hsin hsin ming)*

✸ OLD TESTAMENT

A man of understanding remains silent.

Proverbs 11:12, RSV

✸ ATTRIBUTED TO DIONYSIUS EXIGUUS

(C. 6TH CENTURY)

The higher we soar in contemplation the more limited become our expressions of that which is purely intelligible; even as now, when plunging into the Darkness which is above the intellect, we pass not merely into brevity of speech, but even into absolute silence, of thoughts as well as of words . . . and,

according to the degree of transcendence, so our speech is retrained until, the entire ascent being accomplished, we become wholly voiceless, inasmuch as we are absorbed in Him who is totally ineffable.

✸ OTOMO NO TABITO

(665–731)

To sit silent
And look wise
Is not to be compared with
Drinking sake
And making a riotous shouting.

Saying

✸ WANG WEI

(699–761)

I have always been a lover of
     tranquillity
And when I see this clear stream so
     calm
I want to stay on some great rock
And fish for ever on and on.

"The Green Stream," in *The Poems of Wang Wei*

In my late years I only like
Tranquillity, the world's affairs
No longer exercise my mind
Which I now find unpolicied.

. . . .

                    If
You ask me for a principle
Of poverty and riches, listen
The Fisherman's Song comes clear to
     the shore.

"In answer to Assistant Magistrate Chang," in *The Poems of Wang Wei*

✸ SHANTIDEVA

(8TH CENTURY)

My mind will not experience peace
If it fosters painful thoughts of hatred.

A Guide to the Bodhisattva's Way of Life

❀ CHIA TAO

(777–841)

I asked the boy beneath the pines.
He said, "The master's gone alone
Herb-picking somewhere on the mount,
Cloud-hidden, whereabouts unknown."

My Country and My People

❀ PAO-TZU WEN-CH'I

(c. 900)

Drinking tea, eating rice,
I pass my time as it comes;
Looking down at the stream,
Looking up at the mountain,
How serene and relaxed I feel indeed!

Koan

❀ HAKIM ABU' L-MAJD MAJDUD SANAI OF GHAZNA (HAKIM SANAI)

(12TH CENTURY)

And if, my friend, you ask me the way
    [to God],
I'll tell you plainly, it is this:
to turn your face toward the world of
    life,
and turn your back on rank and
    reputation;
and, spurning outward prosperity, to
    bend
your back double in his service;
to part company with those who deal in
    words,
and take your place in the presence of
    the wordless.

The Walled Garden of Truth

❀ MARIE DE FRANCE

(1160?–1215?)

Whoever has received knowledge and
eloquence in speech from God should
not be silent or secretive but demon-
strate it willingly. When a great good is
widely heard of, then, and only then,
does it bloom, and when that good
is praised by man, it has spread its
blossoms.

Letters

❀ JALAL AL-DIN RUMI

(1207–1273)

But at the very least, by practising God's
remembrance your inner being will be
illumined little by little and you will
achieve some measure of detachment
from the world.

Mathnawi

❀ MEISTER ECKHART

(1260–1327)

Only he to whom God is present in everything and who employs his reason in
the highest degree and has enjoyment in
it knows anything of true peace and has
a real kingdom of heaven.

Sermons

❀ THE BOOK OF COMMON PRAYER

(1549)

The peace of God which passes all
understanding.

Holy Communion: The Blessing

❀ ARJUN

(1563–1606)

I think in love of my Lord, and as I do
so, a peace dawns on my soul, erasing all
worries of the body and mind from the
tablet of my life.

I think of the goodness of Him who fills all things with His presence; whose Name is on the lips of countless various beings. . . .

A particle of that Name coming to reside in the heart of a man gives him a glory beyond all praise.

But he who with a single mind yearns to have a sight of Him sheds a divine influence which is enough to save all men.

This Psalm of Peace is the joy-raining nectar; it is the Name of God which dwells in the hearts of His lovers. Meditate upon it.

The Psalm of Peace

❋ LA FONTAINE
(1621–1695)
People who make no noise are dangerous.
Fables

❋ THOMAS CARLYLE
(1795–1881)
Speech is of time, silence is of eternity.
Sartor Resartus

❋ ALFRED DE VIGNY
(1797–1863),
Only silence is great; all else is weakness.
La Mort du Loup

❋ RALPH WALDO EMERSON
(1803–1882)
I like the silent church before the service begins, better than any preaching.
Self-Reliance

A political victory, a rise in rents, the recovery of your sick, or the return of your absent friend, or some other quite external event, raises your spirits, and you think good days are preparing for you. Do not believe it. It can never be so. Nothing can bring you peace but yourself.
Self-Reliance

❋ HAZRAT INAYAT KHAN
(1882–1927)
The greatest fault of the day is the absence of stillness. Stillness is nowadays often taken as leisureliness or as slowness. Modern man lacks concentration and carries with him an atmosphere of restlessness; with all his knowledge and progress he feels uncomfortable himself, and unintentionally brings discomfort to others. Stillness is therefore the most important lesson that can be taught to the youth of today.
The Sufi Message of Hazrat Inayat Khan:
The Art of Personality

❋ KAHLIL GIBRAN
(1883–1931)
Believe in the unsaid, for the silence of men is nearer the truth than their words.
Jesus, The Son of Man: His Words
and His Deeds as Told and Recorded
by Those Who Knew Him, Zacchæus

❋ FRANZ KAFKA
(1883–1924)
There is infinite hope, but not for us.
Letters

❀ J. KRISHNAMURTI
(1895–1986)

The silence of the mind is the true religious mind, and the silence of the gods is the silence of the earth.

The Second Penguin Krishnamurti Reader

❀ JOHN CAGE
(1912–1992)

We are involved in a life that passes understanding and our highest business is our daily life.

"Where Are We Going and What Are We Doing?," *in Silence*

Try as we may to make a silence, we cannot.

Silence

❀ ALBERT CAMUS
(1913–1960)

In order to understand the world, one has to turn away from it on occasion; in order to serve men better, one has to hold them at a distance for a time. But where can one find the solitude necessary to vigor, the deep breath in which the mind collects itself and courage gauges its strength? There remain big cities.

The Minotaur or The Stop in Oran

The Gods had condemned Sisyphus of ceaselessly rolling a rock to the top of a mountain, whence the stone would fall back of its own weight. They had thought with some reason that there is no more dreadful punishment than futile and hopeless labour. . . . If this myth is tragic, that is because its hero is conscious. Where would his torture be, indeed, if at every step the hope of succeeding upheld him?

The Myth of Sisyphus

If there is a sin against life, it consists perhaps not so much in despairing of life as in hoping for another life and in eluding the implacable grandeur of this life.

The Myth of Sisyphus

❀ U. G. KRISHNAMURTI
(CONTEMPORARY)

Unless you are at peace with yourself, there cannot be peace around the world. When are you going to be at peace with yourself—next life? No chance. Wait, you will see. Even then there is no guarantee that your society will be peaceful. They will not be at peace. When you are at peace with yourself, that is the end of the story.

Mind Is a Myth—Disquieting Conversations with a Man Called U. G.

❀ MOTHER TERESA
(CONTEMPORARY)

God is the friend of silence. Trees, flowers, grass grow in silence. See the stars, moon, and sun, how they move in silence.

For the Brotherhood of Man

⊛ SOGYAL RINPOCHE

(CONTEMPORARY)

We believe in a personal, unique, and separate identity; but if we dare to examine it, we find that this identity depends entirely on an endless collection of things to prop it up: our name, our "biography," our partners, family, home, job, friends, credit . . . [sic] It is on their fragile and transient support that we rely for our security. . . . Without our familiar props, we are faced with just ourselves, a person we do not know, an unnerving stranger with whom we have been living all the time but we never really wanted to meet. Isn't that why we have tried to fill every moment of time with noise and activity, however boring or trivial, to ensure that we are never left in silence with this stranger on our own?

The Tibetan Book of Living and Dying

Sin

OLD TESTAMENT

The soul that sinneth, it shall die.

Ezekiel 18:4

One sinner destroyeth much good.

Ecclesiastes 9:18

There is not a just man upon earth,
that doeth good, and sinneth not.

Ecclesiastes 7:20

Be not ashamed to confess thy sins.

Ecclesiastes 4:26

NEW TESTAMENT

If we say that we have no sin, we
deceive ourselves.

I John 1:8

Christ Jesus came into the world to
save sinners; of whom I am chief.

I Timothy 1:15

Rejoice with me; for I have found my
sheep which was lost.
I say unto you, that likewise joy shall be
in heaven over one sinner that
repenteth, more than over ninety
and nine just persons, which need
no repentance.

Luke 15:6–7

Which man of you, having a hundred
sheep, if he lose one of them, doth
not leave the ninety and nine in the
wilderness, and go after that which
is lost, until he find it?

And when he hath found it, he layeth it
on his shoulders, rejoicing.

Luke 15:4–5

ST. AUGUSTINE
(354–430)

A good conscience is the palace of
Christ; the temple of the Holy Ghost;
the paradise of delight, the standing
Sabbath of the saints.

Confessions

OMAR KHAYYAM
(D. 1123)

Myself when young did eagerly
frequent
Doctor and Saint, and heard great
Argument
About it and about, but evermore
Came out by the same Door as in I
went.

The Rubaiyat

✸ JALAL AL-DIN RUMI
(1207–1273)

Whenever the self-opinionated man sees a sin committed by another, a fire blazes up in him straight out of Hell; he calls that pride the defense of the faith, not seeing in himself that spirit of arrogance. But defense of the faith has a different token, for out of that fire a whole world becomes green.

Tales of the Masnavi

✸ ST. THOMAS AQUINAS
(1224/5–1274)

Three things are necessary for the salvation of man: to know what he ought to believe; to know what he ought to desire; and to know what he ought to do.

Two Precepts of Charity

✸ ST. TERESA OF AVILA
(1515–1582)

How is it that there are not many who are led by sermons to forsake open sin? Do you know what I think? That is because preachers have too much worldly wisdom. They are not like the Apostles, flinging it all aside and catching fire with love of God; and so their flame gives little heat.

Life

It is true that we cannot be free from sin, but at least let our sins not be always the same.

Conception of Love of God

✸ CHRISTOPHER MARLOWE
(1564–1593)

I count religion but a childish toy,
And hold there is no sin but ignorance.

The Jew of Malta

✸ JUDITH SARGENT MURRAY
(1751–1820)

Religion is 'twixt God and my own soul,
Nor saint, nor sage, can boundless
    thought control.

Essay—A Sketch of the Gleaner's Religious Sentiment

✸ OSCAR WILDE
(1854–1900)

I couldn't help it. I can resist everything except temptation.

Lady Windermere's Fan

The only way to get rid of a temptation is to yield to it.

The Picture of Dorian Gray

✸ DOROTHY PARKER
(1893–1967)

Three highballs, and I think I'm St. Francis of Assisi.

Just a Little One

✸ PHYLLIS McGINLEY
(1905–1978)

Sin . . . has been made not only ugly but passé. People are no longer sinful, they are only immature or under privileged or frightened or, more particularly, sick.

For the wonderful thing about saints is that they were *human*. They lost their tempers, got hungry, scolded God, were egotistical or testy or impatient in their turns, made mistakes and regretted them. Still they went on doggedly blundering toward Heaven. And they won sanctity partly by willing to be saints, not only because they encountered no temptation to be less.

The Wisdom of the Saints

☸ ALAN WATTS
(1915–1973)

There is . . . the common scandal of the saint-sinner, the individual who appears in public as the champion of the spirit, but who is in private some sort of rake. Very often his case is not so simple as that of the mere hypocrite. He is genuinely attracted to both extremes. Not only does social convention compel him to publish one and suppress the other, but most often he is himself horribly torn between the two. He veers between moods of intense holiness and outrageous licentiousness, suffering between times the most appalling pangs of conscience. The type is, indeed, especially common in clerical and academic circles, just because these vocations attract highly sensitive human beings who feel the lure of both extremes more strongly than others. Only in the artist is this duplicity more or less accepted, perhaps because beauty is the one attribute shared in common by God and the Devil, because devotion to the beautiful, as distinct from the good and the true, seems to make one a human being who is not altogether serious—neither, man nor devil but some kind of elf, consigned in the Day of Judgment neither to heaven nor to hell but to the limbo of souls without moral sense. It is thus for our society the artist is a kind of harmless clown, an entertainer from whom nothing is expected save proficiency in the realm of the irrelevant, since his function is taken to be no more than the decoration of surfaces. For this reason the artist can get away with a private life that would be scandalous for the priest or the professor.

This Is IT and Other Essays on Zen and Spiritual Experience

☸ OSHO
(1931–1990)

One should never go against one's nature. That is the only sin.

Discourses

☸ DA FREE JOHN (ADIDA)
(CONTEMPORARY)

The *New Testament* declares that there is only one unpardonable sin. Among all of the enumerated sins only one is unpardonable: the denial of the Holy Spirit or the Spirit of God. If that is the one unforgivable sin, then something about that sin must epitomize sin itself. All the forgivable sins must somehow be the lesser versions of this primary sin. Therefore, sin itself has to do with our tendency to deny or dissociate from the Spiritual Divine.

The Fire Gospel

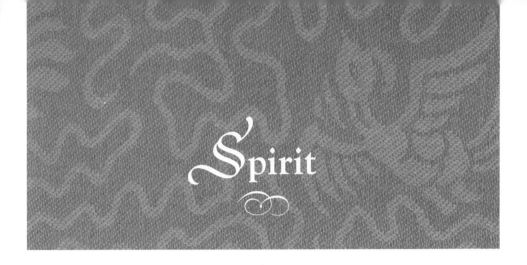

Spirit

◉ THE UPANISHADS
(C. 900–600 BCE)

Spirit is not born, nor deceases ever,
has not come from any, or from it any.
This Unborn, Eternal and Everlasting
Ancient is not slain, be it slain the body.

Katha Upanishad

◉ THE BHAGAVAD GITA
(500? BCE)

It is greedy desire and wrath, born of
passion, the great evil, the sum of destruction: this is the enemy of the soul.

These bodies are perishable; but the
dwellers in these bodies are eternal,
indestructible, and impenetrable.

The soul which is not moved,
The soul that with a strong and constant
    calm,
Takes sorrow and takes joy indifferently,
Lives in the life undying.

Quoted from *The Soul: An Archeology*,
Claudia Setzer

◉ SOCRATES
(469–399 BCE)

Are you not ashamed that you give your
attention to acquiring as much money as
possible, and similarly with reputation

and honour, and give no attention or
thought to Truth and understanding,
and the perfection of your soul.

Shall we believe that the soul, which is
invisible, and which goes hence to a
place that is like herself, glorious, and
pure, and invisible, to Hades, which is
rightly called the unseen world to dwell
with the good and wise God (whither, if
it be the will of God, my soul too must
shortly go)—shall we believe that the
soul, whose nature is so glorious, and
pure, and invisible, is blown away by the
winds and perishes as soon as she leaves
the body, as the world says?

The Phaedo

◉ HIPPOCRATES
(C. 460–357 BCE)

The human soul develops up to the
    time of death.

Aphorisms

◉ HERACLITUS
(C. 4TH CENTURY BCE)

You could not discover the frontiers of
soul, even if you travelled every road to
do so; such is the depth of its meaning.

Cratylus

✸ CHUANG TZU
(369–286 BCE)

Tsech'i of Nan-po was travelling on the hill of Shang when he saw a large tree which astonished him very much. A thousand chariot teams of our horses could find shelter under its shade.

"What tree is this?" cried Tsech'i. "Surely it must be unusually fine timber." Then looking up, he saw that its branches were too crooked for rafters; and looking down he saw that the trunk's twisting loose grain made it valueless for coffins. He tasted a leaf, but it took the skin off his lips; and its odour was so strong that it would make a man intoxicated for three days together.

"Ah!" said Tsech'i, "this tree is really good for nothing, and that is how it has attained this size. A spiritual man might well follow its example of use-lessness."

This Human World

✸ MARCUS TULLIUS CICERO
(106–43 BCE)

. . . so the frail body is quickened by an immortal soul.

De Natura Deorum, II

✸ VIRGIL
(70–19 BCE)

The spirit within nourishes and the mind, diffused through all the members, sways the mass and mingles with the whole frame.

Aeneid

✸ OVID
(43 BCE–17 CE)

Those things that nature denied to human sight, she revealed to the eyes of the soul.

Metamorphoses

✸ SENECA
(C. 4 BCE–65 CE)

The soul alone raises us to nobility.

Epistles

✸ OLD TESTAMENT

Be strengthened with might by [God's] Spirit in the inner man.

Ephesians 3:16

The fruit of the Spirit is love, joy,
  peace, longsuffering, gentleness,
  goodness, faith,
Meekness, temperance.

Galatians 5:22–23

✸ NEW TESTAMENT

It is the spirit that gives life, the flesh is
  of no avail.

John 6:63, RSV

Blessed are the poor in spirit: for theirs
  is the kingdom of heaven.
Blessed are they that mourn: for they
  shall be comforted.
Blessed are the meek: for they shall
  inherit the earth.
Blessed are they which do hunger and
  thirst after righteousness: for they
  shall be filled.
Blessed are the merciful: for they shall
  obtain mercy.
Blessed are the pure in heart: for they
  shall see God.
Blessed are the peacemakers: for

they shall be called the children of God.

Matthew 5:3

For whosoever will save his life shall lose it; but whosoever shall lose his life for my sake and the gospel's, the same shall save it.
What shall it profit a man, if he shall gain the whole world, and lose his own soul?
Or what shall a man give in exchange for his soul?

Mark 8:36

⚙ PLOTINUS
(205–270)
For the soul is the beginning of all things.
It is the soul that lends all things movement.

Enneads

⚙ LUCIAN
(240?–312)
The wealth of the soul is the only true wealth.

Dialogues

⚙ ST. AMBROSE
(C. 340–397)
We know that it [the soul] survives the body and that being set free form the bars of the body, it sees with clear gaze those things which before, dwelling in the body, it could not see.

Hexaëmeron

⚙ ST. AUGUSTINE
(354–430)
The life whereby we are joined into the body is called the soul.

Quoted from *The Soul: An Archeology*, Claudia Setzer

⚙ SOLOMON BEN JUDAH IBN-GABIROL
(1021?–1058)
The created soul is gifted with the knowledge which is proper to it; but after it is united to the body, it is withdrawn from receiving those impressions which are proper to it, by reason of the very darkness of the body.

Fountain of Life

⚙ HILDEGARD OF BINGEN
(1098–1179)
When in the fullness of time
this creation wilts,
its vigour returns to its own source.

This is the underlying natural law.
When the elements of the world fulfil their function,
they come to ripeness
and their fruit is gathered back to God.

Now these things
are in reference to the soul's life:
spiritual vitality is alive in the soul
in the same way as the marrow the hips
   in the flesh.

Out of the soul in good standing,
the vigour of the virtues flows out
as do the elements of creation,
it flows back in the same capacity
in attentive power.

The soul is a breath of living spirit,
that with excellent sensitivity;
permeates the entire body to give it
    life.

Just so,
the breath of the air makes the earth
fruitful.

Thus the air is the soul of the earth,
moistening it,
greening it.

Meditations with Hildegard of Bingen

⊛ JALAL AL-DIN RUMI
(1207–1273)

This body is a tent for the spirit, an ark
for Noah.

Untitled

⊛ MEISTER ECKHART
(1260–1327)

As the soul becomes more pure and bare
and poor, and possesses less of created
things, and is emptied of all things that
are not God, it receives God more
purely, and is more completely in Him;
and it truly becomes one with God, and
it looks into God and God into it, face to
face as it were; two images transformed
into one. Some simple folk think that
they will see God as if He were standing
there and they here. It is not so. God
and I, we are one.

Meditations with Meister Eckhart

⊛ JULIANA OF NORWICH
(1342–1417?)

The soul,
that noble and joyful life
that is all peace and love,

draws the flesh to give its consent
by grace.

And both shall be one
in eternal happiness.
Our soul is one to God,
unchangeable goodness,
and therefore
between God and our soul
there is neither wrath nor forgiveness
because there is no between.

Because of the beautiful oneing
that was made by God
between the body and the soul

it must be
that we will be restored
from double death.

Meditations with Juliana of Norwich

Our soul is made to be God's dwelling
place; and the dwelling place of the soul
is God, which is unmade.

Quoted from *The Soul: An Archeology*,
Claudia Setzer

The soul has a ghostly spot in her where
she has all things matter-free, just as the
first cause harbors in itself all things
with which it creates all things. The soul
also has a light in her with which she
creates all things. When this light and
this spot coincide so that each is the seat
of the other, then, only, one is in full
possession of one's mind. What more is
there to tell?

Meditations with Juliana of Norwich

⊛ MARSILIO FICINO
(1433–1499)

The planets correspond, then, to deeply
felt movements of the soul.

Theologia Platonica

☸ KABIR
(1440?–1518)

I laugh when I hear that the fish in the
    water is thirsty.
You don't grasp the fact that what is
    most alive of all is inside your own
    house;
and so you walk from one holy city to
    the next with a confused look!
Kabir will tell you the truth: go
    wherever you like, to Calcutta or
    Tibet,
if you can't find where your soul is
    hidden,
for you the world will never be real!

The Kabir Book: Forty-Four of the
Ecstatic Poems of Kabir

☸ PARACELSUS
(1493–1541)

Since nothing is so secret or hidden that
it cannot be revealed, everything depends on the discovery of those things
that manifest the hidden.

Essential Readings

☸ ST. TERESA OF AVILA
(1515–1582)

I began to think of the soul as if it were
a castle made of a single diamond or of
very clear crystal, in which there are
many rooms, just as in Heaven there are
many mansions.

Maxims for Her Nuns

Accustom yourself continually to make
many acts of love, for they enkindle and
melt the soul.

Maxims for Her Nuns

Remember that you have only one soul;
that you have only one death to die; that
you have only one life, which is short
and has to be lived by you alone; and
there is only one glory, which is eternal.
If you do this, there will be many things
about which you care nothing.

Maxims for Her Nuns

☸ MICHEL DE MONTAIGNE
(1533–1592)

Physicians might, I believe, make greater
use of scents than they do, for I have
often noticed that they cause changes in
me, and act on my spirits according to
their qualities; which make me agree
with the theory that the introduction of
incense and perfume into churches so
ancient and widespread a practice
among all nations and religions, was for
the purpose of raising our spirits, and of
exciting and purifying our senses, the
better to fit us for contemplation.

Essays

☸ WILLIAM SHAKESPEARE
(1564–1616)

O my prophetic soul!

Hamlet, I, 5, 40

I do not set my life at a pin's fee,
And for my soul, what can it do to that,
Being a thing immortal as itself?

Hamlet, I, 5, 65

Every subject's duty is the King's, but
    every subject's soul is his own.

Henry V, IV, 1, 181

    Be cheerful, Sir.
Our revels are now ended. These our
    actors,
As I foretold you, were all spirits, and
Are melted into air, into thin air:

And, like the baseless fabric of this
   vision,
The cloud-capp'd towers, the gorgeous
   palaces,
The solemn temples, the great globe
   itself,
Yea, all which it inherit, shall dissolve,
And, like this insubstantial pageant
   faded,
Leave not a rack behind. We are such
   stuff
As dreams are made on; and our little
   life
Is rounded with a sleep.

The Tempest

Poor soul, the centre of my sinful earth.

Sonnet 146, line 1

⊛ MR. TUT-TUT
(17TH? CENTURY)

Who is narrow of vision cannot be big-
hearted; who is narrow of spirit cannot
take long, easy strides.

One Hundred Proverbs

⊛ SARMAD
(17TH CENTURY)

Do not ask me questions on my way of
   life.
All writing is useless; useless is all
   interpretation;
All words and sentences are useless,
Unless the Spirit is ready to hear.

Rubaiyats of Sarmad 162

⊛ G. W. LEIBNIZ
(1646–1716)

The soul is the mirror of an indestructible universe.

The Monadology

⊛ J. W. VON GOETHE
(1749–1832)

Our spirit is a being of a nature quite
indestructible and its activity continues
from eternity to eternity. It is like the
sun, which seems to set only to our
earthly eyes, but which, in reality, never
sets, but shines on unceasingly.

Faust

⊛ WILLIAM BLAKE
(1757–1827)

Man has no body distinct from his soul;
for that called body is a portion of the
soul discern'd by the five senses, the
chief inlets of soul in this age.

The Marriage of Heaven and Hell

⊛ J. C. FRIEDRICH VON SCHILLER
(1759–1805)

A beautiful soul has no other merit than
its own existence.

Über Anmut und Würde

⊛ GERMAINE DE STAËL
(1766–1817)

The soul is the fire that darts its rays
through all the senses; it is in this fire
that existence consists; all the obser-
vations and all the efforts of the philosophers ought to turn towards this, the
centre and moving power of our sentiments and our ideas.

Letters

⊛ WILLIAM WORDSWORTH
(1770–1850)

Our birth is but a sleep and a
   forgetting;
The soul that rises with us, our life's star,

Hath had elsewhere its setting,
And cometh from afar.

> Quoted from *The Soul: An Archeology*,
> Claudia Setzer

❀ PERCY BYSSHE SHELLEY
(1792–1822)

Throughout this varied and eternal world Soul is the only element.

> *Queen Mab*

❀ JOHN KEATS
(1795–1821)

Call the world if you Please "The vale of Soul-making."

> *Hyperion*

❀ RALPH WALDO EMERSON
(1803–1882)

Before the revelations of the soul, Time and Space and Nature shrink away.

> *Nature*

❀ ELIZABETH BLACKWELL
(1821–1910)

As I draw near the borderland . . . the wonderful light of the other life seems often to shine so joyfully into this one, that I almost forget the past and present, in an eager anticipation of the approaching awakening.

> *Pioneer Work for Women*

❀ MARY BAKER EDDY
(1821–1910)

Spirit is the real and eternal; matter is the unreal and temporal.

> *Science and Health, with Key to the Scriptures*

❀ EMILY DICKINSON
(1830–1886)

The Soul's distinct connection
with immortality
Is best disclosed by Danger
or quick Calamity—

> *The Complete Poems of Emily Dickinson*

As lightning on a Landscape
Exhibits Sheets of Place
Not yet suspected—but for a Flash—
And Click—and Suddenness.

> *The Complete Poems of Emily Dickinson*

The Soul unto itself
Is an imperial friend—
Or the most agonizing Spy—
An Enemy—could send—

> *The Complete Poems of Emily Dickinson*

❀ SIR EDWARD BURNETT TYLOR
(1832–1917)

The act of breathing, so characteristic of the higher animals during life, and coinciding so closely with life in its departure, has been repeatedly and naturally identified with the life or soul itself.

> *Essential Sacred Writings from around the World*

❀ STÉPHANE MALLARMÉ
(1842–1898)

Every soul is a melody which needs renewing.

> *Crise de vers*

❀ SIGMUND FREUD
(1856–1939)

Man found that he was faced with the acceptance of "Spiritual" forces, that is to say such forces as cannot be apprehended by the senses, particularly not by sight, and yet having undoubted, even extremely strong effects. . . . The idea of the soul was thus born as the spiritual principle in the individual. Now the realm of spirits had opened for man, and he was ready to endow everything in nature with the soul he had discovered in himself.

"A Philosophy of Life," in
New Introductory Lectures on
Psychoanalysis

❀ RABINDRANATH TAGORE
(1861–1941)

That which oppresses me, is it my soul trying to come out in the open, or the soul of the world knocking at my heart for its entrance?

Soul Consciousness

❀ WASSILY KANDINSKY
(1866–1944)

There is nothing on earth so curious for beauty or so absorbent of it, as a soul.

Retrospect

❀ RAMANA MAHARSHI
(1879–1950)

That inner Self, as the primeval Spirit, eternal, ever effulgent, full and infinite Bliss, single, indivisible, whole and living, shines in everyone as the witnessing awareness. That Self in its splendour, shining in the cavity of the heart. . . .

This Self is neither born nor dies, it neither grows nor decays, nor does it suffer any change. When a pot is broken, the space in it is not, and similarly, when the body dies the Self in it remains eternal.

Collected Works, Arthur Osborne

❀ HELEN KELLER
(1880–1968)

It seems to me that there is in each of us a capacity to comprehend the impressions and emotions which have been experienced by mankind from the beginning. This inherited capacity is a sort of sixth sense—a soul-sense which sees, hears, feels, all in one.

The Story of My Life

❀ PIERRE TEILHARD DE CHARDIN
(1881–1955)

Matter is the matrix of Spirit. Spirit is the higher state of Matter.

The Heart of the Matter

❀ HAZRAT INAYAT KHAN
(1882–1927)

Patience is never wasted; patience is a process through which a soul passes and becomes precious. Souls who have risen above the world's limitations and sorrows, the world's falseness and deception, they are the souls who have passed through patience.

The Sufi Message of Hazrat Inayat Khan:
The Art of Personality

There is an Arabian story that when God commanded the soul to enter the body of clay He had made, the first body of man, the soul refused to enter it. The soul said, "I am free to move about in any sphere I like, and I have the limitless strength and power I derive from Thee; I do not want to enter into this body of clay. To me it looks like a prison." Then God asked the angels to play on their harps; and the soul on hearing this music began to dance and went into ecstasy. It entered the body unknowingly and was caught in this prison.

Therefore no soul comes on earth without a feeling for music. It is only when souls have become dense after having come to the earth that they lose that feeling. But when someone has lost interest in music one should know that that person is not living; there is something that was living in that person that is now dead.

The Sufi Message of Hazrat Inayat Khan: The Art of Personality

◉ KAHLIL GIBRAN
(1883–1931)

There is no depth beyond the soul of man, and the soul is the deep that calls unto itself; for there is no other voice to speak and there are no other ears to hear.

Jesus, The Son of Man: His Words and His Deeds as Told and Recorded by Those Who Knew Him

◉ FRANZ KAFKA
(1883–1924)

It's eternity in a person that turns the crank handle.

Letters

◉ NIKOS KAZANTZAKIS
(1885–1957)

The soul of man is a flame, a bird of fire that leaps from bough to bough, from head to head, and that shouts: "I cannot stand still, I cannot be consumed, no one can quench me!"

The Saviours of God

How the soul of man is transformed according to the climate, the silence, the solitude, or the company in which it lives!

Zorba the Greek

◉ D. H. LAWRENCE
(1885–1930)

Let us hesitate no longer to announce that the sensual passions and mysteries are equally sacred with the spiritual mysteries and passions. Who would deny it any more? The only thing unbearable is the degradation, the prostitution of the living mysteries in us. Let man only approach his own self with a deep respect, even reverence for all that the creative soul, the God-mystery within us, puts forth. Then we shall all be sound and free. Lewdness is hateful because it impairs our integrity and our proud being.

The creative spontaneous soul sends forth its promptings of desire and aspiration in us. These promptings are our true fate, which is our business to fulfil. A fate dictated from outside, from theory or from circumstance, is a false fate.

Phoenix II

◉ PAUL TILLICH
(1886–1965)

The most intimate motions within the depths of our souls are not completely our own. For they belong also to our friends, to mankind, to the universe, and the Ground of all being, the aim of our life.

The Shaking of the Foundations

239

❁ ERWIN SCHRÖDINGER

(1887–1961)

This life of yours which you are living is not merely a piece of this entire existence, but is in a certain sense the "whole;" only this whole is not so constituted that it can be surveyed in one single glance. This, as we know, is what the Brahmins express in that sacred, mystic formula which is yet really so simple and so clear: TAT TVAM ASI, this is you. Or, again, in such words as "I am in the east and in the west, I am below and above, I AM THIS WHOLE WORLD."

My View of the World

❁ MIKHAIL NAIMY

(1889–1988)

Rub your eyes and be awake.

The Book of Mirdad

❁ EDNA ST. VINCENT MILLAY

(1892–1950)

The world stands out on either side
No wider than the heart is wide;
Above the world is stretched the sky,
No higher than the soul is high.
The heart can push the sea and land
Farther away on either hand;
The soul can split the sky in two,
And let the face of God shine through.
But East and West will pinch the heart
That can not keep them pushed apart;
And he whose soul is flat—the sky
Will cave in on him by and by.

The Heart of Soul

❁ MEHER BABA

(1894–1969)

All souls were, are and will be in the Over-Soul (paramatma).

Souls are all One.
All souls are infinite and eternal. They are formless.
All souls are One; there is no difference in Souls or in their being and existence as Souls.
There is difference in the consciousness of Souls; there is in the planes of consciousness of souls; there is difference in the experience of Souls and there is difference in the state of Souls.

God Speaks—The Theme of Creation and Its Purpose

❁ SIMONE WEIL

(1909–1943)

The danger is not lest the soul should doubt whether there is any bread, but lest, by a lie, it should persuade itself that it is not hungry.

Quoted in *The Soul: An Archeology*,
Claudia Setzer

❁ PAUL ZWEIG

(1935–1984)

In short, the soul-journey resembles very much the sort of adventure one encounters in folklore and myth. According to archaic view, all men apparently had the chance to become a sort of Odysseus, whether they like it or not.

The Adventurer

❁ RAYMOND CARVER

(1939–1988)

Words lead to deeds. . . . They prepare the soul, make it ready, and move it to tenderness.

No Heroics, Please

WILLIAM BARRATT
(CONTEMPORARY)

Thus at the center of the self there is a hole and a mystery. Our own soul is unknown to us.

Death of the Soul: From Descartes to the Computer

JEAN SHINODA BOLEN
(CONTEMPORARY)

While everyone has a different experience of what is soulful, these experiences do share similar beginnings. We start by giving ourselves permission to be soulful, to take seriously this aspect of ourselves, our soul and our soul needs.

Windows of the Soul, Handbook for the Soul

RAY CHARLES
(CONTEMPORARY)

Some people tell me I'd invented the sounds they called soul —but I can't take any credit. Soul is just the way black folk sing when they leave themselves alone.

Television interview

DAN COHN-SHERBOK
(CONTEMPORARY)

[For Jewish mystics or kabbalists] as far as souls are concerned, they consist of three faculties. The lowest is the *nefesh* (soul, the gross side of the soul), and from the *nefesh* springs all movements, instincts and physical desires. The next faculty is the *ruah* (spirit), which constitutes the moral element. Finally, *neshamah* (super-soul) is the rational component.

Jewish Mysticism: An Anthology

DA FREE JOHN (ADIDA)
(CONTEMPORARY)

You are all spirits. It is not that you "have" a spirit. To have a spirit implies that you are spirit and that you are also something else. Human beings *are* spirits. Being a human being is one of the ways of being a spirit.

The Fire Gospel

ROBERT FULGHUM
(CONTEMPORARY)

For all my good intentions, there are days when things go wrong or I fall into old habits. When things are not going well, when I'm grumpy or mad, I'll realize that I've not been paying attention to my soul and I've not been following my best routine.

Pay Attention, Handbook for the Soul, eds. Richard Carlson and Benjamin Shield

THOMAS MOORE
(CONTEMPORARY)

Everyone should know that you can't live in any other way than by cultivating the soul.

Care of the Soul

UTA RANKE-HEINEMANN
(CONTEMPORARY)

Up till the end of the nineteenth century the doctrine of successive animation had prevailed in theology. This, we recall, maintained that the male embryo received a soul on or about the fortieth day, the female embryo on or about the eightieth.

Eunuchs for the Kingdom of Heaven

❁ SOGYAL RINPOCHE
(CONTEMPORARY)

Recognizing who is and who is not a true master is a very subtle and demanding business; and in an age like ours, addicted to entertainment, easy answers, and quick fixes, the more sober and untheatrical attributes of spiritual mastery might very well go unnoticed. Our ideas about what holiness is, that it is pious, bland, and meek, may make us blind to the dynamic and sometimes exuberantly playful manifestation of the enlightened mind.

The Tibetan Book of Living and Dying

❁ SANGHARAKSHITA
(CONTEMPORARY)

It has been recognised even in the West (by Schopenhauer) that all great Art contains an element of self-transcendence akin to that which constitutes the quintessence of religion. When this element of self-transcendence is consciously cultivated in poetry, in music, or in painting and sculpture, instead of the element of mere sensuous appeal, Art ceases to be a form of sensuous indulgence and becomes a kind of spiritual discipline, and the highest stages of aesthetic contemplation become spiritual experiences.

The Path of the Inner Life

❁ HUSTON SMITH
(CONTEMPORARY)

—a phantom, dew, a bubble,
A dream, a flash of lightning, and a
    cloud:
Thus we should look upon all that was
    made.

The World's Religions

❁ MARIE-LOUISE VON FRANZ
(CONTEMPORARY)

Soul loss can be observed today as a psychological phenomenon in the everyday life of the human beings around us. Loss of soul appears in the form of a sudden onset of apathy and listlessness; the joy has gone out of life, initiative is crippled, one feels empty, everything seems pointless.

Quoted in *The Soul: An Archaeology*,
Claudia Setzer

❁ ALICE WALKER
(CONTEMPORARY)

To such people, your color, your sex, your-*self* make you an object. But an object, strangely, perversely, with a soul. A soul.

"Living by the Word," in *Selected Writings*

❁ RICHARD WILBUR
(CONTEMPORARY)

Teach me, like you, to drink creation whole
And casting out my self, become a soul.

"The Aspen and the Stream," in *Advice to a Prophet*

The Spiritual Path

⊛ THE EPIC OF GILGAMESH
(3RD MILLENNIUM BCE)

May Shamash [the sun god] give you your heart's desire, may he let you see with your eyes the thing accomplished which your lips have spoken; may he open a path for you where it is blocked, and a road for your feet to tread. May he open the mountains for your crossing, and may the night time bring you the blessings of night, and Lugulbanada, your guardian god, stand beside you for victory. May you have victory in the battle as though you fought with a child.

⊛ THE UPANISHADS
(C. 900–600 BCE)

God has bored the opening outward-
    facing,
thus one sees the outer but not the
    inner:
Some wise man desiring the life eternal
inwards turned his sight and beheld his
    Spirit.

Katha Upanishad

When the five senses and the mind are still, and the reasoning intellect rests in silence, then begins the highest path. This calm steadiness of the senses is called yoga. Then one should become watchful, because yoga comes and goes.

Katha Upanishad

⊛ LAO-TZU
(C. 6TH CENTURY BCE)

Manifest plainness, Embrace simplicity, Reduce selfishness, Have few desires.

Tao Te Ching

⊛ BUDDHA
(563–483 BCE)

This Ariyan Eightfold Path, that is to say: Right view, right aim, right speech, right action, right living, right effort, right mindfulness, right contemplation.

Some Sayings of the Buddha

The mighty sea, unmeasured mighty
    lake,
The fearsome home of multitudes of
    pearls—
As rivers, serving countless hosts of
    men,
Flow widely forth and to that ocean
    come:—

Just so, on him that giveth food, drink,
    clothes,

Who bed and seat and coverlet
    provides,
Torrents of merit flood that mortal
    wise,
As rivers, bearing water, reach the
    main.

Samyutta Nikaya

All composite things decay. Strive diligently.

Reputed last words

❈ THE BHAGAVAD GITA

(500? BCE)

For all those who come to me for shelter,
however weak or humble or sinful they
may be—women or Vaisyas or Sudras—
they all reach the Path supreme.

In this world, aspirants may find enlightenment by two different paths. For
the contemplative is the path of knowledge; for the active is the path of selfless
action.

Quoted from The Soul: An Archeology,
Claudia Setzer

❈ PLATO

(C. 428–348 BCE)

For I do nothing but go about persuading
you all, old and young alike, not to take
thought for your persons or your properties, but first and chiefly to care about
the greatest improvements of the soul.

The Phaedo: The Trial and Death of Socrates

❈ HERACLITUS

(C. 4TH CENTURY BCE)

You can never step in the same river
twice.

The Fragments

❈ SOSAN (SENG-S'TAN), THE THIRD ZEN PATRIARCH

The Great Way is not difficult
For those who have no preferences.
When love and hate are both absent
    everything becomes clear and
    undisguised.
Make the smallest distinction, however,
    and heaven and earth are set
    infinitely apart.
If you wish to see the truth then hold
    no opinions for or against
    anything.
To set up what you like against what
    you dislike is the disease of the
    mind.
When the deep meaning of this is not
    understood
the mind's essential peace is disturbed
    to no avail.

Discourses on the Faith Mind; or,
The Book of Nothing (hsin hsin ming)

The Way is perfect like a vast space
Where nothing is lacking and nothing
    is in excess.
Indeed, it is due to our choosing to
    accept or reject
that we do not see the true nature of
    things.
Live neither in the entanglements of
    outer things,
Nor in inner feelings of emptiness.
Be serene in the oneness of things and
    such erroneous views will disappear
    by themselves.
When you try to stop activity to
    achieve passivity your very effort
    fills you with activity.
As long as you remain in one extreme
    or the other you will never know
    oneness.

Discourses on the Faith Mind; or,
The Book of Nothing (hsin hsin ming)

❁ ANONYMOUS
(8TH CENTURY)
Fate has swept our race away,
Taken warriors in their strength and led
    them
To the death that was waiting.

Anglo Saxon song

❁ ZEN SUTRA
(10TH CENTURY)
Kinzan, Ganto and Seppo were doing
Zazen when Tozan came in with the tea.
Kinzan shut his eyes. Tozan asked,
"Where are you going?" Kinzan replied,
"I am entering dhyana." Tozan said,
"Dhyana has no gate; how can you enter
into it?"

The Solitary Bird, Cuckoo of the Forest

❁ NAROPA
(1016–1100)
There where there is no Guru
Not even the name of Buddha is heard.
The Buddhas of a thousand aeons
Depend on the Guru for their
    appearance.

Song

❁ HAKIM ABU' L-MAJD
MAJDUD SANAI OF GHAZNA
(HAKIM SANAI)
(12TH CENTURY)
Why, tell me, if what you seek
does not exist in any place,
do you propose to travel there on
    foot?
The road your self must journey on
lies in polishing the mirror of your
    heart.

It is not by rebellion and discord
that the heart's mirror is polished
    free
of the rust of hypocrisy and unbelief:
your mirror is polished by your
    certitude,
—by the unalloyed purity of your
    faith.

The Walled Garden of Truth

At his [God's] door, what is the
    difference
between Moslem and Christian,
virtuous and guilty?
At his door all are seekers
and he the sought.

The Walled Garden of Truth

Break free from the chains you have
forged upon yourself, for you will be
free when you are free of clay.

The body is dark—the heart is shining
bright; the body is mere compost—the
heart a blooming garden.

The Walled Garden of Truth

❁ JALAL AL-DIN RUMI
(1207–1273)
The spiritual path wrecks the body and
afterwards restores it to health.

It destroys the house to unearth the
treasure, and with that treasure builds it
better than before.

Mathnawi

If you are irritated by every rub,
how will your mirror be polished?

Mathnawi

✦ FAKHRUDDIN IRAQI
(1213–1289)

Beloved, I sought You here and there,
Asked for news of You from all I met.
Then I saw You through myself,
And found we were identical.
Now I blush to think I ever searched
For signs of You.

By day I praised You, but never knew it;
By night I slept with You without
   realizing it,
Fancying myself to be myself;
But no, I was You and never knew it.

✦ KABIR
(1440?–1518)

Tell me, Oh Swan, your ancient tale.
From what land do you come, O Swan?
to what shore will you fly?
Where would you take your rest, O
   Swan,
and what do you seek?

Even this morning, O Swan,
Awake, arise, follow me!
There is a land where no doubt nor
   sorrow have rule:
Where the terror of Death is no more.
There the woods of spring are a-
   bloom,
And the fragrant scent "He is I" is
   borne on the wind:
There the Bee of the Heart
is deeply immersed, and desires no
   other joy.

The One Hundred Poems of Kabir

✦ MIRA BAI
(1450–1547)

O my King,
I relish this loss of good name greatly.

Some will revile me, some will praise
   me,
But I shall follow my unfathomable
   path.
On this narrow path
I have met men of God.

Plain Speaking: Devotional Poems

✦ SARMAD
(17TH CENTURY)

The seeker of the Beloved finds Him
through quiet stillness, not in frantic
   activity.
That search is the purpose of life.

Rubaiyats of Sarmad

✦ MR. TUT-TUT
(17TH? CENTURY)

Be firm in your acts, but easy in your
heart; be strict with yourself, but gentle
with your fellow men.

One Hundred Proverbs

God gives me bad luck, I meet it with a
generous heart. God gives me labor and
toil, I meet it with an easy-going mind.
God gives me trials and adversities, I
understand them by means of Tao.

One Hundred Proverbs

✦ JOHN HENRY NEWMAN
(1801–1890)

It is the saying of holy men that, if we
wish to be perfect, we have nothing
more to do than to perform the ordinary
duties of the day well. A short road to
perfection—short, not because easy, but
because pertinent and intelligible.
There are no short ways to perfection,
but there are sure ones.

Meditations and Devotions

⊛ WALT WHITMAN
(1819–1892)

Afoot and light-hearted I take to the
    open road,
Healthy, free, the world before me,
The long brown path before me
    leading wherever I choose,
Henceforth I ask not good-fortune, I
    myself am good-fortune . . .

Afoot and light-hearted I take to the open road

⊛ SHRI RAMAKRISHNA
(1836–1886)

God can be reached through many
paths; each of these sectarian religions
points out a path which ultimately leads
to Divinity. Yes, all religions are paths,
but the paths are not God. I have seen
all sects and all paths. I do not care for
them any more. People belonging to
these sects quarrel so much! After trying
all religions, I have realized that God is
the Whole and I am His part; that He
is the Lord and I am his servant; again I
realize, He is I; I am He. . . . God is
not only personal and with form but He
can take the form of Krishna, Christ or
any other Incarnation. It is true that
He manifests Himself in infinite
forms to fulfill the desires of His
devotees. It is also true that He is formless, Indivisible Existence-Intelligence-
Bliss Absolute.

Spiritual Teaching

⊛ GEORGE MOORE
(1852–1933)

A man travels the world over in search
of what he needs and returns home to
find it.

The Brook Kerith

⊛ RABINDRANATH TAGORE
(1861–1941)

Man's history is the history of his
journey to the unknown in quest of the
realization of his immortal self—his
soul. Through the rise and fall of
empires, through the building up of
gigantic piles of wealth and the ruthless
scattering of them upon the dust;
through the creation of vast bodies of
symbols that give shape to his dreams
and aspirations, and the casting of them
away like the playthings of an outworn
infancy; through his forging of magic
keys with which to unlock the mysteries
of creation, and through his throwing
away of this labor of ages to go back
to his workshop and work up afresh
some new form; yes, through it all man
is marching from epoch to epoch
towards the fullest realization of his
soul,—the soul which is greater than
the things man accumulates, the deeds
he accomplishes, the theories he
builds; the soul whose onward course
is never checked by death or dissolu-
tion. . . . Yes, they are coming, the
pilgrims, one and all—coming to their
true inheritance of the world, they
are ever broadening their consciousness, ever seeking a higher and higher
unity, ever approaching nearer to the
one central Truth which is all-com-
prehensive.

Soul Consciousness

The song that I came to sing remains
    unsung to this day.
I have spent my days in stringing and
    unstringing my instrument.

Gitanjali (Song Offering)

⊛ GEORGE SANTAYANA
(1863–1952)

Spirituality lies in regarding existence merely as a vehicle for contemplation, and contem-plation merely as a vehicle for joy.

Three Philosophical Poets

⊛ SRI AUROBINDO
(1872–1950)

The spiritual perfection which opens before man is the crown of long, patient, millennial outflowing of the Spirit in life and nature. This belief in a gradual spiritual progress and evolution is the secret of the almost universal Indian acceptance of the truth of reincarnation.

Quoted from *The Soul: An Archeology*, Claudia Setzer

⊛ G. I. GURDJIEFF
(1877?–1949)

Gurdjieff: Eventually, no matter what one starts with, one must go to Philadelphia. After Philadelphia all roads are the same.

R: Does that mean something?

Gurdjieff: Why you ask?

R: It makes me snicker, I think it is cute. I wonder how much I see cuteness when you really are trying to say something.

Gurdjieff: Everyone must go to Philadelphia. Everyone thinks I mean American Philadelphia. But. . . to understand this, they must discover true meaning of "Philadelphia." Everyone must go to "City of Brotherly love," then all roads are the same.

Secret talks with Mr. G.

⊛ HERMANN HESSE
(1877–1962)

When you throw a stone into the water, it finds the quickest way to the bottom of the water. It is the same when Siddhartha has an aim, a goal. Siddhartha does nothing; he waits, he thinks, he fasts, but he goes through the affairs of the world like a stone through water, without doing anything, without bestirring himself; he is drawn and lets himself fall. He is drawn by his goal, for he does not allow anything to enter his mind which opposes his goal. . . . It is what fools call magic and what they think is caused by demons. Nothing is caused by demons; there are no demons. Everyone can perform magic, everyone can reach his goal, if he can think, wait and fast.

Siddhartha

When someone is seeking . . . it happens quite easily that he only sees the thing that he is seeking; that he is unable to find anything, unable to absorb anything, because he is only thinking of the thing he is seeking, because he has a goal, because he is obsessed with his goal. Seeking means: to have a goal; but finding means: to be free, to be receptive, to have no goal.

Siddhartha

⊛ HARRY EMERSON FOSDICK
(1878–1969)

The place where man vitally finds God . . . is within his own experience of goodness, truth and beauty and the truest images of God are therefore to be found in man's spiritual life.

Adventurous Religion

If we hang beautiful pictures on the walls of our souls, mental images that establish us in the habitual companionship of the highest that we know, and live with them long enough, we cannot will evil.

The Hope of the World

❀ KAHLIL GIBRAN
(1883–1931)

And tomorrow, what shall tomorrow bring to the over-prudent dog burying bones in the trackless sand as he follows the pilgrims to the holy city?

The Prophet

❀ J. KRISHNAMURTI
(1895–1986)

So each of us must seek, so each one of us must dance through life, must have tremendous ecstasies, great sorrows and pains and great pleasures; and the greater and stronger they are, the more quickly shall we arrive at that stage of Nirvana, that absolute oneness with Life.

The Pool of Wisdom

❀ WILHELM REICH
(1897–1957)

You think the goal justifies the means, even the vile means. You are wrong: *The goal is in the path on which you arrive at it. Every step of today is your life of tomorrow.* No great goal can be reached by vile means. That you have proven in every social revolution. The vileness or inhumanity of the path to the goal makes you vile or inhuman, and the goal unattainable.

Listen, Little Man!

❀ JOSEPH CAMPBELL
(1904–1987)

Follow your bliss.

Motto

❀ MIRCEA ELIADE
(1907–1986)

In primitive man, as in all human beings the desire to enter into contact with the sacred is counteracted by the fear of being obliged to renounce the simple human condition and become a more or less pliant instrument for some manifestation of the sacred.

❀ ALAN WATTS
(1915–1973)

The central core of the [spiritual] experience seems to be the conviction, or insight, that the immediate *now*, whatever its nature, is the goal and fulfillment of all living. Surrounding and flowing from this insight is an emotional ecstasy, a sense of intense relief, freedom, and lightness, and often of almost unbearable love for the world, which is, however, secondary. Often, the pleasure of the experience is confused with the experience and the insight lost in the ecstasy, so that in trying to retain the secondary effects of the experience the individual misses its point—that the immediate *now* is complete even when it is not ecstatic. For ecstasy is a necessarily impermanent contrast in the constant fluctuation of our feelings. But insight, when clear enough, persists. . . . The terms in which a man interprets this experience are naturally drawn from the religious and philosophical ideas of his culture, and their differences often conceal its basic identity. As water seeks the course of least resistance, so the emotions clothe themselves in the symbols that lie most readily to hand, and the association is so swift and automatic that the symbol may appear to be the very heart of the experience.

This Is IT and Other Essays on Zen and Spiritual Experience

There was never a spiritual movement without its excesses and distortions.

This Is IT and Other Essays on Zen and Spiritual Experience

☯ OSHO

(1931–1990)

Growth is a rare phenomenon. It is natural, yet rare. When the seed has found its right soil, it grows. It is very natural; growth is natural but to find the right soil—that is the very crux of the matter.

Discourses

☯ ROBERTO ASSAGIOLI

(CONTEMPORARY)

Man's spiritual development is a long and arduous journey, an adventure through strange lands full of surprises, difficulties and even dangers. It involves a drastic transmutation of the "normal" elements of the personality, an awakening of potentialities hitherto dormant, a raising of consciousness to new realms, and a functioning along a new inner dimension.

We should not be surprised, therefore, to find that so great a change, so fundamental a transformation, is marked by several critical stages, which are not infrequently accompanied by various nervous, emotional and mental troubles.

These may present to the objective clinical observation of the therapist the same symptoms as those due to more usual causes, but they have in reality quite another significance and function, and need very different treatment.

The incidence of disturbances having a spiritual origin is rapidly increasing nowadays, in step with the growing number of people who, consciously or unconsciously, are groping their way towards a fuller life. Moreover, the heightened development and complexity of the personality of modern man and his more critical mind have rendered spiritual development a more difficult and complicated process. In the past a moral conversion, a simple whole-hearted devotion to a teacher or savior, a loving surrender to God, were often sufficient to open the gates leading to a higher level of consciousness and a sense of inner union and fulfillment. Now, however the more varied and conflicting aspects of modern man's personality are involved and need to be transmuted and harmonized with each other: his fundamental drives, his emotions and feelings, his creative imagination, his inquiring mind, his assertive will, and also his interpersonal and social relations.

Psychosynthesis: A Manual of Principles and Techniques

☯ HUBERT BENOIT

(CONTEMPORARY)

To the question "What must I do to free myself?" Zen replies: "There is nothing you need do since you have never been enslaved and since there is nothing in reality from which you can free yourself."

The Supreme Doctrine

⊛ DA FREE JOHN (ADIDA)

(CONTEMPORARY)

Turning in to a fully developed Master Field, where all of these evolutionary processes have already taken place, permits those changes to be magnified and quickened or, in effect, lived into that system without its having to pass through certain of the processes associated with the individual struggle to evolve.

Therefore, as I have indicated, the Spiritual Adept is a unique mechanism in Nature provided for the sake of the spiritual and altogether human evolution of human beings as well as the transformation and evolution of all beings and all processes that exist in the cosmos.

The Enlightenment of the Whole Body

There is no alternative to practising the Way. The logic of consideration is not an alternative to practice. It does not lead to Realization except in the case of practice.

The Fire Gospel

⊛ U. G. KRISHNAMURTI

(CONTEMPORARY)

There is no path of wisdom, there is no path at all. There is no journey.

The Mystique of Enlightenment—The Unrational Ideas of a Man called U. G.

⊛ STARHAWK

(CONTEMPORARY)

There is no dichotomy between spirit and flesh, no split between Godhead and the World. . . . Spiritual union is found in life within nature, passion, sensuality—through being fully human, fully one's self.

Quoted from *The Soul: An Archeology*, Claudia Setzer

⊛ THICH NHAT HANH

(CONTEMPORARY)

He [Siddhartha] abandoned the desire to escape the world of phenomena, and as he returned to himself, he found he was completely present to the world of phenomena. One breath, one bird's song, one leaf, one ray of sunlight—any of these might serve as his subject of meditation. He began to see that the key to liberation lay in each breath, each step, each small pebble along the path.

Old Path White Clouds: The Life Story of the Buddha

Time

THE VEDAS

Time, like a brilliant steed with seven
    rays,
And with a thousand eyes,
    imperishable,
Full of fecundity, bears all things
    onward.
On him ascend the learned and the wise.

Time, like a seven-wheeled, seven-
    naved car, moves on.
His rolling wheels are all the worlds,
    his axle
Is immortality. He is the first of gods.
We see him like an overflowing jar;
We see him multiplied in various
    forms.

He draws forth and encompasses the
    worlds;
He is all future worlds; he is their
    father;
He is their son; there is no power like
    him.

The past and future issue out of Time,
All sacred knowledge and austerity.
From Time the earth and waters were
    produced;
From Time, the rising, setting, burning
    sun;
From Time, the wind;

Through Time the earth is
    vast;
Through Time the eye perceives; mind,
    breath, and name
in him are comprehended.

    All rejoice
When Time arrives—the monarch who
    has conquered
This world, the highest world, the holy
    worlds,
Yea, all the worlds—and ever marches
    on.

Arthava Veda, book 19, hymn 59

SOSAN (SENG-S'TAN), THE THIRD ZEN PATRIARCH

Words!
The way is beyond language,
for in it there is
no yesterday
no tomorrow
no today.

Discourses on the Faith Mind; or,
The Book of Nothing (hsin hsin ming)

VIRGIL
    (70–19 BCE)
Time bears away all things—even our
minds.

Eclogues

253

⊛ OLD TESTAMENT

To every thing there is a season, and a
time to every purpose under the
heaven:

A time to be born, and a time to die; a
time to plant, and a time to pluck
up that which is planted;

A time to kill, and a time to heal; a time
to break down, and a time to build
up;

A time to weep, and a time to laugh; a
time to mourn, and a time to dance;

A time to cast away stones, and a time
to gather stones together; a time to
embrace, and a time to refrain from
embracing;

A time to get, and a time to lose; a time
to keep, and a time to cast away;

A time to rend, and a time to sew; a
time to keep silence, and a time to
speak;

A time to love, and a time to hate; a
time of war, and a time of peace.

What profit hath he that worketh in
that wherein he laboureth?

I have seen the travail, which God hath
given to the sons of men to be
exercised in it.

He hath made every thing beautiful in
his time: also he hath set the world
in their heart, so that no man can
find out the work that God maketh
from the beginning to the end.

I know that there is no good in them,
but for a man to rejoice, and to do
good in is life.

And also that every man should eat and
drink, and enjoy the good of all his
labor, it is the gift of God.

I know that, whatsoever God doeth, it
shall be for ever: nothing can be
put to it, nor any thing taken from
it; and God doeth it, that men
should fear before him.

That which hath been is now; and that
which is to be hath already been;
and God requireth that which is
past.

And moreover I saw under the sun the
place of judgment, that wickedness
was there; and the place of
righteousness, that iniquity was
there.

I said in mine heart, God shall judge
the righteous and the wicked; for
there is a time for every purpose
and for every work.

I said in mine heart concerning the
estate of the sons of men, that God
might manifest them, and that they
might see that they themselves are
beasts.

For that which befalleth the sons of
men befalleth beasts; even one
thing befalleth them: as the one
dieth, so dieth the other; yea, they
have all one breath; so that a man
hath no preeminence above a beast;
for all is vanity.

All go unto one place; all are of the
dust, and all turn to dust again.

Who knoweth the spirit of man that
goeth upward, and the spirit of the
beast that goeth downward to the
earth?

Wherefore I perceive that there is
nothing better, than that a man
should rejoice in his own works;
that that is his portion: for who
shall bring him to see what shall be
after him?

Ecclesiastes 3

⊛ PLOTINUS
(205–270)

Time was not yet; . . . it lay . . . merged
in the eternally Existent and motionless

with It. But an active principle there . . . stirred from the rest; . . . for the One contained an unquiet faculty, . . . and it could not bear to retain within itself all the dense fullness of its possession.

Like a seed at rest, the nature-principle within, unfolding outwards, makes its way towards what appears a multiple life. It was Unity self-contained, but now, in going forth from Itself, It fritters Its unity away; It advances to a lesser greatness.

Enneads

⚜ HUANG-PO
(800–850)
Beginningless time and the present moment are the same . . . You have only to understand that time has no real existence.

The Zen Teaching of Huang-po

⚜ OMAR KHAYYAM
(D. 1123)
Ah, fill the cup: what boots it to repeat
how time is slipping underneath our feet:
Unborn tomorrow and dead yesterday,
Why fret about them if today be sweet!
One moment in annihilation's waste,
One moment, of the well of life to taste—
The stars are setting and the caravan
Starts for the Dawn of Nothing—Oh, make haste!

Rubaiyat

⚜ MEISTER ECKHART
(1260–1327)
It is an obvious fact that time affects neither God nor the soul. Did time touch the soul she would not be the soul. If God were affected by time he would not be God. Further, if time could touch the soul, then God could not be born in her. The soul wherein God is born must have escaped from time, and time must have dropped away from her.

Meditations

⚜ WILLIAM SHAKESPEARE
(1564–1616)
To-morrow, and to-morrow, and to-morrow,
Creeps in this petty pace from day to day
To the last syllable of recorded time,
And all our yesterdays have lighted fools
The way to dusty death. Out, out, brief candle!
Life's but a walking shadow, a poor player,
That struts and frets his hour upon the stage,
And then is heard no more; it is a tale
Told by an idiot, full of sound and fury,
Signifying nothing.

Macbeth

⚜ MATSUO BASHO
(1644–1694)
The months and days are the travellers of eternity. The years that come and go are also voyagers. . . . I too for years past have been stirred by the sight of a solitary cloud drifting with the wind to ceaseless thoughts of roaming.

The Narrow Road to the Deep North

❈ THOMAS CARLYLE
(1795–1881)

In the midst of winter, I finally learned that there was in me an invincible summer.

On the Choice of Books

❈ RUDOLF STEINER
(1861–1925)

Thus there are these two streams, one from the past and one from the future, which come together in the soul—will anyone who observes himself deny that?

Metamorphoses of the Soul

❈ J. KRISHNAMURTI
(1895–1986)

In the now is all time, and to understand the now is to be free of time. Becoming is the continuation of time, of sorrow. Becoming does not contain being. Being is always in the present, and being is the highest form of transformation.

Commentaries on Living—from the Notebooks of J. Krishnamurti

❈ WEI WU WEI (TERENCE GRAY)
(1895–1986)

It was true before he said it, it is true at this moment, and it will be true forever, for there is no time.

Open Secret

❈ ARTHUR BRYANT (WYNNE MORGAN)
(1899–1985)

Rightly conceived, time is the friend of all who are in any way in adversity, for its mazy road winds in and out of the shadows sooner or later into sunshine, and when one is at its darkest point one can be certain that presently it will grow brighter.

The Spirit of England

❈ THICH NHAT HANH
(CONTEMPORARY)

The Buddha turned to the community and said, "Bhikkus, I will explain what true self-sufficiency is and what is the better way to live alone. A self-sufficient person is a person who dwells in mindfulness. He is aware of what is going on in the present moment, what is going on in his body, feelings, mind, and objects of mind. He knows how to look deeply at things in the present moment. He does not pursue the past nor lose himself in the future, because the past no longer is and the future has not yet come. Life can only take place in the present moment. If we lose the present moment, we lose life. This is the better way to live alone."

Old Path White Clouds: The Life Story of the Buddha

❈ MARIE-LOUISE VON FRANZ
(CONTEMPORARY)

In man's original point of view time was life itself and its divine mystery.

Time: Rhythm and Repose

Truth

THE UPANISHADS
(C. 900–600 BCE)

The Person of a thumb in size
within one's very self abides;
The Lord of past and of future,
from Him, when once he's known,
    none hides
This verily is That.

Katha Upanishad

CONFUCIUS
(551–479 BCE)

Confucius said, "Truth may not depart
from human nature. If what is regarded
as truth departs from human nature, it
may not be regarded as truth."

The Aphorisms of Confucius, VI,
"Humanism and True Manhood"

BUDDHA
(563–483 BCE)

Have confidence in the truth, although
you may not be able to comprehend it,
although you may suppose its sweetness
to be bitter, although you may shrink
from it at first. Trust in the Truth. . . .
Have faith in the Truth and live it.

Dhammapada

MENANDER
(C. 342–292 BCE)

The truth sometimes not sought for
comes forth to the light.

The Questions of Milinda

SARAHA
(1ST OR 2ND CENTURY)

When the deluded in a mirror look
They see a face, not a reflection.
So the mind that has truth denied
Relies on that which is not true.

The Royal Song of Saraha

HAKIM ABU' L-MAJD
MAJDUD SANAI OF GHAZNA
(HAKIM SANAI)
(12TH CENTURY)

When Bayazid said, "Glory unto me!"
he did not speak in ignorance or folly;
and the tongue that uttered that final
    secret
moved truly when announcing, "I am
    God."
When Mansur tried to teach the pack
the secret that the face had taught him,
it turned hangman and destroyed him;

his secret's daylight then became
pitch darkness.
Yet it was God's own word that he
spoke;
and when in the crowd he suddenly
disclosed
the forbidden secret, his outer form
was given to the gallows; but the friend
took his inner being to himself;
and when his life could speak no more,
his heart's blood still disclosed the
secret.
[Bayazid and Mansur were Sufi
masters]

The Walled Garden of Truth

☸ MARTIN LUTHER
(1483–1546)
Here I stand, I cannot do otherwise.

Speech, Diet of Worms, 1521

☸ MICHEL DE MONTAIGNE
(1533–1592)
But truth is so great a thing that we
ought not to despise any medium that
will conduct us to it.

Essays

[Truth] must be loved for its own sake. A
man who speaks the truth because he is
in some way compelled or for his own
advantage, and who is not afraid to tell a
lie when it is of no importance to anyone, is not truthful enough. My soul
naturally shuns a lie, and hates even the
thought of one. I feel an inward shame
and a sharp remorse if an untruth happens to escape me—as sometimes it does
if the occasion is unexpected, and I am
taken unawares.

Essays

☸ FRANCIS BACON
(1561–1626)
There are and can be only two ways
of searching into and discovering
truth. The one flies from the senses
and particulars to the most general
axioms . . . this way is now in fashion.
The other derives axioms from the
senses and particulars, rising by a
gradual and unbroken ascent, so that it
arrives at the most general axioms last of
all. This is the true way but as yet
untried.

Novum Organum

Be so true to thyself, as thou be not false
to others.

"Of Wisdom for a Man's Self," in *Essays*

☸ SIR ISAAC NEWTON
(1642–1727)
I do not know what I may appear to the
world, but to myself I seem to have been
a boy playing on the seashore, and
diverting myself in now and then finding
a smoother pebble, or a prettier shell
than ordinary, whilst the great ocean of
truth lay all undiscovered before me.

Letters

☸ CHARLOTTE LENNOX
(1720–1804)
The only Excellence of Falsehood . . . is
its Resemblance to Truth.

Arabella; or, The Female Quixote

☸ HENRY DAVID THOREAU
(1817–1862)
It takes two to speak the truth,—one to
speak, and another to hear.

Spoken

FRIEDRICH WILHELM NIETZSCHE

(1844–1900)

Now in the beginning, these two Mainyu [the twin aspects of the human mind] revealed themselves in thought, word, and deed as the Better and the Bad; and, from these two, the wise chose aright, but not so the unwise.

And thus, when these two Mainyu first came together, they generated life and the absence of life, and so shall human existence continue till the end of time: The worst life for the Followers of the lie, but the supreme beatific vision for the Followers of Truth.

Songs of Zarathustra

OSCAR WILDE

(1854–1900)

The truth is rarely pure, and never simple.

Letters

RABINDRANATH TAGORE

(1861–1941)

We have come to look upon life as a conflict with death—the intruding enemy, not the natural ending—in impotent quarrel with which we spend every stage of it. When the time comes for youth to depart, we would hold it back by main force. When the fervour of desire slackens, we would revive it with fresh fuel of our own devising. When our sense organs weaken, we urge them to keep up their efforts. Even when our grip has relaxed we are reluctant to give up possession. We are not trained to recognise the inevitable as natural, and so cannot give up gracefully that which has to go, but needs must wait till it is snatched from us. The truth comes as conqueror only because we have lost the art of receiving it as guest.

The Four Stages of Life

EMILY POST

(1873–1960)

To tell a lie in cowardice, to tell a lie for gain, or to avoid deserved punishment—are all the blackest of black lies. On the other hand, to teach him to try his best to avoid the truth—even to press it when necessary toward the outer edge of the rainbow—for a reason of kindness, or of mercy, is far closer to the heart of truth than to repeat something accurately and mercilessly that will cruelly hurt the feelings of someone.

Children Are People

HERMANN HESSE

(1877–1962)

A truth can only be expressed and enveloped in words if it is one-sided. Everything that is thought and expressed in words is one-sided, only half the truth; it all lacks totality, completeness, unity. When the Illustrious Buddha taught about the world, he had to divide it into Sansara and Nirvana, into illusion and truth, into suffering and salvation. One cannot do otherwise, there is no other method for those who teach. But the world itself, being in and around us, is never one-sided. Never is a man or a deed wholly Sansara or wholly Nirvana; never is a man wholly a saint or a sinner.

Siddhartha

J. KRISHNAMURTI
(1895–1986)

Truth is a pathless land and you cannot approach it by any path whatsoever.

Commentaries on Living—from the
Notebooks of J. Krishnamurti

Truth cannot be repeated.

Commentaries on Living—from the
Notebooks of J. Krishnamurti

There is no path to truth. Truth must be discovered, but there is no formula for its discovery. What is formulated is not true. You must set out on the uncharted sea, and the uncharted sea is yourself.

Commentaries on Living—from the
Notebooks of J. Krishnamurti

ALBERT CAMUS
(1913–1960)

I have never seen anyone die for the ontological argument. Galileo who held a scientific truth of great importance abjured it with the greatest ease as soon as it endangered his life. In a certain sense, he did right.

The Myth of Sisyphus

OSHO
(1931–1990)

When you argue, you assert. Assertion is violence, aggression, and the truth cannot be known by an aggressive mind, the truth cannot be discovered by violence.

Discourses

HUBERT BENOIT
(CONTEMPORARY)

Do not try to find the truth,
Merely cease to cherish opinions,
Tarry not in dualism.

Inscribed on the believing mind as quoted
by Hubert Benoit in *The Supreme Doctrine*

THICH NHAT HANH
(CONTEMPORARY)

The Buddha spoke gently, "Once a person is caught by belief in a doctrine, he loses all his freedom. When one becomes dogmatic, he believes his doctrine is the only truth and that all other doctrines are heresy. Disputes and conflicts all arise from narrow views. They can extend endlessly, wasting precious time and sometimes even leading to war. Attachment to views is the greatest impediment to the spiritual path. Bound to narrow views, one becomes so entangled that it is no longer possible to let the door of truth open.

Old Path White Clouds: The Life
Story of the Buddha

YATRI
(CONTEMPORARY)

Truth is a non-transferable ticket which only bears one name.

Unknown Man

Understanding

⊛ THE UPANISHADS
(c. 900–600 bce)

But he who has no understanding,
aye mindful, full of stains,
Never reaches that abode,
only repeated birth obtains.
But he who is with understanding,
ever mindful, free from stain,
Verily reaches that abode
From which he is not born again.

Katha Upanishad

⊛ BUDDHA
(563–483 bce)

It is easy to see the faults of others,
but difficult to see one's own faults.
One shows the faults of others like
chaff winnowed in the wind,
but one conceals one's own faults as a
cunning gambler conceals his dice.

The Dhammapada

⊛ CONFUCIUS
(551–479 bce)

Confucius said, "The superior man understands what is right; the inferior man understands what will sell."

The Aphorisms of Confucius, VII, "The Superior Man and The Inferior Man"

⊛ DEMOSTHENES
(c. 384–322 bce)

You cannot have a proud and chivalrous spirit if your conduct is mean and paltry; for whatever a man's actions are, such must be his spirit.

Third Olynthiac

⊛ MENCIUS
(372–289 bce)

Never has a man who has bent himself been able to make others straight.

Book III

The path of duty lies in what is near, and man seeks for it in what is remote.

Book IV

⊛ ST. AUGUSTINE
(354–430)

God is not what you imagine or what you think you understand. If you understand you have failed.

Quoted in The Soul: An Archeology, Claudia Setzer

❂ SÖREN KIERKEGAARD
(1813–1855)

Life can only be understood backwards, but it must be lived forwards.

Life

❂ MINNIE LOUISE HASKINS
(1875–1957)

And I said to a man who stood at the gate of the year:

"Give me a light that I may tread safely into the unknown."

And he replied: "Go out into the darkness and put your hand into the hand of God. That shall be to you better than a light, and safer than a known way."

The Desert

❂ KAHLIL GIBRAN
(1883–1931)

Your neighbour is your other self dwelling behind a wall. In understanding, all walls shall fall down.

Who knows but that your neighbour is your better self wearing another body? See that you love him as you would love yourself.

He too is a manifestation of the Most High, whom you do not know.

Jesus, The Son of Man: His Words and His Deeds as Told and Recorded by Those Who Knew Him

❂ D. H. LAWRENCE
(1885–1930)

I know I am compound of two waves, I, who am temporal and mortal. When I am timeless and absolute, all duality has vanished. But whilst I am temporal and mortal, I am framed in the struggle and embrace of the two opposite waves of darkness and of light.

Phoenix II

❂ LUSIN
(D. 1936)

When you talk with famous scholars, the best thing is to pretend that occasionally you do not quite understand them. If you understand too little, you will be despised; if you understand too much, you will be disliked; if you just fail occasionally to understand them, you will suit each other very well.

The Epigrams of Lusin

People hate Buddhist monks and nuns, Mohammedans and Christians, but no one hates a Taoist. To understand the reason for this is to understand half of China.

The Epigrams of Lusin

❂ J. KRISHNAMURTI
(1895–1986)

If we can really understand the problem, the answer will come out of it, because the answer is not separate from the problem.

The Penguin Krishnamurti Reader

Ignorance is the lack of self-awareness; and knowledge is ignorance when there is no understanding of the ways of the self. Understanding of the self is freedom from knowledge.

Commentaries on Living—from the Notebooks of J. Krishnamurti

To understand intellectually is not to understand at all.

Commentaries on Living—from the Notebooks of J. Krishnamurti

❀ WEI WU WEI (TERENCE GRAY)
(1895–1986)

There is no need to read books, chant Sutras, recite Scriptures, perform any antics; there is nothing whatever to discuss, argue about, or explain.

There is nothing whatever to teach or to be learned.

Every living (sentient) being knows this and is free to become aware of it and to "live" it.

Open Secret

❀ OSHO
(1931–1990)

Life is always moving into the unknown, and you are afraid. You want life to go according to your mind, according to the known, but life cannot follow you. It always moves into the unknown. That is why we are afraid of life, and whenever we get any chance we try to fix it because with the fixed, prediction is possible.

Discourses

❀ DA FREE JOHN (ADIDA)
(CONTEMPORARY)

The man of understanding is not entranced. He is not elsewhere. He is not having an experience. He is not passionless and inoffensive. He is awake. He is present. He knows no obstruction in the form of mind, identity, differentiation and desire. He is passionate. His quality is an offence to those who are entranced, elsewhere, contained in the mechanics of experience, asleep, living as various forms of identity.

Enlightenment of the Whole Body

❀ U. G. KRISHNAMURTI
(CONTEMPORARY)

When once you have understood that there is nothing to understand, what is there to communicate? Communication is just not necessary, so there is no point in discussing the possibility of communication. Your desire to communicate is part of your general strategy of achievement. Veiled behind that desire for communication is the dependency upon some outside power to solve your problems for you.

Mind Is a Myth—Disquieting Conversations with a Man Called U. G.

❀ RUSSELL SCHWEICHART
(CONTEMPORARY)

You become startlingly aware how artificial are the thousands of boundaries we've created to separate and define. And for the first time in your life you feel in your gut the precious unity of the earth and of all living things it supports. The dissonance between this unity you see and the separateness of human groupings that you know exist is starkly apparent.

On return from an Apollo mission

263

Virtue

❂ ANONYMOUS

Go placidly amid the noise and haste and remember what peace there may be in silence.

As far as possible without surrender be on good terms with all persons.

Speak your truth quietly and clearly and listen to others, even the dull and ignorant; they too have their story.

Avoid loud and aggressive persons, they are vexations to the spirit.

If you compare yourself with others, you may become vain and bitter for always there will be greater and lesser persons than yourself. Enjoy your achievements as well as your plans.

Keep interested in your own career, however humble; it is a real possession in the changing fortunes of time.

Exercise caution in your business affairs; for the world is full of trickery.

But let this not blind you to what virtue there is; many persons strive for high ideals; and everywhere life is full of heroism.

Be careful.

Strive to be happy.

Desiderata

❂ ANCIENT BABYLONIA (SUMERIAN)

(INSCRIBED C. 650 BCE)

Slander not, but speak kindness;
Speak not evil, but show good will;
Who slanders and speaks evil—
Unto him will Shamash requite it
    by . . . his head.
Open not wide thy mouth, guard thy
    lips;
If thou art provoked, speak not at once;
If thou speakest hastily, thou shalt
    afterwards have to atone therefor;
Soothe (rather) thy spirit with silence.
Offer daily unto thy god
Sacrifice, prayer, the incense most meet
    (for the Deity):
Before thy god shalt thou have a heart
    of purity.

Ethical fragment

❂ LAO-TZU

(C. 6TH CENTURY BCE)

Do nondoing, strive for nonstriving, savor the flavourless, regard the small as important, make much of little, repay enmity with virtue; plan for difficulty when it is still easy, do the great while it is still small.

The most difficult things in the world must be done while they are easy; the greatest things in the world must be done while they are small.

Tao Te Ching

Superior virtue is not conscious of itself as virtue, and so really is virtue. Inferior virtue cannot let go of being virtuous, and so is not virtue. Superior virtue does not seem to be busy, and yet there is nothing which it does not accomplish. Inferior virtue is always busy, and yet in the end leaves things undone.

Tao Te Ching

Be humble and you will remain entire. The sage does not display himself, therefore he shines. He does not approve himself therefore he is noted. He does not praise himself, therefore he has merit. He does not glory in himself, therefore he excels.

Tao Te Ching

The best [man] is like water.

Water is good; it benefits all things and does not compete with them.

It dwells in [lowly] places that all disdain.

This is why it is so near to Tao.

Tao Te Ching

❂ CONFUCIUS

(551–479 BCE)

The firm, the enduring, the simple, and the modest are near to virtue.

Analects

❂ AESOP

(C. 550 BCE)

No act of kindness, no matter how small, is ever wasted.

The Lion and the Mouse

❂ MENCIUS

(372–289 BCE)

Benevolence is the tranquil habitation of man, and righteousness is his straight path.

Book IV

Sincerity is the way of heaven.

Book IV

Water indeed will flow indifferently to the east or west, but will it flow indifferently up or down? The tendency of man's nature to good is like the tendency of water to flow downwards. There are none but have this tendency to good, just as all water flows downwards.

Book VI

Benevolence is man's mind and righteousness is man's path.

Book VI

❂ OLD TESTAMENT

Can we find such a one as this is, a man in whom the Spirit of God is?

Genesis 41:38

Whatsoever things are true, whatsoever things are honest, whatsoever things are just, whatsoever things are pure, whatsoever things are lovely, whatsoever things are of good report; if there be any virtue, and if there be any praise, think of these things.

Philippians 4:8

❀ ST. AUGUSTINE
(354–430)

O Lord, help me to be pure, but not yet.

Confessions

❀ HUI HAI
(750–810)

Q: What are the ten evils and the ten virtues?

A: The ten evils are killing, stealing, licentiousness, lying, voluptuous speech, slander, coarse language, covetousness, anger and false views. The ten virtues may be simply defined as absence of the ten evils.

The Zen Teachings of Hui Hai

❀ HROSWITHA OF GANDERSHEIM
(C. 935–1000)

I know that it is as wrong to deny a divine gift as to pretend falsely that we have received it.

Untitled

❀ ST. FRANCIS OF ASSISI
(C. 1181–1226)

Where there is charity and wisdom,
there is neither fear nor ignorance.
Where there is patience and humility,
there is neither anger nor vexation.
Where there is poverty and joy,
there is neither greed nor avarice.
Where there is peace and meditation,
there is neither anxiety nor doubt.

The Counsels of the Holy Father St. Francis, Admonition 27

Lord
Make me an instrument of your
    peace.
Where there is hatred let me sow love;
Where there is injury, pardon;
Where there is doubt, faith;
Where there is despair, hope;
Where there is darkness, light; and
Where there is sadness, joy.
O divine Master,
grant that I may not so much
Seek to be consoled as to console;
To be understood as to understand;
To be loved as to love;
For it is in giving that we receive;
It is in pardoning that we are pardoned;
and
It is in dying that we are born to
    eternal life.

Prayer attributed to St. Francis of Assisi

❀ JAMI
(1414–1492)

Never preen yourself
that you are prideless:
for pride is more invisible
than an ant's footprint
on a black stone
in the dark of night.

The Abode of Spring

❋ JOHN MILTON
(1608–1674)

I cannot praise a fugitive and cloistered virtue, unexercised and unbreathed, that never sallies out and sees her adversary, but slinks out of the race, where that immortal garland is to be run for, not without dust and heat.

Areopagitica

❋ SAMUEL BUTLER
(1612–1680)

Absolute virtue is as sure to kill a man as absolute vice is, let alone the dullness of it and the pomposities of it.

Notebooks

❋ MOLIÈRE
(1622–1673)

I prefer an accommodating vice to an obstinate virtue.

Amphitryon

❋ ROBERT BURNS
(1759–1796)

The upright, honest-hearted man Who strives to do the best he can, Need never fear the church's ban Or hell's damnation.

Epistle to the Rev. John McMath

❋ ADAM LINDSAY GORDON
(1833–1870)

Life is mostly froth and bubble, Two things stand like stone, Kindness in another's trouble, Courage in your own.

Ye Wearie Wayfarer

❋ RUDYARD KIPLING
(1865–1936)

If you can keep your head when all about you
Are losing theirs and blaming it on you.
If you can trust yourself when all men doubt you
And make allowance for their doubting, too.

If

❋ MOHANDAS K. GANDHI
(1869–1948)

I am not a visionary. I claim to be a practical idealist. The religion of non-violence is not meant merely for the rishis [holy men] and saints. It is meant for the common people as well. Non-violence is the law of our species as violence is the law of the brute. The spirit lies dormant in the brute and he knows no law but that of physical might. The dignity of man requires obedience to a higher law—the strength of the spirit. . . . Non-violence in its dynamic condition means conscious suffering. It does not mean meek submission to the will of the evil-doer, but it means the pitting of one's whole soul against the will of the tyrant. Working under this law of our being, it is possible for a single individual to defy the whole might of an unjust empire to save his honor, his religion, his soul and lay the foundation for that empire's fall or its regeneration.

"Statements on Non-violence,"
published in *Young India*

❀ Hazrat Inayat Khan
(1882–1927)

Virtues are virtues because they give joy once they are practised. If a virtue does not give joy, it is not a virtue.

The Sufi Message of Hazrat Inayat Khan:
The Art of Personality

Consideration is the greatest of all virtues, for in consideration all virtues are born. Veneration for God, courtesy towards others, respect of those who deserve it, kindness to those who are weak and feeble, sympathy with those who need it, all these come from consideration.

The Sufi Message of Hazrat Inayat Khan:
The Art of Personality

❀ Osho
(1931–1990)

The question is not of finding in your thoughts what is right and what is wrong, in your actions what is right and what is wrong. The question is of finding a consciousness so total and so intense that only whatever is right remains, and whatever is false burns out. You don't have to decide.

Discourses

Vision

QUINTUS ENNIS
(239–169 BCE)

No one regards what is before his feet; we all gaze at the stars.

De Divinatione

OLD TESTAMENT

Eyes have they, but they see not.

Psalms 115:5

NEW TESTAMENT

For now we see through a glass, darkly; but then face to face: now I know in part; but then shall I know even as also I am known.

I Corinthians 13:12

We look not at the things which are seen, but at the things which are not seen: for the things which are seen are temporal; but the things which are not seen are eternal.

II Corinthians 4:18

SHANKARA
(788–820)

When the vision of Reality comes, the veil of ignorance is completely removed. As long as we perceive things falsely, our false perception distracts us and makes us miserable. When our false perception is corrected, misery ends also.

Crest-Jewel of Discrimination

KABIR
(1440?–1518)

I sell mirrors in the city of the blind.

The One Hundred Poems of Kabir

MACHIAVELLI
(1469–1527)

All armed prophets have been victorious, and all unarmed prophets have been destroyed.

The Prince

MIRA BAI
(1450–1547)

She drinks the honey of her vision.

Devotional Poems

HAYYIM VITAL
(1543–1620)

One Sabbath morning I was preaching to the congregation in Jerusalem. Rachel, the sister of Rabbi Judah Mishnan, was present. She told me that during the whole of my sermon there was a pillar of fire above my head and

Elijah of blessed memory was there at my right hand to support me, and then when I had finished they both departed.

Book of Visions

❁ WILLIAM SHAKESPEARE
(1564–1616)

It adds a precious seeing to the eye.

Love's Labour's Lost, IV, 3, 332

Argus, all eyes and no sight.

Troilus and Cressida, I, 2, 20

❁ WILLIAM BLAKE
(1757–1827)

A fool sees not the same tree that a wise man sees.

The Marriage of Heaven and Hell

❁ FREDERICK LANGBRIDGE
(1849–1923)

Two men look out through the same bars: One sees the mud, and one the stars.

Cluster of Quiet Thoughts

❁ OSCAR WILDE
(1854–1900)

We are all in the gutter, but some of us are looking at the stars.

Lady Windermere's Fan

❁ SIGMUND FREUD
(1856–1939)

When the wayfarer whistles in the dark, he may be disavowing his timidity, but he does not see any the more clearly for doing so.

The Problem of Anxiety

❁ YOGASWAMI
(1872–1964)

It is not a question of analysing yourself. It is a question of seeing yourself.

Positive Thoughts for Daily Meditation

❁ WILL ROGERS
(1879–1935)

The fellow that can only see a week ahead is always the popular fellow, for he is looking with the crowd. But the one that can see years ahead, he has a telescope but he can't make anybody believe that he has it.

The Autobiography of Will Rogers

❁ EDWARD DE BONO
(CONTEMPORARY)

A vision sets direction for thinking and action.

Lateral Thinking

Wisdom

ANONYMOUS

I planted the seed of holy words
in this world.
When long since the palmtree will have
    died,
the rock decayed;
When long since the shining monarchs
have been blown away like rotted
    leaves:
Through every deluge a thousand arks
will carry my word:
It will prevail!

Source unknown, but attributed to "an old sage"
in Wilhelm Reich's *Listen, Little Man!*

ANCIENT CHINESE

(DATE UNKNOWN)
Honour Him, Honour Him
The revealed God.
. . . .
I am still young,
An inexperienced fool,
But day by day
I strive aloft towards wisdom's light.
Help me to bear the burden,
Show me life's revelation

Chinese sacrificial ode

THE UPANISHADS

(C. 900–600 BCE)
The wise, who knows That One hidden
in the cave of the heart as God, is
    liberated
From the fetters of joy and sorrow.
A mortal having realized through
    discrimination the subtle-Self
    (Immortal Spirit)
rejoices, because he has obtained that
    which is the Source of all joy.

Katha Upanishad

LAO-TZU

(C. 6TH CENTURY BCE)
A wise man has no extensive knowledge
He who has extensive knowledge is not
    a wise man.
The sage does not accumulate for
    himself.
The more he uses for others, the more
    he has himself.
The more he uses for others, the more
    he has himself.
The more he gives to others, the more
    he possesses of his own.
The Way of Heaven is to benefit others
    and not to injury.
The Way of the sage is to act but not
    to compete.

Tao Te Ching

273

Knowledge studies others,
Wisdom is self-known.

The Way of Life

☸ CONFUCIUS

(551–479 BCE)

"How dare I allow myself to be taken as sage and humane!," he said. "It may rather be said of me that I strive to become such without ceasing."

Analects

☸ THE BHAGAVAD GITA

(500? BCE)

Even as all waters flow into the ocean, but the ocean never overflows, even so the sage feels desires, but he is ever one in his infinite peace.

Humility, unostentatiousness, non-
    injuring,
Forgiveness, simplicity, purity,
    steadfastness,
Self-control; this is declared to be
    wisdom;
What is opposed to this is ignorance.

Book of Daily Thoughts and Prayers

☸ CHUANG TZU

(369–286 BCE)

For sacrifices to the River God, neither bulls with white foreheads, nor pigs with high snouts, nor men suffering from piles, can be used. This is known to all the soothsayers, for these are regarded as inauspicious. The wise, however, would regard them as extremely auspicious.

This Human World

☸ THE APOCRYPHA

(OLD TESTAMENT TEXTS,

NOT INCLUDED IN THE BIBLE)

Wisdom will not enter a shifty soul, nor make her home in a body that is mortgaged to sin. This holy spirit of discipline will have nothing to do with falsehood; she cannot stay in the presence of unreason, and will throw up her case at the approach of injustice. Wisdom is a spirit devoted to man's good.

The Wisdom of Solomon

Do not stray from the path of life and so court death; do not draw disaster on yourselves by your own actions. For God did not make death, and takes no pleasure in the destruction of any living thing; he created all things that they might have being. The creative forces of the world make for life; there is no deadly poison in them. Death is not king on earth, for justice is immortal.

The Wisdom of Solomon

They said to themselves in their deluded way: "Our life is short and full of trouble, and when a man comes to his end there is no remedy; no man was ever known to return from the grave. By mere chance were we born, and afterwards we shall be as though we had never been, for the breath in our nostrils is but a wisp of smoke; our reason is a mere spark kept alive by the beating of our hearts, and when that goes out, our body will turn to ashes and the breath of our life disperse like empty air. Our names will be forgotten with the passing of time, and no one will remember anything we did. Our life will blow over like the last vestige of a cloud, and as a mist is chased away by the sun's rays and overborne by its heat, so will it too be dispersed. A passing shadow—such is our life, and there is no postponement of our end; man's fate is sealed, and none returns. Come then, let us enjoy the good things while we can, and make full use of the creation, with all the eagerness of youth. Let us have costly wines and perfumes to our heart's content, and let no flower of spring escape us. Let us crown ourselves with rosebuds before they can wither. Let none of us miss his share of the good things that are ours; who cares what traces our revelry leaves behind? This is the life for us; it is our birthright.

"Down with the poor and honest man! Let us tread him under foot; let us show no mercy to the widow and no reverence to the grey hairs of old age. For us let might be right! Weakness is proved to be good for nothing. Let us lay a trap for the just man; he stands in our way, a check to us at every turn; he girds at us as law-breakers, and calls us traitors to our upbringing. He knows God, so he says; he styles himself 'the servant of the Lord.' He is a living condemnation of all our ideas. The very sight of him is an affliction to us, because his life is not like other people's, and his ways are different. He rejects us like base coin, and avoids us and our ways as if we were filth; he says that the just die happy, and boasts that God is his father. Let us test the truth of his words, let us see what will happen to him in the end; for if the just man is God's son, God will stretch out a hand to him and save him from the clutches of his enemies. Outrage and torment are the means to try him with, to measure his forbearance and learn how long his patience lasts. Let us condemn him to a shameful death, for on his own showing he will have a protector."

So they argued, and very wrong they were; blinded by their own malevolence, they did not understand God's hidden plan; they never expected that holiness of life would have its recompense; they thought that innocence had no reward. But God created man for immortality and made him the image of his own eternal self; it was the devil's spite that brought death into the world, and the experience of it is reserved for those who take his side.

The Wisdom of Solomon

I called for help, and there came to me a spirit of wisdom. I valued her above sceptre and throne, and reckoned riches as nothing beside her; I counted no precious stone her equal, because all the gold in the world compared with her is but a little sand, and silver worth no more than clay. I loved her more than health and beauty; I preferred her to the light of day; for her radiance is unsleeping. So all good things together came to me with her, and in her hands was wealth past counting; and all was mine to enjoy, for all follows where wisdom leads, and I was in ignorance before, that she is the beginning of it all. What I learnt with pure intention I now share without grudging, nor do I hoard for myself the wealth that comes from her. She is an inexhaustible treasure for mankind, and those who profit by it become God's friends, commended to him by the gifts they derive from her instruction.

The Wisdom of Solomon

Wisdom concealed and treasure
    hidden—
what is the use of either?
Better a man who hides his folly
than one who hides his wisdom!

Ecclesiasticus

Speak, if you are old—it is your
    privilege—
but come to the point and do not
    interrupt the music.
Where entertainment is provided, do
    not keep up a stream of talk;
it is the wrong time to show off your
    wisdom.

Ecclesiasticus

THE GEMARA
(c. 500)
The highest wisdom is kindness.

The Talmud

SUTRA KRITANGA
(c. 500)
This is the quintessence of wisdom: not to kill anything.

HUANG-PO
(800–850)
The foolish reject what they see, not what they think; the wise reject what they think, not what they see. . . . Observe things as they are and don't pay attention to other people.

The Zen Teaching of Huang-po

NICHOLAS OF CUSA
(1401–1464)
Wisdom in shining in all things invites us, with a certain foretaste of its effects, to be borne to its effects, to be borne to it with a wonderful desire. For life itself is an intellectual Spirit, having in itself a certain innate foretaste through which it searches with great desire for the very Font of its own life.

On Learned Ignorance

MARGUERITE OF NAVARRE
(1492–1549)
Man is wise . . . when he recognizes no greater enemy than himself.

The Heptameron; or, Novels of the Queen of Navarre

Fools live longer than the wise, unless someone kills them . . . for . . . fools do not dissemble their passions. If they are angry they strike; if they are merry they laugh; but those who deem themselves wise hide their defects with so much care that their hearts are all poisoned with them.

The Heptameron; or, Novels of the Queen of Navarre

CATHERINE WILLOUGHBY
(1519?–1580)
Undoubtedly the greatest wisdom is not to be too wise.

Letter to William Cecil

THE BOOK OF COMMON PRAYER
(1549)
The fear of the Lord is the beginning of wisdom.

✺ MR. TUT-TUT
(17TH CENTURY)

Personal talent coupled with a slow temper becomes great talent; wisdom coupled with a pacifist mind becomes true wisdom.

One Hundred Proverbs

✺ EDWARD YOUNG
(1683–1765)

Be wise with speed;
A fool at forty is a fool indeed.

Night Thoughts

✺ MARY WORTLEY MONTAGU
(1689–1762)

People are never so near playing the fool as when they think themselves wise.

Letter to Countess of Bute

✺ SHNEUR ZALMAN OF LIADY
(1747–1813)

The middle course [to reach perfection] is attainable by every individual; each person should try to reach it. A person who pursues the middle course does not despise the evil, which depends on the heart, and the times are not always conducive to such sentiments. But such a person is called on to depart from evil and do good through his behaviour, in deed, word and thought. . . . Therefore, let him delight in God, praised be he, by contemplating the greatness of the Eternal to the full extent of his capacities. Even though he recognises that he will not reach this to its ultimate depth, but only by approximation, it is incumbent upon him to do what he can.

Tanya

✺ JOHN RUSKIN
(1819–1900)

And be sure also, if the author is worth anything, that you will not get at his meaning all at once—nay, that at his whole meaning you will not for a long time arrive in any wise. Not that he does not say what he means, and in strong words too; but he cannot say it all and what is more strange, will not, but in a hidden way and in parable, in order that he may be sure you want it. I cannot see quite the reason of this, nor analyze that cruel reticence in the breasts of wise men which makes them always hide their deeper thought. They do not give it by way of help, but of reward, and will make themselves sure that you deserve it before they allow you to reach it.

Handwritten on front page of
All and Everything, G. I. Gurdjieff

✺ LAURENCE HOPE
(1865–1904)

For this is wisdom: to love, to live,
To take what Fate, or the Gods, may
give.

"The Teak Forest," in *India's Love Lyrics*

✺ LIN-CHI
(1915–1973)

In Buddhism there is no place for using effort. Just be ordinary and nothing special. Eat your food, move your bowels, pass water, and when you're tired go and lie down. The ignorant will laugh at me, but the wise will understand.

Quoted in *This Is IT and Other Essays on Zen and Spiritual Experience*, Alan Watts

⊛ Z'EV BEN SHIMON HALEVI

(CONTEMPORARY)

All complete religions have two faces. The outer facet takes the form of words and public ritual, while the inner aspect is the internal, often an oral instruction which is passed on from teacher to pupil, who face to face have a personal rapport in which the Master knows what and when it can be taught to further the disciple's development. When the pupil becomes a master in his own right he in turn imparts his own wisdom and understanding to the next generation; so that without a break a Tradition may be carried on over several thousand years, without a trace of its outward appearance.

The Tree of Life

World

❈ HOPI PROPHECY

The emergence of the future fifth world has begun. You can read this in the earth itself.

Plant forms from previous worlds have begun to spring up as seeds. . . . the same kinds of seeds are being planted in the sky as stars. The same kinds of seeds are being planted in our hearts. All these are the same, depending on how you look at them. This is what makes the emergence to the next, fifth world.

❈ PTAH-HOTEP

(C. 2600 BCE)

If thou art powerful, respect knowledge and calmness of language. Command only to direct; to be absolute is to run into evil. Let not thy heart be haughty, neither let it be mean. Do not let thy orders remain unsaid and cause thy answers to penetrate; but speak without heat, assume a serious countenance. As for the vivacity of an ardent heart, temper it; the gentle man penetrates all obstacles. He who agitates himself all the day long has not a good moment; and he who amuses himself all the day long keeps not his fortune.

The Book of Ptah-hotep, translated in The Sacred Books and Early Literature of the East

❈ THE UPANISHADS

(C. 900–600 BCE)

Now indeed there are three worlds—the world of men, the world of the ancestors, the world of the gods. This world of men here is to be gained only by a son and by no other means, the world of the ancestors by rites, the world of the gods by meditation. The world of the gods verily is the best of the worlds, therefore they praise meditation.

Brhad Upanishad

❈ HOMERIC HYMN

(7TH CENTURY BCE)

I will sing of well-founded Gaia, Mother of All, eldest of all beings, she feeds all creatures that are in the world, all that go upon the goodly land and all that are in the paths of the sea, and all that fly: these are fed of her store.

❈ LAO-TZU

(C. 6TH CENTURY BCE)

The utility of a house depends on the empty spaces. Thus, while the existence of things may be good, it is the non-existent in them which makes them serviceable.

Tao Te Ching

Those who would take over the earth
And shape it to their will
Never, I notice, succeed.
The earth is like a vessel so sacred
That at the mere approach of the
    profane it is marred.
They reach out their fingers and it is
    gone.

Tao Te Ching

My daily activities are not different,
Only I am naturally in harmony with
    them.
Taking nothing, renouncing nothing,
In every circumstance no hindrance, no
    conflict.
Drawing water, carrying firewood,
This is supernatural power, this the
    marvelous activity.

Tao Te Ching

Put away holiness, throw away knowledge:
thus the people will profit a hundredfold.
Put away morality, throw away duty: thus
the people will return to filial duty and
love. Put away skillfulness, throw away
gain, and there will no longer be thieves
and robbers. In these three things beautiful appearance is not enough. Therefore take care that men have something
to hold on to. Show simplicity, hold fast
to honesty! Give up learnedness! Thus
you shall become free of sorrows.

Tao Te Ching

If all on earth acknowledge the beautiful
as beautiful then thereby the ugly is
already posited. If all on earth acknowledge the good as good then thereby is
the non-good already posited. For
existence and non-existence generate
each other. Heavy and light complete
each other. Long and short shape each

other. Before and after follow each
other. Thus also is the Man of Calling,
He dwells in effectiveness without
action. He practises teaching without
talking. All beings emerge and he does
not refuse himself to them. He gener-
ates and yet possesses nothing. He is
effective and keeps nothing. When the
work is done he does not dwell with it.
And just because he does not dwell he
remains undeserted.

Tao Te Ching

⊛ THE BHAGAVAD GITA
(500? BCE)

Whenever there is a withering of the
Law and an uprising of lawlessness on all
sides, then I manifest Myself. For the
salvation of the righteous and the
destruction of such as do evil, I come to
birth age after age.

Krishna to Arjuna as quoted in
The Soul: An Archeology, Claudia Setzer

⊛ TRIPITAKA
(BUDDHIST SCRIPTURES)
(500 BCE–1 CE)

There are seven ages, each of which is
separated from the previous one by a
world catastrophe.

Visud-dhi-Magga

⊛ MOTSE
(C. 468–401 BCE)

Wu Matse said to Motse: "For all the
righteousness that you do, men do not
help you and ghosts [spirits] do not bless
you. Yet you keep on doing it. You must
be demented." Motse said: "Suppose
you have here two employees. One of

them works when he sees you but will not work when he does not see you. The other one works whether he sees you or not. Which of the two would you value?" Wu Matse said that he would value him that worked whether he saw him or not. Motse then said: "Then you are valuing him who is demented."

Keng Chu

⊛ OLD TESTAMENT

Do not rejoice when your enemy falls,
    and let not your heart be glad
    when he stumbles.

Proverbs 24:17

⊛ APOCRYPHA

(OLD TESTAMENT TEXTS NOT INCLUDED IN THE BIBLE)

Hear then, you Kings, take this to heart; learn your lesson, lords of the wide world; lend your ears, you rulers of the multitude, whose pride is in the myriads of your people. It is the Lord who gave you your authority; your power comes from the Most High.

Wisdom of Solomon

⊛ NEW TESTAMENT

But I say to you, Love your enemies and pray for those who persecute you, so that you may be sons of your Father who is in heaven; for he makes his sun rise on the evil and on the good, and sends rain on the just and on the unjust.

Matthew 5:44–45

If thou wilt be perfect, go and sell all that thou hast, and give to the poor, and thou shalt have treasure in heaven: and come and follow me.

Matthew 19:21

⊛ NEW TESTAMENT

(LOST BOOKS)

Jesus said: He who is near me is near the fire, and he who is far from me is far from the kingdom.

His disciples said to him: On what day does the kingdom come?

Jesus said: It does not come when it is expected. They will not say, Lo, here! Or Lo, there! But the kingdom of the Father is spread out upon the earth, and men do not see it.

The Secret Sayings of Jesus According to the Gospel of Thomas

⊛ THE KORAN

(7TH CENTURY)

In the creation of the heavens and the earth; in the alternation of night and day; in the ships that sail the ocean with cargoes beneficial to man; in the water which God sends down from the sky and with which He revives the earth after its death, dispersing over it all manner of beasts, in the disposal of the winds, and in the clouds that are driven between sky and earth: surely in these there are signs for rational men.

⊛ RABI'A AL-ADAWIYYA

(717–809)

I spun some yarn to sell for food
And sold it for two silver coins.
I put a coin in each hand
Because I was afraid
That if I put both together in one hand
This great pile of wealth might hold
    me back.

Doorkeeper of the Heart

One day Rabi'a was sick,
And so her holy friends came to visit
    her, sent by her bedside,
And began putting down the world.
"You must be pretty interested in this
    'world,'" said Rabi'a, "otherwise—
    you wouldn't talk about it so much:
"Whoever breaks the merchandise
"Has to have bought it first."

Doorkeeper of the Heart

⊛ DEVARA DASIMAYYA
(10TH CENTURY)

Whatever It was
That made this earth
the base,
the world its life,
the wind its pillar,
arranged the lotus and the moon,
and covered it all with folds
of sky
with Itself inside.
To that Mystery
indifferent to differences,
to It I pray,
O Ramanatha.

Speaking of Siva

⊛ HÉLOISE
(C. 1098–1164)

Riches and power are but gifts of blind
fate, whereas goodness is the result of
one's own merits.

Letters

⊛ FARID UD-DIN ATTAR
(1120?–1193?)

This love is not divine; it is mere greed
For flesh—an animal, instinctive need.

How long then will you seek for beauty
    here?
Seek the unseen, and beauty will appear

The Conference of the Birds

⊛ JALAL AL-DIN RUMI
(1207–1273)

Know, my son, that this whole world is a
pitcher filled to the brim with wisdom
and beauty. The world is a single drop of
the Tigris [a river of present-day Iraq] of
God's beauty which on account of its
fullness cannot be contained within any
vessel.

Tales of the Masnavi

⊛ JAMI
(1414–1492)

Justice without religion is better for the
order of the universe than the tyranny of
a pious prince.

The Abode of Spring

⊛ MARTIN LUTHER
(1483–1546)

War is the greatest plague that can afflict
humanity; it destroys religion, it
destroys states, it destroys families. Any
scourge is preferable to it.

Table Talk

⊛ MR. TUT-TUT
(17TH? CENTURY)

All the universe is an inn; search not
specially for a retreat of peace: all the
people are your relatives; expect therefore troubles from them.

One Hundred Proverbs

✸ SIR WILLIAM JONES
(1746–1794)

My opinion is that power should always be distrusted, in whatever hands it is placed.

Letters

✸ WILLIAM BLAKE
(1757–1827)

He who loves his enemies betrays his friends; this surely is not what Jesus meant.

The Everlasting Gospel

✸ CHIEF SEATTLE
(1786–1866)

Whatever befalls the Earth befalls the sons of the Earth. Man does not weave the web of life, he is merely a strand in it. Whatever he does to the web he does to himself.

His address, 1853

✸ RALPH WALDO EMERSON
(1803–1882)

For every thing you have missed, you have gained something else; and for every thing you gain, you lose something else.

Nature

✸ ALEXIS DE TOCQUEVILLE
(1805–1859)

America is a land of wonders, in which everything is in constant motion and every change seems an improvement. . . . No natural boundary seems to be set to the efforts of man; and in his eyes, what is not yet done is only what he has not yet attempted to do.

Democracy in America

✸ HENRY WADSWORTH LONGFELLOW
(1807–1882)

If we could read the secret history of our enemies, we should find in each man's life sorrow and suffering enough to disarm all hostility.

Driftwood

✸ THE SHIVAPURI BABA
(1826–1963)

All the things in this universe, men, and materials, all nature and its different phenomena, are simply bewildering. We cannot make out what they are. The reality behind them, the secret of secrets is quite hidden to our view and, as it were, hermetically sealed.

Quoted in Long Pilgrimage, *J. G. Bennett*

Q: Does the world grow and degenerate periodically? Why do people build and destroy what they build—even civilisations?

S.B.: Everything we build must be discharged and rebuilt. This is a periodical process. Every 100 years some change takes place. Every 1,000 years some great change. Every 2,000 years the end of an epoch. Every 6,000 years a major disaster to civilisation. Every 12,000 years a complete change. We are now at the end of a 6,000 year cycle.

Q: Will the destruction you foresee be localised?

S.B.: No. It will be everywhere. In cities and villages. Something will be left behind to carry on this world with people have who have sensed and seen the results of material living.

Q: How does one prepare for this? Not escape this—but prepare for this?

S.B.: There is only one way. Begin to do your duty now. And meditate on the meaning of one's life.

Quoted in Long Pilgrimage, J. G. Bennett

⊛ SHRI RAMAKRISHNA
(1836–1886)

This very world is a mansion of mirth; here I can eat, here drink and make merry.

Meditations

⊛ E. A. WALLIS BUDGE
(1857–1934)

The [Ancient] Egyptian believed that every word spoken under certain circumstances must be followed by some effect, good or bad; a prayer uttered by a properly qualified person, or by a man ceremonially pure, in the proper place, and in the proper manner, must necessarily be answered favourably; and similarly the curses which were pronounced upon a man, or beast, or thing, in the name of a hostile supernatural being were bound to result in harm to the object cursed. This idea had its origin in the belief that the world and all that therein is came into being immediately after Thoth [a god] had interpreted in words the will of the deity, in respect of the creation of the world, and that creation was the result of the god's command.

Translation of The Egyptian Book of the Dead

⊛ A. E. HOUSMAN
(1859–1936)

I, a stranger and afraid
In a world I never made.

Last Poems

⊛ MARIE CURIE
(1867–1934)

You cannot hope to build a better world without improving the individuals. To that end each of us must work for his own improvement, and at the same time share a general responsibility for all humanity, our particular duty being to aid those to whom we think we can be most useful.

Pierre Curie

⊛ BERTRAND RUSSELL
(1872–1970)

The secret of happiness is to face the fact that the world is horrible, horrible, "horrible."

Quoted in Bertrand Russell:
The Passionate Sceptic, Alan Wood

⊛ YOGASWAMI
(1872–1964)

If you catch hold of the cat by its tail, it will bite you. The world will do the same. Live in the world like water on a lotus leaf.

Positive Thoughts for Daily Meditation

⦾ PIERRE TEILHARD DE CHARDIN
(1881–1955)

True enough, there are days when the world appears to be one vast chaos. Great, indeed, is the confusion; so great that if we look at ourselves we may very well reel with dizziness at the prospect of our very existence. With such heavy odds against us, is it not most improbable that we should find ourselves whole and entire, and living—as single individuals, let alone as two? We wonder, then, whether true wisdom may not consist in holding on to every chance that comes our way, and immediately drawing all we can from it. It would be madness, surely, to take any further risk with the future and to strive after a life that is even more improbable because even more elevated.

For years now, Jean, my work has been such that every day of my life has necessarily been lived under the shadow of the improbability of life's successes. And once again it is this improbability which I meet today when I look at the happiness of both of you together.

Three Wedding Addresses

I imagine that when Mankind has understood *en bloc* that it is sealed in upon itself and that in all the world (if not in the heavens) there is only itself on which it can rely to save itself (experimentally, I need hardly say) it will first feel a great thrill of charity vibrate in the fabric of its being—There are times when, in a sudden flash, we see what treasures of goodness towards his fellow man lie hidden in the heart of man. But these treasures are nearly always locked up, so that what we know of society is hardly more than its conflicts and tyrannies: the men of today live as chance dictates, they do not seek one another out nor love one another. . . . If the pressure of an undeniable necessity could succeed in overcoming our mutual repulsions and in breaking the barrier of ice which isolates each one of us, who can judge what well-being and what tenderness would not emerge form the harmony of such vast numbers?—When men feel that they are really alone in the world, then (unless they tear one another to pieces) they will begin to love one another.

Moreover, I like to think, instead of withdrawing into despairing inactivity, they will see how fruitless and chaotic has been the work to which they have so far applied themselves.—Even in this century, men are still living as chance circumstances decide for them, with no aim but their daily bread or a quiet old age. You can count the few who fall under the spell of a task that far exceeds the dimensions of their individual lives. . . . At this very moment we are being given a glimpse of what a *national effort* can mean. Even so, unless adult Mankind is to drift aimlessly and so perish, it is essential that it rise to the concept of a specifically and integrally *human effort*. After having for so long done no more than allow itself to live, Mankind will one day understand that the time has come to undertake its own development and to mark out its own road.

The Great Monad

⊛ NIKOS KAZANTZAKIS
(1885–1957)

You have seen what happens when you hold a glass out to the sun and concentrate all the rays onto one spot, Zorba? That spot soon catches fire, doesn't it? Why? Because the sun's power has not been dispersed but concentrated on that one spot. It is the same with men's minds. You do miracles, if you concentrate your mind on one thing and only one.

Zorba the Greek

⊛ D. H. LAWRENCE
(1885–1930)

Debacles [such as war or violent revolution] don't save men. In nearly every case, during the horrors of a catastrophe the light of integrity and human pride is extinguished in the soul of the man or the woman involved, and there is left a painful, unmanned creature, a thing of shame, incapable any more. It is the great danger of debacles, especially in times of unbelief like these. Men lack the faith and courage to keep their souls alert, kindled and unbroken. Afterwards there is a great smouldering of shamed life.

Phoenix II

I know that, first and foremost, we must be sensitive to life and to its movements. If there is power, it must be sensitive power.

Phoenix II

⊛ T. S. ELIOT
(1888–1965)

I must tell you that I should really like to think there's something wrong with me.

Because, if there isn't, then there's something wrong with the world itself—and that's much more frightening!

Letters

⊛ MIKHAIL NAIMY
(1889–1988)

Yours is a world divided 'gainst itself, because the "I" in your is so divided. Yours is a world of barriers and fences, because the "I" in your is one of barriers and fences. Some things it would fence out as alien to itself. Some things it would fence in as kindred to itself. Yet that outside the fence is ever breaking in; and that within the fence is ever breaking out.

The Book of Mirdad

⊛ RICHARD BUCKMINSTER FULLER
(1895–1983)

I am a passenger on the spaceship, Earth.

Operating Manual for Spaceship Earth

⊛ J. KRISHNAMURTI
(1895–1986)

If you find the garden that you have so carefully cultivated has produced only poisonous weeds, you have to tear them out by the roots; you have to pull down the walls that have sheltered them. You may or may not do it, for you have extensive gardens, cunningly walled-in and well-guarded . . . but it must be done, for to die rich is to have lived in vain.

Notebooks

Self-expansion in any form, whether through wealth or through virtue, is a process of conflict, causing antagonism and confusion.

Commentaries on Living—from the Notebooks of J. Krishnamurti

PHYLLIS MCGINLEY
(1905–1978)

We live in the century of the Appeal . . . . One applauds the industry of professional philanthropy. But it has its dangers. After a while the private heart begins to harden. We fling letters into the wastebasket, are abrupt to telephone solicitations. Charity withers in the incessant gale.

Aspects of Sanctity

ALAN WATTS
(1915–1973)

Money is a way of measuring wealth but is not wealth in itself. A chest of gold coins or a fat wallet of bills is of no use whatsoever to a wrecked sailor alone on a raft.

The Book—On the Taboo Against Knowing Who You Are

For there is a growing apprehension that existence is a rat-race in a trap: living organisms, including people, are merely tubes which put things in one end and let them out at the other, which both keeps them doing it and in the long run wears them out. So to keep the force going, the tubes find ways of making new tubes, which also put things in at one end and let them out at the other. At the input end they even develop ganglia of nerves called brains, with eyes and ears, so that they can more easily scrounge around for things to swallow. As and when they get enough to eat, they use up their surplus energy by wiggling in complicated patterns, making all sorts of noises by blowing air in and out of the input hole, and gathering together in groups to fight with other groups. In time the tube grows such an abundance of attached appliances that they are hardly recognisable as mere tubes, and they manage to do this in a staggering variety of forms. There is a vague rule not to eat tubes of your own form, but in general there is serious competition as to who is going to be the top type of tube.

The Book—On the Taboo Against Knowing Who You Are

We do not "come into" this world; we come *out* of it, as leaves from a tree. As the ocean "waves," the universe "peoples." Every individual is an expression of the whole realm of nature, a unique action of the total universe. This fact is rarely, if ever, experienced by most individuals. Even those who know it to be true in theory do not sense or feel it, but continue to be aware of themselves as isolated "egos" inside bags of skin.

The Book—On the Taboo Against Knowing Who You Are

JOHN F. KENNEDY
(1917–1963)

The supreme reality of our time is . . . the vulnerability of our planet.

Speech, June 28, 1963

✸ PAOLO SOLERI
(1919–1989)

It is only logical that the pauperization of our soul and the soul of society coincide with the pauperization of the environment. One is the cause and the reflection of the other.

Quoted in The Soul, An Archeology,
Claudia Setzer

✸ JOHN COLLIER
(1928–1971)

They had what the world has lost: the ancient, lost reverence and passion for human personality joined with ancient, lost reverence and passion for the earth and its web of life. Since before the Stone Age they have tended that passion as a central, sacred fire. It should be our long hope to renew it in us all.

Speech

✸ OSHO
(1931–1990)

All the religions of the world teach charity, service, giving. But look at the world they have created—there is neither any charity nor any service nor any giving. They have used beautiful words, but their beautiful words are like the words of a blind man who is talking about light.

Discourses

Merit should be decisive, not the power of votes. And the meritorious should be invited because the meritorious are not the ones who are going to beg for votes. A man of merit has a certain dignity. Politicians don't have any dignity. They are beggars.

Discourses

The degree of attachment decreases as the field of attachment spreads.

Discourses

Stopping the world is the whole art of meditation. And to live in the moment is to live in eternity. To taste the moment with no idea, with no mind, is to taste immortality.

The Orange Book

✸ STOCKHOLM CONFERENCE
(1972)

We have forgotten how to be good guests, how to walk lightly on the earth as its other creatures do.

Only One Earth

✸ THE ECONOMIST
(1995)

Doomsday is a grave event. One does not simply reschedule it, therefore, without a good explanation.

November 18–24, 1995

✸ DOUGLAS ADAMS
(CONTEMPORARY)

There is a theory which states that if ever anybody discovers exactly what the universe is for and why it is here, it will instantly disappear and be replaced by something even more bizarre and inexplicable.

There is another theory which states that this has already happened.

The Hitchhiker's Guide to the Galaxy

✺ CARLOS CASTANEDA

(CONTEMPORARY)

This is a weird world. . . . The forces that guide men are unpredictable, awesome, yet their splendour is something to witness.

Journey to Ixtlan

✺ LAWRENCE DURRELL

(CONTEMPORARY)

We are the children of our landscape.

Justine

✺ MARILYN FERGUSON

(CONTEMPORARY)

We have had a profound paradigm shift about the Whole Earth. We know it now as a jewel in space, a fragile water planet. And we have seen that it has no natural borders. It is not the globe of our school days with its many colored nations.

The Aquarian Conspiracy

✺ ROLLO MAY

(CONTEMPORARY)

I need my enemy in my community. He keeps me alert, vital. . . . But beyond what we specifically learn from our enemies, we need them emotionally; our psychic economy cannot get along well without them. . . . [O]ur enemy is as necessary for us as is our friend. Both together are part of authentic community.

Power and Innocence

✺ THOMAS MOORE

(CONTEMPORARY)

I think we would be able to live in this world more peaceably if our spirituality were to come from looking not just into infinity but very closely at the world around us—and appreciating its depth and divinity.

Quoted in *Embracing the Everyday: Handbook for the Soul*, eds. Richard Carlson and Benjamin Shield

✺ CHET RAYMO

(CONTEMPORARY)

The silence of the stars is the silence of creation and re-creation.

The Soul of the Night

✺ SOGYAL RINPOCHE

(CONTEMPORARY)

The [Buddhist] master knows that if people believe in a life after this one, their whole outlook on life will be different, and they will have a distinct sense of personal responsibility and morality. What the masters must suspect is that there is a danger that people who have no strong belief in a life after this one will create a society fixated on short-term results, without much thought for the consequences of their actions. Could this be the major reason why we have created a brutal world like the one in which we are now living, a world with little real compassion?

The Tibetan Book of Living and Dying

❁ SANGHARAKSHITA

(CONTEMPORARY)

For Buddhism, no less than for modern physics and psychology, all the apparently stable and solid material and mental objects in the universe are in reality temporary condensations of energy.

The Three Jewels

❁ ROGER ZELAZNY

(CONTEMPORARY)

The universe did not invent justice. Man did. Unfortunately, man must reside in the universe.

The Dream Master

Biographical Index

Abelard, Peter (1079–1142) Priory of Saint-Marcel, Burgundy (now France). French theologian best known for his original use of dialectics, also for his poetry and celebrated love affair with Héloise.

Abraham ben Samuel Abulafia, (1240–after 1292) Jewish patriarch and writer.

Abram, Morris B. (Contemporary) Journalist for *The Wall Street Journal*.

Adams, Douglas (Contemporary) Science fiction writer.

Adams, Henry Brooks (1838–1913) American historian and author.

Addison, Joseph (1672–1719) English essayist, poet, and dramatist, leading spirit in the creation of the English magazines *Tatler* and *Spectator*.

Adler, F. (1851–1933) German who emigrated to the U.S. as educator and founder of the Ethical Movement.

Aeschylus (525–456 BCE) First of the Greek classical tragic dramatists.

Aesop (c. 550 BCE) Presumed compiler of Aesop's Fables, known to be crippled and a beggar.

Allen, Woody (Contemporary) U.S. comedian, film actor, and director.

Ambrose, St. (c. 340–397) Bishop of Milan, Italy, and biblical critic.

Amenhotep IV (14th century BCE) Egyptian Pharaoh who tried to force monotheism in place of polytheism on his people. Changed his own name to Ikhn-aton after the name of his god.

Amiel, Henri Frédéric (1821–1881) Swiss writer known for his masterpiece *Journal intime*.

Andrews, Joel (Contemporary) American writer and compiler of religious and spiritual work.

Anselm, St. (1033–1109) English saint, founder of Scholasticism, a philosophical school of thought that dominated the Middle Ages.

Aquinas, St. Thomas (1224/5–1274) Italian Dominican theologian, the foremost medieval Scholasticist who formed the classical systemization for the Roman Catholic Church.

Arden, Elizabeth (1878–1966) Founder of the Arden cosmetic products.

Aristotle (384–322 BCE) Greek philosopher. Studied with Plato and taught Alexander the Great. His influence even into the present day is immense, probably because he developed such an all-encompassing system that continues to affect physics, natural science, biology, drama, metaphysics, ethics, philosophy, and logic.

Arjun (1563–1606) Indian who was fifth in the succession of Sikh gurus (teachers). He lived in Amritsar in the West Punjab, giving away all his wealth and devoting his life to religion, including doing good works (including the establishment of a leper colony). He was burned to death by the Moslem ruler of the area when he refused to accept the Moslem faith.

Asoka (c. 269–232 BCE) Last major Emperor in the Mauryan dynasty of India. Vigorously supported Buddhism.

Asquith, Margot (1864–1945) Prominent member of the English aristocratic and political family.

Assagioli, Roberto (Contemporary) Proponent of Psychosynthesis and author of *Psychosynthesis: A Manual of Principles and Techniques*.

Atisa (Dipankara) (982–1054) Indian Buddhist reformer whose teachings formed the basis for the Tibetan Bkag-dams-pa sect of Buddhism. Also taught the way of life as dream.

Augustine, St. (354–430) Born in what is now Algeria, studied and worked across the Roman Empire. A philosopher-theologian of early Christianity, more than any other he shaped and defined the problems characterizing Christian theology. His early dilemma was in the attempt to reconcile his classical education with Christianity. Later, his struggles with various Christian movements of the times emphasized the unity of Christianity rather than its division and helped forge a Christianity to survive the barbarian invasions of the 5th century and become the religion of medieval Europe.

Aurelius, Marcus (121–180) Roman writer and spiritual teacher, author of *Meditations*.

Aurobindo, Sri (1872–1950) Born in Calcutta, India, son of wealthy Bengali parents, educated at Kings College Cambridge in England. A highly evolved Yogic master.

Ba'al Shem Tov (Isael ben Eleazar) (1700–1760) Founder of Hasidic movement and miracle worker.

Bacon, Francis (1561–1626) English essayist, lawyer, statesman, and philosopher. Major influence in the philosophy of science. Began studying at Cambridge at the age of twelve and went on to become a successful politician until he was removed from office for accepting bribes.

Bancroft, Anne (Contemporary) Originally from a Quaker family, she turned to Buddhism and worked as a teacher and lecturer in America for most of her life.

Barratt, William (Contemporary) American philosopher.

Basho, Matsuo (1644–1694) Born in the city of Ueno in the province of Iga (now part of Mie Prefecture), his father was a minor samurai in the service of the Todo family that ruled the city. He studied the art of linked verse and acquired the pen name of Sobo. His most famous work is The Narrow Road to the Deep North.

Baudelaire, Charles (1821–1867) French poet attacked in his time for obscenity and blasphemy. He died unrecognized, many of his works unpublished.

Bayly, T. H. (1797–1839) Writer and creator of the famous line, "Absence makes the heart grow fonder."

Bazin, René (1853–1932) Influential French novelist of provincial life and love of nature.

Beatles, The British rock group performing during the 1960s. Band members included John Lennon, Ringo Starr, Paul McCartney, and George Harrison.

Beaumarchais, Pierre-Augustin de (1732–1799) French author of outstanding comedies of intrigue: *The Barber of Seville* and *The Marriage of Figaro*.

Beecher, Henry Ward (1813–1887) Liberal U.S. congregational minister, one of the most influential Protestant spokesmen of his age.

Bennett, Alan (Contemporary) U.K. dramatist and author, one of the founding members of the British comedy series, *Beyond the Fringe*.

Bennett, William (Contemporary) American author.

Benoit, Hubert (Contemporary) French philosopher and first to elaborate what came to be called process philosophy, which rejected static values and expounded change and movement in all things.

Berenson, Bernard (1865–1959) U.S. art critic, especially of Italian Renaissance art. One of the great spiritual thinkers of this century.

Bergson, Henry (1859–1941) Author of *The Supreme Doctrine*.

Bernard, St. (1091–1153) French Cistercian monk and mystic, founder of the abbey of Clairvaux.

Besant, Annie (1847–1933) British social reformer and Theosophist.

Bhagavad Gita, The (500? BCE) A poem from the Mahabharata. One of the most widely studied sacred writings of Hinduism.

Bierce, Ambrose (1842–1914) American newspaper man, wit, satirist, and short-story writer, whose life ended in an unsolved mystery rather similar to his stories.

Bird, Christopher (Contemporary) American biologist.

Blackwell, Elizabeth (1821–1910) First woman physician in the United States.

Blake, William (1757–1827) Visionary English poet and artist, precursor of English Romanticism.

Blavatsky, H. B. (1831–1891) Russian Theosophist.

Bly, Robert (Contemporary) Poet, storyteller, translator, and lecturer. Author of *Iron John*, a major bestseller that started the men's movement in America in the early 1990s.

Boethius (470?–524) Roman scholar, Christian philosopher, and statesman.

Bogan, Louise (1897–1970) Poet and literary critic who served as poetry critic for the *New Yorker* from 1931 to 1969.

Bohm, David (Contemporary) Scientist and teacher.

Böhme, Jakob (1575–1624) German peasant who was said to have had visions even as a child. After traveling as a cobbler and returning to his home town to marry the butcher's daughter, his great illumination took place at the age of twenty while he was gazing at a polished pewter dish reflecting the sun's rays. He wrote several books that brought him both a reputation among Germany's scholars and accusations of heresy for which he was sent to trial in Dresden. There the chief theologians of the day were deeply impressed by his piety and earnestness and refused to uphold the charge.

Boleyn, Anne (1507–1536) Queen of England, mother of Elizabeth I, and second wife to Henry VIII.

Bonaparte, Napoleon (1791–1821) French statesman.

Boodin, John Elof (Contemporary) American writer.

Booth, Leo (Contemporary) Spiritual writer.

Borges, Jorge Luis (1899–1986) Argentine poet and short-story writer.

Bridges, Robert (1844–1930) English poet. Poet laureate from 1913.

Bridget of Sweden (1303–1373) Patron saint of Sweden and a mystic.

Brindley, T. H. (Contemporary) English theologian.

Brontë, Emily (1818–1848) One of the three sisters who lived together and wrote Romantic novels in England.

Brooks, Phillips (1835–1893) American Episcopal clergyman, renowned as a preacher.

Broughton, James (Contemporary) American writer and compiler of religious and spiritual work.

Browne, Lewis (Contemporary) American religious writer.

Browne, Sir Thomas (1605–1682) 17th-century English author and physician.

Browning, Robert (1812–1889) Major English poet of the Victorian age noted for his mastery of the dramatic monologue.

Bruce, Lenny (1926–1966) American comedian, noted for his harsh social criticism.

Brunton, Paul (Contemporary) American writer and theorist.

Bryant, Sir Arthur (Wynne Morgan) (1899–1985) British historian and biographer particularly noted for his biography of Samual Pepys.

Bucke, Richard (Contemporary) Author and mystic.

Buddha, Gautama (563–483 BCE) One of the greatest mystics of all time, born into Indian royal family in Sakya Republic, Kosala Kingdom, India. Founder of the Buddhist religion and philosophy. Buddha is a title meaning "the awakened one."

Budge, E. A. Wallis (1857–1934) Orientalist and curator of Egyptian and Assyrian antiquities at the British Museum, London.

Buñuel, Luis (1900–1983) Spanish director and filmmaker, noted especially for his early surrealist films.

Burke, Edmund (1729–1797) British statesman and political thinker.

Burne-Jones, Edwin (1833–1898) Leading English Romantic painter and designer.

Burns, Robert (1759–1796) National poet of Scotland, also famous for his rebellion against orthodox religion.

Burton, Robert (1577–1640) English mathematician, astrologer, and scholar. Author of "Anatomy of Melancholy" under a pseudonym.

Buson, Yosa (1715–1783) Japanese poet and philosopher.

Butler, Katy (Contemporary) American feminist writer.

Butler, Samuel (1612–1680) English poet and satirist, famous as author of *Hudibras*, one of the most memorable burlesque poems in the English language.

Byron, Lord George Gordon (1788–1824) English Romantic poet and satirist whose poetry and romantic personality captured the imagination of Europe. Friends with Percy and Mary Shelley, and other famous writers of the 19th century.

Cage, John (1912–1992) American composer whose work profoundly influenced mid–20th-century music.

Campbell, Joseph (1904–1987) Brilliant American theorist, writer, and lecturer. Interested in mythology since childhood, he expressed human behavior through mythological storytelling.

Camus, Albert (1913–1960) Algerian-born novelist and essayist. Won the Nobel Prize for Literature in 1957. Somewhat against his will, became a leading moral voice of his generation during the 1950s.

Cardozo, Benjamin (1870–1938) American jurist, common law judge, and legal essayist.

Carlyle, Thomas (1795–1881) British historian and essayist.

Carnegie, Dale (1888–1955) American lecturer, author, and teacher who worked as a pioneer in the art of public speaking and the psychology of the successful personality.

Carrington, Dora (1872–1941 Twentieth century artist and socialite.

Carver, Raymond (1939–1988) American author.

Castaneda, Carlos (Contemporary) While a graduate in anthropology at the University of California at Los Angeles, Castaneda was gathering medicinal herbs used by the Indians in Sonora, Mexico, when he met the old Yaqui Indian, don Juan. His books on the subject of this master's teachings include *The Teachings of Don Juan, A Separate Reality, Journey to Ixtlan, Tales of Power, The Second Ring of Power,* and *The Eagle's Gift.*

Cather, Willa (1873–1947) American novelist noted for her stories of frontier life on the American plains.

Catherine of Genoa (1447–1510) Italian mystic admired for her work among the poor.

Catherine of Siena (1347–1380) Dominican tertiary mystic and patron saint of Italy.

Cavell, Edith (1865–1915) English nurse who became a popular heroine in World War I. She was executed for assisting Allied soldiers to escape from German-occupied Belgium.

Céline (1894–1961) Pseudonym of Louis-Ferdinand Destouches, French writer and physician. Became famous as a novelist.

Chamfort, Sébastien R. N. (1740–1794) French playwright and conversationalist, famous for his wit during the French Revolution.

Chanel, Coco (1883–1971) French fashion designer.

Charles, Ray (Contemporary) Popular jazz and blues singer.

Chaucer, Geoffrey (1340?–1400) British author and poet whose work, *The Canterbury Tales,* is among the greatest classics of history.

Chesterfield, Earl of (Philip Dormer Stanhope) (1694–1773) British statesman, diplomat, and wit, chiefly remembered for his *Letters to His Son* and *Letters to His Godson.*

Chesterton, G. K. (1874–1936) English critic and author of verse, essays, novels, and short stories. Known also for his exuberant nature and rotund figure.

Chia Tao (777–841) Spiritual poet of the T'ang dynasty in China.

Chopra, Deepak (Contemporary) Trained in India and the United States, Chopra (M.D.) practices endocrinology and is a Fellow of the American College of Physicians. His books include *Creating Health*, *Return of the Rishi*, *Quantum Healing*, *Unconditional Life*, and *Perfect Health*.

Chuang Tzu (369–286 BCE) Chinese thinker. Founder (with Lao-tzu) of Taoism—the Way of Nature. Chose personal freedom over premiership. Freedom is a key issue in his philosophy.

Churchill, Winston (1874–1965) British statesman and prime minister who brought the British people to victory over Hitler and Nazi Germany during World War II. Also a writer, artist, and orator.

Cicero, Marcus Tullius (106–43 BCE) Roman statesman and author.

Clark, Sir Kenneth (1903–1983) British art historian and leading authority on Italian Renaissance art.

Clement of Alexandria (150–211) Christian apologist and missionary theologian to the Hellenistic world.

Climacus, St. John (525–600) Byzantine monk and author of *The Ladder of Divine Ascent*.

Clinton, Elizabeth (1574–1630?) English aristocrat and author.

Cohn-Sherbok, Rabbi Professor Dan (Contemporary) Jewish professor and author in the United Kingdom.

Coklin, Edwin Grant (Contemporary) American author.

Coleridge, Mary (1861–1907) Author and poet.

Coleridge, Samuel Taylor (1772–1834) British poet, critic, and philosopher. Author of *The Rime of the Ancient Mariner.*

Colette (1873–1954) One of the greatest French writers of the first half of the 20th century, whose novels dealt with the pains of love.

Collier, John (1928–1971) Onetime United States Commissioner of Indian Affairs.

Confucius (551–479 BCE) Chinese sage who founded Confucianism. The sayings of Confucius were later gathered into the Analects.

Congreve, William (1670–1729) English neo-classical dramatist who shaped the English comedy of manners.

Connolly, Cyril (1903–1974) English critic, novelist, and founding editor of *Horizon* magazine.

Conroy, Pat (Contemporary) American novelist considered to be one of the greatest writers of the late 20th century. Author of *The Prince of Tides* and *Beach Music*.

Cousins, Norman (Contemporary) Essayist and editor, long associated with the *Saturday Review*.

Cousteau, Jacques (Contemporary) French naval officer and ocean explorer known for his extensive undersea explorations.

Cowper, William (1731–1800) One of the most widely read English poets of his age whose most characteristic work is *The Task*.

Craighead, Meinrad (Contemporary) Born of Native American and German parentage. She had a Roman Catholic upbringing and works as a teacher and writer.

Curie, Marie (1867–1934) Scientist.

Da Free John (Adida) (Contemporary) Franklin Albert Jones was born on Long Island in 1939. It is claimed that he was born enlightened, and by the 1960s he began experiencing psychic phenomena. While staying in the ashram of Swami Muktananda he reached higher states of spiritual awakening and is said to have seen an apparition of the Virgin Mary. He then assumed the name of Bubba Free John and then Da Free John and finally Love Ananda, each name celebrating new stages of his rise to full enlightenment. He lives on an island in Fiji with close friends and devotees.

Darrow, Clarence (1857–1938) Lawyer, whose work in dramatic criminal trials earned him a place in U.S. legal history.

Dasimayya, Devara (10th century) Poet and mystic.

Davi Kopenawa Tanomami (Contemporary) Chief of a Brazilian Yanomami tribe.

Davies, Paul (Contemporary) Scientist and author, particularly interested in popular science subjects.

Davies, William Henry (1871–1940) English poet of particular wit and simplicity, uncharacteristic during his lifetime.

de Bono, Edward (Contemporary) Author and advisor to British industry. Famous for his creation of the concept of *Lateral Thinking*.

Declaration of Independence, The (1776) The formal statement, written by Thomas Jefferson and adopted July 4, 1776, by the Second Continental Congress, declaring the thirteen American colonies free and independent of Great Britain.

Deffand, Marie Anne du (1697–1780) Woman of letters and leading female figure in French society.

Defoe, Daniel (1661?–1731) English novelist, pamphleteer, journalist, and author, whose most famous work was *Robinson Crusoe*.

Demosthenes (c. 384–322 BCE) Athenian statesman and one of the greatest of Greek orators.

Descartes, René (1596–1650) French philosopher and mathematician. Sometimes called the founder of modern philosophy. Developed the method of systematic doubt. Sought to provide a conceptual foundation for the new mechanical physics based on the Copernican system.

Dhammapada (3rd century BCE) Buddhist text.

D'Holbach, Baron (Contemporary) French commentator and writer.

Dickens, Charles (1812–1870) One of the greatest English writers of all time.

Dickinson, Emily (1830–1886) One of the foremost American poets of the 19th century. Hailed as perhaps the best female poet since Sappho (see separate entry).

Dionysius Exiguus (c. 6th century) Roman monk and Christian theologian, born in Scythia. He is believed to have introduced the current system of numbering years on the basis of the Christian era.

Disraeli, Benjamin (1804–1881) British politician, prime minister, and wit.

Dodge, Mabel (1879–1962) American writer and patron of the arts.

Donne, John (1572–1631) Most outstanding of the English Metaphysical poets. A churchman who became Dean of St. Paul's Cathedral. Famous for mixture of wit and seriousness in his poetry.

Dostoyevsky, Fyodor (1821–1881) Russian novelist, journalist, and short-story writer of the greatest influence.

Dryden, John (1631–1700) British poet, dramatist, and literary critic who was so important in his day that it became known as the Age of Dryden.

D'Souza, Fr. Alfred (Contemporary) Roman Catholic priest, writer, and spiritual theorist.

Dubuffet, Jean (1901–1985) French printer, sculptor and print maker, best known for his development of art brut or raw art.

Duncan, Isadora (1878–1927) Popular entertainer, dancer, author, and feminist.

Durrell, Lawrence (Contemporary) English novelist, poet, and writer of topographical books, verse plays, and farcical short stories. Widely regarded as one of the most important writers of his time.

Eckhart, Meister (1260–1327) German Dominican theologian, writer, and mystic. One of the world's greatest spiritual masters and exponents of the connection between the individual soul and God.

Eddington, Arthur (Contemporary) Scientist and popular science writer.

Eddy, Mary Baker (1821–1910) American theologian, writer, and founder of Christian Science.

Egyptian Book of the Dead, The (c. 3000 BCE) A collection of prayers, hymns, and instructions for the departing souls of the Egyptian dead, each one written and tailored for individuals, mostly of royal or higher standing. Believed to help the departing soul find the next world more easily and with more joy.

Einstein, Albert (1879–1955) American (German-born) physicist and Nobel Prize winner. Probably the most loved and celebrated scientist of the second millennium.

Eleazar ben Judah of Worms (c.1165–c.1230) One of the greatest Jewish philosophers and writers of all time.

Eliade, Mircea (1907–1986) American religious historian and researcher into symbolic languages.

Eliot, T. S. (1888–1965) British (American-born) poet, playwright, and literary critic. A leader of the modernist movement.

Ellis, Havelock (1859–1939) English essayist and physician who studied human sexuality and challenged Victorian taboos against open discussion of the subject.

Emerson, Ralph Waldo (1803–1882) American lecturer, essayist, and poet. Leading Transcendentalist.

Empedocles (490–430 BCE) Greek philosopher, poet, and religious teacher.

Enoch (3rd Century BCE–CE 3rd Century) One of the most important figures in the Old Testament.

Epic of Gilgamesh, The (c. 3rd millennium BCE) Collection of tales in the Akkadian language about Gilgamesh, the best-known of all ancient Mesopotamian heroes.

Epictetus (55–135) Greek philosopher associated with the Stoics. Began life as a slave and attained freedom but lived his life lame and in ill-health. Expelled from Rome in 90 for his beliefs.

Epicurus (341–270 BCE) Greek philosopher-founder of Epicureanism, mistakenly taken as a school of debauchery due to teachings on pleasure.

Erasmus, Desiderius (1466?–1536) Humanist and great scholar of the Northern Renaissance. First editor of the New Testament.

Euripides (485?–406? BCE) Last of the three greatest Athenian classical tragic dramatists, following Aeschylus and Sophocles.

Farid ud-Din Attar (1142–1220) Persian Sufi poet. Educated as a theologian. After traveling widely, settled in his home town but was tried for heresy and banished.

Ferguson, Marilyn (Contemporary) American writer and author of *The*

Aquarian Conspiracy, one of the most influential works in the beginning of the "New Age" movement in America.

Ferguson, Sheila (Contemporary) African-American singer and author.

Ficino, Marsilio (1433–1499) Italian philosopher, theologian, and linguist.

Fielding, Henry (1707–1754) Humorist, novelist, and social commentator.

First Book of Enoch, The (c. 168 BCE) Also called the Ethiopic Book of Enoch. A compilation of works, most of which are apocalyptic. The oldest portion is the Apocalyptic of Weeks, which was written shortly before the Maccabean uprising of 168 BCE against Rome. Other sections deal with astrology and cosmology.

Flaubert, Gustave (1821–1880) Novelist, regarded as the prime influence of the Realist school of French literature, and best known for his masterpiece, *Madame Bovary*.

Forster, E. M. (1879–1970) English novelist, essayist, and social and literary critic whose fame rests largely on the novels *Howards End* and *A Passage to India*.

Fosdick, Harry Emerson (1878–1969) Liberal Protestant minister, author, and teacher. Pastor of the interdenominational Riverside Church in New York City.

Francis of Assisi, St. (c. 1181–1226) Founder of the Franciscan orders of men and women. Leader of the church reform movements of the early 13th century within the Roman Catholic Church. Mystic and enlightened master.

Frank, Anne (1929–1945) Young Jewish girl whose diary records the years that her family spent in hiding from the Nazis during World War II.

Franz, Marie-Louise von (Contemporary) Swiss Jungian analyst, scholar, and author. Founder of the Jung Institute in Zurich.

Freud, Sigmund (1856–1939) Austrian neurologist and founder of psychoanalysis and Freudian theory.

Fulghum, Robert (Contemporary) American writer.

Fuller, Richard Buckminster (1895–1983) U.S. engineer and architect who developed the geodesic dome, the only practical kind of building that has no limiting dimensions.

Fuller, Thomas (1608–1661) British scholar, preacher, and one of the most witty and prolific authors of his time.

Galileo (1564–1642) Italian mathematician, astronomer, and physicist. Considered the founder of the experimental method.

Gandhi, Mohandas K. (1869–1948) Leader of the Indian nationalist movement against the British Empire, and considered to be the father of India.

Garcia Marquez, Gabriel (Contemporary) Probably the greatest

South American novelist of this century.

Gardiner, John W. (Contemporary) U.S. journalist and writer for the *New York Times.*

Gay, John (1685–1732) English poet and dramatist, chiefly remembered as the author of *The Beggar's Opera.*

Gemara, The (c. 500) Jewish scripture that forms part of the Talmud.

George, Henry (1839–1897) American land reformer and economist.

Gerber, William (Contemporary) Lecturer in philosophy at the University of Maryland.

al-Ghazzali (born 1058)

Gibran, Kahlil (1883–1931) Lebanese poet who emigrated to the United States. Influenced by Nietzsche, but highly religious. He was also a writer of Arabic poetry and a skillful artist.

Gide, André (1869–1951) French writer, humanist, and moralist. Received the Nobel Prize in 1947.

Gilbert, W. S. (1836–1911) English playwright and humorist.

Gilman, Charlotte Perkins (1860–1935) Leading U.S. theorist of the women's movement, author of *The Forerunner.*

Goethe, Johann Wolfgang von (1749–1832) One of Germany's greatest poets. Author of many lyric poems, plays, and novels including the epic poem "Faust." Also a statesman and scientist.

Gogh, Vincent van (1853–1890) World-famous Dutch artist and social commentator.

Gordon, Adam Lindsay (1833–1870) English poet.

Gotama Aksapada (2nd century BCE) Also known as Dirghatapas. The name Gotama is his family name, while the other name refers to his meditation practices of long penance. His background is obscure, but he is said to be the son of Rahagana and priest for the royal family of Kurusrmjaya. Mentioned in the Rig Veda, he is said to have lived on the banks of the Ganges in the town of Chapra around 550 BCE, so he is almost a contemporary of Gautama the Buddha.

Govind-Singh or **Gobind Rai Singh (1666 or 1675–1708)** Tenth and last Guru of the Sikhs.

Graham, Janet (1723?–1789) Scottish poet and author of *The History of Emily Montague.*

Graham, Martha (1894–1991) American dancer and choreographer. Founder of the Martha Graham Dance Company. Pioneer of modern dance.

Grant, Ulysses S. (1822–1885) American general and eighteenth president of the United States.

Graves, Robert (1895–1985) English poet, novelist, critic, and classical scholar. Wrote more than 120 books, including *I, Claudius*.

Greenberg, Sidney (Contemporary) Author and social comentator.

Grumback, Argula von (1492–1563?) Author of *Letter to Her cousin, Adam von Torring*.

Guevara, Marina de (c. 1510–1559) Spanish nun, burned as a heretic during the Catholic Inquisition.

Guhyasamajatantra, The Part of the fundamental elements of Tantra, which appear in the Sanatana-dharma, the eternal religion of Hinduism.

Guizot, François (1787–1874) French political figure and historian.

Gurdjieff, G. I. (1872?–1949) Born in Georgia, Russia. One of this century's most remarkable teachers, he gathered a group of disciples in revolution-torn Russia and led them out of the country through Germany and eventually to Paris in 1922. He created the Institute for the Harmonious Development of Man. After a mysterious and near-fatal road accident he devoted himself to writing his now famous series of three books under the title *All and Everything*.

Hakim Abu' L-Majd Majdud Sanai of Ghazna (Hakim Sanai) (12th century), Born Adam Sanai in Ghazna in the reign of Bahramshah (1118–1152). While still young, became one of the most learned, devout men of his age. A Sufi philosopher. The *Hadiqa* was his main contribution to Sufism,

consisting of 11,500 lines, and one of the greatest works, placing the author as one of the great trio of Sufi teachers, with 'Attari and Rumi.'

Hammarskjöld, Dag (1905–1961) Swedish economist and statesman, second secretary general to the United Nations.

Hamsun, Knut (1859–1952) Norwegian novelist, dramatist, poet, and winner of the Nobel Prize.

Harding, Douglas (Contemporary) Brilliant and absorbing British author of spiritual works.

Harris, Sydney J. (Contemporary) American writer and religious commentator.

Harris, T. George (Contemporary) Author and journalist.

Haskins, Minnie Louise (1875–1957) English educator and writer. Author of *The Desert*.

Hazlitt, William (1778–1830) English writer remembered for his essays.

Heine, Heinrich (1797–1856) German poet remembered for his *Buch der Lieder*.

Hellman, Lillian (1905–1984) American playwright and movie script writer who attacked injustice, exploitation, and selfishness in society.

Héloise (c. 1098–1164) Wife of the theologian and philosopher Peter Abelard, with whom she was involved in one of the best-known love tragedies in history.

Henry, Matthew (1662–1714) English writer and religious philosopher.

Heraclitus (c. 4th century BCE) Greek philosopher. Maintained that all things were in a state of flux and that fire was their origin. Known as the "Weeping Philosopher" because of his melancholy views on the changing character of life.

Herbert, George (1593–1633) English religious poet and metaphysical poet. Author of *The Church-Porch*.

Hesburgh, Theodore M. (Contemporary) Writer and theologian.

Hesse, Hermann (1877–1962) German novelist, poet, and winner of the Nobel Prize for Literature in 1946.

Heywood, Carter (Contemporary) Priest and spiritual writer.

Highwater, Jamake (Contemporary) Native-American commentator.

Hildegard of Bingen (1098–1179) German prophet and mystic.

Hippocrates (c. 460–357 BCE) Greek geometer who compiled the first known work on the elements of geometry nearly a century before Euclid.

Homer (c. 900 BCE) Presumed author of the *Iliad* and the *Odyssey*, two of the greatest epic poems of ancient Greece.

Hope, Laurence (1865–1904) Author.

Hopkins, Gerard Manley (1844–1889) English poet and Jesuit priest, one of the most important Victorian writers.

Housman, Alfred Edward (1859–1936) English scholar and celebrated poet.

Hroswitha of Gandersheim (c. 935–1000) The first German woman poet.

Hsueh-tou (950–1052) Japanese poet and writer of Koans.

Huai-Nan Tzu (1st century BCE) Anonymous work compiled at the court of Liu An Cd. (122 BCE) from "Sources of Chinese Tradition" edited by William Tehodore De Bary.

Huang-po (800–850) One of the greatest Chinese Zen masters; a student of the dharma and master of Lin-chi. Described as more than six feet tall with a bead-shaped protuberance on his forehead and a sonorous voice, he is said to have been of a simple character and great spiritual beauty.

Hubbard, L. Ronald (Contemporary) Founder of the Scientology movement of spiritual understanding, and science fiction author.

Hugo, Victor (1802–1885) French poet, dramatist, and novelist and later politician and political commentator.

Hui Hai (750–810) Zen teacher. Author of *The Zen Teachings of Hui Hai*.

Hungerford, Margaret (1855–1897) Irish author.

Husayn ibn Mansur al Hallaj (858–922) Persian Islamic mystic who broke away from Sufism to preach publicly, causing Sufis to criticize him for revealing secret experiences. Charged with blasphemy for his phrase "I Am the Truth." The manner of his execution gave rise to legends of resurrection similar to that of Christ.

Huxley, Aldous (1894–1963) English novelist and essayist. Coming from a distinguished literary and scientific family, he intended to study medicine, but an eye ailment almost blinded him at the age of sixteen and he turned to literature.

Huxley, Thomas Henry (1825–1895) English biologist who speculated on spiritual and philosophical subjects.

Hymns Ancient and Modern (1861) A compilation of hymns drawn from Judeo-Christian heritage, updated most recently during the Victorian era.

Ingersoll, Robert Green (1833–1899) American politician and orator known as "the great agnostic," who popularized criticism of the Bible.

Iraqi, Fakhruddin (1213–1289) Born in Persia, according to legend, was famous for his religious devotion by the age of eight, and giving lectures before he was seventeen. A Sufi who traveled throughout Persia and India, his most famous work is the *Lama'at*.

Isaac of Acco (13th–14th century) Jewish mystic.

Jalal al-Din Rumi (1207–1273) Persian mystic, teacher, and poet revered both for his spiritual teachings and poetic innovations. Founder of the Sufi order known as the Whirling Dervishes.

James, William (1842–1910) American philosopher and psychologist, a leader of the Pragmatism movement.

Jami (1414–1492) Persian scholar, mystic, and poet who is regarded by many as the last great Sufi poet. Wrote *The Abode of Spring* translated by David Pendelbury in *Four Sufi Classics*.

Jefferson, Thomas (1743–1826) Third president of the United States.

Jerome, Jerome K. (1859–1927) English novelist and playwright.

John of Damascus, St. (c. 700–c. 760) Eastern monk and theological doctor of the Greek and Latin churches.

John of the Cross, St. (1542–1591) Spanish Catholic priest, lived during the height of the Protestant Reformation's rebellion against the Catholic Church in northern Europe, though not yet in Spain. Worked with the Carmelite order. Stood only five feet in height. Works include *The Ascent of Mount Carmel*.

Johnson, Samuel (1709–1784) English poet, essayist, critic, and journalist. Regarded as one of the most important literary figures of his century.

Jones, Sir William (1746–1794) British orientalist and jurist.

Jonson, Ben (1573?–1637) English Jacobean dramatist, lyric poet, and critic.

Jowett, Benjamin (1817–1893) British classical scholar and one of the greatest teachers of the 19th century.

Joyce, James (1882–1941) Irish novelist noted for experimental writing. Most famous work is *Ulysses*.

Judah ben Samuel of Regensburg (12th century) Jewish kabbalist who lived in the Rhineland.

Juliana of Norwich (1342–1417) English mystic.

Jung, Carl Gustav (1875–1961) Austrian psychologist, theorist, philosopher, and originator of the concept of global and universal (collective) consciousness.

Juvenal (55–127) Most powerful of all Roman satiric poets, whose epigrams have entered common usage. From a well-to-do family, he became an officer in the army of the Emperor Dominitian. Wrote sixteen satiric poems entitled *The Satires*, dealing with life in Rome at that time.

Kabir (1440–1518) Indian Sufi master, born near Banaras, of Mohammedan parents, probably about 1440. Became a disciple of the Hindu ascetic Ramananda early in life. Earned his living as a weaver. Married and had a family, unlike other ascetics of the time.

Kaddish In Judaism, a hymn in praise of God, recited as part of the daily service or, in one form, a mourner's prayer.

Kafka, Franz (1883–1924) Bohemian. One of the 20th century's most influential writers. Virtually unknown in his lifetime, his works have since been recognized as symbolizing modern man's anxiety-ridden and grotesque alienation in an unintelligible, hostile, or indifferent world. Worked in a law firm and regarded writing (which he did at night) as the curse and blessing of his life.

Kandinsky, Wassily (1866–1944) Russian artist.

Kazantzakis, Nikos (1885–1957) Greek novelist.

Keats, John (1795–1821) English Romantic poet. Between the ages of eighteen and twenty-four produced some of the most powerful poetry in the English language. Died young and the myth is that he died of criticism.

Keen, Sam (Contemporary) American author.

Keller, Helen (1880–1968) Blind and deaf American author and lecturer.

Kempis, Thomas à (1380–1471) Dutch theologian, probably author of *Imitation of Christ*.

Kennedy, John F. (1917–1963) Thirty-fifth president of the United States. Assassinated in Dallas, Texas, November 22, 1963.

Kepler, Johannes (1571–1630) German astronomer who discovered the elliptical orbit of the solar system.

Kerr, Jean (Contemporary) American playwright.

Key, Ellen (1849–1926) Swedish writer and feminist.

Khan, Hazrat Inayat (1882–1927) Sufi born into a family of great musicians. Master musician at an early age and worked for revival of spiritual heritage in Indian music. Initiated into Sufism and trained in four major schools. At age twenty-eight, his training was complete and he left India for the West, lecturing extensively in Europe and the United States.

Khan, Imajat (1889–1988) Middle-Eastern Sufi philosopher.

Kierkegaard, Soren (1813–1855) Danish philosopher and theological writer.

King, Martin Luther, Jr. (1929–1968) Eloquent Baptist minister who led mass civil rights movement in the mid-1960s. Nobel Peace Prize winner, 1964. Assassinated in Memphis, Tennessee, 1968.

Kipling, Rudyard (1865-1936) English novelist short-story writer, and poet.

Kobayashi, Issa (1763–1827) Japanese poet.

Koran, The (7th century) Islamic sacred scripture.

Krishnamurti, Jiddhu (1895–1986) In 1908, at only thirteen years of age, he was "discovered" by C. W. Leadbeater and Annie Besant and declared to be the Lord Maitraya—World Teacher, or returned Buddha. In 1929, he disbanded the organization set up by the Theosophists to support this belief and spent the rest of his long life speaking to millions of people about the need to avoid religious organizations, among many other subjects. He is one of the few great "gurus" to escape the normal public anxiety of such unique beings. He was still giving discourses at the age of ninety-one.

Krishnamurti, Uppalura Gopala (1918–?) From south India. He was raised by his grandparents and educated in a highly religious background. He met Ramana Maharshi while still in his teens and asked the old sage: "Can you give me what you have?" Raman answered, "I can give you but can you take it?" Later he became the General Secretary of the Theosophical Society and met J. Krishnamurti, but left without becoming a follower. At forty-nine, while penniless, living on the streets of London, he entered what he calls "the calamity," a natural state of enlightenment. He lives between India, Switzerland, and America each year, and is little known to the West, largely because of his fundamental message: "I can't help you."

Kübler-Ross, Elisabeth (Contemporary) Swiss-American thanatologist, psychiatrist, and author.

Kushner, Harold (Contemporary) Author and Rabbi.

Lacordaire, Jean Baptiste (1802–1861) Leading Catholic ecclesiastic following the Napoleonic wars.

La Fontaine, Jean de (1621–1695) Poet whose *Fables* are among the greatest French literary works.

Laing, R. D. (1927–1989) British psychoanalyst who gained a particular reputation among the British and European medical profession for outspoken attitudes, particularly towards family psychology. Also author and brilliant speaker.

Langbridge, Frederick (1849–1923) Poet and author.

Lao-tzu (c. 6th century BCE) Chinese sage and founder of Taoism. Putative author of the Taoist classic *Tao Te Ching*.

Lauder, Leonard (Contemporary) Of Estee Lauder cosmetics.

Lawlor, Robert (Contemporary) Australian author and artist.

Lawrence, D. H. (1885–1930) One of the outstanding British authors of the early 20th century. Best known for works considered shocking for their frankness in dealing with themes of love and sexual passion.

Leibniz, Gottfried Wilhelm von (1646–1716) German philosopher, political advisor, and mathematician.

Lennox, Annie (Contemporary) British popular songwriter and performer.

Lennox, Charlotte (1720–1804) U.S.-born English novelist who wrote the much-admired *Arabella*, or, *The Female Quixote*.

Leon, Moses de (1250–1305) Author of the *Zohar*.

Lessing, Gotthold Ephraim (1729–1781) German dramatist, writer, and philosophical writer.

Levin, Bernard (Contemporary) Columnist for the *Times* (London), author, and television satirist.

Lewis, C. S. (1898–1963) British author, lecturer, and educator.

Lin-Chi (1915–1973) Chinese T'ang master.

Lippman, Walter (1889–1974) American journalist and author.

Locke, John (1632–1704) English political and educational philosopher who created the epistemological foundations of modern science.

Lodge, Thomas (1558?–1625) British writer.

Longfellow, Henry Wadsworth (1807–1882) One of the most popular American poets of the last two centuries.

Lorie, Peter (Contemporary) Pseudonym of Philip Dunn, British publisher and author.

Lowell, James Russell (1819–1891)
Poet, critic, and diplomat who dominated American literature in his time.

Lucian (240?–312) Christian theologian and martyr.

Lucretius (99–55 BCE) Latin poet and philosopher known for his single long poem, *On the Nature of Things.*

Lusin (died 1936) More warrior than literary man, his writings represent the Literature of Revolt and advocated a complete rejection of China's ancient ideals.

Luther, Martin (1483–1546) German priest, biblical scholar, and linguist whose Ninety-Five Theses precipitated the Protestant Reformation.

Lyly, John (1554?–1606) English prose stylist.

Lynd, Robert (1892–1970) American sociologist, who, with his wife, Helen Lynd, collaborated on a series of books entitled *Middletown.*

Ma, Anandamayi (1896–1982) Indian guru and teacher born a Hindu, and one of the greatest spiritual teachers of this century.

Maccall, William (died c. 1830) Poet.

Machiavelli (1469–1527) Italian writer and political philosopher of the Renaissance period.

Macy, Joanna (Contemporary) American Buddhist writer and teacher.

Mahabharata (4th–5th century BCE) Classical Indian epic compiled by many anonymous poets and Hindu priests. With the Ramayana, principal source of Hindu social and religious doctrine.

Mahadevi (12th century) Indian woman initiated to Siva worship at the age of ten. Her writings are often about the conflict between Divine and human love. Recognized by fellow saints as the most poetic. She died in her twenties in "oneness with Siva" according to legend.

Mahavira (599–527 BCE) Last of the twenty-four Tirthankaras (fully enlightened teachers) who founded Jainism, and reformer of the Jaina religious order. Records show that he followed an extreme ascetic life, and taught a doctrine of austerity, nonviolence, vegetarianism, and renunciation. He also spent the greater part of his life completely naked as part of his doctrine.

Mallarmé, Stéphane (1842–1898) French symbolist poet.

Mann, Thomas (1875–1955) German novelist and essayist, who won the Nobel Prize for Literature in 1929.

Marguerite of Navarre (1492–1549) Author of *The Heptameron,* or *Novels of the Queen of Navarre.*

Marie de France (1160?–1215?) Earliest known French poet.

Marlowe, Christopher (1564–1593) English poet. Shakespeare's most important predecessor.

Marx, Karl (1818–1883) Political theorist, sociologist, and economist whose work was the foundation of Marxism.

Maugham, W. Somerset (1874–1965) British playwright, novelist, and short-story writer.

Mauriac, François (1885-1970) Novelist, essayist, poet, playwright, journalist, and winner of the Nobel Prize for Literature in 1952.

May, Rollo (Contemporary) American writer.

McGinley, Phyllis (1905–1978) American poet, humorist, and Pulitzer Prize winner.

Mechtild of Magdeburg (1207–1249) German Benedictine mystic.

Medici, Cosimo de' (1389–1464) Founder of the Medici family that ruled Florence.

Meher Baba (1894–1969) Indian mystic and enlightened master.

Melville, Herman (1819–1891) American novelist, short-story writer, and poet, best known for his novel *Moby Dick*.

Menander (c. 342–292 BCE) Greek comedic dramatist—his work has had a profound influence on European theater from the Renaissance to modern times.

Mencius (372–289 BCE) Chinese philosopher who lived 107 years after Confucius and developed his ideas. He believed in the innate goodness of human nature, which culture should seek and retrieve.

Mencken, H. L. (1880–1956) Controversial American writer, humerous journalist, and critic of American life. Powerfully influenced American fiction writing during the 1920s.

Merriam, G. S. (Contemporary) American writer.

Merton, Thomas (1915–1968) American 20th-century trappist monk and philosopher.

Metchnikoff, I. I. (1845–1916) Russian zoologist and microbiologist who received the Nobel Prize for Medicine in 1908.

Milarepa or **Jetsun Mila (1040–1123)** Milarepa means a wearer of cotton garments. Milarepa was born in Nepal to a wealthy trader and man of influence in the local village, who died when the child was seven years old and left his fortune to him, including herds of cattle and vast estates, which were lost through the perfidy of an uncle and aunt. Milarepa traveled to a black magician named Lama Yungtun-Trogyal (Wrathful and Victorious Teacher of Evil) and learned his arts to use against his aunt and uncle, bringing down their house and destroying their lives. He then moved to the path of religion and spent the rest of his life on the path of love.

Mill, John Stuart (1806–1873) English philosopher, economist, and exponent of Utilitarianism.

Millay, Edna St. Vincent (1892–1950) American poet, dramatist, and feminist.

Milner, Marion (Contemporary) British psychoanalyst and writer. She is in her nineties and still teaching in England.

Milton, John (1608–1674) One of the greatest English poets of his time. Best known for his work, *Paradise Lost.*

Mira Bai (c. 1498–1547) Indian noblewoman who married a prince, but her devotion to Krishna caused her to reject all conventional values. Leaving the women's quarters, she would mix with holy men and dance before the image in the temple. This flouting of social mores led to her persecution, including an attempt at poisoning.

Mishna, The (c. 200) Jewish scripture that gives some four thousand legal decisions regulating every phase of Jewish life and incorporated into the Talmud.

Mistral, Gabriela (1889–1957) Chilean poet.

Molière (Jean Baptiste Poquelin) (1622-1673) French actor and one of the greatest comedy playwrights.

Montagu, Mary Wortley (1689–1762) Colorful English personality and brilliant writer.

Montaigne, Michel Eyquem de (1533–1592) French courtier during the reign of Charles IX.

Montesquieu, Charles, Baron de (1689–1755) French political philosopher.

Montessori, Maria (1870–1952) Founder of the Montessori education system.

Moore, George (1852–1933) Irish novelist and man of letters.

Moore, Marianne (1887–1972) American poet.

Moore, Thomas (1779–1852) English theologian and writer.

Moore, Thomas (Contemporary) American psychologist and bestselling author.

Morris, William (1834–1896) English designer, craftsman, and poet who created unique and beautiful furnishings and wallpapers.

Moses ben Shem Tov (13th century) Spanish kabbalist (Jewish mystical tradition). Is attributed by some with composing the *Zohar* or *The Book of Splendour.*

Mother, The (1878–1990) French disciple of the Indian enlightened master Aurobindo, who took over the administration of his ashram and then became enlightened herself.

Mother Teresa (Contemporary) Roman Catholic nun who has created a reputation for her charitable philosophy and work with the poor and sick of India.

Motse (c. 468–401 BCE) The only indigenous religious teacher produced in China, his teachings were enormously influential for a time and were then completely neglected until fairly recently. His teachings are the closest to Christianity of all the Chinese philosophers as he believed in universal love as the basis of society and of peace.

Mr. Tut-Tut (17th? century) Compiler of *One Hundred Proverbs*. An anonymous Chinese inheritor of a tradition of folk and literary wisdom, also adding some of his own. *One Hundred Proverbs* is a "popular" collection of games, riddles, jokes, verse oddities, and anecdotes.

Muhi 'I-Din Ibn Arabi-al-Futu hat al-Makkiyya (1165–1240) Celebrated Muslim mystic philosopher who gave first form to Islamic thought.

Muir, John (1838–1914) Naturalist and advocate of U.S. forest conservation. Muir Woods National Monument is named after him.

Murasaki, Shikibu (974–1031?) Court lady and author of *The Tale of Genji*.

Murray, Judith Sargent (1751–1820) American author, feminist, poet, and playwright.

Naimy, Mikhail (1889–1988) Mystic and author of *The Book of Mirdad*, one of the least well known and most beautiful spiritual works written in the last century.

Nanak, Guru (1469–1539) Born in the small jungle village of Talwandi (now Nanakana) in what was then India, now in the Punjab, a territory of Pakistan. Spawned as one of the many gurus who followed the genius of Kabir, he had very similar beliefs and teachings, though was not so original.

Naropa (1016–1100) Indian Tibetan Buddhist who became a disciple of Guru Tilopa and began a new and rich era of Buddhist thought in Tibet. Born in Bengal of royal parentage. At eleven he traveled to Kashmir to begin his learning as a Buddhist. After many visions and transformations, which made him one of the most significant teachers within the Buddhist tradition, Naropa died and his remains were preserved in the Kanika monastery in Zangskar.

Nehru, Jawaharlal (1889–1964) One of the greatest Indian politicians and political commentators of this century.

Neruda, Pablo (1904–1973) Chilean poet.

Neusner, Jacob (Contemporary) American journalist.

Newman, John Henry (1801–1890) British Catholic cardinal.

Newton, Sir Isaac (1642–1727)
English physicist and mathematician, who laid the foundation for calculus and the mechanics of planetary motion.

Nicholas of Cusa (Nicholas Krebs) (1401–1464) Born on the Moselle river in the Rhineland to a well-to-do barge captain. Studied law at the university and then entered the priesthood to become a Church reformer and writer. His works include *On Learned Ignorance*, *The Vision of God*, and *De sapientia* (On Wisdom).

Niebuhr, Reinhold (1892–1971)
American theologian who had extensive influence on political thought and whose criticism of the prevailing theological liberalism of the late 1920s significantly affected the intellectual climate within American Protestantism.

Nietzsche, Friedrich Wilhelm (1844–1900) German philosopher. One of the forefathers of existentialism. His writings expound the idea that man must learn to live without any kind of god or other metaphysical consolation.

Nightingale, Florence (1820–1910)
Famous nurse and compassionate healer from the Crimean War.

Nurbakhsh, Javad (Contemporary)
Middle-Eastern poet and romantic writer.

O'Brien, John A. (Contemporary)
British writer.

O'Brown, Norman (Contemporary)
Philosopher, historian, and academic author.

Oliphant, Margaret (1828–1897)
Prolific Scottish novelist and biographer, famous for her writing on small town life.

Omar Khayyam (died 1123) Persian poet, mathematician, and astronomer. Author of *The Rubaiyat of Omar Khayyam*.

O'Neill, Eugene (1888–1953) American philosopher and playwright. A three-time recipient of the Pulitzer Prize for Drama. Also won the Nobel Prize for Literature in 1936.

Origen (185–254) The most important theologian and biblical scholar of the early Greek period.

Orpingalik (c. 20th century) A Netskilik Eskimo.

Osho (Bhagwan Shree Rajneesh) (1931–1990) One of the most important spiritual mystics of the 20th century, though shrouded toward the end of his life in scandals created by followers in the American commune set up in Oregon. His philosophies encompassed the search for freedom and individuality with a strong emphasis on love and human psychology. His ashram in Poona, India, is the largest meditation center in the world.

Otomo No Tabito (665–731) Japanese poet.

Ovid (Publius Ovidius Naso) (43 BCE–CE 17) Roman poet noted specially for his work the *Art of Love*.

Paine, Thomas (1737–1809) American (English-born) writer and political pamphleteer.

P'ang-yun (c. 800) Chinese poet.

Pao-tzu Wen-ch'I (c. 900) Chinese poet.

Paracelsus (Theophrastus Bombastus von Hohenheim) (1493–1541) German-Swiss physician and alchemist who established the role of chemistry in medicine.

Parker, Dorothy (1893–1967) American critic, satirical poet, and short-story writer remembered for her flashing verbal exchanges and malicious wit.

Parry, Idris (Contemporary) Writer and broadcaster.

Pascal, Blaise (1623–1662) French mathematician, physician, writer, and religious philosopher who founded the theory of probabilities.

Patanjali, Bhagwan Shree (2nd? century BCE) Author of two great Hindu classics: *Yoga Sutras* and the *Great Commentary*.

Petronius (died c. 66) Reputed author of the *Satyricon*, a portrait of Roman society.

Philo of Alexandria (1st century BCE) Preeminent Jewish thinker of the Hellenistic period.

Pilkington, Laetitia (1712–1750?) British poet, playwright, and printer.

Pius XII, Pope (1876–1958) Head of the Roman Catholic Church during World War II.

Plath, Sylvia (1932–1963) American poet and dramatist.

Plato (c. 428–348 BCE) Greek philosopher. Among the most important and creative thinkers of the ancient world, his influence has extended to the present day. His work set forth most of the important problems and concepts of Western philosophy.

Plotinus (205–270) Roman philosopher and founder of the Neoplatonic movement of philosophy.

Plutarch (c. 46–119?) Greek biographer and author whose work strongly influenced the evolution of the essay, the biography, and historical writing in Europe.

Pope, Alexander (1688–1744) English poet, satirist, and translator of Homer.

Post, Emily (1873–1960) American educationalist and writer.

Powys, Llewelyn (Contemporary) American author.

Pritchett, V. S. (Contemporary) British novelist, short-story writer, and critic.

Protagoras (c. 481–411 BCE) Greek thinker and teacher who was the first and most famous of the Greek Sophists.

Ptah-hotep (c. 2600 BCE) Egyptian sage. Most ancient author known to us by name.

Pugh, Emerson (Contemporary) American writer.

Purva-Mimamsa Though many writers contributed to the Vedanta, which contains five hundred and five sutras that form part of the basis for Hinduism, Badarayana is the name given as the main source of this extraordinary work of which the Purva-Mimamsa is a part. The basis of the Vedas are seen as perception and inference, while the realm of *Brahman*, the essence of the Vedanta's understanding of life, lies beyond all reasoning, and can only be reached by intuition acquired from meditation and devotion. This is the very source of the most ancient definable religion in the world, that reasoning and logic are born out of intuition or the Brahman, and the Brahman is the basis for reality—the material and final cause of existence. In creating the world, God had no purpose to fulfill: what seems to be His activity is nothing but sport. Cause and effect are therefore one and the same, happening from different perspectives, before and after, but nevertheless identical.

Quintus Ennis (239–169 BCE) Greek poet.

Rab (3rd century) Jewish sage.

Rabelais, François (1494?–1553) French writer, physician, and humorist.

Rabi'a al-Adawiyya (717–809) A saint of Islam and one of the central Sufi figures. She lived in Basra, which is now Iraq. Sold as a slave after her parents' death from famine, she later was freed and became a flute player, living always in poverty.

Radhakrishnan, Sarvepalli (1888–1975) Indian born in Madras. Taught philosophy in various colleges and universities in India and at Oxford University in England. From 1949 held public office: Indian ambassador to the Soviet Union, vice president of India, and president of India.

Raine, Kathleen (Contemporary) American poet and spiritual writer.

Ramakrishna, Shri (1836–1886) A religious genius of the last century, he experimented with virtually all the evolutionary paths and pronounced that all religions were directed toward the same God but used different paths. He was initiated into Tantric practices when he was twenty-five years old. He tried, "scientifically," to explain each stage in the ascent of the Kundalini, but each time he came to the penultimate Samadhi, he became lost to the outside world and would pass into unconsciousness.

Ramana Maharshi (1879–1950) Hindu-enlightened master and yogi, one of the greatest of this century.

Ramtha (35,000 years ago) Channeled entity, using Z. Z. Knight, contemporary American.

Ranke-Heinemann, Uta (Contemporary) German theologian.

Raymo, Chet (Contemporary) American astronomer.

Reade, Charles (1814–1884) English novelist and exposer of social injustice.

Recéjac, E. (died 1899) French occultist and writer.

Reich, Wilhelm (1897–1957) Author of *The Golden Bough*, he is one of the most important authors of this century.

Rhodes, Cecil (1853–1902) Financier, empire builder, and statesman of British South Africa.

Rig Veda (c. 1200–900 BCE) One of the most ancient forms of Hindu scripture which is derived from the still more ancient Vedic scriptures.

Rilke, Rainer Maria (1875–1926) German writer and poet.

Rimbaud, Arthur (1854–1891) French poet, who wrote some of the most remarkable poems between the ages of sixteen and twenty-one. At twenty-one he abandoned writing to travel.

Rinpoche, Sogyal (Contemporary) Buddhist monk and author of *The Tibetan Book of Living and Dying*.

Rochefoucauld, Duc de la (1613–1680) French writer.

Rogers, Will (1879–1935) American actor, columnist, and humorist famous for his homespun wit.

Roquette, Adrien-Emmanuel (Contemporary) Writer.

Rossetti, Christina (1830–1894) Artist and writer.

Rostand, Jean (1894–1977) French biologist and author of *Pensées biologiste*.

Ruether, Rosemary Radford (Contemporary) Twentieth-century American scholar and theologian.

Ruskin, John (1819–1900) English writer, critic, and artist who championed the Gothic Revival movement.

Russell, Bertrand (1872–1970) British mathematician, philosopher, social and political agitator, and pacifist.

Saigyo, Hoshi (1118–1190) Japanese Buddhist priest celebrated for his piety as well as his poetic genius.

Salinger, J. D. (Contemporary) American author. Most noted for his novel *The Catcher in the Rye*.

Sangharakshita (Contemporary) Author of *The Three Jewels*.

Santayana, George (1863–1952) Spanish-born philosopher, poet, and literary critic. Remained philosophically a Naturalist throughout his life and was concerned with the ideal factors in human existence.

Sappho (c. 610–635 BCE) Celebrated Greek lyric poet greatly admired for the beauty of her writing, of which only fragments remain.

Saraha (1st or 2nd century) Indian Brahmin Buddhist teacher.

Sarashina, Lady (1008–?) Birth name unknown. The author of *As I Crossed a Bridge of Dreams*. Lived at the height of the Heian Period. Her early years were spent in the capital of what is now Kyoto. At thirty-one she became a lady-in-waiting to one of the Imperial Princesses, and thereafter gave birth to three children. Little else is known about her life.

Sarma, D. S. (Contemporary) Indian spiritual writer.

Sarmad (17th century) Middle-Eastern writer and philosopher.

Sartre, Jean-Paul (1905–1980) French novelist, poet, and exponent of Existentialism—a philosophy acclaiming the freedom of the individual human being. Awarded the Nobel Prize for Literature in 1964, but declined it.

Schiller, J. C. Friedrich von (1759–1805) Leading German dramatist and poet.

Schopenhauer, Arthur (1788–1860) German philosopher known for his atheistic and pessimistic concepts.

Schrödinger, Erwin (1887–1961) Austrian. One of the most prominent scientists involved in developing the theories of quantum physics. Shared a Nobel Prize in 1933.

Schurz, Carl (1829–1906) Political leader, journalist, and orator in Germany and the United States.

Schweichart, Russell (Contemporary) Astronaut on an Apollo mission.

Seattle, Chief (1786–1866) Native American, Suqwamish and Duwamish chieftain, a Christian and an ally of the white American. He agreed to settle the Washington tribes on reservations in 1855, and gave a speech to the government of Washington Territory in 1853.

Segal, Erich (Contemporary) American popular novelist.

Seneca, Lucius Annaeus (c. 4 BCE– CE 65) Born in Spain and lived in Rome and Corsica. One of most influential Stoic writers, known as a moral teacher rather than an original philosopher. Major influence on medieval and Renaissance literature and theatre.

Sertillages, Antonin (Contemporary) Writer and religious philosopher.

Sévigné, Marie de (1626–1696) French writer.

Shabistari, Mahmud (1250–1320) Persian mystic.

Shakespeare, William (1564–1616) British dramatist, who is one of the most celebrated English playwrights and poets of all time.

Shankara (788–820) One of the greatest and most influential seers of India, born at Kaladi in southern India. His life remains shrouded in legend and folktale, but he was probably born of a poor brahmin family and recognized as a precociously intelligent child at a very early age. By the time he was ten he was studying the Vedanta and speaking with holy men in the area where he lived. He was initiated into "sannyas" by the guru Govindapada. His best known work is a commentary on the Vedanta sutras.

Shantideva (8th century) Indian Buddhist master.

Shaw, George Bernard (1856–1950) British dramatist, playwright, author, wit, and satirist.

Sheen, Fulton J. (Contemporary) Journalist for *Look* magazine.

Sheldrake, Rupert (Contemporary) Biologist, author, and founder of the theory of morphic resonance.

Shelley, Percy Bysshe (1792–1822) British poet and romantic during the same period as Lord Byron.

Shinoda Bolen, Jean (Contemporary) American author specializing in Goddess mythology.

Shivapuri Baba (1826–1963) Indian mystic.

Shneur Zalman of Liady (1747–1813) Jewish mystic. Founder of *Habad* mysticism emphasizing the ability of each individual to advance spiritually through study and meditation.

Shore, Eliezer (Contemporary) American writer.

Siegel, Bernie (Contemporary) American author.

Smedley, Francis Edward (1818–1864) British writer.

Smith, Charlotte (1749–1806) English novelist and poet.

Smith, Huston (Contemporary) American teacher and author of *The World's Religions*.

Smith, Lillian (1897–1966) Author of *The Journey*.

Smith, Paul Jordan (Contemporary) American storyteller and author.

Socrates (469–399 BCE) Born to the sculptor Sophroniscus and Phaenarete, a midwife, in a suburb of Athens called Alopece. He was probably a journeyman stonecutter for his father in his youth, but we know nothing of this. He became an armed infantryman in the Athenian army and served for ten years in the field during the Peloponnesian war. Plato also served with him in this war and praised him highly, telling of his powers of endurance and his bravery. He had three children by Xanthippe. One of the greatest and most enlightened thinkers of ancient Greece, he was executed (by poisoning) for his beliefs and teachings.

Soleri, Paolo (1919–1989) Italian-born American architect and city planner who coined the term arcology.

Solomon ben Judah Ibn-Gabirol (c. 1021–1058) Born in Malaga,

Spain, and reared and educated in Saragossa, he began composing spiritual verse at sixteen. Wrote some three hundred poems in Hebrew, some of which still form part of the Spanish Jewish liturgy. Main work: *The Fountain of Life*.

Sophocles (496?–406 BCE) One of the three great Greek tragedians.

Sosan (Seng-s'tan) (dates unknown) Ancient Chinese spiritual master and writer.

Soseki, Natsume (1867–1916) Popular Japanese haiku poet. His work was published by Weatherhill, Inc., in the United States.

Spinoza, Baruch (1632–1677) Dutch Jewish philosopher who exponded the theory of Rationalism.

Staël, Germaine de (1766–1817) German author and philosopher.

Starhawk (Miriam Samos) (Contemporary) Twentieth century American feminist thinker.

Steiner, Rudolph (1861–1925) German anthroposophist, speaker, and educator, who founded the Rudolph Steiner schools. Believed in the spiritual nature of children.

Stevenson, Robert Louis (1850–1894) Scottish essayist, poet, and author of fiction and travel books.

Stewart, David (Contemporary) British popular songwriter and performer.

Stowe, Harriet Beecher (1811–1896) American writer and social critic.

al-Suhrawardi, 'Umar (Contemporary) Middle-Eastern philosopher, religious writer, and poet.

Suzuki, D. T. (Contemporary) Writer and spiritual teacher.

Swift, Jonathan (1667–1745) Author and Dean of St. Patrick's Cathedral, Dublin.

Szasz, Thomas (Contemporary) American author.

Tacitus (c. 55–117) Roman orator and public official, probably the greatest historian and prose stylist who wrote in Latin.

Tagore, Rabindranath (1861–1941) Indian poet. He was born in Calcutta, studied in London, and returned to India, where he founded a school. He became India's most popular poet, won the Nobel Prize for Literature in 1913, and was knighted in 1915. He lectured worldwide and was in personal contact with renowned thinkers of his day from Europe and India. He wrote about one hundred books of verse, about fifty plays, about forty works of fiction, and about fifteen books of essays.

Tales from the Thousand and One Nights (18th century) Derived from a lost Persian book of fairy tales called *Hazar Afsanah* ("A Thousand Legends"), these lay and secular stories of the fantastic were taken from Indian, Persian, and Arab culture.

Tanemura, Kenneth (Contemporary) Japanese poet.

Teilhard de Chardin, Pierre (1881–1955)   French Roman Catholic priest, theologian, and paleontologist who developed a religiously oriented doctrine of cosmic evolution. Widely attacked in his time, his ideas have inspired and broadened the thought of theologians, philosophers, and scientists.

Tennyson, Lord Alfred (1809–1892) British poet.

Teresa of Avila, St. (1515–1582) Spanish Carmelite nun.

Thich Nhat Hanh (contemporary) Vietnamese Zen Buddhist monk. Scholar, poet, peace activist, and author of many books, he lives in his community in France, Plum Village.

Thomas, Dylan (1914–1953)   Irish poet, famous for his outrageous opinions. One of the greatest writers of the 20th century.

Thompson, Keith (Contemporary) American author.

Thomson, James (1700–1748)   Scottish poet of the Romantic movement.

Thoreau, Henry David (1817–1862) American essayist, poet, and practical philosopher, renowned for having lived the doctrines of Transcendentalism.

Tillich, Paul (1886–1965)   German-born American theologian and philosopher.

Tocqueville, Alexis de (1805–1859) French political writer and commentator.

Tolstoy, Count Leo (1828–1910) Russia's greatest novelist and one of its most influential moral philosophers.

Tompkins, Peter (Contemporary) American author.

Traherne, Thomas (1637–1674) Last of the Anglican clergy's mystical poets.

Trueblood, Elton D. (Contemporary) American spiritual thinker and writer.

Turgenev, Ivan Sergeyevich (1818–1883)   Russian novelist, poet, and playwright.

Tutu, Desmond (Contemporary) African priest, political activist, author, and religious philosopher.

Twain, Mark (1835–1910)   One of the most famous of American writers.

Tylor, Sir Edward Burnett (1832–1917)   British anthropologist.

Ullathorne, W. Bernard (1806–1889) Roman Catholic missionary to Australia.

Underhill, Evelyn (1875–1941)   English novelist, poet, and mystic.

Upanishads, The (Compiled and written between 900 and 600 BCE) The most recent portions of the Vedas, which are the sacred texts of Hinduism. Their fundamental concern is the nature of reality.

Valéry, Paul (1871-1945) French poet, essayist, and critic.

Vallejo, Cesar (1892–1938) Peruvian poet and revolutionary activist.

van Dyke, Henry (1852–1933) Writer and commentator.

Vaughan, Henry (1622–1695) British poet.

Veblen, Thorstein (1857–1929) American economist and social scientist, born of Norwegian stock in Wisconsin, sought to revolutionize the study of economic institutions. His books include *The Theory of the Leisure Class* and *An Economic Study of Institutions*.

Vigny, Alfred de (1797–1863) Foremost French romantic writer, poet, and novelist.

Virgil (Publius Virgilius Maro) (70–19 BCE) The greatest Roman poet, best known for the *Aeneid*.

Vital, Hayyim (1543–1620) Jewish speaker and writer.

Vivekananda, Swami (1863–1902) Indian whose real name was Narendranath Datta and was a disciple of Ramakrishna (see separate entry). Traveled worldwide including America where he made a strong impression with his combination of spiritual consciousness and social responsibility. Founded the Vedanta movement.

Voltaire (François-Marie Arouet) (1694–1778) One of the greatest 18th-century European authors, remembered as a crusader against tyranny and bigotry.

Waley, Arthur (Contemporary) Academic writer and translator of ancient Chinese scripture.

Walker, Alice (Contemporary) African-American author.

Walton, Izaak (1593–1683) English biographer and author of *The Compleat Angler*.

Wang Wei (699–761) Chinese poet.

Washington, Martha (1731–1802) The first First Lady of the United States.

Watson, Lyall (Contemporary) Author, anthropologist, known particularly for his book *Supernature*.

Watts, Alan (1915–1973) One of the leading figures of the California "Renaissance" of the 1960s and 1970s, with a particular presence in the interpretation of Zen, though his greatest contributions were probably also related to the processes of enlightenment and how to discover it.

Watts, Isaac (1674–1748) English writer of poems and hymns for children.

Waugh, Evelyn (1903–1966) English writer. Regarded as one of the most brilliant satirical novelists of his era.

Wei Lang (80? BCE) Philosopher and religious writer.

Wei Wu Wei (Terence Gray, 1895–1986) Zen/Taoist writer, wine grower, and racehorse owner.

Weil, Simone (1909–1943) French social activist and religious writer.

Welles, Orson (1915–1985) American actor and director.

West, Morris (Contemporary) Novelist, author of *The Shoes of the Fisherman* and *The Devil's Advocate*.

Whichcote, Benjamin (1609–1683) English moralist and religious writer.

White, E. B. (1899–1985) Leading American essayist, children's novelist, and literary stylist.

Whitman, Walt (1819–1892) One of the greatest 19th-century American poets. The first American poet to abandon previous poetic conventions and create a distinctly national idiom celebrating and affirming democracy, freedom, the self, and the joys of living.

Wilbur, Richard (contemporary) American author and poet.

Wilde, Oscar (1854–1900) One of the most important Irish literary figures of the last century, poet, dramatist, and social figure.

Willoughby, Catherine (1519?–1580) English noble, lady-in-waiting to Catherine of Aragon.

Wittgenstein, Ludgwig (1889–1951) British (Austrian-born) philosopher,

known best for his "picture theory" of language.

Wodehouse, P. G. (1881–1975) English-American author and humorist, author of the Jeeves novels.

Woodman, Marion (Contemporary) American writer.

Woolf, Virginia (1882–1941) English author and member of the Bloomsbury set.

Wordsworth, William (1770–1850) One of England's leading lyric poets. The birth of the Romantic movement was marked by the publication of his *Lyrical Ballads*.

Wyman, Jane (Contemporary) American actress.

Xenophanes (570–475 BCE) A contemporary in ancient Greece of Heraclitus, a native of Colophon, banished to Sicily, where he taught his mystical philosophy. He is said to have lived to a very old age, but little more is known of him. The quotation in this book is the one fragment of his writing that is left to us.

Yatri (Contemporary) Yatri is the *sannyas* name of Malcolm Godwin, a "Sunday Mystic" who lives in Dorset, England, and has written a number of books, including *Angels—An Endangered Species* and *Lucid Dreamer*. He is a disciple of the spiritual master, Osho.

Yeats, William Butler (1865–1939) Irish poet, dramatist, and nationalist politician. Winner of the Nobel Prize for Literature in 1923.

Yogaswami (1872–1964) Sri Lankan. He had an early education in Christian Missionary school, where he was given the name John although not christened. Later known as Johnswami, which came to be corrupted to Johanswami, then Yogaswami, most of his followers were Hindus and his teaching was usually expressed in Hindu terms.

Young, Edward (1683–1765) English poet, dramatist, and literary critic.

Zelazny, Roger (Contemporary) Science fiction author.

Zell, Katherine (1497/8–1562) German church worker and hymnist.

Zeno (335–263 BCE) Greek thinker who founded the Stoic school.

Z'ev ben Shimon Halevi (Contemporary) Writer and religious philosopher. Author of *The Tree of Life*.

Ziyad B. al-Arabi (9th century) One of the three great Sufi writers who created the foundation of Sufism.

Zukav, Gary (Contemporary) American philosopher and author.

Zweig, Paul (1935–1984) American author.

Key-Phrase Index

The following entries include both first lines and random phrases from selections included in *The Quotable Spirit*. Each entry is followed by the page on which the complete selection may be found and the author (last name only) or other source when no author is known.

ℬ

C

G

H

I

J

K

M

O

𝒫

R

S

U

Without mysticism man can achieve nothing great, 182, Gide

woman sheds blood, 25, Craighead

Word was with God, 44, New Testament

world in a grain of sand, 67, Blake

world is but a school of inquiry, 130, Montaigne

world is our playground, 189, Nanak

world stands out on either side, 240, St. Vincent Millay

world would be poorer without the antics of clergymen, 212, Pritchett

world's a bubble, 52, Bacon

Ye behold Him face to face, 90, *Hymns Ancient and Modern*

You are That, 185, The Upanishads

You can never step in the same river twice, 244, Heraclitus

You cannot hope to build a better world, 284, Curie

You think heaven's prettier than Venice, 104, Conroy

Name Index